THE

GEORGIA and SOUTH CAROLINA

EXPEDITIONS

*of Clarence
Bloomfield Moore*

Classics in Southeastern Archaeology

Stephen Williams, Series Editor

Publication of this work has been supported in part by grants
and donations from the following agencies and institutions.

Southeastern Archaeological Conference
Panamerican Consultants, Inc.
Southeastern Archeological Services, Inc.
Georgia Council of Professional Archaeologists
Council of South Carolina Professional Archaeologists
South Carolina Institute of Archaeology and Anthropology
Savannah River Archaeological Research Program
Archaeological Society of South Carolina

T H E
GEORGIA and
SOUTH CAROLINA
EXPEDITIONS
of Clarence
Bloomfield Moore

Edited and with an Introduction by
LEWIS LARSON

The University of Alabama Press
Tuscaloosa and London

The works by Clarence B. Moore reproduced by facsimile in this volume were
published originally in the *Journal of the Academy of Natural Sciences of
Philadelphia* in 1897 and 1898.

∞

The paper on which this book is printed meets the minimum requirements of
American National Standard for Information Science-Permanence of Paper
for Printed Library Materials, ANSI Z39.48-1984.

Library of Congress Cataloging-in-Publication Data

Moore, Clarence Bloomfield.
 The Georgia and South Carolina expeditions of Clarence Bloomfield
Moore / edited and with an Introduction by Lewis Larson.
  p. cm. — (Classics in southeastern archaeology)
  Includes bibliographical references (p.) and index.

  ISBN 0-8173-0941-1
  1. Indians of North America—Georgia—Antiquities. 2. Indians of
North America—South Carolina—Antiquities. 3. Mounds—Georgia.
4. Mounds—South Carolina. 5. Georgia—Antiquities. 6. South Carolina—Antiquities. I. Larson, Lewis H., 1927– II. Title. III. Series
  E78.G3 M66 1998
  975.7'01—ddc21   98-19728

British Library Cataloguing-in-Publication Data available

Contents

Maps

Acknowledgments

I was very pleased to have been asked to write the introduction to the reprint of Clarence B. Moore's archaeological investigations in Georgia and South Carolina. I am also grateful for the assistance that I have received from several quarters, beginning with the encouragement of Judith Knight at The University of Alabama Press. I am particularly appreciative of the kind cooperation of the Huntington Free Library, Bronx, New York, in making available the microfilm of Clarence Moore's notebooks and logs that record his work on the Georgia and South Carolina coasts and the Savannah and Altamaha rivers. I appreciate the comments of the several anonymous individuals who reviewed an earlier draft of my manuscript; I have attempted to utilize their suggestions. I also wish to thank Ms. Nancy Farmer, Ingram Library, State University of West Georgia, for arranging and renewing the microfilm loan from the Huntington Free Library and for obtaining several needed references. Brian Valimont, as a student assistant, transcribed sections of the notes and log on microfilm, and from the log developed a chronology of Moore's work. I am especially grateful for the forbearance, energy, and understanding that Sharon Chapoton brought to the thankless tasks of transcribing the microfilm notes, reading and correcting the manuscript, and undertaking the thousand and one other activities that resulted in the completion of this introduction.

THE
GEORGIA and
SOUTH CAROLINA

EXPEDITIONS
of Clarence
Bloomfield Moore

Introduction

Lewis Larson

It is fitting that the centenary of the archaeological investigations of Clarence B. Moore on the Georgia coast is marked by reprinting his *Certain Aboriginal Mounds of the Georgia Coast* (1897), *Certain Aboriginal Mounds of the Coast of South Carolina* (1899a), *Certain Aboriginal Mounds of the Savannah River* (1899b), and *Certain Aboriginal Mounds of the Altamaha River* (1899c). Moore, born in 1852, was one of the first to examine the prehistory of the southeastern states in an organized and systematic manner. Beginning in 1891 and continuing for 27 years he investigated the prehistoric remains lying within many of the major river drainages in the Southeast, spending the winter months in the field using his steam-powered riverboat *Gopher* as a base for his operations. The remainder of the year he spent in the analysis of the excavated materials and in the preparation of reports covering his work. He was one of that small breed of savants who, because of their wealth, intellect, and interest, contributed to the creation of a science of archaeology in the United States. Perhaps his most singular contribution to southeastern archaeology is to be found in the regularity with which he published the results of his work, along with the quantity and quality of the illustrations he included therein. He wrote and published the reports on his fieldwork promptly, in no inconsiderable measure because he seems to have simply transcribed his field notes for publication.[1] Vernon James Knight, Jr., has discussed Moore's archaeological work, his methods, and his contributions to the field in an earlier volume in this series, in which the Moore reports on the Moundville investigations have been reprinted (Knight 1996:1–20). For more information on Moore, the reader is also referred to the brief summary of Moore's life by H. Newell Wardle, which has recently been reprinted by the Huntington Free Library (Davis 1987:11–15).

Prior to his arrival on the Georgia coast in the late autumn of 1895, the several previous winter archaeological seasons had seen Moore, aboard the *Gopher,* employed

[1]The archival record of Moore's investigations is to be found in a series of notebooks containing the field notes of his archaeological activity in the Southeast. These field notes are held by the Huntington Free Library, Bronx, New York, and are available on microfilm. The field notes made by Moore covering his Georgia and South Carolina work from 1895 to 1898 are to be found on *Roll 2: Field notebooks 8–16 (1894–1899),* Huntington Free Library, Bronx, New York. Here, the references to these notes are to the microfilm copy of Moore's notes. All of the original notes referenced in this introduction are contained on Microfilm Roll 2, which is abbreviated in the citations as *R2*. The letter *B* is used to designate the cited notebook number; for example, *B12* refers to notebook number 12. The letter *p* is used to identify the referenced pages within the notebook.

just south of the Georgia-Florida border in the lower drainage of the St. Johns River. During the following several seasons he seemingly worked his way northward along the Atlantic coast. Ultimately, he got as far north as St. Helena Sound on the South Carolina coast: he went no farther north, perhaps because he had reached a latitude where winter weather made his work too uncomfortable and also perhaps because he did not find the kind of archaeology there that interested him. In the interval, however, he had investigated several of the barrier islands, as well as portions of the adjoining mainland in all of the Georgia coastal counties. He had in effect initiated the archaeological investigation of the region. To be sure the methods and objectives of American archaeology have changed fundamentally since the *Gopher* made its way through tidal rivers and along the marshes of the southeastern Atlantic coast, but such changes have in no way negated the considerable value of Moore's research and his published record of those investigations.[2] I have always considered the evaluation of Moore that was made by John Goggin to have been a pragmatic and fair one:

> Moore's position is a peculiar one. He is alternately condemned or praised by present workers, both amateur and professional. In terms of his period, though he was considered good—a competent worker whose results were respected [e.g., Putnam 1896]. . . . Although our present standards are more critical, we cannot casually dismiss Moore's work. By using his publications and specimens with care, considerable information can be derived from them. He was a careful recorder and a cautious interpreter, but one who was nevertheless, willing to back his postulates. . . . Aside from the mere recording of data, some of Moore's postulates have been important and have stood the test of time. These include the recognition of historic as well as prehistoric burial mounds, proof of the existence of prehistoric Indian dogs . . . and the recognition of the prehistoric use of copper [see Moore 1903]. . . . These points are all accepted as a matter of course now, but in the 1800s they were sources of controversy. (Goggin 1952:34)

We are told by Moore that "five months of continual work have been devoted by us to the coastal mounds of Georgia" (Moore 1897:6).[3] In addition to covering the immediate coastal areas, he extended his activities the following year up the Altamaha River, almost to the point where the river is created by the union of the Ocmulgee and Oconee Rivers, and up the Savannah River into Burke County, Georgia, and adjacent Barnwell County, South Carolina. The Savannah River explorations reached

[2]Although the published Moore narrative of archaeological investigations on the Georgia coast appears to progress naturally from the southernmost site at Fairview in Camden County to the northernmost site on Skidaway Island in Chatham County, the notes reveal that in reality the actual work took place in a much more erratic fashion, moving between sites in a manner that appears to be a consequence of Moore's ability to secure permission to excavate at particular locales.

[3]In point of fact the work was not continual, if Moore meant the statement to be taken literally. Moore began his investigations on the Georgia coast in the first week of November in 1895. However, he left Georgia at the end of November after his examination of the two Fairview, Camden County, mounds to return to Florida. He returned to the Georgia coast in the middle of March 1896 and began work in the Woodbine area of Camden County. He was to continue working on the Georgia coast with month-long breaks during the Christmas holidays of 1896 and 1897 and a six-month-long break from May through October of 1896. He concluded his Georgia coastal investigations at the end of April 1897.

a point on the river just south of the Fall Line where the Coastal Plain is separated from the Piedmont. Again it may have been the northerly and cooler weather of the Piedmont that deterred him from proceeding, although certainly the shoals of the Savannah River would have been a real barrier to moving the *Gopher* farther upstream.

In this introduction it is my intention to discuss the sites that Moore investigated within the framework of our current understanding of Georgia and South Carolina coastal archaeological chronology. I will also attempt to bring the archaeological investigations that Moore initiated on the Georgia and South Carolina coasts up to the present by briefly surveying the major research activity that has taken place in these areas during this century.

The Georgia Coast

The Georgia coast extends for about 164 kilometers in a north-northeast direction from the St. Marys River on the Florida border to the Savannah River on the South Carolina border. Between the entrances of these two freshwater streams are those of three additional freshwater rivers flowing into the Atlantic. They are, from south to north, the Satilla, Altamaha, and Ogeechee rivers. Of the five streams two, the Altamaha and Savannah, drain the Piedmont and Blue Ridge provinces across the Coastal Plain Province. The Satilla and the Ogeechee drain only the Coastal Plain.

A series of barrier islands backed by an extensive system of tidal creeks and rivers, salt marsh, marsh islands, and hammocks provide a buffer between the mainland and the ocean. From south to north, the major barrier islands include Cumberland, Jekyll, St. Simons, Sapelo, St. Catherines, Ossabaw, Wassaw, and Tybee. Each barrier island is separated from the islands to the south and north of it by a sound, several of which are quite broad. For example, St. Andrews Sound separating Cumberland Island from Jekyll Island to the north is about five kilometers wide. The salt marsh behind the islands is equally broad and in some places extends for more than seven kilometers from the barrier island to the mainland. Until relatively recently, access to the islands was only by boat and the boat landings were limited to those few locations where a tidal creek or river flowed against the high ground of the island.

For the most part, Moore appears to have remained inside the barrier islands as he moved along the coast. The *Gopher* was navigated through the tidal creeks and rivers that laced the broad expanses of the coastal salt marsh. To some extent it seems that Moore's decisions about investigating archaeological sites were determined, not only by the sites that were reported to him and at which he was given permission to dig, but also by the proximity of the site to a landing that was accessible to the *Gopher*.

At the time that Moore was on the Georgia coast the state had only two coastal cities of any size: Savannah, on the northern end of the coast, and Brunswick, a small port that was situated at the midpoint of the coast in Glynn County. In Moore's time Brunswick had fewer than 10,000 inhabitants, while the population of Savannah was only about 50,000. Darien, in McIntosh County, a lumber port already in decline at the time of Moore's visit, had a population of fewer than 1,500. All in all, in

1896, the area was largely rural and isolated. Communication was almost solely by water along the coast, although a north-south rail line ran parallel to the coast some twenty miles to the west. The population was supported by the timber and naval stores industries, by subsistence farming and fishing, and to a limited extent by coastal shipping.

For the most part Moore's presence seems to have attracted relatively little attention. A brief note on Moore's McIntosh County visit appeared in the Darien newspaper, *The Darien Gazette,* for Saturday, March 28, 1896. Entitled "A Unique Mission," the story read as follows:

> Professor C. B. Moore and Surgeon Miller, both connected with the Academy of Natural Sciences of Philadelphia, arrived here from Florida on Tuesday on the steamer "Gopher." Their mission is to explore the numerous Indian mounds located in the county, and they will probably be here for ten or twelve days. For the last five years the professor has been engaged in similar work in Florida, and he evidently feels convinced from the description given by noted local archaeologists that along our rivers, the Altamaha, the Ocmulgee and the Oconee, he will find rich fields for his researches. Both Prof. Moore and Dr. Miller are noted scientists and the institution with which they are connected is one of the most celebrated and wealthy in the country.
>
> Speaking of the exploring party, the Brunswick Call says:[4]
>
> "The beautiful and commodious stern wheel steamer Gopher came into port on Sunday, and her mission is unique as it is interesting. The owner, M. Clarence B. Moore, is a member of the academy of Natural Sciences of Philadelphia, and this steamer and a crew of eighteen men are exploring the southern waters in search of Indian mounds, from which relics are gathered for the academy at Piladelphia [*sic*]. The party yesterday explored a mound at South Brunswick, but unfortunately it was a small one without any relics [see Moore 1897:15]. At Woodbine, on the Satilla river, they found a mound, on the property of Mr. J. C. Bedell, full of hatchets, tomahawks, arrowheads and shell ornaments [see Moore 1897:11\14 for an accurate account of the mound contents]. At Fernandina [just south of the Georgia-Florida border on Amelia Island, Nassau County, Florida] one mound alone contained the skeletons of seventy-five Indians, which of course was a big find. These various articles are shipped to Philadelphia as fast as they are unearthed, and are placed on exhibit in the archaeological department of the academy. Mr. Moore says he has been engaged in the work for five summers, and finds it both interesting and pleasant. The steamer's name, `Gopher,' is decidedly significant of her errand." (microfilm of *The Georgia Gazette* on file in the Ingram Library, State University of West Georgia)

The Savannah press intercepted Moore as he came to Savannah in late November 1896, as he broke off his Georgia coastal work in order to go north to Philadelphia for the holidays. He was to return after the first of the year to conclude the Georgia coast portion of his investigations the following April. Moore's arrival in

---

[4]The lengthy quotation from the *Brunswick Call,* the local Brunswick, Georgia, newspaper, suggests that the author of the Darien news article relied entirely on the Brunswick news story and in all likelihood never interviewed Moore.

Savannah was of sufficient interest to merit printing a rather extended interview with him by the *Savannah Morning News* on November 22, 1896 (Trowell 1992:43–45). The Savannah press story suggests that Moore was somewhat peevish with what he perceived as a misunderstanding of what he was about and also that he probably did not suffer fools, or reporters, gladly. The interview should be of interest to any archaeologist working in the Southeast who has ever been interviewed by the local press. Moore was called upon to answer the inevitable reporter's inquiries concerning "the unknown race that built the mounds," "giant skeletons," and whether the *real* purpose of archaeological inquiry was not the recovery of lost treasure. Moore's obvious impatience and barely maintained forbearance with the press can be detected just below the surface of his responses to questions that he had undoubtedly answered many times before. One cannot help but conclude that, in the Southeast at least, the journalist's repertoire of questions for the archaeologist has remained unchanged for the past one hundred years. No wonder archaeologists often find public information and public relations a difficult business at best.

The local press stories were undoubtedly responsible for the number of people who regularly sought out Moore to tell him of the location of mounds. Thus, it would seem that the local residents had some measure of awareness of his work, if not a complete understanding of his motivations. Certainly the awareness that resulted from the press coverage was to his profit in that it brought him new information.

MOORE IN CAMDEN COUNTY, GEORGIA

Moore's work in Georgia began in Camden County, the southernmost of the coastal Georgia counties. His arrival on the Georgia coast marked the beginning of serious and, for its time, professional archaeological investigation of the area. The St. Marys River, a relatively short stream draining the Okefenokee Swamp eastward to the Atlantic, serves to divide coastal Georgia from Florida and the northern St. Johns River area within which Moore had been working. The port of St. Marys was, at the time of Moore's arrival, a small fishing town occupying the north-side entrance to the St. Marys River. Subsequently, the construction in the 1980s of the Kings Bay Naval Submarine Base dramatically increased the size of the town. In the 1890s it was both the county seat and the largest town in the county and in all likelihood served as an important supply and communications base for Moore and his operations as well as providing proper mooring for the *Gopher*. Moore related in a much later publication that he examined the area along the St. Marys River on both the Florida and Georgia sides without result. He observed: "The [St. Marys] river was carefully searched by us on either side, all landings and settlements being visited, and diligent inquiry made, resulting in the conclusion that no mounds of importance, and an extremely limited number of any size, were present. . . . No shell-heaps [such as he had found in Florida] were noticed on the banks" (Moore 1922:69–70). As was his wont throughout the time he spent in Georgia and South Carolina, Moore made his primary focus the earthen burial mounds of the region. The investigations he carried out in Camden County were no exception to this practice; here he dug into four mounds. In the vicinity of the town of St. Marys he examined two mounds near an old plantation called Fairview. In addition, one mound near the town of Woodbine, the present county seat, and a mound at Owen's Ferry were investigated.

The mound identified by Moore as the **Low Mound at Fairview, Camden County** (Moore 1897:10), appears to have been a Mississippi Period structure. Under a layer of oyster shell at a depth of only 1 foot was a deposit of cremated bone that was accompanied by "a sheet copper ornament with a repoussé decoration" (ibid.). This embossed copper, actually two fragments of perhaps two larger plates, was illustrated a number of years ago (Larson 1958a:427, fig. 2) and is unquestionably a part of a Mississippi Period embossed copper plate of the type usually identified as a falcon dancer plate. The larger of the two fragments very clearly shows a human head carried by a hand in the manner and style of the familiar copper plate recovered from Mound C, Etowah, by Rogan in 1885 (Thomas 1887:101, fig. 43). The remainder of the fragment is covered with the spotted wing feather patterning characteristic of these embossed copper plates. The second fragment again has what appears to be the spotted wing feather patterning, but there is also a curious series of five parallel lines that in part form three sides of a rectangular figure. This fragment appears to be a part of an entirely different plate, in a different style, from the plate that was the source of the first fragment. One can only speculate about the failure of Moore to draw attention to the resemblance of the Etowah copper plate to the fragments of similar plates he recovered from the mound at Fairview. The Etowah material along with excellent drawings had been published in the *Fifth Annual Report of the Bureau of American Ethnology* by Cyrus Thomas (1887:96–102, figs. 42 and 43) some ten years prior to the publication by Moore of his Georgia coast investigations. It would hardly appear likely that Moore was unaware of the mound investigations of Thomas. Interestingly, Moore was in communication with William Henry Holmes of the Bureau of American Ethnology, Smithsonian Institution (Moore 1897:69) concerning archaeological questions and was obviously familiar with the Bureau and its publications.

The **Low Mound near Fairview, Camden County** (Moore 1897:11), not to be confused with the "low mound *at* Fairview" (see above), was dismissed by Moore with five sentences within which there was little in the way of information that would permit the identification of a context for the mound. The "small and gracefully-shaped vessel of earthenware and several sherds, most of which bore an incised cross-hatched decoration" (ibid.) do not immediately call to mind any specific ceramic types.

While the **Mound near Woodbine, Camden County** (Moore 1897:11–14), was but one of four Camden County mounds Moore examined, it was the only excavation that was described in any detail. The mound was situated a short distance from the Satilla River, a freshwater stream draining the southern portion of the Georgia Coastal Plain. At the point on the river where the town of Woodbine is situated the tidal influence is still apparent and the water is brackish. The mound was undoubtedly a Mississippi Period construct. Although sherds were encountered in the mound fill, they were few in number. Moore stated that most of the sherds were "undecorated, though the complicated form of stamp, so well known in Georgia was present" (ibid.:12). In describing some of the sherds as decorated with complicated stamping "well known in Georgia," Moore was probably referring to the ceramic type presently identified as Irene Complicated Stamped (named after Irene, a Mississippi Period site in Chatham County, Georgia, and initially identified as Irene Filfot Stamped by the authors of the original type description, Joseph Caldwell and

Antonio Waring [1939b:5–6]). The location of the site on the Satilla River placed it on or just south of the presumptive boundary between the historic Guale towns of the northern portion of the Georgia coast and the Timucua towns of northeastern Florida and the southern portion of the Georgia coast. This boundary is thought to have been either St. Simons Sound immediately to the north of Jekyll Island or St. Andrews Sound immediately to the south. The Satilla River drains into St. Andrews Sound. Therefore, the presence of the type Irene Complicated Stamped, a ware characteristic of the northern Georgia coast, in the Woodbine Mound should not be considered too surprising.

On the other hand complicated stamping of an earlier period is known from Camden County. The recent excavations at archaeological sites at the Kings Bay Naval Submarine Base identified several sites with Swift Creek Complicated Stamped wares present (Adams 1986; Smith 1986; Smith, Council, and Saunders 1985). It is thus possible that the Woodbine Mound was a Woodland Period structure.

Moore noted that "an undecorated tobacco pipe of earthen ware" was also recovered from the Woodbine Mound, apparently in association with a burial. The pipe was identified as "of a type common to the mounds of the lower thirty miles of the St. Johns river and other sections, where the aperture for the stem rivals that of the bowl in size" (Moore 1897:12). A pipe of this type, from the Low Mound at Point La Vista, Duval County, Florida, was referenced by Moore (ibid.) and illustrated by him (1922:21, fig. 1) a quarter century later. Two similar ceramic pipes, found by Moore in the Grant Mound, Duval County, Florida (Moore 1896:480), are illustrated by Goggin (1952:pl. 11, *a* and *b*). The Grant Mound has been recognized as falling within the St. Johns II Period, the local manifestation of the Mississippi Period in the lower St. Johns drainage of Florida (Goggin 1952:70). While it is not particularly diagnostic, the presence of this type of pipe in the Woodbine Mound suggests a relationship with the northern St. Johns River area and the possible chronological placement of the mound in the late Prehistoric Period. Other than the sherds and the pipe, there is little in Moore's description of the mound and its contents that allows it to be placed within a specific cultural or temporal context.

The **Mound at Owen's Ferry, Camden County** (Moore 1897:14–15), like the mound at Woodbine, was on the Satilla River, upstream from the latter mound, but still within the zone where the river is brackish and the tidal pull is felt. Moore reported, "A few sherds, some plain and some ornamented with the usual diamond or square stamp, lay loose in the sand" (ibid.:15). The "ornamented" sherds undoubtedly belong to a checked stamped type. However, the question is which one? They could be a St. Johns ware, a Deptford ware, or a Savannah ware. Each of these wares serves to denote a different set of cultural and temporal relationships.

Interestingly, Moore carried out no investigations on Cumberland Island, the largest of the Georgia barrier islands. This is striking in view of the fact that it has since been demonstrated that the island is the locale of many archaeological sites, including a number of burial and midden mounds of the type favored by Moore for excavation. Although Moore made no reference to the island in the account of his Georgia work, it seems very probable that his agent, who routinely sought access to promising sites prior to the onset of the winter work season, was unable to gain permission to work on the island. At the time Moore was on the Georgia coast, most of Cumberland Island was owned by Lucy Carnegie, the widow of Andrew's brother

Thomas. Here Mrs. Carnegie and her nine children built great houses and quietly enjoyed great wealth. The island was operated as a very private fiefdom and it is unlikely that Moore and his excavators would have been viewed as other than an unnecessary intrusion by the Carnegies.

After Moore there was no formal archaeological work in Camden County for almost forty years. In 1934 James Ford excavated two test squares at the nineteenth-century John Houstoun McIntosh tabby sugar mill near St. Marys (Ford 1937:213–16).[5] More recently, however, there has been considerable archaeological activity in the county as the result of two major development projects undertaken there beginning in the 1970s. The first of these was the incorporation of Cumberland Island, in 1972, into the National Park System as Cumberland Island National Seashore. The second was the construction of the Kings Bay Naval Submarine Base beginning in 1977. Both of these developments triggered intensive archaeological survey of the respective areas and subsequent excavation where dictated by cultural resource management requirements. As is too often the case when archaeological work is the consequence of cultural resource management demands, the results of a portion of the Camden County archaeological investigations have been available only in reports that have had a very restricted distribution, constituting a part of the infamous grey literature of archaeology.[6] An important exception is the series of five reports of the investigations carried out under U.S. Navy contracts by the University of Florida and published by the Department of Anthropology, University of Florida under the editorship of William H. Adams (Adams 1985a, 1985b, 1986, 1987; Eubanks and Adams 1986). It is worthwhile to note that none of the later archaeological work was able to relocate the sites examined by Moore, although the Fairview mounds may well have been within the boundaries of the naval base development.

MOORE IN GLYNN COUNTY, GEORGIA

Glynn County must have been a disappointment for Moore. He dug at only two sites, both of them mounds and neither of which produced anything of interest to their investigator. The **Two Mounds South of Brunswick, Glynn County** (Moore 1897:15), were low, each no more than 2 feet high and respectively 25 feet and 28 feet in diameter. Moore located the first of the mounds at South Brunswick about 200 yards south of the railroad wharf. A recent quadrangle sheet, *U.S. Geological Survey, Brunswick West Quadrangle, Georgia, 7.5 Minute Series* (1956), locates an

---

[5]At that time the ruined tabby structure was widely thought to be the remains of a seventeenth-century Spanish mission. Ford was investigating a number of such Georgia coastal structures as part of a project to establish their true function as processing facilities for locally grown sugar cane and to debunk the romantic notion that they were seventeenth-century Franciscan missions.

[6]At the time of this writing, information about the Cumberland Island reports and the pertinent curated collections is available from the National Park Service Southeastern Archaeological Center, Tallahassee, Florida. Information about the Kings Bay Naval Submarine Base limited-distribution reports is available from the Antonio J. Waring, Jr. Archaeological Laboratory, State University of West Georgia, Carrollton. As a result of the Department of Anthropology, University of Florida archaeological work at Kings Bay, a number of theses and dissertations were produced by graduate students in the department. Information about this research can be obtained from the Department of Anthropology, University of Florida, Gainesville. Most of the pertinent collections from the Kings Bay surveys and excavations are curated at the Florida State Museum, Gainesville.

abandoned pier on the south side of the South Brunswick River where the Georgia Route 303 bridge touches high ground after crossing the river. Apparently the first mound was just south of this point. Moore stated that "a total demolition of the mound was without result" (Moore 1897:15).

The second mound was located "about 1.5 miles inland from Fancy Bluff" (ibid.). If by *inland* Moore meant west, the second mound would then have been found about where Georgia Route 303 and U.S. Highway 17 intersect. If indeed this was the mound location, then the two mounds were within a short distance of one another—less than a mile. In fact, the *Gopher* may well have been moored at a dock at Fancy Bluff as the archaeological investigations proceeded ashore. Moore dismissed the second mound with a phrase equally as terse as that used for the first, relating that "no discoveries of any sort were made" (ibid.).

We now know that there are archaeological sites throughout the coastal area of Glynn County; why Moore selected only the two small mounds in the southern part of the county is not at all clear. Again, he avoided the nearby barrier islands. Jekyll Island at the harbor entrance at Brunswick may well have been off limits to him in the same way that Cumberland Island probably had been. The Jekyll Island Club had been organized only ten years earlier in 1886. On the island a number of the wealthiest families in the United States, to escape to the milder winter climate and simpler life of the Georgia coast, had built grand houses that were, with inappropriate modesty, called "cottages." I suspect that Moore was not welcome on the island, lacking, as he did, a membership in the very exclusive club. On the island were the kinds of archaeological sites that would have interested Moore. A case in point is the Rockefeller cottage, built in 1892, which has a burial mound on the front lawn. The mound is such a notable feature of the property that the family used it to provide the name for the cottage: *Indian Mound.*

Moore carried out no investigations on St. Simons Island, the largest barrier island located within Glynn County. Again the reasons for his avoidance of the island are not clear. The southern one-half of the island, unlike Jekyll and Cumberland islands, was divided into many small land holdings. It was also a much more densely populated area, which may have deterred Moore.[7]

After the brief visit by Clarence Moore, Glynn County was to see no renewal of organized archaeological activity until the depression years saw the creation of several projects under the auspices of one or another of the federal relief agencies that operated during this period. The first of these investigations occurred during the winter of 1936–1937. At that time Preston Holder was brought in by the Works Progress Administration to supervise the excavation of a number of sites on St. Simons Island and adjoining Sea Island (Holder 1938:8–9). Because the limited information about these sites is not generally accessible, it seems justified to include a brief summary of the data here. A discussion of the sites investigated by Holder will, I believe, serve to demonstrate the randomness Moore used in his approach to the

[7]The log of Moore's travels indicated that he did stop at St. Simons Island and at Frederica, a settlement on the inland waterway on the western side of the island. At Frederica the *Gopher* collided with a raft on March 24, 1896, at 2:30 P.M. Moore must have been made aware of some of the archaeological sites on the island because he made a reference to the "considerable shell deposit on St. Simons Island" (Moore 1897:5, fn. 2). In all probability his reference was to the huge midden piles on Cannons Point.

archaeology of the coastal area, even limiting, as he did, his interest to burial mounds.

The largest of the sites investigated and that with the most extensive excavation carried out by Holder was the Airport site, located within the area now occupied by the Malcom McKinnon Airport. The site was initially examined by Frank M. Setzler of the United States National Museum, Smithsonian Institution, and Holder was assigned the task of subjecting it to a more thorough examination (Larsen 1982:170–71). Holder described it as a "flat-land [and] midden covered" area. Writing to A. R. Kelly on August 31, 1936, Holder characterized the midden as composed primarily of shell, relatively shallow, only about 18 inches deep, and overlying a sterile sand subsoil. In an earlier letter to Kelly written June 2, 1936, he stated that "the pottery bearing horizon [was] only six to eight inches thick, of which from four to six inches have been *thoroughly* plowed" (Holder 1936). The site also included a large number of prehistoric burials that appeared to have constituted a sizable cemetery. Although no published final report of the excavation exists, after the conclusion of his investigations on St. Simons Holder wrote a brief summary report that was submitted to the Society for Georgia Archaeology for publication in the March 1938 *Proceedings* of the society (Holder 1938:8). In that statement he reported that he encountered the remains of some 200 individuals during the excavation of the Airport site.[8] Some of the individuals were included in what he called "group-secondary" burials, apparently large charnel house–like collections of disarticulated and fleshed bone, while the majority of the others were interred as extended primary burials. The Airport site also embraced a considerable village occupation distinguished by an extensive shell midden. Holder stated that he recorded more than 3,000 postholes on the site, all in such profusion that no complete patterning was discernable. Along with the postholes were a large number of pits containing shell, animal bone, and sherds. In addition, Holder recovered some 200 nonceramic artifacts during the excavation. Of these, fifty, or one-quarter of the total, were described as bone awls or pins. Some 21,077 sherds were collected from the site, which, Holder informed the readers of his report, "established a grit-tempered complicated stamp ware as the typical decorated pottery" (ibid.).[9] In a letter to Kelly written on October 5, 1936, he provided an analysis of a ceramic sample consisting of 8,678 sherds that had been recovered. The majority of the sherds, eighty-seven percent, were plain and of that percentage sixty-six percent were grit tempered. Of the decorated wares of all kinds (complicated stamped, cord marked, etc.) eighty-five percent were grit tempered. Eighty-four percent of the decorated sherds were "complex paddle stamps," with both rectilinear and curvilinear motifs (Holder 1936).

[8]Clark Larsen (1982:171–73), utilizing Holder's field notes, stated that "a minimum of 147 individuals [were recovered] from 85 single and multiple interments" by Holder at the Airport site. I am unable to account for the contradiction between Holder's statement in his field notes and that in the report to the Society for Georgia Archaeology regarding the number of individuals that he found buried at the site.

[9]There were probably more than 21,077 sherds found. Holder wrote to Arthur Kelly on December 12, 1936, from St. Simons Island as follows: "A total of 21,077 sherds has been collected, identified and catalogued. This sample will be considered definitive for the pottery types at the Airport site, and in the future only decorated ware and rims will be kept in hopes of getting as large a sample as possible, not only to determine the accuracy of decoration percentages, but also for museum display purposes" (Holder 1936).

On the basis of Holder's description of the ceramics recovered from the Airport site, the data suggest that the site is late—very likely a Mississippi Period site or perhaps even a historic town of the Mission Period Guale. However, in 1973 a new hanger was constructed at the airport whose location was to the south of the probable location of Holder's excavations. Thomas H. Eubanks carried out a salvage excavation for the Georgia Department of Natural Resources in the area of the new hanger construction. The area had been badly disturbed by a variety of activities, but he did recover a ceramic sample. The Eubanks sample is in marked contrast to that which Holder recovered. Whereas Holder recovered mostly plain, grit-tempered sherds, Eubanks recovered plain, sand-tempered sherds that can be typed as Refuge Plain.[10] The few decorated sherds from the most recent excavation were Deptford Checked Stamped. It is almost certain that the midden excavated by Eubanks was either from the Refuge or Deptford Phase of the Woodland Period.[11] The description by Holder of the burial placement suggests a cemetery rather than a mound. This in turn suggests that Holder was working in a late site because, prior to the Mississippi Period or perhaps even the Historic Period, coastal burials were exclusively in mounds. However, it is very likely that the entire Airport site had been disturbed, not only by deep plowing (letter from Holder to Kelly, June 2, 1936) but also by the Glynn County Road Department (Holder to Kelly, August 31, 1936), and that the area of the burials was really a mound that had been plowed down and probably robbed of its shell for road surfacing. Holder's description of the burials as occurring within a defined area and including primary and bundle burials of individuals, as well as several mass interments consisting of many individuals, and his description of the use of hematite in graves recall many of the burial situations that Moore encountered on St. Catherines and Ossabaw islands farther north on the Georgia coast (see below).

The Charlie King Mound was located on the southern half of St. Simons Island, approximately one mile south of the airport, off of Demere Road, in an established African-American community. Here Holder excavated eight burials that contained the remains of twenty-five individuals, "nearly all" of which were covered with hematite. The ceramic types comprising the 3,000 sherds recovered included "a well-executed cord mark" (cf. St. Catherines Fine Cord Marked), "a muck-ware-stamp" (?), and a "crude vegetal-tempered ware" (cf. St. Simons Fiber Tempered). The Charlie King Mound would seem to have belonged to the Deptford or Wilmington Phase of the Woodland Period of the Georgia coastal sequence.

Sea Island is a small island separated from St. Simons Island by a tidal creek. Actually, it is geologically recent and structurally a part of St. Simons Island. It is a product of the long shore current development, that is, a relict beach of the main island. Holder's excavation of the "mound on the north end of Sea Island" determined that the mound was the result of the capping with "two or more layers of shell and midden debris" of a naturally formed sand dune. The burials, most of which

---

[10]Throughout this introduction I use the ceramic type names and the ceramic chronology established by Chester DePratter (1979:109–32) for the American Museum of Natural History excavations on St. Catherines Island, Liberty County, Georgia (see below).

[11]Larsen (1982:72), following Milanich (1977:138–39, table 1) assigns the Airport site to the Wilmington Phase of the Woodland Period.

were primary, had been placed into the dune prior to the addition of the midden cap. Holder reported that one-third of the forty-five individuals buried in the mound were infants and children. Sherd-tempered cord-marked pottery (cf. St. Catherines Fine Cord Marked) recovered from the midden layer would place the Sea Island Mound within the pre-Irene Woodland Period.

Holder also carried out limited excavations at a site on Cascoigne Bluff, apparently near the point where the causeway connecting St. Simons Island with Brunswick reaches the island. This would have placed the site at the Sea Island Yacht Club. The description of the sherds recovered suggests that this site, like the Airport site, belongs to the Irene Phase or later Mission Period.

The work that Holder carried out in the very large shell mounds at Cannons Point on the north end of St. Simons Island overlooking Buttermilk Sound resulted in little information. Seemingly, they were composed only of shell and contained little or no cultural material. In an adjoining field marked by low midden mounds Holder found one burial and a large sample of "finely executed cord-mark pottery" (cf. Savannah Fine Cord Marked). The site would appear to belong in the same period as the Charlie King and Sea Island mounds. The University of Florida, working at Cannons Point in the 1970s, replicated Holder's experience.

In the years immediately after World War II there was no archaeology carried out in Glynn County. In the early 1950s archaeological activity was renewed by the National Park Service with investigations at Fort Frederica, initially under the direction of Charles Fairbanks and continued later under Joel Shiner. Fort Frederica, the ruins of a Colonial Period military installation and town on St. Simons Island, was not the sort of archaeological site that would have interested Moore.

Beginning in the 1970s the University of Florida initiated several field seasons of investigations that focused generally on the historic antebellum plantations on the northern half of St. Simons Island (Otto 1984). Historic sites, however, were not the sole concern of the archaeological work by the university on the island. Prehistoric sites in the area were examined, including two Archaic Period shell rings, the Taylor Mound, and Cooper and Indian fields on the northern half of the island. The results of the prehistoric archaeology were the subject of several theses and dissertations produced by graduate students in the Department of Anthropology at the University of Florida.

MOORE IN MCINTOSH COUNTY, GEORGIA

In March 1896 Moore crossed the Altamaha River from Glynn County into McIntosh County. From this point on Moore seemed to have hit his stride and to have worked more intensively. He certainly investigated a larger number of sites in each of the northern counties on the Georgia coast and seemingly with more result.

Moore began his investigations on the northern edge of the town of Darien, the county seat and a lumber port located on the northern side of the Altamaha River estuary. He commenced with the excavation of three **Mounds in Lawton's Field, Darien, McIntosh County** (Moore 1897:15–20). The first mound, designated Mound A by Moore, was reported to have suffered the consequences of years of plowing and additionally had been superficially trenched. It was slightly more than 4 feet in height and had a basal diameter of 46 feet. Moore encountered disturbed as well as undisturbed burials in the mound. Though "infrequent," there were plain, checked stamped, and complicated stamped sherds recovered. Despite the characterization by Moore that the mound was "unusually devoid of artifacts," shell beads, two celts, and "one bit of earthenware" were found associated with the burials (ibid.:16). Mound A, considering the ceramic sherds found, should probably be attributed to the Irene Phase of the coastal Mississippi Period.

The most interesting of the three mounds excavated was Mound B. It lay some 30 feet to the south of Mound A and was comparable to it in basal area and height. Like Mound A, Mound B had also been superficially trenched, which had resulted in the disturbance of several burials. In all Moore encountered thirty-two burials in the mound. Thirty of these were primary burials with the remaining two burials deposits of cremated bone. A number of the primary burials had been placed in log tombs. Moore referred to the log tombs as "pens" or "coops." He provided a drawing of one of these burials that, although undoubtedly accurate and clearly conveying the archaeological situation, presents a rather comically bizarre picture (ibid.:17, fig. 9). It is one of my favorite archaeological illustrations.

Moore reported that both plain sherds and sherds "with variously stamped patterns" were found in the fill of Mound B. In addition, two complete pottery vessels were found with one burial. While the larger of the two was dismissed as "a bowl of ordinary pattern" and not illustrated, the other was depicted full size (ibid.:18, pl. 1). This vessel has a notched rim strip and is incised over the upper half of the body. The vessel can be identified readily as belonging to the ceramic type Irene Incised (Caldwell and Waring 1939b:3–4).

Fragments of two pottery tobacco pipes, apparently unassociated with burials, were recovered from the mound (Moore 1897:19, figs. 10 and 11). Pottery pipes similar to the human head effigy pipe (ibid.:fig. 10) have been found at several sites in the northern coastal Georgia counties. Moore himself recovered and illustrated two almost identical pipes from the mound at Bourbon (ibid.:62, fig. 38) and from the mound in Dumoussay's Field, which are both sites on Sapelo Island, McIntosh County, Georgia (ibid.:fig. 46). Moore (ibid.:19) called attention to the fact that Charles C. Jones, Jr., illustrated two very similar pipes he identified as having been recovered from coastal shell mounds on Colonels Island in Liberty County, Georgia (Jones 1873:411, pl. 24, figs. 3 and 5). The pipes from Mound B as well as the ceramic types are typical of Irene Phase coastal sites.

The third mound in Lawton's Field, Mound C, as in the case of the other mounds, had been disturbed by a "small and superficial trench" prior to its excavation by Moore. The burials encountered in this mound had also been placed in log tombs. In all Moore found seven individual primary burials, none with mortuary accompaniments (Moore 1897:19–20). Moore commented that Mounds B and C in Lawton's Field were noteworthy because they contained the only log tomb burials that he met with during his entire coastal investigations, although he was told that log tomb burials were "in vogue" upstream on the Altamaha River (ibid.:20).[12]

Moore next excavated the **Townsend Mound, McIntosh County** (ibid.:20–

[12]The archaeological investigations of the American Museum of Natural History on St. Catherines Island, Liberty County, Georgia, encountered a log tomb, or at least a log-lined pit, in Stage I of Marys Mound on St. Catherines Island (Larsen and Thomas 1982:279), suggesting that such mortuary features were more widespread on the coast than Moore's experience indicated.

23), located "about one mile east of Darien." It was apparently situated on the high ground overlooking the salt marsh along Black Island Creek.[13] Moore reported that the mound was almost 4 feet high and some 42 feet in diameter, and although there had been no previous digging in the mound, it had sustained many years of plowing. Moore encountered human skeletal material at fifty-nine locations within the mound, and he estimated that this material represented the remains of some seventy-five individuals. The burials comprised not only primary burials but also bundle burials and cremations (ibid.:20).

There were no pottery vessels recovered from the mound. Moore wrote that "a small number of sherds, probably accidentally introduced, plain, with the ordinary square stamp, with intricate stamped decoration and in one case, incised, were present" (ibid.:21–22). The presence of the incised and the complicated stamped sherds argues that chronologically the mound belongs in the Irene Phase of the Mississippi Period. Savannah Checked Stamped, probably Moore's "ordinary square stamp" because it appears to be associated with Irene Phase wares, is recognized as a part of the Irene Phase ceramic complex. It should be pointed out, however, that a checked stamped ware of one or another of several types is found earlier in the coastal sequence.

Other artifacts with diagnostic value included pottery tobacco pipes and shell ear ornaments. The pipes, described by Moore as "of the same type as those from the mound at Darien" (ibid.:22, figs. 12 and 13), that is, Mound B at Lawton's Field, serve to further identify the mound as an Irene Phase structure (cf. Caldwell and McCann 1941:pl. 18).

The shell ear ornaments, because they are unillustrated, are less surely identified. Moore stated that "eleven pins of shell of the familiar type, none over 2.5 inches in length, were with various crania" (Moore 1897:22). The assumption here is that Moore has made reference to a familiar southeastern artifact, the shell earpin. These ornaments were produced from whelk columella; in form they had a knob head with a straight shank, and they have occurred in lengths up to 4.5 inches. Moore reported that the eleven pins from the Townsend Mound were associated with skulls. Elsewhere they have been regularly found on either side of skulls in primary burials, thus producing their identification as ear ornaments. In the Georgia coastal area the pins have been found in the Norman Mound, McIntosh County (Larson 1957:42, fig. 5B), and in the mortuary at the Irene site, Chatham County, Georgia (Caldwell and McCann 1941:27–28, pl. 19h). At these two coastal sites the earpins were in an undoubted late chronological context, the Irene Phase of the Mississippi Period. Writing recently about the Lake Jackson site, Leon County, Florida, Brain and Phillips had the following comment about these earpins, one of which was recovered from the Florida site: "The latter [a knobbed shell earpin] is a well-known type that was broadly distributed throughout the Southeast during the protohistoric period, and continued in use in some areas well into the eighteenth century" (Brain and Phillips 1996:181).

[13]The mound almost certainly lay in the vicinity of Fort King George, an early colonial establishment but also the site of a large Mission Period Guale town. Interestingly, on the *U.S. Geological Survey, Darien Quadrangle, Georgia, 7.5 Minute Series* sheet, about one-quarter mile north of Fort King George there is marked "Indian Cem." One can only wonder, given Moore's description of the archaeological situation, whether this is not the location of the Townsend Mound.

Of special interest within the artifact inventory of the Townsend Mound are the "considerable number of glass beads [that] lay with a burial two feet from the surface" (Moore 1897:23). Moore was well aware of the importance of these beads to the chronological identity of the mound. Although the burial was shallow, Moore was careful to point out that "the burial with which [the beads] lay had no appearance of being intrusive" (ibid.). The presence of glass beads argues that the mound was in use into the Historic Period. With the beads was "a minute piece of copper or of brass, of about the area of twice that of the head of a pin" (ibid.). This piece of metal may well have been a copper or brass bead. Unfortunately, we will never know the relationship in the mound of the burial with the glass beads to the other burials and their associated artifacts. One is tempted to identify the historic burial with the historic Mission Period, but until the beads are found, probably accidentally, in one of the many museums to which portions of the Moore collection were scattered, we will be unable to date the burial.

The **Passbey Mound, McIntosh County** (ibid.:23–24), located about one mile northwest of Darien, was 5.5 feet high and some 48 feet in diameter. Of the eleven burials found by Moore, one was a cremation, while those remaining were primary burials of individuals placed on their sides in a flexed position. There were no artifacts accompanying the burials, although "four or five" checked stamped sherds were found in the mound fill along with a single quartz projectile point. The description of the sherds is not sufficient to permit assignment of the mound to a temporal context given that checked stamped wares were present throughout the coastal sequence. The checked stamped wares of a particular type are distinguished by vessel shape, rim form, paste, and the kind of stamping.

In the general area of the boat landing of the same name Moore examined five **Mounds near "The Thicket," McIntosh County** (ibid.:24–26). The landing is located about five miles northeast of Darien.[14] Three of the mounds were on the Mansfield property and one each was on the King property and the Ravenel property. Moore supplied no information that would allow for an easy identification of any of the five mounds with a currently recognized temporal or cultural entity. Burials were encountered during the excavation of all the mounds, with the exception of the mound on the King property. The mound on the King property appears to have been a midden rather than a burial mound in that not only did it contain no burials but it was made up largely of shell and was of an irregular shape.

The mound on the Ravenel property was of some interest in that it contained two secondary burials. The smaller of the burials lay at the center of the mound 2 feet below the surface and contained two skulls along with other bone. Lying 4 feet below the surface and 2 feet below the first burial was a massive mortuary deposit consisting of twenty-seven skulls and a "confused mass of human bones" 10 inches thick and covering an area of 5 by 6 feet. With this mass of bone the only artifacts retrieved were two shell beads.

[14]The Thicket can be located on *U.S. Geological Survey, Ridgeville Quadrangle, Georgia—McIntosh Co., 7.5 Minute Series* south of Carnigan where a road runs east to the marsh and an unnamed tributary of the Carnigan River flows against the high ground. At this point there is a notation "Tolomato Spanish Mission Ruins" that marks a property locally identified as The Thicket. The ruins are those of a nineteenth-century sugar mill erroneously equated with a sixteenth-century Franciscan mission in the 1930s.

The third mound on the Mansfield property also contained at least one large mortuary deposit of bone including at least thirteen fragmentary skulls. Although the description of the artifacts found with these burials does not permit the ready identification of the mound with a particular archaeological complex, several of the artifacts are worthy of comment in that they represent an assemblage of materials exotic to the coastal area and perhaps provide some indication of the temporal position of the mound. Included in this assemblage were what appear to have been copper-covered wooden ear discs, described by Moore as follows: "parts of two copper discs each about 2.3 inches in diameter and having three concave-convex concentric circles by way of ornamentation" (ibid.:26). In addition to the copper discs, other artifacts fashioned from exotic materials included a small sheet of mica, a grooved hammer or maul of igneous rock, chert chips or flakes, and a pottery vessel with three compartments. Coastal Georgia is without local deposits of stone of any sort so the mica, chert, and igneous rock were almost certainly brought to the area. Moore found the pot "similar in style" to a vessel that he recovered from the Monroe Mound, Duval County, Florida. Goggin placed the Monroe Mound in the St. Johns Ja, late, Period and noted that mica and copper are often present in the Florida mounds of this period along with groups of flint chips (Goggin 1952:50). The Monroe Mound vessel that Moore likened to that from the third mound on the Mansfield property was illustrated by Goggin, who identified it as the type Weeden Island Plain (ibid.:144, pl. 3i). If the comparisons with the Duval County, Florida, Monroe Mound are valid, this suggests that the third of the mounds near The Thicket that Moore investigated on the Mansfield property can be assigned to the Woodland Period and is probably contemporary with Weeden Island and Swift Creek manifestations elsewhere.

The fifth mound that Moore examined in the vicinity of "The Thicket" was that owned by a man by the name of King (Moore 1897:26). The mound was apparently a large shell midden some 5 feet in height. Nothing indicating its use for mortuary purposes was found.

Moore next excavated on the Attwood property in the **Mound at Shell Bluff, McIntosh County** (Moore 1897:26–28). The mound was probably located at or near the place where the Shellbluff River, a tidal stream, flows against the high ground at Valona, a small settlement north of Darien (see *U.S. Geological Survey, Doboy Sound Quadrangle, Georgia—McIntosh Co., 7.5 Minute Series*). Moore reported that the mound had been almost obliterated by cultivation and that digging on the part of the landowner had further disturbed it. The mound fill contained few sherds, and none was identified as complicated stamped or for that matter as having any other distinctive characteristics (Moore 1897:27). Despite the disturbed condition of the mound Moore found thirty-one burials, six of which he briefly described.

Burial No.12 was apparently an urn burial contained within a checked stamped vessel. Burial No. 20 consisted of four pottery vessels, two of which contained calcined human bone. The first of these latter urn burials was in a plain jar about 10.5 inches high with a maximum diameter of 10.5 inches (ibid.:27, pl. 2). It was covered by a second plain vessel that, because of its fragmentary condition, was not described by Moore. The second urn burial was also contained within a plain jar 7.5 inches high with an orifice 7.5 inches wide (ibid.:27–28, pl. 3). A fourth vessel, a checked stamped bowl, lay crushed beside the second urn. It may, in fact, have been the cover for the second urn. There is a comparability between the two plain burial urns in

Burial No. 20 and several of the vessel shapes associated with the ceramic type Savannah Burnished Plain (Caldwell and Waring 1939b:7 with accompanying illustration; see also Caldwell and McCann 1941:fig. 19). It should be noted that Caldwell and Waring (1939b:7) identified the Shell Bluff site as one of the sites where this ceramic type occurred. Although the fragmentary checked stamped vessels associated with Burials Nos. 12 and 20 cannot be identified with certainty, it is very likely that they can be equated with the type Savannah Checked Stamped, especially when considered in conjunction with the probability that the two urns belong to the type Savannah Burnished Plain. If my suppositions are correct, then the mound at Shell Bluff can be placed within the Savannah Phase of the Mississippi Period.

Creighton Island is a little more than two and a quarter miles long and three-quarters of a mile wide and is completely surrounded by marsh. It lies east of Belleville Point and just south of the Sapelo River (see *U.S. Geological Survey, Shellman Bluff Quadrangle, Georgia—McIntosh Co., 7.5 Minute Series*). A large archaeological site overlooking the Sapelo River covers a sizable portion of a pasture on the north end of the island. The site, designated by Moore as **Creighton Island, McIntosh County—North End** (Moore 1897:28–43), is characterized by a considerable number of shell middens that have been reduced in height and spread through years of cultivation. Here, Moore dug into a substantial mound from which he recovered many burials. It is difficult to be certain as to the exact location of the mound. Moore described it as being about "one mile S.E. by E. from the landing" (ibid.:28). Today, however, the landing currently in use lies on the southwestern side of the island about two miles from the northern end. At the present there is no apparent place suitable for a north-end landing. The high ground of the island in the north-end area is everywhere separated from all of the creeks and rivers that might serve as an approach to the island by substantial stretches of marsh that are impossible to cross either on foot or by watercraft.

As described by Moore, the mound was quite large in comparison to other coastal mounds. Moore gave the dimensions of the structure as extending 116 feet along a northwest by southeast axis with a maximum width of approximately 100 feet. Its greatest height was 34 inches. Moore pointed out that the mound contained the "usual fireplaces and fragments of charcoal" and that throughout the mound were layers and pockets of oyster shell alternating with areas of sand (ibid.:28–30). This description suggests that the mound was the result of the building up of an occupational midden. On the other hand, if it is the product of accretion, it is difficult with the information available to characterize such growth as either deliberate or unintentional. Further, the reported presence of 220 individuals found throughout the mound suggests that the growth of the mound was as a cemetery rather than as a burial mound of the type heretofore encountered by Moore on the coast. This suggestion is supported by the observation by Moore that a number of the burials were disturbed by aboriginal pits.

There is one further possibility for the function of the mound that comes to mind, one that is dictated by the large size and nature of the mound, as well as its temporal position. Conceivably the earthwork could have been a platform mound supporting a mortuary temple or other public structure. It has always seemed strange to me that there has been but one platform mound identified on the coast: that at the Irene site. Mississippi Period sites are numerous, well distributed, and large throughout the northern half of the Georgia coast. In addition, there is a considerable body of archaeological and ethnohistorical evidence that the coastal occupations were as socially complex as most of the sites of the interior. I suspect that the nature of the sandy coastal soils made it difficult if not impossible to construct high stable temple mounds that would withstand regular usage. Mounds that were built of sand would have been subject to severe erosion in the high rainfall environment of the coastal area, arguing against the construction of steep-sided mounds of very great height. For the most part, reported mounds of any type in the coastal area are not very steep sided or very high. The Irene Mound was demonstrably a platform mound; however, the several mound stages were not particularly high—Mound 5 was 4.5 feet high, Mound 6 was 5.5 feet high, and Mound 7 (the last of the apparently functional platform mounds) was 7.5 feet high. The slope angle of the sides ranged from twenty-five degrees for Mound 5, to twenty degrees for Mound 6, to forty-five degrees for Mound 7. These stages, although constructed of sand, were each stabilized in part by clay or oyster shell (Caldwell and McCann 1941:14–17). Most of the reported mounds were of such an inconsiderable elevation that they were brought under cultivation without any real effort. Continued cultivation served to reduce the height until even the very identification of the mound as such is at best difficult. Thus, I would argue that it would be almost impossible, without excavation, to distinguish a platform mound from a burial mound except in terms of the relatively large areal extent of the former compared to the latter and the identification of construction stages across a profile.

It is perhaps appropriate to note here an unpublished comment that appeared as an entry in the Moore notes and one that was repeated in the log (this seems to have covered the daily schedule of Moore or the *Gopher;* it is not clear which). The entry indicated that Moore went to see a mound at Cedar Point, McIntosh County, on about March 11, 1897. The notes stated that the mound was "considerably leveled at [the] top by a church for colored people (we were informed), [it is] now removed. Deep depression at portions of margin [is this a borrow pit?]" (R2, B11, p. 155). I recall that on a number of occasions Antonio J. Waring, Jr., stated that there was supposedly a platform mound at Cedar Point, but he never took me to see it. A mound large enough to support a church and one that might have had a top level enough for the construction of a church may well have been a platform mound. A platform mound, the base for a mortuary temple, on the north end of Creighton Island may have existed, and if so reexamination of the mound explored by Moore might provide confirmation.

The types of burials in the Creighton Island Mound ranged from large deep pits with thick deposits (e.g., 6 inches) of calcined bone, to primary extended burials, to primary flexed burials, to urn burials of infants. In all there appeared to have been eight urn burials and in cases in which Moore was able to identify the skeletal remains contained within the urn the identification was that of an infant. An additional point of interest is that the urn burials, when their location was stated, appeared to be either beyond the margins of the mound as it was defined by Moore or else just under the margin of the earthwork. Unfortunately, with but two exceptions, Moore made no attempt to describe the type of pottery used either for the urns themselves or for the vessels employed as covers. Moore referred to these vessels repeatedly by the maddeningly ambiguous phrase "a vessel of the ordinary type" (Moore 1897:32–33). Given this characteristic type of reportage, one wonders how Moore could state, with an apparently straight face, the following: "*A detailed description of vessels used, or probably used, for interments has been given*" (ibid.:39, italics added for emphasis). One exception was a significant description given for the burial urn called Vessel G. This pot was described as "a bowl of about 4 gallons capacity, with marginal incised decoration surmounting the complicated stamp" (ibid.:32). On the basis of the reference to incising and complicated stamping in the description, the bowl can undoubtedly be typed as Irene Complicated Stamped. The second exception was an illustration (ibid.:fig. 23) that depicted a small jar 5 inches high with a globular body below a relatively long but only slightly constricted neck leading to a minute flaring of the rim. Decoration consists of two horizontal rows of small appliquéd nodes or rosettes, each with a centered hollow reed punctate. The first of these rows follows the break between the body of the vessel and the neck while the second lies immediately below the exterior of the vessel lip. Between the two defining rows of nodes, the surface of the neck is decorated with a large checked stamping. The body of the vessel is plain. The use of the appliquéd hollow reed punctated nodes, especially those placed just below the lip, is a variant of a very common rim treatment associated with the Mississippi Period Irene Phase wares (Caldwell and Waring 1939b:2–5).

Although he stated that such were not abundant, Moore did briefly discuss the sherds recovered from the mound fill. The sherds were characterized as "complicated stamp and various patterns of incised decoration" (Moore 1897:38). Again, the use of incised and complicated stamped decoration on the sherds argues that we are dealing with the Irene Phase wares Irene Incised and Irene Complicated Stamped.

Moore illustrated two of the nine tobacco pipes that he found associated with burials (ibid.:figs. 21 and 22). The illustrated pipes, presumably representative of the other seven, were typical of those associated with the Irene Phase.

Other artifacts recovered from the Creighton Island Mound that have contextual significance include a series of three shell gorgets (ibid.:35–37, figs. 17 through 19). The first of these gorgets (ibid.:fig. 17) was found with the burial of an adolescent and is a rather crude affair some 3 inches in diameter. Its decoration consists of a series of concentric perforations. Brain and Phillips, in their recent encyclopedic study of shell gorgets in the eastern United States, placed this gorget within the geometric category but did not assign it to a particular style (Brain and Phillips 1996:42, Ga-MI-CI6). The second gorget with a 3.8-inch diameter was found with an adult male "having many objects in association" (Moore 1897:36, fig. 18). The design is composed of two concentric bands of small cut-out half circles contained within a plain gorget rim. The effect is that of two bands that appear as a series of rays around a central area with an incised cross. This gorget was also categorized by Brain and Phillips as geometric and identified as falling within their Claflin style (Brain and Phillips 1996:38, Ga-MI-CI2). The third gorget, placed with an infant, has a diameter of 2.4 inches and bears the design of a conventionalized coiled rattlesnake (Moore 1897:37, fig. 18). Brain and Phillips placed this gorget in their rattlesnake category and assigned it to the Lick Creek style (Brain and Phillips 1996:84, Ga-MI-CI3).

In their discussion of the temporal considerations of gorgets in the geometric and rattlesnake categories, Brain and Phillips had the following comments: "[R]attlesnake gorgets . . . first appear in the archaeological record during the early protohistoric period. More briefly restricted to the early protohistoric are . . . probably the other eastern geometric styles [i.e., the gorgets in Moore's figures 17 and 18]" (ibid.:395). If we accept this analysis, the Creighton Island gorgets are late and are compatible with a late Mississippi or Protohistoric Period date for the Irene Phase.

With burials in the Creighton Island Mound Moore found sixteen shell earpins, the other shell artifact with chronological significance. He stated that "they are invariably found near the skull" (Moore 1897:37). Although they were not illustrated and he referred to them simply as "pins" while speculating that they were probably used in the hair, they were almost certainly the knobbed ear ornaments made from whelk columella that are so widely distributed in the Southeast and, on the Georgia coast, associated with the Irene Phase.

Moore recovered a copper celt from a pit containing a primary burial (ibid.:41). The celt was almost 8 inches in length, a little more than 1 inch wide along the shank, and slightly more than 0.25 inch thick and was characterized by a flared bit 2 inches wide. It was comparable to copper celts found at Mississippi Period sites throughout the Southeast, although the type more commonly occurred at Etowah, Moundville, and Spiro where relatively large numbers of these axes were placed in graves.

In 1951 I visited the northern end of Creighton Island as part of a survey to locate possible Spanish mission sites on the mid-Georgia coast (Larson, n.d.). At the time of my visit much of the northern portion of the island had been cleared and recently cultivated in preparation for its use as a pasture. Low shell middens, composed mostly of oyster shell, covered most of the exposed acreage. Conditions were ideal for a surface collection and it was possible to make an unstructured collection over a rather extensive portion of the site. The sherd types found on the surface included Savannah Checked Stamped, Irene Incised, Irene Complicated Stamped, Altamaha Complicated Stamped, Altamaha Incised, and Altamaha Red Filmed. The Altamaha wares are associated with the seventeenth-century historic Guale occupation of the Georgia mid-coastal region. Along with the aboriginal Altamaha wares from the Creighton Island survey, there were several historic sherds of European origin found, including two Spanish olive jar sherds and one Fig Springs Polychrome majolica sherd.[15] The analysis of the materials from my site examination would seem to confirm the assessment of the results of Moore's work, that is, that the site dates to the Mississippi Period and into the Historic Period if a Mission Period occupation at the site is acknowledged.

Moore dug into a second, smaller mound near the landing on Creighton Island (Moore 1897:43). This mound can also be equated with the Irene Phase on the basis

[15]The Altamaha wares have been regularly found in northeastern Florida where they have been identified as San Marcos wares. They have been associated with the historic Spanish sites of that area of Florida (Smith 1948:314–15, pl. 31). The complicated stamped ware was initially identified by Joseph Caldwell and named King George Malleated. He found it at Fort King George, Darien, McIntosh County, Georgia, during depression-era excavations at that site. There the ware was associated with a supposed seventeenth-century Spanish mission (Caldwell 1943). Later Georgia usage saw the type name changed to Altamaha Line Block Stamped. Other wares of the Altamaha series include Altamaha Incised, Red Filmed, and Check Stamped.

of the description of the sherds found in the fill of the mound. These were described by Moore as decorated with incising as well as complicated stamping. The description would almost certainly serve to identify Irene Incised and Irene Complicated Stamped. The fill of the mound also yielded a small clay human female figurine (ibid.:fig. 26) that had lost its head, arms, and legs. Following his very brief discussion of the figurine, Moore noted: "Another effigy of a woman, in a like state of mutilation was shown us by a gentleman living on the mainland a few miles from Creighton Island, who stated it had been washed from a shell bluff on Cedar Creek, fronting his residence. This figure tapered gracefully at the waist and bore incised ornamentation front and back" (ibid.:43). Cedar Creek, a tidal stream, flows against a low bluff for about one-half mile immediately south of Cedar Point, which in turn lies about one mile due west of the southern tip of Creighton Island. For most of its length the bluff along Cedar Creek was the location of a large Irene Phase site. Today, little of the site remains as a result of the bluff erosion and residential development that have taken place in the past fifty years.

Although Moore did not illustrate or describe the incised ornamentation on the Cedar Creek figurine, it should be noted in passing that two clay figurines were recovered from the Pine Harbor site, across the Sapelo River, about three miles northwest of the northern end of Creighton Island. A description of one of these figurines has been published (Larson 1955). The Pine Harbor figurines are almost certainly representations of males in that unlike the Creighton Island and Cedar Creek figurines they lack modeled breasts. However, like the Cedar Creek figurine, the Pine Harbor figurines have incised decoration front and back. The decoration on the Pine Harbor figurines delineates the costume of what has come to be called the falcon dancer, and although both of the ceramic effigies lack a head, what seems to represent a raptorial bird mask is depicted with incised lines, pendant, upside down on the back of the figurine, as if it had been simply pushed back off of the head and was suspended from the neck.

Moore's investigation of the **Hopkins Mound, Belleville, McIntosh County** (Moore 1897:43–44), which he located on the south side of the Sapelo River, one and a half miles north of Crescent,[16] did not produce results that were considered worthy of extended description or discussion. The mound was a high one, slightly more than 13 feet, which is perhaps the highest that Moore encountered on the Georgia coast, with a basal diameter of 76 feet. Again, the Hopkins Mound was quite possibly a platform mound. The size of the mound and the shell strata suggest that it may have served as the base of a mortuary temple or other public building.

The limited information presented by Moore focused on a physical description of the Hopkins Mound construction rather than its contents. Here is as good a point as any to make several comments about the kind of mound construction with which Moore contended during his traversal of the Georgia coast. Moore noted no soil lenses or other evidence of what might be considered "basket loading" in the Hopkins Mound. This situation was one that was almost uniformly true of all of the coastal mounds that he examined. I suspect that, in fact, there was basket loading in the mounds

[16]The 1954 *U.S. Geological Survey, Shellman Bluff Quadrangle, Georgia—McIntosh Co., 7.5 Minute Series* identifies the area of the mound location as Belleville Point rather than simply as Belleville.

and that early in the history of these earthworks it was possible to observe the lenses created through this manner of construction. Such lenses would initially have been marked by organic matter in the soil taken from the surface or by color differences in the subsoil sources exploited. In the coastal areas of Georgia the soil is composed, almost without exception, of fine sand. These soils are remarkably porous and when found, as they are, in an environment with high annual rainfall will leach to a uniform appearance in a relatively short time. Moore regularly reported that the coastal mounds he investigated were composed of a light yellow sand, the soil color a mound might well be expected to attain following several hundred years of exposure to heavy rain after its construction. The first and third of the Mansfield mounds near The Thicket (ibid.:24–25) were other examples of mounds composed entirely of undifferentiated yellow sand or, in the case of the third mound, yellowish-brown sand. As a result of the recent archaeological excavation of a number of mounds on St. Catherines Island, Liberty County, Georgia, by the American Museum of Natural History, a similar interpretation of the construction history of coastal burial mounds was advanced (Larsen and Thomas 1986:8).

Although the Hopkins Mound was without soil lensing, it did contain several shell strata. Moore reported that five or six layers of oyster shell occupied the central portion of the mound. He did not, however, provide a profile nor did he state that the strata were horizontal. Each of these shell strata was reported as being some 4 inches thick and separated from the shell stratum lying above or below by slightly more than 1 foot of sand. It is entirely possible that these strata were laid down in an attempt to contain erosion on the summit and slopes of a platform mound as it was enlarged from time to time over the period of its active use, with each stratum having been at one time a functional mound surface. Given the manner in which Moore reported on the excavations of the mounds he examined, it is difficult to be certain whether the strata were confined only to the central section of the mound or whether they remained horizontal throughout their length and width and followed the slope of earlier surfaces. On the other hand, acknowledging the manner in which the mound was dug and reported, in this instance it is impossible to insist that my explanation of the use of the oyster shell for erosion control on a platform mound is more than conjecture.

Oyster shell was a regular feature of coastal mounds and its abundance in middens made it an obvious element for use in burial mound fill, as well as for use as a material to stabilize the mounds. In a number of instances subfloor burial pits were lined with shell before the placement of the body. In many of these examples the pits were also filled with shell. In other instances, a body might be covered with a layer of shell after it had been placed on a cleared surface. Sometimes the bodies were placed around an existing mound of naturally accumulated midden shell and then covered with sand or more shell. This latter situation was suggested in those mounds in which Moore commented on encountering the "usual fireplaces," as was the case with the Creighton Island Mound (Moore 1897:29).

There was another feature of the Hopkins Mound noted by Moore that is worthy of comment. He recorded that "a well-marked black band at about the level of the surrounding territory extended [from the margin of the mound] to the center [of the mound]" (ibid.:44). This feature appears to represent the old topsoil, protected from the leaching effects of rain, that had been buried at the time the mound was constructed. Moore remarked on this feature in mounds repeatedly. He observed it under the Creighton Island Mound where the numerous pits cutting through the black band gave the band a broken and irregular appearance (ibid.:29). The black layer was also present beneath Mounds A and B in Lawton's Field (ibid.:15, 16), as well as under the Passbey Mound (ibid.:23–24).

The excavation of the Hopkins Mound at Belleville revealed burials "at ten points," including flexed burials, large masses of human bone, and cremations. Burial accompaniments were meager, consisting of hematite and a few shell beads. "Practically no sherds were met with" in the mound fill (ibid.:44).

The Moore excavation of the **Mound near Crescent, McIntosh County** (ibid.:44–45), provided us with no useful information for determining the cultural or temporal position of the mound, although it was little disturbed by previous digging and of a relatively large size. Again, there were cremations, bundle burials, and one primary burial. Moore wrote that he found no complicated stamped ware among the few sherds that were encountered in the mound fill. Once more grave goods were sparse and consisted solely of a few pearl beads and hematite (ibid.).

The **Walker Mound, McIntosh County,** located in Cooper's Field, was identified by Moore as "about 1.5 miles in a westerly direction from Contentment" (ibid.:45). Moore was probably confused about the settlement name. He almost certainly intended to locate the mound with reference to Shellman Bluff. Today Shellman Bluff is a small fishing and resort community located on the upper reach of the Broro River, a tidal stream connecting the Sapelo River to the south and the Julienton River to the north (see *U.S. Geological Survey, Shellman Bluff Quadrangle, Georgia—McIntosh Co., 7.5 Minute Series*). At the time of Moore's visit Shellman Bluff was certainly in existence and would have provided a mooring for the *Gopher* while he was engaged in his mound explorations. The log indicates that on most days the *Gopher* would depart from the site under investigation at the end of the seven-hour work day and then tie up for the night at either Darien or Belleville Point. In the instance of the Walker Mound exploration the *Gopher* returned to Belleville at the end of the day. It hardly seems likely that Moore would have used Contentment as a place to tie up during the work day. Contentment Bluff is two miles north of Shellman Bluff in a northeasterly direction and on a small tidal extension of the Broro River. Further, the Walker Mound would have been at least two and a half miles southwest of Contentment Bluff, not the one and a half miles that Moore gave for the distance.

At the time of the Moore visit, the mound was almost 6 feet high and had a basal diameter of 46 feet. Moore described the mound as follows:

> The mound had previously been dug into to an inconsiderable extent. On its northern margin grew a live-oak 5 feet in diameter, 3 feet from the ground. This tree was not removed, though otherwise the mound was totally demolished, being dug through at a depth considerably below the level of the surrounding territory.
>
> The mound was composed of rich, loamy, brown sand with many local layers of oyster shells. The usual charcoal and fireplaces were present. A black layer from 3 inches to 1 foot thickness, made up of sand mingled with charcoal in minute particles, ran through the mound at about the level of the surrounding territory. At the center of the mound, measurements showed this layer to be 5 feet 9 inches below the surface. (Moore 1897:45)

The mound would appear to have been built up of midden material removed from the area surrounding the mound, while the "black layer" seemingly represented the buried topsoil preserved beneath the mound construction. In about 1953 I was taken to the Walker Mound remnant by a U.S. Coast and Geodetic Survey geologist who was at that time engaged in the plane table mapping of the area in preparation for the publication of the *U.S. Geological Survey, Shellman Bluff Quadrangle, Georgia—McIntosh Co., 7.5 Minute Series* sheet. At that time the huge live oak described by Moore was still standing in an open field, marking that portion of the mound that Moore did not excavate. These trees were frequently left standing in cultivated fields and in pastures to provide shade for field hands and herds during the hot summers. Unfortunately, within the next year or so of my visit to the mound, the entire area, consisting of hundreds of acres, was planted in a pine plantation, effectively losing the mound amidst thousands of slash pine. I assume the huge live oak continues to mark its location; however, several attempts to return to the mound have ended in failure.

Moore reported that he encountered the remains of some seventy-five individuals at "thirty six points," a phrase that presumably meant thirty-six burials. Seemingly, fifteen of these burials were primary burials of individuals, approximately ten of the interments were bundle burials apparently of single individuals, six were cremations in urns, and five were deposits of burned and unburned bone composed of multiple individuals. Immediately adjacent to one of the larger deposits of bone was a heavily charred and rectangular log structure 32 inches long within which were burned human bones. Moore identified the structure as a pyre. Fires had been built against several of the primary burials. Also, a number of primary burials as well as the massed bone deposits had been placed in pits that were then filled with oyster shell.

Grave goods in the mound were rare and consisted primarily of shell beads of various types. A number of undecorated whelk bowls or cups accompanied several burials. With one deposit of bone were four of the shell bowls along with three stone celts and two shell earpins, while associated with eight shell bowls was a group of five urn burials. With one burial, an isolated skull, was a shell bowl with a simple incised decoration on the exterior surface consisting of "three incised lines forming a parallelogram with a portion of the margin of the opening as one of the shorter sides" (Moore 1897:50).

Of considerable interest are the pottery vessels that were encountered during the excavation of the Walker Mound. Of the nine vessels found in the mound, Moore was able to recover and restore six. Seven of the vessels were containers or covers for urn burials while the other two accompanied bundle burials. Three of the vessels, part of a group of five urn burials that occupied a more or less central position in the mound, were so fragmentary that "all hope of restoration was abandoned" (ibid.:51). The other two vessels are illustrated. One is a large, 15-inch-high Irene Incised bowl (ibid.:pl. 5). The peculiarly shaped second vessel, also 15 inches high, has a short undecorated neck that rises from a depressed portion at the top of a globular body that has Irene Complicated Stamped decoration (ibid.:pl. 6). Of the remaining two vessels, one served as a cover for the other, an urn that contained an infant cremation. They were undecorated and were not illustrated by Moore (ibid.:47). The two vessels that accompanied bundle burials were decorated in the most interesting and elaborate manner. The first of these, found with the burial numbered 27 by Moore, was incised with a design redolent of Southeastern Ceremonial Complex relationships. The decoration consisted of lines incised into the exterior surface of the vessel, and, in addition, areas of the polished or smoothed vessel surface within the incised lines had been scraped away and filled with red pigment creating a champlevé-like effect (ibid.:50, pl. 1, fig. 2). The second vessel found with Burial No. 28, a bundle burial, was similar in shape, decoration technique, and decorative motif to that just described. Elsewhere I have identified the pottery type characteristic of the bowls found with the Walker Mound Burials Nos. 27 and 28 as McIntosh Incised (Larson 1958a:428). The type is a minority ware that serves to distinguish the Pine Harbor ceramic complex of the central Georgia coast from the Irene ceramic complex found at the Irene site and elsewhere on the northern Georgia coast.

It should be noted that W. H. Holmes illustrated, with excellent photographs, three of the vessels Moore recovered from the Walker Mound including the Irene Incised bowl, the Irene Complicated Stamped jar with the short neck, and the McIntosh Incised bowl with Burial No. 28. He also provided roll-outs of the designs found on the two McIntosh Incised bowls from the bundle burial (Holmes 1903:pl. 119 through 121).

The **Mound near Contentment, McIntosh County** (Moore 1897:53–55), was described by Moore as located "on the bank of the Broro River, a water-way joining the Sapelo River and Julianton [sic] creek . . . about one-half mile in a northerly direction from Contentment" (ibid.:53). As pointed out in the discussion of the Walker Mound, Moore appears to have confused the Shellman Bluff and Contentment settlements. Shellman Bluff is on the Broro River just south of its junction with the Julienton River (as it is identified on the 1954 quadrangle sheet). The map provided by Moore at the beginning of the report of his Georgia coast investigations lacks the detail that would make it useful for locating the sites with any precision. Nevertheless, the map does appear to erroneously place Contentment at the location of Shellman Bluff. Further, except for Shellman Bluff, today there is no other settlement located on the Broro River. It is almost certain that the name of the settlement that he used for the location and orientation of his sites in this area should be Shellman Bluff rather than Contentment.

The diagnostic materials that were recovered from the mound near Contentment, whose identities and characteristics can be determined from the text descriptions, were exclusively ceramics. These comprised a number of pottery vessels used to contain the cremated remains of individuals. Moore described them as "undecorated or with an ordinary stamp" (ibid.:54). In several instances the urn burial utilized two vessels, one to contain the cremation and the second to serve as a cover for the first. One such cover bowl is described as "an inverted, undecorated pot somewhat resembling in shape a reversed cone with rounded apex" (ibid.:54). This description could well apply to the type Savannah Burnished Plain (Caldwell and Waring 1939b:2). These conical, carinated bowls have been found to have been used elsewhere as urn covers; for example, Burial 14 in the Norman Mound, Belleville Point, McIntosh County, Georgia (Larson 1957:42). If the identification of the vessel type as Savannah Burnished Plain is correct, then the ware associated with it, the "ordinary stamp" ware found by Moore in the mound near Contentment, may well be Savannah Complicated Stamped. If the identification of these two wares is correct, it would argue that the chronological position of the mound in which they were found is the Savannah II Phase of the Mississippi Period.

The two **Low Mounds near Broro Neck, McIntosh County** (Moore 1897:55), provided Moore with little that serves to position them within the presently defined Georgia coastal chronology or cultural framework. The use of hematite and cremations in both mounds echoed mortuary practices frequently encountered by Moore elsewhere in the McIntosh County burial mounds.

Moore excavated on a Georgia barrier island for the first time when he initiated the investigation of the large mound on **Sapelo Island, McIntosh County, Bourbon** (ibid.:55–66).[17] Reached from Sapelo Sound via Blackbeard Creek, the African-American settlement at Bourbon was still occupied in 1897 at the time of Moore's visit. The excavated mound stood some 8 feet high and was 72 feet in diameter. Moore noted that its surface was covered with shell and made up of "local layers of bright yellow sand dug from beneath the surface loam of the field; of dark sand containing occasional shell, mostly belonging to the oyster; of shell with admixture of dark sand and, at the surface, of a layer of midden refuse made up of crushed shell and loam, varying from 8 inches to 2 feet in thickness and occasionally extending still farther down over burials let in from above" (ibid.:56). Moore found 192 burials in the mound with this total made up of primary burials, cremations, deposits of burned and unburned bone, and urn burials. Few sherds were included in the mound fill and those that he observed were reported to be undecorated or cord marked. He was specific about not having found complicated stamped sherds in the mound fill. Among the whole vessels recovered, most often in fragments, were several that he described in enough detail to have diagnostic value. Burial No.134, a bundle burial, was contained within a vessel with an incised decoration below the rim and a complicated stamped decorated body (ibid.:59). This vessel was almost surely a pot with an Irene Incised upper body and an Irene Complicated Stamped lower body. Contained within what Moore described as a complicated stamped vessel was Burial No. 135, another bundle burial (ibid.). Moore gave the same description to the vessel that contained Burial No. 137 (ibid.). Although it is possible that one or the other or both of these two vessels were Savannah Complicated Stamped burial urns, the probabilities are greater that both could be classified as Irene Complicated Stamped ware. Accompanying Burial No. 26, that of a child, was a jar with a flared rim, a constricted neck, and a hemispherical body. The exterior was decorated immediately below the rim with an encircling row of appliquéd clay nodes (ibid.:60) of the sort typical of one type of jar rim decoration characteristic of Irene Phase ceramics.

Another vessel, found in "caved sand" and therefore without a burial association, was described as having on "such parts as were recovered . . . on the base and sides—an unusual occurrence—an intricate incised decoration" (ibid.:61). The vessel was tiny, only about 2 inches in diameter. Although certainty is impossible, the description of the decoration may well refer to a McIntosh Incised vessel, some of

---

[17]Bourbon Field apparently acquired its name, as did several other places on the island, subsequent to the settlement there in 1790 of a small group of the petite French nobility who had fled the revolutionary turbulence in France. Today the African-American residents of Sapelo refer to the old settlement as "Babbune" or, as Moore renders the phonetics of the Geechee dialect (cf. Gullah) pronunciation, "Boobone" (Moore 1897:55).

which are of odd shapes and sizes. Found with Burial No. 113 was a small cord-marked bowl (ibid.), which, given the other pottery types in the mound, may be assignable to the Savannah Fine Cord Marked type. Accompanying Burial No. 154 was a small fragmentary checked stamped bowl, very likely Savannah Checked Stamped. Using what are interpreted as diagnostic pottery descriptions provided by Moore, it seems likely that the mound at Bourbon can be positioned within either the Savannah II or the Irene Phase of the Mississippi Period.

Although found in "caved sand" and lacking a burial provenience, a human head effigy pottery pipe of the same type as that from the Townsend Mound further argues for an Irene Phase temporal position for the mound. Supporting this argument was the recovery from the mound of twelve earpins, the longest about 4.5 inches, all lying in association with skulls (ibid.:63). In addition, two gorgets were found (ibid.). The first, 2 inches in diameter and with "a rough diamond-shaped figure" incised in the center (ibid.:fig. 41), was recovered from shell that formed a midden layer in the mound. Brain and Phillips were not able to assign this gorget to one of the types they developed for gorget classification (Brain and Phillips 1996:42). The second gorget, circular and about 1.7 inches in diameter, was found with Burial No. 92, that of a child about seven years old. Incised on its surface was the familiar conventionalized rattlesnake (Moore 1897:63). Brain and Phillips consider the rattlesnake gorget type protohistoric (Brain and Phillips 1996:395), thus also providing support for a late temporal position for the mound at Bourbon.

Other funerary inclusions in the mound were thirty-four conch shell bowls (Moore identified three cut from the channeled whelk [*Busycon canaliculatum*]; the remainder were from the lightning whelk [*Busycon contrarium*]). Ten of the total number were recovered from a single deposit (Moore 1897:63). Several steatite objects were found in the mound. Burial No. 137 included a circular piece of steatite approximately 2 inches in diameter and half an inch thick. One surface of the object bore a series of spiral lines that appeared to be a conventionalized representation of a coiled rattlesnake complete with rattles; the reverse side carried a series of cross-hatched lines arranged in a diamond pattern. With Burial No. 45 was a small human effigy 1.8 inches long carved from steatite. While no legs were represented, the arms, head, and upper torso are present. A somewhat similar steatite effigy, but with a more detailed face, was found with a burial in the Norman Mound at Belleville Point, McIntosh County (Larson 1957:42, fig. 5B). It should also be noted that a "small bead of blue glass" was found at the surface of the mound during its excavation (Moore 1897:66). Moore recognized the potential significance of the bead, but because the mound burials lacked historic materials its presence was attributed to Indians that were known to have been on Sapelo during the Historic Period.

A second mound located some 150 yards south of the first mound was excavated by Moore at **Sapelo Island, McIntosh County. Low Mound at Bourbon** (Moore 1897:66–67). Only slightly more than 3 feet high and 38 feet in diameter, it was considerably smaller than the first mound. Although Moore found evidence of burials at twelve locations within the mound, no diagnostic grave goods were recovered. Seemingly all were primary burials; however, there was great variation in burial positions including extended, flexed, and "semi-sitting" placement (ibid.).

The shell middens in Bourbon Field have since been mapped, the entire field was cultivated, and a surface collection was done within a tightly controlled grid.

Finally, a series of test excavations was made over the entire site. The site was determined to cover approximately 14 hectares with 119 shell middens that were defined and mapped along with what is presumably a small burial mound. The site occupation covers the range of Georgia coastal aboriginal history from the Late Archaic Period to the Mission Period (Crook 1984, 1985). The two mounds excavated by Moore could not be relocated with certainty, but one, probably the large mound, appears to have been situated on the western edge of the southern half of the site (ibid. 1985:fig. 1).

The **Sapelo Island, McIntosh County. Mound in Dumoussay's Field**[18] was a little more than one mile north-northwest of Bourbon (Moore 1897:47). Reached by McCoy Creek, a tidal stream that drains into Blackbeard Creek, the landing was situated at the north end of an old field now planted in pine. The mound lay about one-quarter of a mile northwest of the landing. The field itself, like the other old fields on the island, Bourbon, Drawbar, Kenan, and Long Row, was characterized by hundreds of low shell middens 20 to 50 feet in diameter. The burial mound, apparently having suffered as much as one hundred years of cultivation, was reported by Moore to have been only 18 inches high and of an indeterminate circumference. Moore encountered fifty-one burials in the mound, which included primary burials, bundle burials, uncremated bone in burial urns, and one burial of cremated bone in a burial urn. Sherd inclusions in the mound fill were described as undecorated, cord marked, checked stamped, and complicated stamped (ibid.:71). Because Moore did not refer to these sherds as few in number, as was usually the case, perhaps we are justified in concluding that they occurred rather frequently in the mound fill.

Diagnostic burial accompaniments were relatively few, but of some interest were the artifacts associated with the burials, which are addressed in the discussion that follows. Burial No. 5 included a pottery tobacco pipe with the modeled and incised features of a human head (ibid.:fig. 46). It was almost identical to the human head pipe recovered from Mound B in Lawton's Field (ibid.:fig. 10): both heads were depicted without the lower jaw and both possessed a prominent pointed nose. On the other hand, there were differences in the manner in which the incised forked eye was depicted. At the back of each head was a modeled arrangement that extended from the back of the pipe bowl onto the stem, a step-like series of rectangular blocks on the pipe from the mound in Dumoussay's Field and a handle-like device on the pipe from Mound B in Lawton's Field. Presumably these additions at the back of the heads represented conventionalized hair arrangements or headdresses.

Lying above Burial No. 8 was a layer of charcoal, burned shell, and human bone within which was found a calcined shell earpin. Along with Burial No. 30 were two "rectangular" pottery vessels, the smaller of the two inverted inside the larger. Incising on the base of the smaller vessel would seem to argue that the pot can be typed as McIntosh Incised (ibid.:fig. 47). Moore found the design to be "curious" and apparently submitted either the pot or a drawing of the design to William H. Holmes at the Smithsonian and to Frederic Ward Putnam and Charles C. Willoughby at Harvard

[18]Francois-Maria Loys Dumoussay de la Vause purchased all of Sapelo Island in 1789 as a basis for an agricultural joint-venture proposal, the future French co-partners of which at that point were yet unselected. The purchase was to provide the group of his co-partners fleeing the French Revolution the promise of a safe haven and a new life on the Georgia coast (Thomas 1989).

seeking their opinions about the interpretation of the design. Holmes responded that he thought it to be "representative of some life form or forms," while Putnam, responding for both himself and Willoughby, suggested that it was "probably a conventionalized figure, which in time will be traced back to its realistic form" (ibid.:69). If nothing else these exchanges indicated that Moore did not carry on his work in a professional vacuum. The Burial No. 30 incised design, in its entirety, lacks familiarity. Nevertheless, the left-hand portion of the design as presented in the Moore drawing recalls parts of similar designs, identified as the windmill motif, engraved on pottery vessels from Moundville (Moundville Engraved, var. *Hemphill;* Steponaitis 1983:54, 56, 62–63). A number of these vessels were recovered by Moore during his several seasons at the Alabama site (Moore 1905:figs. 30, 35, 53, 1907a:fig. 12). The remainder of the incised design fails to bring to mind any comparable southeastern motifs.

Burial No. 35, a primary burial of a child, contained the remains of a tortoise-shell rattle lying on the chest. Along with the rattle was a shell gorget, 2.6 inches in diameter, on whose surface was engraved a rattlesnake (Moore 1897:70). A number of sherds, the scattered remains of a cord-marked vessel, were described by Moore as being found near the knee of Burial No. 48. These might have been considered simply an inclusion in the mound fill except that apparently the sherds present comprised most of the vessel, suggesting that a whole pot had been buried (ibid.). If the vessel were truly contemporary with the shell gorget, and it certainly seems to have been, it was probably a Savannah Fine Cord Marked pot. Although the burial accompaniments from the mound just discussed are not a complete inventory of those recovered by Moore, they do constitute the materials recognized as providing a temporal or cultural context for the mound and suggest a late Mississippi Period, Irene Phase setting for the mound in Dumoussay's Field.

By far the largest extant prehistoric structure on Sapelo Island is that which Moore called the **Aboriginal Enclosure at Sapelo High Point, Sapelo Island, McIntosh County** (ibid.:71–73). Although in the past it has been referred to as "the Indian Fort" or "the Spanish Fort," in recent decades the site has been called simply the Sapelo Shell Ring. Even though it has suffered damage as a result of the removal of some of its shell mass over the years for use in island tabby construction or for island road surfacing, it may well be the largest and most intact of a number of shell rings that have been identified on the southeastern coast. It was first brought to the attention of prehistorians by William McKinley in 1873, the same year that Charles C. Jones published his *Antiquities of the Southern Indians, Particularly of the Georgia Tribes,* an indication of a growing interest in Georgia prehistory. McKinley, in his brief note published in the *Smithsonian Annual Report, 1872,* stated that there were three shell rings in the area south of High Point (McKinley 1873:422–23).[19] McKinley described each of the rings he supposedly recognized; however, two of the rings were stated to be "in an open field long cultivated" and only 3 feet high (ibid.:422).

---

[19]William McKinley, a lawyer from Milledgeville, Georgia, was the father of Archibald C. McKinley, who married Sarah Spalding. Sarah, called Sallie by her husband, was the granddaughter of Thomas Spalding, who owned most of Sapelo Island during the first half of the nineteenth century. William McKinley presumably became familiar with the shell ring and other mounds on the island while visiting his son and daughter-in-law.

One quarter of a century later Moore observed the shell ring and area wherein the other two shell rings lay and made the following comments: "[R]eference is made to two circular enclosures in the vicinity [of the large shell ring]. One is at present indistinct and has by no means the height assigned to it [by McKinley]. The other escaped our attention" (Moore 1897:73).

In the plantation period it appears the entire western side of the island was a series of cultivated fields. The cultivation plowed down hundreds of small shell middens, until today only a few remain more or less intact in the old field beyond the drain north of the shell ring. The plow not only leveled the middens but scattered their shell over the surface of the fields. The area of the shell ring has not been cultivated for many years and certainly not since the time Moore visited the site, if one is to judge by the size of the large live oak trees that cover the acreage. I have been over the area on foot many times in the past few decades, on more than one occasion with the specific purpose of finding the other two shell rings McKinley stated were present. I have not been able to locate these structures or even to identify a situation that would fit that of the "indistinct" ring mentioned by Moore. The area is one characterized by much midden shell, but none of this shell assumes a configuration, distinct or indistinct, disturbed or undisturbed, that allows recognition as a shell enclosure or ring. I have come to the conclusion that McKinley was misled in his identifications by the large amount of scattered midden shell and that he assumed that at least some of it formed other rings (see also Simpkins 1975:23–25).

In 1950 I excavated a trench across the Sapelo Ring from the center through the west embankment to its outer edge. Although it is not possible to tell from the description of his excavations where he dug in the ring, I more or less replicated the results obtained by Moore. Inside of the area circumscribed by the wall or embankment of shell forming the ring there was little or no midden material, only a few sherds and a like amount of oyster shell. In the central portion of the ring, sterile sand lay immediately below a topsoil layer little more than 15 centimeters thick. As the embankment itself was approached and cut into there was an increase in midden until a nearly solid mass of shell was encountered in the enclosing embankment (Waring and Larson 1968:270–73). Moore was absolutely correct in his conclusion that the ring was aboriginal in origin and he apparently rejected the suggestion that the structure was a fortification by his reference to it as an "enclosure" or a "mound" (Moore 1897:71–73). The ring was composed entirely of midden material including primarily oyster shell but also quahog clam shell, marsh mussel, and whelk. The cultural material included fiber-tempered sherds, antler projectile points, polished and engraved bone pins, and a ground and polished quartz winged atlatl weight. Inclusive in the midden material were areas of ash and charcoal, some of which appeared to be hearths, and horizontal layers of crushed shell that appeared to be living floors (Waring and Larson 1968:273). The presence of fiber-tempered pottery, of the types usually identified as St. Simons Plain, St. Simons Incised, and St. Simons Punctated, established a Late Archaic to Early Woodland Period date for the site. The shell ring has produced two radiocarbon dates from oyster shell collected in 1949 by A. J. Waring, Jr., out of the eroding western face of the shell midden. As published, these uncorrected dates were (M-39) 3600 ± 350 B.P. and 3800 ± 350 B.P. (Crane 1956:665). In 1975 a two x five meter excavation was made approximately thirty meters south of the shell ring. A concentration of midden material in a small refuse pit was encountered at a depth of 80 to 135 centimeters. In the pit were fish bones, charred and fragmentary hickory nut shell, and unidentified seeds; however, no shell was found in the pit or in the stratum wherein the pit originated. Within the stratum containing the pit was a large section of a St. Simons Plain fiber-tempered bowl. Using hickory nut shell from the stratum, a radiocarbon date of (RL-580) 4120 ± 200 B.P. was obtained, which was compatible with the earlier dates obtained using shell (Simpkins 1975:34).

Moore commented in passing that situated on the property of "a Mr. Keenan or Kennon, with whom we were unable to come to terms" was a large mound (Moore 1897:73). Kenan Field, to use the current designation of the location and the correct spelling of the name, is a major site on Sapelo Island. It covers some 60 hectares and comprises some 589 separate shell middens and two burial mounds. Complete mapping of the site and limited excavation in the vicinity of the largest mound was carried out by Morgan R. Crook in 1976 and 1977. The work served as the basis for his dissertation (Crook 1978a) and two papers (ibid. 1978b, 1980). The major occupation of the site was during the Savannah and Irene phases of the Mississippi Period and during the Mission Period. The limited excavation immediately west of the large mound revealed a complex of wall trenches and postholes of considerable magnitude suggesting the locale of extensive public structures and areas.

The **Mounds at Bahama, McIntosh County** (Moore 1897:73), were to be the last of the sites in McIntosh County that Moore investigated during his 1895–1896 field season. Bahama, according to Moore, was located "at the union of Barbour's Island river and South Newport river" (Moore 1897:73). The name, Bahama, was the name of the post office established in 1891 on Harris Neck. In 1895 the post office was closed, only to be reestablished in 1896 as the Lacey Post Office at the same location (Fryman, Griffin, and Miller 1979:72). The mid-1870s saw the development of a strong and stable settlement of African-American freedmen in the Harris Neck area with the establishment there of both a school and church. Thus, from 1870 until the early 1940s, the area was the locale of a modest-sized community supported by subsistence agriculture and fishing. By 1940 there were 171 separate private landholdings on Harris Neck. For the most part these were held by African-Americans (ibid.:69–72).

Moore described the area as covered with "numerous low shell heaps," but noted that his investigations were with "meagre result." Two small mounds, elevated but slightly above the surrounding surface, were examined. Although Moore reported that several burials were encountered in each of the two mounds that he excavated at Bahama, he provided no information that would permit the assignment of the earthworks to a cultural or temporal context. The exact location of these mounds is difficult to determine. That Moore placed them at Bahama suggests they may have been situated in the vicinity of the post office, which in turn was probably at or near Gould Landing. On the other hand, Moore placed Bahama at the junction of the South Newport and Barbour Island rivers,[20] which would seem to indicate that the mounds were on the northern tip of Harris Neck in the vicinity of Thomas Landing.

Harris Neck is a remnant Pleistocene beach ridge, bounded on the north by the

---

[20]These tidal rivers actually unite in an extensive area of salt marsh more than a mile east of the northern end of Harris Neck.

South Newport River, on the west by marsh and the Julienton River, on the east by marsh and the Barbour Island River, and on the south by the Sapelo River. The northeastern quadrant of Harris Neck comprises a huge archaeological site. There is an almost continuous expanse of shell midden stretching from Thomas Landing, at the northern end of the neck, southward along the eastern edge of the neck for a distance of approximately two and a half miles. In some places the midden area is almost three-quarters of a mile wide.[21] I first recorded the site in 1952. At that time, I was unable to believe that the entire acreage constituted a single site and as a result I assigned three separate site file numbers to the area. I now believe that the area should be treated as a single site.

Although over a century and a half of cultivation during the nineteenth and early twentieth centuries certainly had its destructive effect on the midden areas, it was not until the 1940s that profound site destruction occurred. During the first years of the United States's involvement in World War II, the northern one-third of the Neck, comprising most of the African-American–held land, was taken by the federal government for the construction of an army airfield.[22] The development of this facility destroyed or seriously disturbed sizable portions of the archaeologically significant areas. In 1962 the area was acquired by the U.S. Fish and Wildlife Services for management as a wildlife refuge. In the decade prior to its acquisition by the Fish and Wildlife Services and during the period of development of the area as the Harris Neck National Wildlife Refuge there were a number of excavations in several portions (or sites if one insists) of the northern part of Harris Neck.

In 1953 I excavated a limited area several hundred feet southeast of the Livingston house site at Thomas Landing.[23] I had found Spanish majolica and olive jar ware sherds there during my 1952 survey to locate the sixteenth- and seventeenth-century Spanish missions known to have been located in the coastal area (Larson, n.d.). The area was badly disturbed as a consequence of the World War II development, and while I found no Spanish mission I did uncover six aboriginal house floors contemporary with the coastal Mission Period (Larson 1980:40, fig. 2).

In 1981 and 1984 the U.S. Fish and Wildlife Services contracted with the Carolina Archaeological Services (Drucker 1982) and Southeastern Archeological Services, Inc. (Braley 1986) to carry out limited excavations in the vicinity of Gould Landing, on the eastern side of the Neck about two miles south of its northern end. The excavations, conducted as a compliance action, were designed to mitigate the

[21]The limits of the site, and for the most part the boundaries of other sites in McIntosh County, have been determined by the extent of Palm Beach Fine Sand. This soil type is invariably coincident with archaeological sites that exhibit extensive areas of shell midden, including Bourbon Field, Kenan Field, and Dumoussay Field on Sapelo Island; the north end of Creighton Island; and the Pine Harbor site on the mainland.

[22]A much smaller airfield, without services, had been built on Harris Neck in the late 1930s by the Civil Aeronautics Authority to serve as an emergency landing facility (Fryman, Griffin, and Miller 1979:78).

[23]Late in the nineteenth century Pierre Lorillard, a wealthy New Yorker, developer of Tuxedo Park, and founder of the tobacco company that bore his name, came to have an interest in Harris Neck (the local lore provides a colorful explanation for this interest). Subsequently, Miss Lily Allien (later Mrs. Livingston), reputed to be Lorillard's mistress, built a large home at Thomas Landing. This home, used as an officers' club during the time the Neck was an army airfield, survived into the 1950s.

adverse effects of the construction of a service road on the refuge. Ceramics representing all of the aboriginal periods of the Georgia coastal sequence, as well as Spanish mission and antebellum plantation activity, were recovered from the excavations. A surprisingly large number of subsurface features, postholes, food-processing pits, refuse pits, and daub-processing pits were exposed during the excavation of the area by Southeastern Archeological Services. Most of these features were assigned to the Irene Phase of the Mississippi Period. Unfortunately it was not possible to completely define a structure within the area covered by a myriad of postholes (ibid.:49–59).

McIntosh County, like Camden and Glynn counties, has been the focus of considerable archaeological interest and activity since the end of World War II. Much of the activity has been the result of the Historic Preservation Act of 1966 and the 106 Compliance Process that was developed to implement it. The investigation of the historic Darien waterfront and numerous excavations in Darien attendant to the installation of a sewer line; the excavations carried out in the slave-quarter areas of the antebellum Butler Island Plantation by the University of Florida and West Georgia College (Singleton 1980) and supported by the Georgia Department of Natural Resources; and the Sapelo Island archaeological survey and excavations in the 1970s at Bourbon, Kenan Field, the Shell Ring, and Chocolate (Juengst 1980), also funded by the Georgia Department of Natural Resources, are all examples of relatively recent archaeological activity in McIntosh County.

MOORE IN LIBERTY COUNTY, GEORGIA

Moore moved northward across Sapelo Sound and the South Newport River into Liberty County, the county immediately to the north of McIntosh County. The first of the sites Moore investigated in Liberty County was the **Mound at Laurel View, Liberty County** (Moore 1897:74–75). The site is described as one mile south of the high bluff called Laurel View located on the south side of the Medway River. This would place the site about one and a half miles west of Sunbury, on the north side of the Sunbury Road. The site consisted of two mounds, the larger of which had been disturbed by a trench through the middle of the mound and by the removal of one side. The smaller mound, while not vandalized, had suffered the effects of many years of cultivation. Moore related no information about these earthworks that permitted their contextual identification and classification. There were apparently no ceramics accompanying burials and there was no mention of sherds in the mound fill. Both mounds contained burials; the larger of the two held about twenty cremations along with "several solitary skulls very badly decayed." Within the smaller mound Moore found seven cremations and a single skull "unaffected by fire" (ibid.).

Moore next shifted his operations to St. Catherines Island, the barrier island immediately north of Sapelo Island and separated from the latter by the mile-and-one-quarter expanse of Sapelo Sound. The first of the St. Catherines mounds explored by Moore was the **St. Catherines Island, Liberty County. Mound near South-end Settlement** (ibid.:75–81). The mound was described by Moore as lying about three-quarters of a mile north of the South-end Settlement. Today there is no settlement in the area. The location of the mound was at the end of an open field on the high ground of the western side of the island. The field in turn was separated from Johnson Creek to the west by some 500 meters of marsh. The mound was described as 3 feet high with a basal area 68 feet in diameter. The central portion of the mound was occupied by a layer of oyster shell some 2 feet thick and from 10 to 20 feet across. In all, Moore located fifty burials within the mound, which were, with few exceptions, primary burials. The exceptions included cremations (e.g., Burial No. 30), bundle burials (e.g., Burial No. 45), and urn burials (e.g., Burials Nos. 3, 4, 5, 7, and 23) (ibid.:75–80).

Moore stated that the mound fill contained undecorated, cord-marked, and complicated stamped sherds (ibid.:80). The presence of the complicated stamped sherds, assumed to be the majority ware Irene Complicated Stamped rather than the minority wares Deptford or Savannah Complicated Stamped, argues for placement of the mound in the Irene Phase of the Mississippi Period. Such placement is confirmed by an examination of the whole vessels that, for the most part, contained secondary burials. Six of these vessels were reexamined and described by Debra Peter in 1985 and 1986 (Larsen and Thomas 1986:14–15). Vessel A, which contained Burial No. 3 (Moore 1897:frontispiece), was 40 centimeters high with a rim diameter of 34 centimeters. Although Peter identified the vessel type as Irene Complicated Stamped, the vessel, both as it is figured by Moore in his frontispiece and as shown in the drawing found with the analysis by Peter (Larsen and Thomas 1986:fig. 8a), appears to me to be an Altamaha Line Block Stamped vessel. Peter's identification of the vessels designated by Moore as Ca and Fa, with Burials Nos. 5 and 23, as the type Irene Complicated Stamped is readily supported by the illustrations of the vessels accompanying her analysis (ibid.:14–15, figs. 9a and 10a). Two of the remaining three vessels, designated Cb (Burial No. 5) and Fb (Burial No. 23) by Moore, are cazuelas in form and are typed as Irene Plain by Peter. The third vessel, found with Burial No. 8, described by Moore as "boat-shaped" and designated by him as vessel E, was identified as Irene Plain by Peter (ibid.:15, fig. 8c). Larsen and Thomas concluded that the mound near South-end Settlement was assignable to the Irene Phase of the Mississippi Period (ibid.:21). There is every reason to agree with that conclusion.

The mound near South-end Settlement was relocated during the archaeological program conducted by the American Museum of Natural History in the 1970s. At that time a series of test pits was placed in the mound. In 1991 and for two additional field seasons Clark Larsen returned with a Purdue University field crew to excavate a large portion of the interior of the mound. He described the excavation as follows:

> This excavation revealed a number of important aspects of Moore's excavation strategy for this, and probably, other mounds. That is, it appeared that his crews worked across the mound, placing dirt behind them as they excavated. As they encountered burials, skeletal remains were disturbed, but the remains were left essentially in the same place as where found. Thus, using Moore's published map of the site, we were able to match the concentrations of skeletal remains with actual burials that he figured in his map [Moore 1897:fig. 43]. This also indicates that, though crude looking, the published map is highly accurate. Indeed, we were able to predict within a few centimeters the periphery of Moore's excavation and location of burials during our own excavations. In addition to the ceramics described by Debra Peter, we found mostly Irene period ceramics, confirming the late prehistoric construction of the mound. (Clark Larsen, personal communication, July 1997)

Moore excavated the **St. Catherines Island, Liberty County. Mound near Middle Settlement** (Moore 1897:81), an earthwork some 5 feet high and 54 feet in diameter, "without result." The archaeological work by the American Museum of Natural History on St. Catherines Island identified this mound and excavated a north-south stratigraphic trench as well as several adjoining test units in the central portion of the structure referred to as the South New Ground Mound (Thomas and Larsen 1979:78–83). Using radiocarbon dates from their South New Ground Mound (i.e., Mound near Middle Settlement) excavation, and from their excavations in the nearby Cunningham Mound group, Thomas and Larsen assigned the mound excavated by Moore to the Refuge-Deptford Phase of the Woodland Period. They commented that

> The 1976 American Museum excavation . . . established not only the aboriginal character of South New Ground Mound [i.e., Mound near Middle Settlement], but also explained why Moore's 1896 fieldwork failed to locate any cultural materials here. C. B. Moore was a man accustomed to finding obvious, and rather striking features in his work along the Georgia coast and elsewhere. . . .
>
> From the preceding descriptions of the Cunningham Mound group, it is clear that Refuge-Deptford mounds are not spectacular at all. The skeletons generally lack grave goods, and bones crumble at the slightest touch. Little wonder that Moore dismissed his mound near Middle Settlement as a mere house foundation. (ibid.:81–83)

Moore next turned his attention to the **St. Catherines Island, Liberty County. Mound in King's New Ground Field** (Moore 1897:81–86). The mound was located in an antebellum agricultural field on the eastern side of the northern half of the island, overlooking the headwaters of the northern portion of McQueen Inlet, a tidal stream that drains the marsh separating the active dunes and beach from the older late Pleistocene portions of the island (Thomas, Jones et al. 1978:161). Despite the fact that the mound was built in the midst of a number of shell middens that presumably constituted a village area, little shell was employed in the mound construction. Some shell was used in the fill of subsurface pits, and small and localized pockets of shell were encountered in a few instances. Curiously, one of the latter deposits was said by Moore to have been composed of freshwater mussel shells (Moore 1897:82). One might well ask, from whence came freshwater shells?[24] It is unlikely that they came from the fresh water occupying one or more of the low-lying sloughs that characterize central portions of the island, and the question of how those shells would have reached the island remains. It hardly seems plausible that freshwater shellfish would have been brought to the island, which itself had extensive oyster and clam beds. The shells alone may have been brought to the island and cached within the mound with the intention of using them in some craft production.

The King's New Ground earthwork had apparently suffered years of cultiva-

---

[24]Moore also recovered freshwater mussel shells from somewhat similar situations in mounds D and F at Middle Settlement on Ossabaw Island, Chatham County, Georgia (for comments on the habitat requirements of the genus *Unio* see below in this introduction the section on Ossabaw Island, Bryan County [i.e., Chatham County]. Middle Settlement, Mound D).

tion; it had a height of only 22 inches and was barely discernable above the surrounding field level at the time Moore investigated it (ibid.:81). In his description of the mound and its structure Moore called attention to "the usual great outlying pits" associated with the mound. These were not only large but also filled with topsoil, and they contained no burials (ibid.). These pits appear, from the descriptions by Moore, to occur just beyond the margins of the mound and were probably borrow pits whose configurations were obscured by years of cultivation.

Of the thirty-eight burials found by Moore within the mound, most were primary extended burials. Burial No. 5 was a bundle burial, while Burial No. 26 consisted only of a single skull. Burial No. 38 was described as "a confused mass of human bones about 7 inches thick and 4 feet wide" (ibid.:86). At least a portion of the bone in this deposit was calcined. There was little reported by Moore that would allow the mound to be placed in a cultural or chronological context. With Burial No. 36 were "small perforated marine shells" identified as *Olivella,* while Burial No. 37, that of a very young child, was accompanied by "the base of a cord-marked vessel of clay." Along with Burial No. 38, the deposit of human bone, were found "hematite; a few shell beads; two small, imperforate clay bowls, inverted within the larger; and a marine shell . . . in two fragments" (ibid.:85–86). Sherds found within the mound fill "were coarse and either undecorated or cord-marked" (ibid.:82).

Chester DePratter has identified four different cord-marked wares that are the constituents of four ceramic complexes with chronological significance on the northern portion of the Georgia coast (DePratter 1979:111–12). These cord-marked wares are Deptford Cord Marked, Wilmington Heavy Cord Marked, St. Catherines Fine Cord Marked, and Savannah Fine Cord Marked, and their respective ceramic complexes are Deptford, Wilmington, St. Catherines, and Savannah. Thus, the description by Moore of the King's New Ground Field Mound ceramics as "cord-marked" is too ambiguous to be of much assistance in placing the mound in a presently defined archaeological complex.

Although the antebellum field that was the location of Moore's mound in King's New Ground Field can still be identified on St. Catherines Island (Thomas, Jones et al. 1978:fig. 4), the American Museum of Natural History archaeological investigations on the island were not able to determine the site of Moore's excavation (ibid.:174).

The **St. Catherines Island, Liberty County. Mound in the Greenseed Field** (Moore 1897:86–89) was located in yet another antebellum agricultural field. In fact, the name *Greenseed* refers to a type of cotton grown during the antebellum period on the coast. The field, like that of King's New Ground Field, can still be recognized on St. Catherines Island (Thomas, Jones et al. 1978:fig. 4) and is situated a short distance to the south and west of the other field. As with the mound just discussed, the height of the Greenseed Field Mound was barely greater than the surrounding field level. Again, as with the King's New Ground Field Mound, the fill evidenced little use of shell in the mound construction (Moore 1897:86). And once more, "The usual outlying pits, in this case two in number, were present in this mound. Both were filled with black loam and scattering oyster shells. One began 42 feet from the center, was 21 feet across and extended inward 18 feet. Its maximum depth was 3 feet 7 inches. The second pit began 47 feet out, was 23 feet across and extended inward 15 feet. Its average depth coincided with that of the other. As usual, no burials were present in them" (ibid.). In large measure the Greenseed Field Mound replicated the mound in King's New Ground Field in the form and manner of the placement of the burials that it contained. The two mounds were also similar in that most of the burials in the Greenseed Field Mound were primary and extended. Of the thirty-one burials found, twenty-nine were apparently primary burials and of these it could be determined that twenty-three were placed in the extended position lying face down while two were extended and placed lying on the back. The bones of four infants were badly crushed and no burial position for them was given (ibid.:88, fig. 52).

Two of the burials were deposits of bone. Burial No. 11 was described by Moore as "a layer of calcined fragments of human bone" 23 inches long, 15 inches wide, and 6 inches thick. Moore pointed out that unburned bone was intermixed with the calcined bone in the deposit (ibid.:88). Burial No. 28 lay in the center of the mound on sterile subsoil and beneath a deposit of shell. The burial was "a layer of the bones of numerous individuals, inextricably mixed." The layer was some 8 inches thick and extended over an area 4 feet 9 inches long and 2 feet 4 inches wide. Here again Moore noted the presence of a few fragments of calcined bone in the deposit. "Numbers" of tubular shell beads, the largest 2 inches long; a pointed bone tool; and several cut carnivore mandibles accompanied this burial. These latter had the lower margins, including the roots of the teeth, ground away. Frederic W. Putnam, apparently in response to an inquiry from Moore, saw comparability between the cut mandibles from the Greenseed Field Mound and cut human and animal jaws from the "mounds of Ohio." Presumably the reference by Putnam was to similar Middle Woodland specimens held by the Peabody Museum at Harvard with which he was certainly familiar. It was Putnam who directed the excavation of the Turner Earthworks in Hamilton County, Ohio. Two cut wolf jaws were found with a burial beneath a portion of the embankment defining the "Great Enclosure" of the site (Willoughby 1922:13, fig. 6d). The cut wolf, wildcat, and mountain lion mandibles that were recovered from burials in Mound 25 of the Hopewell Group were illustrated by H. C. Shetrone (1926:241, fig. 89). These mandibles, if they came from Warren K. Moorehead's excavations (Moorehead 1922), may have been known to Putnam. Shetrone stated that the holes that were drilled in the Hopewell artifacts were for "attachment or suspension" (Shetrone 1926:241). On the other hand, Moore suggested that the cut mandibles were the surviving parts of wooden masks that had been placed with the burials (Moore 1897:88–89). William S. Webb and Raymond Baby proposed a similar use for cut animal jaws from the Ohio area, in particular a cut wolf maxilla found in an Adena mound in Montgomery County, Kentucky (Webb and Baby 1957:61–71).

Although it is not specifically mentioned, the Greenseed Field Mound was apparently not relocated during the American Museum of Natural History anthropological research on St. Catherines Island (Thomas, Jones et al. 1978:174).

Moore continued his work on St. Catherines by next turning to a mound that lay, as best as one can tell, in the general vicinity of the two previous mounds on the eastern side of the island. Moore stated that the **St. Catherines Island, Liberty County. Mound near the Light-House** (Moore 1897:89) was located "near the site of the projected light-house." To my knowledge the lighthouse was never built and its projected location is not presently known. In any event, the mound was not relocated by the American Museum of Natural History investigators during their work on the island in the 1970s and 1980s (Thomas, Jones et al. 1978:174). Moore described the mound as a small, symmetrical earthwork 3 feet high and 56 feet in diameter and composed entirely of sand. The mound held two primary burials and a cremation of several individuals. In addition, there were a number of places where what are described as "decayed bits of human bone" occurred (Moore 1897:89). Nothing.of identifiable diagnostic value was recovered.

Moore completed his investigations on St. Catherines Island with the excavation of two **St. Catherines Island, Liberty County. Low Mounds at the North-End** (ibid.). These mounds were described as being located about one mile east of the "main" landing on the island. This would have placed them again on the east side of the island, probably overlooking the marsh and the headwaters of the tidal creek that cuts across the beach and empties into the ocean at Black Hammock. The two mounds, approximately 50 yards apart, were low, with heights of 36 inches and 14 inches, respectively, and diameters of 42 feet for the higher mound and 36 feet for the lower. Other than "a few fragments of decaying human cranium" in the smaller of the two mounds, Moore reported having found nothing in the two structures (ibid.). Again, it was not possible for the American Museum of Natural History archaeologists to identify the locations of these mounds (Thomas, Jones et al. 1978:174).

Although he did not identify the sites to which he was referring, Moore reported that he did examine the shell midden sites on St. Catherines Island as well as the burial mounds there: "Careful attention was paid to numerous low shell-heaps studding the island of St. Catherine's. In some, results were negative, while from others came sherds incised and with complicated stamped decoration in use in the best class of the burial mounds of the coast" (Moore 1897:89). The midden sites that Moore investigated were, at least in part, Irene Phase sites. The incised ware coupled with complicated stamped ware argues for this conclusion. The brief statement also suggests that Moore was interested in more than burial mounds, but because the statement was never repeated it is difficult to determine how frequently midden areas were examined elsewhere. In addition, the statement reveals Moore's preference for Mississippi Period mortuary structures. In this regard he was not the first, nor was he to be the last, of the archaeologists in the Southeast to express this view.

In 1969 and 1970 Joseph Caldwell directed a University of Georgia excavation of two burial mounds on St. Catherines Island, Johns Mound and Marys Mound. The American Museum of Natural History completed the excavation of Marys Mound as a part of the archaeological program carried out by that institution in 1977 and 1978. The contents, archaeology, bioarchaeology, and skeletal biology of the two mounds were described and discussed by Clark Larsen and David Thomas (1982) in the monograph series covering the American Museum of Natural History research on St. Catherines Island.

The most recent archaeological work on St. Catherines Island has been the extensive program of research begun in 1974 and carried out by the American Museum of Natural History under the direction of David Hurst Thomas. This work has produced an impressive series of papers and monographs published by the museum. The research activity has covered a broad range of anthropological interests including a summary of previous archaeological investigations on the island; an archaeological survey of the island; a record and description of the island's cultural ecology; a description of the island's ethnohistory; reports on the excavation of several island burial mounds and their physical anthropology; and finally the major research focus of the program—the excavation, analysis, and historical interpretation of a sixteenth-century Spanish mission along with the biocultural analysis of its associated mortuary population (see Bushnell 1994; Larsen 1982, 1990; Larsen and Thomas 1982, 1986; Thomas 1987; Thomas, Jones et al. 1978; Thomas and Larsen 1979; Thomas, South, and Larsen 1977; Worth 1995).

MOORE IN BRYAN COUNTY [I.E., CHATHAM COUNTY], GEORGIA[25]

Leaving St. Catherines Island, Moore moved north to Ossabaw Island in Chatham County, the next of the Georgia barrier islands. Moore was to excavate nine mounds on Ossabaw Island at two locations. Six of these mounds were at Middle Settlement, an antebellum slave quarters occupied by tenant farmers at the time of Moore's visit in 1896. This location and the ruins of the tabby slave cabins marking the plantation slave quarters are now identified on contemporary maps as Middle Place. Middle Settlement was located on the eastern side of the island overlooking Buckhead Creek, a tidal stream that drains a large section of the salt marsh west of Ossabaw (see *U.S. Geological Survey, Raccoon Key Quadrangle, Georgia—Chatham Co., 7.5 Minute Series*). The three additional mounds excavated by Moore were at Bluff Field, thought to be the large site at the bluff where Cabbage Garden Creek flows against the eastern side of the high ground of the western half of the island. Cabbage Garden Creek, a tidal creek, is a part of the western drainage of the salt marsh that divides the northern portion of the island into eastern and western halves.

The first of the Ossabaw Island sites investigated was **Ossabaw Island, Bryan County. Middle Settlement, Mound A** (Moore 1897:89–101). The mound stood only some 18 inches high and had a diameter of 45 feet. Within the mound Moore found thirty-seven burials of which fifteen were probably primary burials. There were apparently seventeen urn burials, four of which Moore counted as a single burial, Burial No. 22. The burial urns contained cremations as well as unburned bone. Burials Nos. 13, 16, and 20 were areas of calcined human bone. Each of these constituted a fairly large deposit: the largest, Burial No. 20, measured 4.5 feet wide, 5.75 feet long, and up to 5 inches thick, and Burial No. 13 almost duplicated these dimensions. Burial No. 16 covered an area about 2 feet in diameter and was 2 inches thick. Moore did not, as he had done with calcined bone from other mounds, state that the bone was found with charcoal in an area subjected to intense heat. Rather it was implied that the burning took place elsewhere with the calcined bone having been brought to the mound for burial. There was in addition one bundle burial, Burial No. 15, which was described as "a bunched burial of the bones of a child." Finally, Moore found the primary burial of a dog, Burial No. 37. This last appeared to be sufficiently isolated from the remainder of the burials that its inclusion as a mound burial could well be an artifact of the manner in which Moore defined the limits of the mound (ibid.:fig. 55).

[25]Ossabaw Island has not been a part of Bryan County since the early part of the nineteenth century when the state legislature placed it within Chatham County. Why Moore thought that the island was part of Bryan County is difficult to explain. Perhaps he assumed that it was a part of Bryan County after looking at a map on which the demarcation of the county boundaries was not clear. A hasty examination of almost any contemporary road map of Georgia would lead one to repeat Moore's error.

Moore recovered forty-five pottery vessels he specifically identified as such. For the most part these vessels constituted burial urns, either containing the burned or unburned bone of the burial or serving as a cover for the container. Some vessels were covered only by what Moore described as large sherds. One suspects that because, almost without exception, the identified vessels were found crushed, some of the large sherds that covered them may also have been from vessels buried whole.

With great and infuriating monotony Moore described almost all of the vessels that he recovered in the most ambiguous of terms. The vessels were characterized as "plain," "the usual type," "the ordinary type," or "the common type." Fortunately several of the vessels were illustrated in carefully drawn plates (Moore 1897), including vessel D, Irene Complicated Stamped, one of five vessels with Burial No. 3 (plate 9); vessel Rb, Irene Incised, inverted over vessel Ra constituting Burial No. 10, an urn burial (plate 10); vessel Sb, Irene Plain, inverted over vessel Sa constituting Burial No. 11, an urn burial (plate 11); vessel AA, Irene Complicated Stamped, one of a group of four burial urns constituting Burial No. 22 (plate 12); vessel II, Irene Incised, an isolated vessel found near Burial No. 27 (plate 13, fig. 1); vessel I, Irene Incised, seemingly an isolated vessel found near Burial No. 6 (plate 13, fig. 2); and vessel LL, Irene Incised, probably associated with Burial No. 28, a primary burial (plate 14, fig. 1). Without exception these vessels belong to the Irene Phase of the Mississippi Period, and therefore the mound and its contents can almost certainly be assigned to this cultural and chronological niche.

In 1974 Chester DePratter relocated Mound A and collected Irene Complicated Stamped and Irene Plain sherds from the surface of the area (DePratter 1974a:14). The work of DePratter, Patrick Garrow, and others was part of an archaeological survey carried out by the University of Georgia for the owner of the island.

The mound that Moore identified as **Ossabaw Island, Bryan County. Middle Settlement, Mound B** (Moore 1897:101–9), was located about one-half mile northeast of Mound A: it stood slightly more than 7 feet high and was approximately 46 feet in diameter. It was covered with a layer of shell of varying depth but up to 2 feet thick in places. Moore recorded and described forty-five burials in the mound. The majority of these burials, thirty-seven in number, were primary burials. Two of the interments contained more than a single person: Burial No. 22 held three children while Burial No. 33 comprised an adult male and an adult female. From the description given by Moore it is not clear whether the two adults in this latter burial were part of the same mortuary event. It is almost certain that the dog burial found beneath these individuals constituted a discrete, prehistoric burial. Seven of the primary burials were described as interments of seated adults, while one young adult male was reported as having been interred in a kneeling position.

Burials Nos. 3, 4, 6, and 9 were bundle burials, the burial form that Moore referred to as "bunched burials." Interestingly, these four burials were located on the extreme southern margin of the major burial activity in the mound. If the bundle burials were the result of mortuary activity contemporary with the activity that was responsible for the majority of the other burials in the mound, the primary burials, then we might well ask why these four burials were so different in form and location from the others.

In addition to the primary and bundle burials in Mound B, there was a sizable deposit of burned and unburned human bone placed within a large pit identified by

Moore as Burial No. 45. The deposit covered an area 3 by 3.5 feet and had an average thickness of 7 inches at the base of the pit. The upper portion of the pit was probably close to 10 feet in diameter (ibid.:fig. 56). This deposit was shown on the profile drawn following a northeast-southwest transect of the mound along a midline (ibid.:fig. 57). The deposit was seemingly indicated as the finely dotted area at the base of the central shell-filled depression or pit, with the shell having been shown as the coarser circles. Moore described this deposit as having been placed in a fireplace, by inference suggesting that the contents had been burned in the pit. If the contents of the pit had been subjected to fire, then the fire had been kindled on the top of the mortuary deposit rather than under it. Moore stated that the material at the base of the pit was unburned, including a quantity of human bone and numerous shell beads. The cremated bone presumably lay over the unburned bone, although Moore provided no definite statement to that effect. Nor did Moore indicate whether charcoal and burned shell were mixed into the upper portion of the deposit. Such would be expected if indeed the fire had been laid over the top of the pit contents.

Adjoining the pit and its contents immediately to the west was a second feature identified by Moore as XXX on his plan of Mound B (ibid.:fig. 56). Moore described this feature as follows: "A little W. of the center was a layer of calcined earth and lime presumably from oyster shell, showing intense and prolonged heat. Its length was 11 feet; its breadth about 6 feet. It had an average thickness of about 1 foot. This curious layer, whose upper surface was 6 feet from the surface of the mound, upon careful examination seemed not to have been subjected to fire upon the spot, since oyster shells, bits of deer horn, bones of lower animals, etc., showing no trace of fire, were scattered through it" (ibid.:109). Unfortunately Moore identified this feature only on the plan of Mound B, omitting it from the profile drawing of the mound. Consequently its relationship to Burial No. 45, if any, is not clear. The feature XXX would appear to be on or only slightly above the surface on which the mound was built.

Finally, two dog burials were encountered in the mound, one of which may have been associated with Burial No. 33. These appear to have been deliberate burials. The presence of one of the dogs beneath the two adult burials that constituted Burial No. 33 presents a very strong argument that at least this burial was contemporary with the mound construction and was not a pet burial from the plantation days of the Middle Settlement.

Moore reported: "Throughout the mound, but principally in the midden refuse, were fragments of earthenware vessels. These, with several exceptions found at the base, were of gritty ware, while all were either undecorated, cord-marked, basket-marked, or stamped with the well-known square impression. To the best of our knowledge, none bore any variety of the complicated stamped decoration present in the low neighboring mounds" (ibid.:102–3). In addition to the sherds identified in the mound fill, there were many sherds found mixed in the material comprising Burial No. 45; unfortunately they remained undescribed. Two small pots were found with Burial No. 16, that of an infant. Moore described them as undecorated. The smaller of the two vessels was further described as "elongated at one end and terminating in an extension for a handle, resembling in shape and size a type found in Florida" (ibid.:105).

Using the somewhat ambiguous descriptions of the ceramics from the mound fill we can be somewhat assured that the mound does not belong to the Irene Phase because there is no complicated stamped ware mentioned. Irene Complicated Stamped pottery is a dominant ware associated with any Irene Phase occupation. Chester DePratter concluded from the Moore descriptions that the sherds from the mound fill were Savannah Cord Marked and Savannah Checked Stamped (DePratter 1974a:15). If his identification is correct the mound belonged to the Savannah Phase of the Mississippi Period. There is also a possibility that the sherds belong to the Deptford Phase of the Woodland Period. The Deptford Cord Marked, Deptford Checked Stamped, and Deptford Simple Stamped (Moore's "basket-marked"?) wares are all grit tempered according to the original type descriptions, as well as according to the restatement of these descriptions by DePratter himself (Caldwell and Waring 1939a:4 and 8, 1939b:1; DePratter 1979:123–26). The descriptions by Moore of the sherds from Mound B conformed to the type descriptions for the Deptford wares as well as to those of the Savannah wares.

The DePratter archaeological survey of Ossabaw Island was successful in relocating the remnants of Mound B. DePratter reported that he collected grit-tempered checked-stamped, clay-tempered cord-marked, and clay-tempered plain ware from the surface of the Mound B area. The sherds were not, however, assigned to specific ceramic types.

The mound Moore referred to as **Ossabaw Island, Bryan County. Middle Settlement, Mound C** (Moore 1897:109–12), lay some 300 yards north of Mound B. It was 8 feet high and had a diameter of approximately 68 feet. In all, Moore encountered ninety-two burials, some of which contained more than a single individual. Moore did not provide details of the Mound C burials: "Though careful notes of all burials were taken, yet, owing to similarity of form to interments in Mound B, we deem it unnecessary to go into detail" (ibid.:111). The detailed information, such as there is, is indeed in the Moore notebooks and is available to those who desire to go beyond my summary of that information.[26]

As was the case with Mound B, the majority of the burials were primary burials. Moore identified at least seventy-one of the burials in terms that indicated they were primary burials. At least four of the remaining burials were bundle burials. However, it is difficult to be certain because some of the scattered bone, including crania, may have originated with bundle burials rather than disturbed or poorly preserved primary burials; for example, Burial No. 92 was described as two femurs and a pelvis. Moore also encountered five deposits of cremated human bone (ibid.:112). Only three of these deposits were identified in the notes and only one was described in the published report. One of them, Burial No. 30, covered an area about 1 foot in diameter and was from 3 to 5 inches thick. Burial No. 86, a second cremation, covered an area only 5 inches in diameter and was 3 inches thick.

The largest burial, Burial No. 82, was also a deposit of calcined bone that occupied the base of a large central pit (ibid.). The pit, some 13 feet in diameter at its opening, narrowed to a base 3 to 5 feet in diameter. The calcined bone formed a layer at the base of the pit 5 inches thick and 7 feet in diameter. Mixed with the bone were materials that appeared to constitute mortuary accompaniments. These included

[26]Moore's notes on the excavation of Middle Settlement, Mound B, are found in R2, B10, p. 72–90.

shell and pearl beads, bone pins, several cut carnivore mandibles, a number of chert spalls and chips, and a collection of "pea-sized" quartz pebbles in a compact placement suggesting perhaps the remains of a rattle. The pit fill contained several burials apparently placed in the pit as it was filled. As determined from the Moore notes they were all primary burials and included Burials Nos. 77, 79, 80, and 83.

Although sherds were "of frequent occurrence" in the mound fill, Moore was, as usual, parsimonious with his ceramic descriptions. The Mound C ceramics were "undecorated or cord-marked—the latter predominating" (ibid.:110). Pottery vessels, presumably placed with burials, were encountered in the sand of the collapsed profile as the mound was sliced away vertically moving from the northern edge of the mound southward toward the middle of the mound. In the notes (R2, B10, p. 86) there was a reference to a small vessel with a cord-marked decoration lying with a larger crushed vessel in Burial No. 64. This was undoubtedly the same vessel that the published report identified as a "rough" checked stamped vessel recovered from "caved sand" in the excavation (Moore 1897:111). Moore was emphatic in his assertion that there were no complicated stamped sherds found in the fill of the mound.

Almost certainly we can again safely conclude that because of the absence of complicated stamped ware the mound predates the Irene Phase. Moore's use of the adjective *rough* in his description of the checked stamping on the pot in Burial No. 64 suggests that the ware is Deptford Checked Stamped rather that Savannah Checked Stamped. The latter ware usually is characterized by a small check with fine lands and grooves, a stamping that would not normally be adjudged as "rough."

Ossabaw Island, Bryan County. Middle Settlement, Mound D (ibid.:113–28), was located about 200 yards southwest of Mound B. It stood some 3 feet 9 inches high with an apparent diameter of 82 feet. The central portion of the mound was occupied by a large pit, approximately 20 feet in diameter and 7 feet deep. It was filled with shell to within 1 foot of the pit base. Moore reported that eighty-five burials were encountered in the mound. The majority of these were primary burials, although cremations and urn burials were found. Moore apparently collected and preserved very little of the skeletal material that he excavated, a practice that seems to have been true of all of his work on the Georgia coast. The following statement regarding the manner in which Moore treated the skeletal bone from Mound D probably could be applied to his investigations at other coastal mounds. "Skeletal remains, so numerous in this mound . . . were in a fairly good state of preservation compared to many we have encountered elsewhere, though with one exception . . . no crania were saved, owing to their crushed state" (ibid.:114). Evidently, Moore's practice was to collect only the skeletal material that was perceived to have some medical interest, for example, fractured limb bones that had mended well or badly. These bones were sent to the Army Medical Museum in Washington, D.C. (see also Middle Settlement, Mound E, Burial No. 4 [ibid.:129]).[27] The experience of Clark Larsen

___

[27]Coincidentally, while writing this introduction I received a telephone call from an individual working with the Army Medical Museum collections, now part of the National Museum of Health and Medicine, Armed Forces Institute of Pathology. The person calling had the responsibility for developing the compliance summaries required by the Native American Graves Protection and Repatriation Act (P.L. 101-601, November 16, 1990). The human skeletal material from coastal Georgia that Moore sent to the Army Medical Museum still exists, and it has remained a part of the Army museum collections. The person was calling in an attempt to develop an ethnic affiliation for this material.

with respect to his reexcavation of Moore's mound near South-end Settlement on St. Catherines Island, described above in the personal communication of Larsen, would appear to bear out this assumption.

Among the eighty-five burials in the mound were ten primary dog burials, including three dogs "buried singly within a few feet of each other." Most of the dogs were placed in the mound in situations that precluded interpretation of the interments as intrusive burials from a later time, that is, during the occupation of the plantation settlement. At least one of the dog burials was overlain by a human burial. Although no such burials were recovered from the other coastal mounds that Moore excavated, the presence of primary dog burials in the Middle Settlement Mounds B and F suggests that there may have been a particular mortuary practice that was peculiar to the inhabitants of Ossabaw Island.[28] Dog burials are certainly not a rare phenomenon in the prehistoric Southeast. For example, they were recovered in considerable numbers at the Perry site, Lu°25, in the Pickwick Basin (Webb and DeJarnette 1942:68–69), where at least some of the burials were in a Late Archaic context. To my knowledge, there has been but one other archaeological dog burial reported on the Georgia coast. Jerald Milanich reported that the University of Florida excavation of the Taylor Mound, St. Simons Island, found "a late Savannah [Phase] charnel house [that] contained a dog burial with a musket ball between the ribs" (Milanich 1977:140). There is probably little cultural relationship between the dogs buried in the Refuge or Deptford Phase, Woodland Period, mounds excavated by Moore on Ossabaw Island and the Historic Period dog recovered on St. Simons Island. Nevertheless, we can say that generally the disposal of dogs was not casual in the aboriginal Southeast.

Also worthy of note was the recovery by Moore of two groups of freshwater mussel shells in the mound. One such deposit, composed of six unmodified shells stacked one within the other, was found unassociated with a burial near the southeastern margin of the mound (Moore 1897:118). The second deposit lay near Burial No. 52 and consisted of approximately fifty shells, each of which appeared to have two holes drilled in it for suspension. The freshwater origin of the shells in the latter deposit was affirmed, presumably by a conchologist, who identified three species of *Unio* (ibid.:123). The presence of freshwater shells in the mound is of interest. There is no likely source for the shells on Ossabaw Island given the fact that in order to reproduce the *Unio* genus requires specific freshwater fish to act as vectors. The nearest habitat imperatives for the genus probably existed only in the stretches of the Ogeechee River that lay above the tidal reach. The freshwater shell encountered by Moore in the mound in King's New Ground Field on St. Catherines Island appears to have constituted a different kind of deposit from that on Ossabaw Island. Moore described the St. Catherines deposit as "one mainly of freshwater mussel shells . . . 13 inches by 20 inches by 10 inches thick" (ibid.:82). Certainly the St. Catherines shells formed a much more massive deposit than the two deposits from Middle Settlement, Mound D. Moore also recovered *Unio* shells from the Lawton's Field, Mound B and from the Townsend Mound, both in McIntosh County. In the

___

[28]The dog burial that Moore described as associated with Mound A was, in all likelihood, not actually buried within the mound.

former mound the shells were apparently not found with a burial; however, in the latter mound the shells not only lay near a skeleton but also were pierced for suspension. The McIntosh County mounds were both late Mississippi Period mounds. It should be noted that both of these mounds existed in proximity to a major freshwater environment, the Altamaha River. The Middle Settlement occurrences of *Unio* were from mounds within a major saltwater environmental setting.

Moore reported the finding of twenty-three pottery vessels in the mound. Most of these were urns that contained the bones from primary infant burials or the calcined bones of one or more cremated individuals. As usual, Moore described the vessels in the most laconic and dismissive manner. The descriptions that follow offer the best opportunity for establishing a cultural context for the mound. Vessel Ab, with Burial No. 2, was described as having a complicated stamped decoration. Vessel C was found in an area described as "a layer of fragments of earthenware vessels, 22 inches by 3 feet 8 inches, 18 inches below the surface. It was made up of overlapping sherds of large size, at times single, and again double, and not of several vessels placed on their sides and crushed by the weight of sand, since cord-marked pottery lay with that having the complicated stamp, and when a fragment was imposed upon another, it often occurred that the convex portion of an upper sherd fitted into the concave portion of a lower, which could not be the case were two sides of a previously entire vessel brought into apposition through breakage" (ibid.:117). Vessel G, which contained the cremated remains of a child (Burial No. 12), was described as having a "bell-jar shape" and a "faint" checked stamped decoration (ibid.:118). With Burial No. 39 was "a bit of cord-marked pottery—possibly of accidental introduction—[that] lay near the foot" (ibid.:121). Included with Burial No. 52 was a small cord-marked bowl (ibid.:123). Accompanying Burial No. 62 were a number of pottery vessels, among them Vessel Mc, which was described as a "black ware, having a globular body and flaring rim with decoration around the margin consisting of raised circles, enclosing projections" (ibid.:125). Burial No. 70, the primary burial of a child, included "a cord-marked bowl imposed upon a basket-marked cup" (ibid.:125). Burial No. 73, comprising the calcined bones of a child, was contained within Vessel N, an "urn-shaped vessel with a faint diamond-stamped decoration" (ibid.:125). This last vessel was illustrated by Moore and appeared on plate 15 (ibid.). Close by Vessel N was a second vessel, Vessel O, described as having a complicated stamped decoration (ibid.:126). It too was illustrated by Moore (ibid.:pl. 14, fig. 2). Finally, Burial No. 82, consisting of a primary infant burial, was contained within Vessel P, which was identified as a "cord-marked pot" (ibid.:127).

The Middle Settlement, Mound D, vessels illustrated by Moore are of little real help in establishing the chronological or cultural identity of the mound. It can be argued that the "faint diamond-stamped" decoration on the urn, Vessel N, shown in the drawing on plate 15 (ibid.:125), appears to be simple stamping rather than checked stamping. On the other hand, the vessel shape with its slightly flaring rim is somewhat reminiscent of a Savannah Checked Stamped jar form. The other illustrated vessel from the mound, Vessel O, although described by Moore as having a complicated stamped decoration, does not call to mind any complicated stamped motif with which I am familiar. Further, the vessel shape is not distinctive of a particular ceramic type. It should be noted that complicated stamped wares occur throughout the coastal sequence, beginning at least as early as the Deptford Phase; however, sherds of these wares never comprise more than a tiny fraction of the types recovered until the onset of the Irene Phase.

The other pottery vessels recovered from the mound were described by Moore in terms that serve to baffle and frustrate: "[a] vessel of the common type," "a vessel of the ordinary type," and "a vessel of the usual type" are all phrases employed by Moore to describe the majority of the vessels. One can never be reasonably sure what Moore was describing when he used one of those phrases.

During his archaeological survey of Ossabaw Island in 1974, Chester DePratter reported recovering sand-tempered and grog-tempered plain and cord-marked pottery from the surface of the mound (DePratter 1974a:15). These types are not incompatible with the meager information that Moore provided. In summary, it is difficult to characterize the cultural and chronological position of Mound D. The ambiguous nature of the Moore ceramic descriptions and the absence of other distinctive artifacts, coupled with the singular occurrence of such things as the dog burials and the freshwater shells, create circumstances wherein there exists a lack of comparative archaeological situations. Middle Settlement Mounds B and F, from all appearances, were probably the product of the same cultural forces as those of Mound D. Although perhaps not to the same degree, the three mounds seemingly share the same characteristics: the dog burials, freshwater shells, and cord-marked pottery. It seems likely that the Middle Settlement mounds were built during one of the phases of the Woodland Period on the coast; perhaps the Wilmington Phase is a reasonable candidate.

Moore described **Ossabaw Island, Bryan County. Middle Settlement, Mound E** (Moore 1897:128–30), located approximately 300 yards west of Mound D, as only 14 inches high, a low height that was a consequence of decades of cultivation (ibid.:128–30). Its diameter was estimated to be 38 feet. Moore reported a total of seven burials in the mound along with two areas of calcined shell that were identified as "fireplaces." Several of the burials were badly disturbed, undoubtedly as a result of cultivation. Burial No. 6 held the skeletal remains of three children along with sherds that were described as occurring in layers and a small undecorated vessel "with a curious knob" near the base. The notes (R2, B12, p. 33), but not the printed text, referred to three "fragments of Vessel A" that accompanied Burial No. 1 but were apparently not collected. Unfortunately these ceramics were not otherwise described, and thus we are deprived of specific information about what appears to be the only material with diagnostic value found in the mound. An engraved bone pin was found in "the shell debris" covering the mound (Moore 1897:129, fig. 74), but engraved pins occur in various coastal cultural complexes from the late Archaic Period through the Mississippi Period. Without an understanding of the context in which the Mound E pin occurred it is difficult to regard it as having diagnostic value.

The sixth of the Middle Settlement mounds, **Ossabaw Island, Bryan County. Middle Settlement, Mound F** (ibid.:130), lay some 200 yards to the west of Mound B, although in the same field as that mound. Again, decades of cultivation had blurred the contours of the mound to the extent that Moore found its elevation to be only 20 inches at the time of his excavation. The basal diameter was apparently more or less arbitrarily established as 76 feet (ibid.:130).[29] Moore explored only one half of the

[29]Moore seemingly established the outer boundaries of the mounds he excavated on the Georgia coast by defining the extent to which burials extended from the center of the mound. The center was

mound, in which he encountered twenty burials. Apparently all were primary burials, with the majority flexed and lying on the left side. No deposits of cremated bone were found nor were there urn burials in the mound (ibid.).

Cord-marked sherds were identified as being present throughout the mound fill. A few complicated stamped sherds were found just below the mound surface. Interestingly, two freshwater mussels had been placed with one burial, but mortuary accompaniments were for the most part nonexistent and without great diagnostic value (ibid.).

It perhaps is worth noting that while Moore presented few particulars in print concerning individual burials from Mound F, his notes described each of the burials in turn (R2, B12, p. 33–37). Lest anyone think that Moore denied us important information in his refusal to describe the burials in print, let me state that there is assuredly little significant detail that the notes add to his published summary of burial information from the mound (Moore 1897:130). The archaeological survey of Ossabaw Island carried out by Chester DePratter in 1974 was not able to relocate Middle Settlement, Mound F.

Taken as an archaeological complex rather than as a series of burial mounds, it would appear that the largest number of Middle Settlement mounds were probably constructed as a result of a more or less sedentary Deptford, Wilmington, or St. Catherines Phase of the Woodland Period occupation of this portion of the island.

Moore next turned his attention to an area of Ossabaw Island that lay two and a half miles to the northeast of the Middle Settlement sites, on the eastern edge of the western half of the island. The Bradley River, a tidal stream, bisects the northern portion of the island as it meanders across a broad expanse of salt marsh fed by numerous smaller tributary creeks. Here, in a field behind a steep bluff overlooking one of these tributaries, Cabbage Garden Creek, Moore investigated two mounds. The first of the mounds, **Ossabaw Island, Bryan County. Bluff Field, Mound A** (ibid.:131), was a low mound some 75 yards from the bluff edge. Moore determined its height to be 2 feet 3 inches above the surrounding field and its diameter to be 56 feet. Once again he was apparently working with a mound that had been subjected to cultivation for over two hundred years. Moore encountered thirteen primary burials and one deposit of cremated human bone. In a manner similar to that of burials in the mounds at Middle Settlement, the primary burials appeared to lack any semblance of formal orientation or body position. The cremated bone was placed in a shallow pit dug 18 inches into the subsurface level beneath the mound. At the premound level, the area of the pit was covered by "a layer of four thicknesses of large cord-marked sherds" (ibid.). Once more Moore encountered a primary dog burial in an Ossabaw Island mound. The burial, the only dog burial in this mound, lay at some distance from the human interments. In his field notes Moore stated that the dog burial was "not near any human remains as is the case in other mounds" (R2, B11, p. 96). The only ceramic vessel found was one that accompanied a child burial. It was plain, although Moore described it as "a practically undecorated pot," which

---

determined to be the highest elevation of earthwork. An examination of the plats of Middle Settlement, Mound A (Moore 1897:91, fig. 53, 97, fig. 55), suggests that he may have initially miscalculated the outer limits of the mound. He found nothing in the western side of the mound, as he first defined the basal area, only to find that the burials extended eastward of his original eastern margin.

leads me to wonder what he meant by "practically," as he provided no description of that portion of the pot that was minimally decorated (Moore 1897:131). He illustrated the vessel, but it is difficult to tell from the drawing whether any sort of decoration is being depicted (ibid.:132, fig. 75). A few sherds, undescribed, were found in the mound fill.

The 1974 Ossabaw Island archaeological survey by Chester DePratter relocated Bluff Field, Mound A, but reported no material specifically collected from the mound area. Sherds collected from the general area of Bluff Field included types representative of the Wilmington, St. Catherines, Savannah, and Irene phases. DePratter tentatively assigns the mound to the Savannah Phase on the basis of his reading of Moore's description of the archaeology of the earthwork (DePratter 1974a:20).

The second mound that Moore examined in the same area, **Ossabaw Island, Bryan County. Bluff Field, Mound B** (Moore 1897:131–33), was another small, low mound that had suffered the effects of many years of cultivation. As was the case with the previous mound, there was a dearth of diagnostic material that would allow the mound to be unequivocally placed within one of the coastal cultural and chronological categories. With Burial No. 2 were two small vessels, one a plain open bowl with a slightly incurving rim. Within the bowl was a smaller jar with a notched rim and an angular shoulder. Moore illustrated this latter vessel (ibid.:133, fig. 36), which has a shape that can be characterized as "Mississippian."

Although noting that the "pottery from this mound is hard to identify," DePratter concluded that the mound was probably a Savannah Phase mound (DePratter 1974a:20). He was unable to determine the location in Bluff Field of Mound B.

The last of the mounds that Moore explored on Ossabaw Island was **Ossabaw Island, Bryan County. Bluff Field, Mound C** (Moore 1897:134–36). The mound was only 30 inches high and approximately 50 feet in diameter, and it rewarded the efforts of its excavator with three burials. Burials Nos. 1 and 3 were cremations within the lower sections of large urns. The upper halves of the vessels had been carried away by the plow when the mound was cultivated during the plantation period. According to Moore's notes, the base of Burial No. 3 was only 5 to 6 inches below the surface (R2, B11, p. 103). The vessel holding Burial No. 1 was described as complicated stamped. No description of the surface treatment of the vessel with Burial No. 3 was given. Burial No. 2 was a deposit of cremated bone, a portion of which was covered by large sherds. Moore singled out two of the sherds for an extended discussion because their decoration interested him. His interest was sufficient to prompt him to send either illustrations of the sherds or the actual sherds to William Holmes at the Bureau of American Ethnology, Smithsonian Institution, and to Frederic Putnam and Charles Willoughby at the Peabody Museum, Harvard, for comment on the apparent symbolism of the sherd decoration. Both sherds were illustrated by Moore (1897:135, figs. 78 and 79).[30] One of the sherds, that in figure 78, appears to have a rosette appliqué of the sort that is fairly common on Irene Plain, Irene Complicated Stamped, and Irene Incised wares (Caldwell and McCann 1941:46–49). The drawing suggests that it is a rimsherd from an Irene Plain vessel with a

---

[30]The captions accompanying each of these illustrations erroneously attributed the sherds to Bluff Field, Mound B. Moore's text, however, leaves no doubt that rather than being from Mound B, they should be identified as coming from Bluff Field, Mound C.

cazuela form. The sherd in figure 79 also appears to be from a plain vessel with an appliqué decoration; Putnam referred to this decoration as a "peculiar Z-shaped figure with . . . two dots." In this instance the drawing recalls the appliqué representations of legs that are often associated with effigy bowls, for example, those representing the frog, belonging to the late Mississippi cultural manifestations throughout the Southeast (cf. Phillips, Ford, and Griffin 1951:fig. 108, e, f, g).

The DePratter 1974 archaeological survey of Ossabaw Island was unable to relocate the mound, although Bluff Field was identified. Nevertheless, on the basis of his reading of Moore, Chester DePratter concluded that Mound C was an Irene Phase mound (DePratter 1974a:20). I see no reason to dispute this conclusion.

Other than the recent archaeological surveys of Ossabaw Island already mentioned, there have been no formal archaeological investigations on the island since the work carried out by Moore. Today the island is owned by the state of Georgia and is managed by the Georgia Department of Natural Resources. It is assumed that those archaeological resources that survived the cultivation of the plantation occupation and Moore's visit will enjoy a considerable measure of protection.

Following his investigations in Bluff Field, Moore departed Ossabaw Island for Skidaway Island in Chatham County, where he excavated at three locations. Skidaway Island is not a barrier island in the same sense that Sapelo, St. Catherines, and Ossabaw islands are. Although it is undoubtedly a product of the same geological and hydrological forces as the others, in the recent past Skidaway has lost its barrier beach and today is surrounded by tidal streams and salt marsh (see *U.S. Geological Survey, Isle of Hope Quadrangle, Georgia—Chatham Co., 7.5 Minute Series Orthophotomap, 1979*).

The first of the Skidaway Island sites, **Skiddaway[31] Island, Chatham County. Third Settlement, Mound A** (Moore 1897:136–37), was a small mound some 74 feet in diameter with a summit that "scarcely rose above the general level." Moore excavated only the southern half of the mound, within which he found burials at twenty-seven locations. Determinations about the nature of the burials were made in twenty-two instances. Four of these burials were deposits of cremated bone while eighteen of them were primary burials laid out in a wide variety of positions. The most common position, found in nine burials, was extended and face down. Moore noted the rare occurrence of sherds of any type in the mound. He specifically called attention to a complete absence of complicated stamped pottery in the structure. The mound may well belong to either the Deptford or Wilmington phases of the Woodland Period. However, nothing was recovered from the mound that can be recognized as having particular diagnostic value for establishing the chronological or cultural context of the mound.

The **Skiddaway Island, Chatham County. Third Settlement, Mound B** (ibid.:137), was located about 300 yards to the north of Mound A. The mound had an elevation of only 18 inches above the surrounding surface and its diameter, as determined by Moore, was 60 feet. Only the eastern half of the mound was excavated and eleven burials were encountered. All of the burials appeared to be primary and in-

---

[31]The present spelling of the island name, accepted as correct on all modern maps, is *Skidaway.* Moore persistently spelled the name *Skiddaway,* which is probably one of several unstandardized nineteenth-century spellings.

cluded both males and females as well as a range of ages. Moore reported nothing of diagnostic value in the mound, although he noted that no complicated stamped ceramics were found. As was the case with Mound A, Mound B was probably a Woodland Period mound that could be identified with the Deptford or Wilmington phases of the coastal sequence.

The final coastal Georgia mound investigation reported by Moore was of a mound found in an old field at the **Skiddaway Island, Chatham County. North-end Settlement** (ibid.). Moore supplied precious little in the way of information about this excavation. The mound was small, only 2 feet high and 45 feet in diameter. He apparently encountered burials, but they "offered no points of especial interest." He also found the lower portion of a pottery vessel, but it was dismissed as being of "the ordinary type." The notes, fortunately, supplied a little more information (R2, N10, p. 89–90). We are told in the notes that while sherds within the mound fill were not numerous, those that were encountered were either plain or cord marked. In addition, we learn that while the basal portion of the pot that was found, some 20 feet from the center of the mound, was of the "ordinary type," it bore a complicated stamped decoration and was accompanied by two good-sized fragments of a red ware vessel that also had a complicated stamped decoration. These last two sherds were thought to be the remnants of a bowl used as a cover for the first vessel.

Skidaway Island, which now lies within the Savannah metropolitan area, has experienced massive development in the interim since Moore worked there. The island is now the location of a gated upper-income housing development, a state park, and a marine research facility. Archaeological survey preceded the development in the instances of each of these facilities. These reports have not been published, but they are on file at the Georgia State Archaeological Site Files, University of Georgia, Athens (DePratter 1974b, 1975; Simpkins 1990).

The account by Moore of the North-end Settlement site and his work on Skidaway Island strikes me as a regrettable way for Moore to conclude his archaeological narrative of the Georgia coast. Unfortunately it is not atypical of the kind of reporting that characterized his investigations of the area. An even cursory examination of his later reports provides a clear demonstration of how his methods and interests, as well as the reporting of his work, matured and gained a nature and character that was more truly scientific in every way. The Georgia coastal investigations, while not the first that he undertook, were certainly improved upon as he continued his winter sojourns on the rivers of other areas of the Southeast in subsequent years. Nevertheless, it should be pointed out that Moore was well aware of the archaeological significance of the situations and objects that he found during his work. He saw the importance of similarities in artifact types; for example, he noted the resemblance between the Townsend Mound pipe and one reported by Charles C. Jones from Colonels Island, Liberty County, Georgia, and the resemblance of a pipe he recovered from the Woodbine Mound to one he had found in the Point La Vista Mound, Duval County, Florida. Certainly the recognition of dog burials as a part of the Refuge or Deptford Phase mortuary complex on Ossabaw Island should be especially noted. Also recognized should be his identification of the presence in the mortuary accompaniments of freshwater mussel species in the saltwater environment of the Ossabaw Island mounds.

Moore's work on Skidaway Island was his last on the Georgia coast. He departed Savannah for Philadelphia on April 28, 1897, after leaving the *Gopher* in a safe berth on the Savannah River. He did, however, return to Georgia in 1898 to examine the archaeology of the Altamaha and Savannah rivers.

The Coast of South Carolina

Moore had returned to Philadelphia for the summer of 1897 after having concluded his archaeological investigations on the Georgia coast in late April. With the onset of cooler weather in the north Moore again turned southward to resume his examination of coastal burial mounds. He was to spend the excavation season of 1897–1898 on the coast of South Carolina and on the Savannah and Altamaha rivers. The *Gopher* had been anchored in the Savannah River during the summer and, with his arrival in Savannah, Moore was ready to continue the pursuit of his archaeological interests to the north of the Savannah River entrance.

MOORE IN BEAUFORT COUNTY, SOUTH CAROLINA

Once more on the *Gopher,* Moore concentrated his attention in South Carolina within a single coastal county, Beaufort County. In particular he focused on that part of the coast that lay between St. Helena Sound and the Savannah River, a relatively short stretch of the South Carolina coast approximately thirty-five miles long as the crow flies. The coast between St. Helena Sound and Charleston was subjected to only a cursory series of inquiries that produced "nothing but tar kilns and comparatively modern fortifications" (the Civil War had ended only thirty-two years earlier). In part this lack of significant information was the result of the coastal Carolinians' "total ignorance of the existence of mounds on [that] part of the coast" (Moore 1899a:147). In all Moore investigated fourteen mounds at nine sites in Beaufort County before returning to Georgia to explore the Coastal Plain stretches of the Altamaha and Savannah rivers (ibid.:148).

The first of the sites that Moore investigated was the **Mound near Bluffton, Beaufort County** (ibid.:148), on Cresson Plantation. It was a small mound some 3 feet in height and 58 feet in diameter, which produced two small central deposits of cremated bone and fragments of a child's skull. The mound was composed of sand without the inclusion of midden shell in the fill. Moore reported nothing of diagnostic value that allows the mound to be fitted into the current coastal archaeological sequence. Other than noting that they were not complicated stamped, Moore did not describe the sherds he encountered in the mound fill.

The **Mound on Callawassie Island, Beaufort County** (ibid.:148–49), provided Moore with more of interest than did his initial endeavor. The mound was located on the northwestern portion of the island and showed some evidence of previous digging. The mound was about 3 feet high with a basal diameter of 48 feet, and Moore excavated its northern half, as well as a considerable area lying beyond what had been determined as mound base. A total of nine human burials plus two dog burials was recovered from the mound. The human burials all appeared to be primary with the possible exception of Burial No. 10. The dog burials were also primary and were apparently recovered from situations that allowed for no other interpretation than that they were interred contemporaneously with the mound construction.

The mound fill produced plain and cord-marked sherds along with a single "rude" checked stamped sherd.

The Callawassie Island Mound was subsequently relocated during a recent archaeological survey by the Institute of Archaeology and Anthropology, University of South Carolina, and was assigned the site file number 38Bu19 (Michie 1982:35, 38). In February and March 1982 the Institute excavated that portion of the mound left undisturbed by Moore and published a preliminary report on these investigations (Brooks et al. 1982). The report places the mound construction during the St. Catherines Phase of the Late Woodland Period, A.D. 1000–1150 (ibid.:56). The chronological position of the mound was based on the comparability of the ceramic assemblage found in the Callawassie Island Mound to that defined for the St. Catherines Phase on the Georgia coast by the American Museum of Natural History (DePratter 1979). The Institute work not only provides considerable detail about the mound construction and its mortuary complex but also contributes valuable human osteological, zooarchaeological, paleobotanical, and palynological data from the mound as a consequence of the recent investigations. Moore stated that the Callawassie Island Mound lay in the vicinity of a number of shell middens, suggesting that a village area was adjacent to the mound (Moore 1899a:148). The Institute carried out a preliminary survey of the area to the north and west of the mound and concluded that indeed a village area was associated with the mound (Brooks et al. 1982:56).

Moore shifted his efforts to two **Mounds near Hasell Point, Beaufort County** (Moore 1899a:150–51). The first of these mounds, 4 feet high with a basal diameter of 34 feet, was found to have been disturbed by previous digging. Although Moore excavated more than one-half of the mound, he recovered only a few plain and cord-marked sherds from the fill.

The second of the Hasell Point mounds, about 1 foot high and 32 feet in diameter, was characterized by a central core composed of oyster shell. It produced six burials represented by both cremated and primary forms. Plain and cord-marked sherds were recovered from the mound fill.

The existence of the **Aboriginal Enclosure, Guerard Point, Beaufort County,** was noted by Moore but does not seem to have been excavated by him (ibid.:151). The structure, which was on the order of the shell ring on Sapelo Island, had suffered considerably from cultivation and in all likelihood had been robbed of its shell for road or tabby construction. Its walls were only 28 inches high while its basal diameter was about 130 feet, which is only half that of the Sapelo Shell Ring.

Although Moore did excavate the **Mound at Indian Hill, Beaufort County** (ibid.), he found little he deemed worthy of discussion. The mound, on the Paget property, was greatly reduced by continuous cultivation and as a consequence was only 17 inches high and 47 feet in diameter. The central deposit, cremated bone and bone from what may have been primary burials, was badly disturbed. Moore encountered sherds in the mound fill that he characterized as "few," "rough," and "mostly cord-marked." This site should not be confused with the mound called Indian Hill, which was also excavated by Moore (see below) but which was located on the Chaplin property near the Frogmore Post Office on St. Helena Island.

Perhaps the most interesting of the South Carolina sites examined by Moore, and certainly the site about which he provided us the greatest detail, was the **Larger Mound, Little Island, Beaufort County** (ibid.:152–62). The mound was probably one of the largest mounds that Moore encountered on either the Georgia or South Carolina coast. It stood 14 feet high. At the base, oval in outline, it was 150 feet long on the north-south axis and 100 feet wide on the east-west axis. The mound was characterized by a "markedly level" summit 38 feet wide and 61 feet long. Moore described the sides of the mound as too steep for any cultivation. The mound, a well-preserved platform mound, had not been vandalized. Moore spent twelve days in the excavation of this mound, which was more time than he devoted to any other site in the Georgia or South Carolina coastal areas. He employed twenty-eight laborers with four supervisors before he completed the excavation of the mound. Apparently he also employed a person to plot the excavations, including the exposed features. The publication of the excavation of the Little Island mound site also marked the first time Moore used photographs, particularly field photographs, to illustrate his work. If Moore was using a camera to record his work, are there photographs of his earlier fieldwork during the Florida and Georgia excavations—or even of later excavations for that matter? If they exist, where are they? There is no mention of photographs contained within the archives of Moore's work held by the Huntington Free Library (Davis 1987). The brief introduction to the microfilm guide to Moore's field records published by the library notes that Moore was an award-winning photographer (ibid.:8). I am informed by Stephen Williams that a search of the records that were at the Museum of the American Indian failed to locate any of Moore's photographs.

Within the mound at Little Island Moore found the walls of a large rectangular building that had been buried with the construction of the large earthwork. The building, about 40 feet by 35 feet in plan, had been filled and surrounded with oyster shell in the construction of the mound, which served to preserve its clay daub walls more or less intact. On the upper edges of the walls Moore found rafter impressions of the roof, which had apparently been removed in order to fill the building with shell. A clayey sand layer was placed over the shell used to bury the building. The mound that resulted from these actions was covered with a thin layer of midden. Subsequently the mound was enlarged several times, apparently to create surfaces on which buildings were constructed as evidenced by the large number of postholes and the occupational debris that Moore found associated with these strata.

Moore collected and presumably preserved sections of the building walls that were discovered beneath the mound. A colored drawing of the excavation showing the exposed building that lay beneath the mound forms the frontispiece for Moore's South Carolina coastal report.

Associated with the building at the mound base was an infant burial beneath the central fire basin. Sherds found in the fill were described as plain, as checked stamped, or as having a complicated stamped decoration. One of the complicated stamped sherds illustrated by Moore appears to be related to Irene Complicated Stamped (Moore 1899a:160, fig. 7). The most obvious conclusion to be drawn about the site is that it was a Mississippi Period site probably related to the Irene Phase.

The **Smaller Mound, Little Island, Beaufort County** (ibid.:162–63), lay some 35 yards to the south-southeast of the larger platform mound. At the time of his visit, Moore estimated that at least one-half of the mound had eroded into the adjacent tidal stream. Moore thought the size of the mound to have been originally almost 4 feet high with a basal diameter of 50 feet. The mound consisted of a shell core with a central depression that held four deposits of cremated human bone. Two of the deposits contained shell beads as well as other artifacts without particular diagnostic importance. Sherds from the mound fill were described as bearing a complicated stamped decoration. This suggests not only that the mound was contemporary with the larger of the Little Island mounds, but also that along with the larger mound it probably comprised a part of a formal site ritual complex.

The Institute of Archaeology and Anthropology, University of South Carolina, relocated the site of Moore's Little Island mounds during an archaeological survey of Port Royal Sound and the Broad River Estuary in 1979–1980, at which time the site was assigned the number 38Bu23 in the South Carolina archaeological site files (Michie 1980). In his description of the survey and its results Michie had the following comment about the site:

> *38BU23* This Mississippian mound was partially excavated by C. B. Moore. . . . Presently, the eastern portion is eroding into the marsh of Whale branch. The small burial mound located to the south appears totally excavated. Both mounds have suffered vandalism. (ibid.:45)

Only three platform mounds have been described for the Georgia and South Carolina coasts: they are the larger of the two Little Island mounds; Indian Hill Mound on the Chaplin property, near the Frogmore Post Office, St. Helena Island (discussed below); and the Irene Mound at the juncture of Pipemakers Creek and the Savannah River. It may be of significance that they are located relatively close to one another—probably no more than fifty miles separate them. The scarcity of such structures on the coast would seem to provoke questions about the nature of the aboriginal cultures in the area during the Mississippi Period.

The four **Mounds near Button Hill, Port Royal Island, Beaufort County** (Moore 1899a:163–64), were in part seriously damaged by cultivation, digging by those whom Moore referred to as "treasure seekers," or both. The fill of the third mound produced plain and cord-marked sherds. On the surface near the fourth mound was a celt with a tapered poll. The meager diagnostic evidence suggests that the Button Hill mounds probably could be assigned to the St. Catherines Phase of the Woodland Period and are representative of what appears to be a rather widespread and intensive coastal occupation during this time.

Moore investigated a second platform mound at **Indian Hill, St. Helena Island, Beaufort County** (ibid.:164–65). The mound was located one-half mile from the Frogmore Post Office, St. Helena Island (R2, B13, p. 19). Although Moore discussed little of diagnostic value in findings encountered during his examination of the mound, there is no doubt that the mound was a platform mound. Its 15-foot height, its flat summit 62 feet in diameter, and the postholes "found at four distinct levels" would appear to unequivocally establish its identity as a temple mound probably referable to the Irene Phase of the Mississippi Period.

The last mound investigated by Moore on the South Carolina coast was the **Mound on Polleewahnee Island, Beaufort County** (Moore 1899a:165–66), from which he reportedly recovered nothing: no "artifacts or burials."

In the summary of his relatively brief coastal South Carolina experience Moore provided us with a clear statement that reflected not only his archaeological interests centered almost solely on burial mounds, burials, and the artifacts recovered from a mortuary context—witness Moore's refusal to examine midden areas. After having generalized about the nature of the mounds he encountered on the South Carolina coast and the perceived absence of practical results stemming from his efforts, he stated, "On the whole, it would seem probable the South Carolina coast has little to offer from an archaeological standpoint" (ibid.:166). Few statements can be cited that serve as well to measure how far archaeology in the southeastern United States has progressed in the past one hundred years.

The Savannah River

Concluding his examination of coastal South Carolina, primarily the tidewater portions of Beaufort County, Moore departed Charleston on February 10, 1898, for Savannah after a disappointing search for sites along the Stone River. The investigation of the Savannah River took place February 12 through March 7, 1898. During this time he examined thirteen mounds, eleven on the Georgia side of the river and two on the South Carolina side. The work was confined to the area below the Fall Line, that is, that portion of the river valley and adjacent uplands below Augusta, Georgia. Augusta was and remains the head of navigation on the Savannah River. Consequently the *Gopher* could not proceed beyond the shoal waters that close the river to traffic upstream from Augusta. The Savannah River valley below the Fall Line is typical of that of many of the large streams in the region as they cross the southeastern Coastal Plain. The valley is characterized by back swamps on both sides of the river over much of its length except where the river flows against the uplands at the edge of its alluvial floodplain. The floodplain is subject to inundation in almost any month of the year. Once the floodwaters have broken across the natural levees along the banks of the river, they will only slowly drain back into the main river channel as a flood recedes. The back swamps and other low areas of the floodplain, not unusually, retain water for weeks following the end of a flood. Consequently there are few areas suitable for human occupation, and thus few archaeological sites, within the alluvial valley itself except where elevated areas create "swamp islands" on the floodplain. Most of the sites are found on the nearby uplands. Because he focused his investigations exclusively upon mounds, particularly burial mounds, Moore found few sites that excited his interest along the Savannah River.

MOORE IN CHATHAM COUNTY, GEORGIA

The first site Moore described embraced two **Mounds near Pipemaker's Creek, Chatham County, Georgia** (Moore 1899b:168). The site, which lay only four miles above Savannah as the city existed at the time, was treated by its investigator in three paragraphs. Moore described the site as consisting of a large mound, a truncated cone with a circular base, and an adjacent small mound composed largely of midden. The larger mound was 19 feet high and had a diameter of 130 feet. Moore examined a portion of the mound that had been exposed by a large pot hunter's hole, but finding no evidence of burials moved on to the smaller of the two mounds, which was 3 feet high and 60 feet in diameter. Eighteen burials were encountered, the largest number of which were apparently flexed. The only grave goods were small shell beads found with two burials and a pebble hammer accompanying a third. The fill of the small mound was described as containing sherds bearing checked stamped, complicated stamped, and "diamond-shaped" stamped motifs. There are checked stamped and complicated stamped wares characteristic of both the Woodland and Mississippi periods on the Georgia coast, and the Pipemakers Creek site is by most measures a coastal site. Without illustrations or more detailed descriptions of the sherds it is difficult to assign the mound to a particular archaeological context using the information supplied by Moore.

Today the site no longer exists. It has been destroyed by the expansion of the Savannah port operations and presently lies beneath one of the massive container facilities of the Georgia Ports Authority, Savannah. Fortunately, the destruction of the site occurred several decades after the completion of extensive excavations that attended a reexamination of the site during the depression years preceding World War II. The results of the reexamination have been published and consequently more information is available about the Pipemakers Creek site than almost any other site on the Georgia coast. The site that Moore identified as the Pipemakers Creek site is now better known as the Irene site (Caldwell and McCann 1941). The excavation of the mound as a Works Progress Administration (WPA) project took place over twenty-nine months between September 1937 and January 1941 and was directed successively by Preston Holder, Vladimir J. Fewkes, Claude Schaeffer, and finally Joseph Caldwell. This excavation was a major contributor to the establishment of the coastal Georgia chronology and ceramic sequence. Edwin A. Lyon summarized the history of this excavation in his recent discussion of archaeology in the Southeast during the New Deal era (Lyon 1996:109–11).

The site, as revealed by the WPA excavations, occupied a more or less triangular piece of land some 6 acres in extent and some 15 feet above the river and the surrounding area. The Savannah River flowed south along its eastern edge and was eroding that edge as it cut laterally westward into the site. Pipemakers Creek bounded the site on the north and west sides while the south side of the area was defined by a shallow defile that was apparently an old channel of Pipemakers Creek. The large mound at the site, the mound that Moore found of so little interest as to dismiss it in seven sentences, consisted of a series of seven, and possibly eight, superimposed platform mounds. The surfaces of the first seven stages of mound construction were each apparently occupied by a building while the last construction stage was the conical mound described by Moore.[32] The first seven construction stages were attributed to the Savannah Phase of the Mississippi Period. The final stage was identified as belonging to the Irene Phase of the Mississippi Period.

The smaller mound, the burial mound from which Moore removed eighteen burials, lay immediately west of the large mound. In addition to the large mound and the burial mound, the site features included a mortuary structure within two

---

[32]A careful reading of the descriptions of these structures and examination of the accompanying drawings in the report of Caldwell and McCann (1941:18–20) suggests that the first four phases of construction may well represent a series of superimposed buildings with earth-banked walls rather than superimposed mounds. There is no doubt, however, that mounds five, six, and seven were functional platform mounds with ramps and summit structures. Mound eight, the final mound construction, was described by Caldwell and McCann as having a rounded summit and a circular base, rather than a flat summit and rectangular base with a ramp, as was found on the earlier mounds.

concentric post enclosures; a wall trench that defined the outline of a rotunda 129 feet in diameter; at least four houses, apart from the structures associated with the mounds and others already mentioned; and several palisade systems that served to define and perhaps defend particular areas of the site. The rotunda lay across a large plaza, some 90 feet south of the large mound. The plaza was further defined by palisades on its north, west, and south sides. The absence of a palisade on the east side was undoubtedly a consequence of the Savannah River's having cut into that part of the plaza. One hundred two burials were recovered from within the mortuary building and its enclosing palisades, 106 interments were found in the burial mound, and forty more burials were excavated at other locations on the site (Caldwell and McCann 1941:4–5, 22–39, fig. 13).

Although Moore stated that he had excavated one-half of the burial mound, the later WPA excavation indicated that he had placed a trench approximately 25 feet wide and 40 feet long into the mound. The area within which burials were located was approximately 70 feet in diameter (ibid.:fig. 11). In all Moore probably excavated less than one-quarter of the mound.

MOORE IN SCREVEN COUNTY, GEORGIA

Leaving the city of Savannah sixty-eight miles downriver Moore moved up the Savannah River to investigate two **Mounds near Hudson's Ferry, Screven County, Georgia** (Moore 1899b:169–71). At Hudson Ferry Landing (the current place name usage) the Savannah River flows on the western side of its floodplain and a high bluff rises abruptly some 110 feet from the river edge to the relatively flat upland (see *U.S. Geological Survey, Kildare Quadrangle, Georgia—South Carolina, 7.5 Minute Series*). About one mile west of Hudson Ferry Landing, Moore excavated a mound measuring 2 feet 5 inches in height with a basal diameter of 74 feet. Four burials were encountered, each of which was apparently placed in a shallow pit dug no more than a few inches into the original ground surface. Moore found no pottery vessels in the mound nor was mention made of sherds found in the mound fill. Moore found two ceramic pipes that are of particular interest. One, recovered from Burial No. 2, was a type of pipe that is regularly found with manifestations of the Mississippi Period in the interior areas of Georgia (Moore 1899b:fig. 9). This pipe, an elbow pipe with a flaring bowl, had several concentric incised lines on and just below the bowl rim as well as around the end of the short stem. The bowl was further ornamented with a number of rounded bosses, probably eight in number, that covered the base and body of the bowl below the flaring of the bowl opening. The second pipe, an owl effigy, was taken from Burial No. 3. The bowl of the pipe was the body of the owl while the legs of the bird were extended along the sides of the short stem. The owl pipe resembles a pipe found during the excavations carried out by Henry Reynolds for Cyrus Thomas at the Hollywood Mound, Richmond County, Georgia, as part of the Bureau of American Ethnology mound exploration in 1891 (Thomas 1894:fig. 205). The two pipes from the Hudson Ferry Mound argue for a Mississippi Period chronological position for the mound.

A second mound was trenched by Moore but produced little of interest to him. The mound, slightly higher than the first mound, yielded only fragments of calcined bone. These were encountered as a central deposit in the mound.

Moore next applied his efforts to the excavation of two **Mounds near Mill's**

Landing, Screven County, Ga. (Moore 1899b:171). The first of these mounds, described as 11 feet high and "a mound with circular base and marked summit plateau, also circular," may well have been a platform mound. Finding no burials, Moore moved his operation one-half mile in a northwesterly direction to another smaller platform mound only to meet with a similar lack of interesting results.

MOORE IN BARNWELL COUNTY [I.E., ALLENDALE COUNTY], SOUTH CAROLINA

Continuing upriver, Moore stopped next at the two **Mounds near Brook's Landing, Barnwell County, S.C.** (ibid.:171). He investigated only the northernmost of the two mounds at the site. This mound, slightly more than 5 feet high with a basal diameter of 68 feet, was described by Moore as a platform mound. The trenches Moore placed in this mound encountered no burials and revealed no stratification. Although several "fireplaces" were met with, only a handful of sherds were identified in the fill. The second mound, "almost contiguous" to the first mound, was not examined.

David Anderson described this site as possessing not only the two platform mounds but also a fortification ditch and embankment with a site area of 3.5 acres (Anderson 1994:187, 189).[33] Anderson also noted that the South Carolina Institute of Archaeology and Anthropology carried out limited examinations of the site in 1970 and 1989 and as a consequence found evidence that the mounds were the product of construction stages and that a wattle-and-daub building was associated with the mound. The sherds collected by the later work at the site appear to be related to Savannah Phase coastal occupations (ibid.:189). There is no doubt that the site can be assigned to the Mississippi Period.

MOORE IN BURKE COUNTY, GEORGIA

At **Stony Bluff, Burke County, Ga.** (Moore 1899b:172), Moore viewed an area of extensive chert quarrying and chert workshop activity. The site is located just north of the Screven-Burke county line atop a bluff some 70 to 80 feet above the Savannah River floodplain. Moore seemingly did no digging at the site, and apparently confined his activity there to surface collecting. The archaeological area has been designated as 9Bk6 in the Georgia State Archaeological Site Files. Present at several locations in Burke County, in the general area of Brier Creek, are exposures of Cenozoic deposits containing the type of chert that produced the raw material for chipped stone tools and weapons during much of the prehistoric period. The Burke County chert enjoyed a wide distribution in the state, although as might be expected it was most extensively employed locally.

The two **Mounds near Demerie's Ferry, Burke County, Ga.** (ibid.), produced little of interest for Moore. The mounds had been vandalized and although in the larger of the two Moore found human bone at two locations, nothing was apparently recovered from the smaller mound.

The final investigations in the Savannah River valley were made at the three **Mounds near Shell Bluff, Burke County, Ga.** (ibid.). Shell Bluff, located only

---

[33]The site is presently identified in the South Carolina archaeological site files as the Lawton mound group (38Al11), and the portion of the county occupied by the site has been renamed Allendale County.

about two miles above Demerie's Ferry, is more famous for its huge fossil oyster shells than for its archaeology. The mounds that Moore examined were located on the high ground adjacent to the Shell Bluff Landing slightly more than 100 feet above the river floodplain. Two of the mounds had been damaged by cultivation and vandals; the third mound had apparently been used historically as a family burial plot. Moore suggested that it may have originally been a small platform mound.

Moore was undoubtedly disappointed with the results of his trip up the Savannah River. He seems to have been motivated to undertake the trip by references made by William Bartram to mounds at Silver Bluff just below Augusta (Harper 1958:199) and by Charles C. Jones to large mounds at Mason's Plantation also just below Augusta but on the South Carolina side of the river (Jones 1873:150–56; Moore 1899b:167–68). Strangely, Moore provided no map of the Savannah River marked with the locations of the sites he investigated. Such maps accompanied his coastal Georgia, coastal South Carolina, and Altamaha River research. The map he published to illustrate his traverse of the Altamaha River was based on U.S. government charts, and perhaps such charts did not exist for the Savannah River.

The Altamaha River

The Altamaha is one of the major streams draining the interior of Georgia. It is formed by two rivers that are part of large drainage basins originating in the Piedmont Physiographic Province. These rivers, the Ocmulgee and the Oconee, flow south toward the Atlantic from the drainage divide that carries the waters of the Chattahoochee River and its tributaries into the Gulf via the Apalachicola River. The Ocmulgee and the Oconee unite at Lumber City, Georgia, to form the Altamaha River. The river then flows more than 120 miles across the Coastal Plain to the point at which it enters the Atlantic Ocean through a broad area of cypress swamps and braided streams that finally empty into the Altamaha and Doboy sounds.

Operating from the *Gopher*, Moore examined thirty-nine mounds at eighteen different locations along the Altamaha River.[34] If one follows the published text, the sequence of sites visited by Moore would seem to indicate that he steamed steadily upriver examining one site after another in the order presented. This was not the case. If instead one follows the daily log of the *Gopher* kept for the Altamaha trip, it is readily apparent that Moore spent a great deal of time going up and down the river, probably investigating the sites as he became aware of them from his local informants.

Moore in Wayne County, Georgia

The first site that was described was the **Mound Opposite Fort Barrington, Wayne County** (Moore 1899c:175). Today it is difficult to locate the site. Fort

[34]In 1920 the Georgia legislature created Long County out of the southwestern one-third of Liberty County. Consequently all of the sites that Moore identified as located in Liberty County would presently be placed within the boundaries of Long County. It should also be noted that although Moore listed five mounds in the vicinity of Darien along with those that he examined during his Altamaha investigations, these mounds were those that he had excavated during his traversal of the Georgia coast a year earlier, and they are described in *Certain Aboriginal Mounds of the Georgia Coast* (Moore 1897).

Barrington has been not only a steamboat landing but also a ferry landing. At one time the ferry moved the Old Barrington Road traffic across the Altamaha River to a landing some two miles below Sansavilla Bluff. It may be that the mound was located on the bluffs some 45 feet above the river floodplain on Aleck Island (see *U.S. Geological Survey, Everett Quadrangle, Georgia, 7.5 Minute Series*). There is also a real possibility that the mound may have been at or near Sansavilla Bluff. The Sansavilla Bluff area was the location of an important crossing of the Altamaha River, the site of an eighteenth-century trading post, and possibly the site of a seventeenth-century Spanish mission. During the colonial era, the principal route south along the Georgia coast from Savannah to Florida crossed the Altamaha River from Fort Barrington on the north side of the river to Sansavilla Bluff on the south. Fort Barrington was built by colonial Georgia authorities not only to control traffic on the river but also to control the roadway. Today it is still possible to trace portions of the earthworks that constituted elements of Fort Barrington's defenses.

The results of the examination of this Wayne County mound must have been disappointing to Moore if we are to judge by his description of the venture. The mound, according to Moore, "was two-thirds dug through by us yielding nothing beyond a few decayed human bones here and there" (Moore 1899c:175).

Moore in Liberty County [i.e., Long County], Georgia

Moore carried his investigations to the edge of the north side of the Altamaha floodplain where he examined a **Mound near wood landing, Liberty County** (ibid.), a low sand mound that "was trenched and dug centrally without result." Note that *wood landing* is not the name of the landing, but rather the descriptive term applied by Moore to the "nameless landing used by raftsmen" (ibid.). The mound, which was trenched, may have been near Big Bug Landing on Bug Island in what is now Long County, because this is the only landing between Sansavilla Bluff opposite Fort Barrington and Joyner Island (see below), the excavation Moore reported next.

The two **Mounds on Joiner's Island, Liberty County**[35] (ibid.), proved to be of no more interest to Moore than the two previous earthworks he examined. The first mound, a low, small sand mound, had been vandalized and Moore found only one pocket of cremated human bone. The second mound, although almost 7 feet high and 68 feet in diameter at the base, produced no more than two or three sherds despite the rather extensive excavation that Moore carried out at the site.

The **Mounds near Lake Bluff, Liberty County** (ibid.:175–79), seven in all, must have provided Clarence Moore some satisfaction and thus allowed him to justify his expenditure of effort, time, and money on the Altamaha venture. Lake Bluff lies on the eastern side of the river on a low, one-half-mile-wide ridge, probably a natural levee, near the western edge of the river floodplain. At this point the floodplain is approximately six miles wide (see *U.S. Geological Survey, Doctortown Quadrangle, Georgia, 7.5 Minute Series*). Although the first mound, 5 feet 10 inches high with a basal diameter of 52 feet, had been the object of extensive vandalism, Moore was able to locate seven burial areas (Moore 1899c:176). From these burials he removed a number of objects that have diagnostic value, including five pottery vessels.

---

[35]The name of the island now appears on current maps, such as *U.S. Geological Survey, Bug Island Quadrangle, Georgia, 7.5 Minute Series,* as "Joyner Island."

One of the pots, identified as E, a large jar used to cover a deposit of cremated bone, was illustrated in a drawing (ibid.:fig. 15) and in a photograph, at full scale, of the complicated stamped motif found on the exterior of the vessel (ibid.:fig. 16). The vessel shape and the complicated stamped motif argue that the vessel should be classified as Savannah Complicated Stamped. A second vessel, A, also used to contain a cremation, was stated to have had a faintly applied complicated stamped design, but was not otherwise described (ibid.:178). A third vessel, D, was described as decorated with a checked stamped design (ibid.:179). The second and third vessels, in all likelihood, would not be out of place in a Mississippi Period Savannah Phase assemblage.

The other six low mounds at Lake Bluff were excavated; one produced a primary burial of an infant under an inverted undecorated pottery vessel. Another mound, upon excavation, revealed a central pit at the mound base that contained a mass of bones covered with hematite and placed without any apparent order. This mass included the parts of skulls of eight individuals (ibid.:178).

The three **Mounds near Old River, Liberty County** (ibid.:179–80), were apparently located on the east side of an Altamaha cutoff meander identified on maps as "Hughes Old River" (see *U.S. Geological Survey, Doctortown Quadrangle, Georgia, 7.5 Minute Series*). Here Moore found little he considered of importance. The first of the mounds had been vandalized and Moore found fragments of human bone in the back dirt of the vandal's pit, an indication that it had held burials at one time. The second mound contained a central pit, but from this pit Moore recovered only a few fragments of unburned and burned bone.

MOORE IN WAYNE COUNTY, GEORGIA

Moore found that the **Mound near Oglethorpe Bluff, Wayne County** (Moore 1899c:180), had been vandalized, as was the case with many of the Altamaha River mounds. Although Moore excavated the remaining undisturbed margins of the mound, he went unrewarded for his efforts. The site was located due west and upriver on the opposite side of the Altamaha from the Old River site, probably near Oglethorpe Branch, a small stream (recently dammed) that drained into the Altamaha at Oglethorpe Bluff (see *U.S. Geological Survey, Jesup NW Quadrangle, Georgia, 7.5 Minute Series*).

The five **Mounds near Mitchell's Lake, Wayne County** (Moore 1899c:180–81), were next to receive Moore's attention. The mound sites were apparently located on an abandoned meander of the Altamaha. However, a search of the recent and relevant U.S. Geological Survey quadrangle sheets revealed no lake by that name. Presumably Mitchell's Lake lay between the Old River sites and those at Beard's Bluff, the sites that Moore described after Mitchell's Lake. However, while both Old River and Beard's Bluff can be located on sheets of the *U.S. Geological Survey, Jesup NW Quadrangle, Georgia, 7.5 Minute Series* and *U.S. Geological Survey, Glennville SW Quadrangle, Georgia, 7.5 Minute Series* (editions with the field surveys dated 1958), as well as on the *Georgia, Jesup Quadrangle* sheet (with a field survey dated 1917), no lake is identified on either edition as Mitchell's.

Moore excavated in all five of the Mitchell's Lake mounds. Human burials were found in four of the mounds. The fifth and last mound that Moore described was stated to be "1.5 miles west by north from the swamp landing near Mitchell's Lake"

(Moore 1899c:181). The directions given in the description would seem to place this mound in a location that was above the Altamaha floodplain on the high ground overlooking the river valley.

Moore found "bunched burials" at six locations in the mound. A small shell disc, 0.8 inch in diameter with two perforations, lay with the skull of an adult. With the skull of a child was a shell pin, very likely the knobbed shell earpin type that Moore encountered in some of the Irene Phase mound burials on the northern half of the Georgia coast. Along with the pin was a shell gorget about 4.5 inches in diameter. It was decorated with an engraved design, much eroded when found, and with portions of the background cut away. There is little doubt that this gorget belongs to the style that Brain and Phillips refer to as the Spaghetti style (Brain and Phillips 1996:62–67). This style is associated with the knobbed shell earpins and is generally regarded as a late form.

In his published account, Moore made no mention of ceramics having been encountered during the Mitchell's Lake investigations. However, the handwritten notes that described the work at the mounds at Mitchell's Lake did refer to sherds in the fill of several of the mounds. The absence of any reference to sherds in the published report was apparently deliberate because the published accounts of the investigations were, largely, literal transcriptions of the text contained in the notebooks. In the handwritten notes describing the investigations of the first mound, which contained a "circular implement of rough sandstone," Moore reported that "several undecorated sherds, and one with complicated stamp lay loose in the sand" (R2, B13, p. 54). For the second mound the notes indicated that "several sherds with rude cross-hatched decoration were loose in the sand" (R2, B13, p. 55). The notes covering the work on the last mound, the one with the shell gorget, stated that "several sherds with rude cross-hatched decoration lay in the sand" (R2, B13, p. 57). The descriptions of these sherds do not allow for their identification. Complicated stamped ware occurs throughout the Woodland and Mississippi periods in this area of the Coastal Plain. The "rude cross-hatched" ware may well be one of several cord-marked types that have been noted in the region.

MOORE IN LIBERTY COUNTY [I.E., LONG COUNTY], GEORGIA

Of the two **Mounds near Beard's Bluff, Liberty County** (Moore 1899c:181–82), Moore reported that one, a previously disturbed earthwork 3 feet high and 56 feet in diameter at the base, was probably a domiciliary mound. The second mound, also disturbed by a small trench through its center, was encircled by a series of shallow borrow pits. The mound was 2.5 feet high with a basal diameter of 36 feet. Only a small deposit of cremated human bone was found in the mound. The first mound was located on a relatively narrow elevated area, a natural levee, in the river swamp on the north side of the Altamaha River in what is now Long County. The second mound, also in the river swamp, lay about one-half mile to the north of the first mound, across Beards Creek and in Tattnall County.

MOORE IN WAYNE COUNTY, GEORGIA

The investigation of the **Mound near Fort James, Wayne County** (ibid.:182), was "without result." Interestingly, there is no reference to such a mound in the notes or in the log. The site was located on the south side of the river probably in the area where the Altamaha River first swings against the high-ground bluffs after it leaves Appling County and enters Wayne County in its eastward course (see *U.S. Geological Survey, Glennville SW Quadrangle, Georgia, 7.5 Minute Series*). Presently, several roads lead from the high ground down the bluff to the river. One or another of these roads probably gave Moore access from the landing to the location of the mound.

The **Mound near Reddish's Landing, Wayne County** (Moore 1899c:182), was stated to be two miles in a northwesterly direction from the landing. However, an examination of the relevant U.S. Geological Survey quadrangle sheets tracing the Altamaha River as it flows along the northern boundary of Wayne County demonstrates that it is impossible to travel northwest from any possible Altamaha River landing in Wayne County. Almost certainly Moore was in error and should have said "southwesterly" in giving directions to the site. The mound, 4 feet high and with a basal diameter of 45 feet, had been vandalized. Moore encountered a large deposit of cremated human bone within the mound. Again, for some inexplicable reason, Moore omitted mention of the occurrence of ceramic sherds although the notes indicated that "sherds plain and complicated stamp" were found in the mound fill (R2, B13, p. 53). Unfortunately this information is not helpful in attempting to place the Reddish's Landing Mound in a cultural or temporal context.

Moore in Tattnall County, Georgia

The two **Mounds near Matlock Water Road, Tattnall County** (Moore 1899c:182), were located on the north side of the river on what appears to have been a natural levee (see *U.S. Geological Survey, Altamaha SE Quadrangle, Georgia, 7.5 Minute Series*). Moore was able to locate deposits of cremated and unburned bone in the larger of the two mounds. The smaller mound, although much disturbed by cultivation, also yielded evidence of burials.

Moore encountered disappointment in the two **Mounds near the Ohoopee River, Tattnall County** (Moore 1899c:182). The mounds were so vandalized that he turned from them without making any attempt to dig.

Moore in Appling County, Georgia

The investigation of the **Mound below Tilman's Ferry, Appling County** (ibid.:182–83), proved to be more rewarding. The ferry no longer appears on the appropriate topographic map or on the Georgia Department of Transportation Appling County road map. Nevertheless, the mound must have been located on the south side of the Altamaha River about one mile upstream from its juncture with the Ohoopee River (see *U.S. Geological Survey, Altamaha Quadrangle, Georgia, 7.5 Minute Series*). Despite the fact that the mound had a large crater in its center, the product of vandals, Moore encountered the remains of several primary burials. One of the burials was accompanied by two shell earpins, undoubtedly of the knobbed type that had been found in late burials along the coast. The burial also contained many large shell beads. Complicated stamped sherds were recovered from the mound fill. Given the presence of the shell earpins, the sherds were probably a Mississippi Period complicated stamped type.

Moore found little of apparent interest in the two **Mounds near Iron Mine Landing, Appling County** (Moore 1899c:183). The site was almost certainly located near what today appears on the quadrangle sheet as Iron Mine Bluff (see *U.S. Geological Survey, Altamaha Quadrangle, Georgia, 7.5 Minute Series*). Moore noted a bundle burial with some fragments of cremated bone and shell beads in association in the mound.

Moore next investigated a small sand **Mound near Hell's Shoal, Appling County** (Moore 1899c:183). The colorful name of the location reflects the fact that the Altamaha River was a major waterway for steam-powered, shallow-draft riverboats in the latter half of the nineteenth century and the first quarter of the twentieth century. The river was also an important route, after the Civil War, for huge rafts of longleaf pine timber cut on the Coastal Plain and floated to the port at Darien for milling and shipment by sail to East Coast ports and to Europe. The destruction of the longleaf forest and construction of rail routes between the coast and the interior across the Coastal Plain brought an end to the use of the river as a transportation route, a fact reflected in the complete absence of navigational cautions and references on the modern quadrangle sheets. Only the old place names persist, but Hell's Shoal is still not among them. This location was three miles upriver from Iron Mine Landing, which would place Hell's Shoal on or near the point at which the Tattnall-Tombs county line reaches the river (see *U.S. Geological Survey, Altamaha Quadrangle, Georgia, 7.5 Minute Series*).

The mound was typical of those that Moore encountered previously during his investigation of the Altamaha. The mound was of modest dimensions measuring about 2 feet in height with a basal diameter of 35 feet. It was also typical in that it had been vandalized. The mound contained both a primary and a cremated burial. The primary burial had been disturbed by the earlier digging. The cremation had been placed in an undecorated pottery vessel, the rim of which had been carried away by the plow.

The investigation of the **Mound near Buckhorn Bluff, Appling County** (Moore 1899c:183–84), placed Moore about 100 miles up the Altamaha River from Darien. Buckhorn Bluff does not appear on the relevant quadrangle sheets. Landings on the Appling County side of the river are not numerous and the most likely location of Buckhorn Bluff is near what is presently called Davis Landing. Davis Landing is approximately three miles from the supposed location of Hell's Shoals, a distance that would agree with Moore's estimated distance (see *U.S. Geological Survey, Altamaha Quadrangle, Georgia, 7.5 Minute Series*). The mound, another of the familiar small sand mounds that Moore regularly explored on his way upriver, contained a deposit of cremated bone and also several primary burials. The latter were accompanied by several celts.

MOORE IN TATTNALL COUNTY [I.E., TOOMBS COUNTY], GEORGIA

The last site explored by Moore was the **Mound at Gray's Landing, Tattnall County** (Moore 1899c:184). At the time of Moore's Altamaha investigations Gray's Landing was located in Tattnall County; however, in 1905 the Georgia legislature created Toombs County out of portions of three existing counties. The portion of Tattnall County that included Gray's Landing then became a part of Toombs County. Gray's Landing remains as a named location (see *U.S. Geological Survey, Gray's Landing Quadrangle, Georgia, 7.5 Minute Series*). The mound was yet another of the usual low sand mounds along the Altamaha. Although he found no human remains, Moore did encounter "abundant" sherds and chert fragments. Unfortunately the sherds were not otherwise described.

The archaeological investigations of the Altamaha River by Moore carried him to within five or six miles of the juncture of the Ocmulgee and Oconee rivers, the two rivers that unite to form the Altamaha. Moore, as was his regular practice, concentrated his efforts on the excavation of the burial mounds that were reported to him by local residents. The amount of information that resulted from his activities is very limited. The excavations of only two mounds recovered materials and were reported in the kind of detail that permits speculation about cultural and chronological affiliation: the first of the mounds near Lake Bluff and the fifth mound near Mitchell's Lake. These two mounds appear to be the product of Mississippi Period cultural manifestations. It is probably impossible to establish a context for the other thirty-four mounds that were examined at some seventeen locations along the Altamaha.

Since the investigations by Moore, relatively little attention has been given to the areas along the Altamaha. The principal recent archaeological work in the area was a survey carried out by Frankie Snow (1977). The Snow survey focused largely on that portion of the Ocmulgee River that lies upstream from its junction with the Oconee River, that is, immediately upstream from where Moore turned the *Gopher* around and headed back downriver to Darien and the coast. Snow reported a full range of archaeological complexes in the area, including those found within the Early Man, Archaic, Woodland, and Mississippi periods.

There has been but a single reported excavation of a site in the immediate area of the Altamaha since the work by Moore. This excavation, that of the Lowe site, was located in Telfair County near Jacksonville, Georgia, on the Ocmulgee River some twenty-two miles upstream from the point where Moore ended his work. The work revealed a long archaeological sequence from a Dalton occupation to a late protohistoric occupation (Crook 1987).

In the 1980s Dennis Blanton succeeded in relocating a number of the mound sites that were investigated by Moore (Blanton, personal communication, May 1997). Blanton found that a number of these sites were associated with middens that undoubtedly represent village area occupations.

Leaving the Altamaha River and the Atlantic coast of the Southeast for good, Moore centered his later operations on the Gulf Coast and the streams that drained into it. He was to briefly return to Georgia to carry out the investigations published in his *Mounds of the Lower Chattahoochee and the Lower Flint Rivers* (Moore 1907b) almost a decade after his traversal of the Georgia coast. His later work was to be his most important. The archaeological investigations of the Weeden Island Period mounds, Moundville, and the Mississippi River sites were certainly significant contributions to our understanding of prehistory in the Southeast.

Recent Acquisitions

A COPPER PLATE

Moore was able to obtain a large copper gorget found in a mound near Rockmart in Polk County, Georgia, for his collection at the Academy of Natural Sciences, Philadelphia, as a result of the intercession of the state geologist of Georgia (Moore 1899d). Polk County is in the northwest quadrant of Georgia. Rockmart sits astride the boundary between the Great Valley Section of the Ridge and Valley Physiographic Province and the Piedmont Physiographic Province and commands the access from the Great Valley Section to the upper drainages of the Tallapoosa and Little Tallapoosa rivers. These unite with the Coosa River, which drains the upper portion of the Great Valley and the Piedmont via a series of tributary streams that include the Conasauga, Coosawatee, Oostanaula, and Etowah rivers. The Coosa and Tallapoosa rivers in turn create the Alabama River, which flows into Mobile Bay via the Mobile River. Rockmart also commands access to the middle and lower reaches of the Chattahoochee River flowing out of the Piedmont and thence into Apalachicola Bay and the eastern portion of the upper Gulf of Mexico.

The gorget, made of a heavy sheet of copper, had a maximum thickness of 7 millimeters and weighed approximately 46 grams (17 ounces). In outline, the gorget recalled the expanded center bar gorget type. However, there are several important ways in which it was unlike the expanded center bar gorget. The Rockmart specimen had flaring ends and wide angled points whereas the bar gorget regularly has squared and unflared ends. The typical bar gorget has two holes placed in the midsection, drilled at spots equidistant from the ends. The copper gorget had but a single hole placed in the middle of one of the pointed ends, about 1 centimeter from the edge. The Rockmart gorget was "found with . . . stone implements" (ibid.). Unfortunately Moore did not record what these stone implements were, if indeed he knew.

Copper gorgets are not unknown in the northwest Georgia area. Over fifty years ago Antonio Waring (1945) reported a large copper gorget from an extended burial beneath a stone mound on the Shaw property located on the south slope of Ladd Mountain just south of Cartersville, Bartow County, Georgia. Ladd Mountain is only about fifteen miles northeast of Rockmart on the eastern edge of the Great Valley Section. The Shaw Mound gorget, although damaged by the rock crusher into which it had been thrown during the destruction of the mound, had slightly concave ends. It had a length of 19.5 centimeters (7.5 inches), which compared favorably with the 20.5-centimeter (8-inch) length of the Rockmart gorget. The sides of the Shaw Mound gorget were slightly concave whereas the upper and lower edges were straight. The thickness of the copper sheet from which the gorget was made was within the range of that of the Rockmart specimen.

The Shaw Mound was a rock mound and was apparently associated with a rock wall or "fort" that encircled a portion of Ladd Mountain. The associated artifacts included a copper celt, tapered poll ground stone celts, and simple stamped pottery. Cumulatively the Shaw Mound traits add up to a Woodland Period site.

A third site from which a large copper gorget was recovered is the Tunacunnhee site in Dade County in the extreme northwest corner of Georgia. Tunacunnhee was professionally excavated by the University of Georgia Department of Anthropology in 1973 (Jefferies 1976). The site lies in a narrow valley on the western edge of the Cumberland Plateau Physiographic Province with Sand Mountain to the west and Lookout Mountain to the east. Lookout Creek flows northeast along the floor of the valley into the Tennessee River and hence into the Gulf via the Ohio-Mississippi river system. Because it was properly excavated there is much more information available about the Tunacunnhee site than exists for either the site that produced the Rockmart gorget (we do not even know the exact location of the site) or the Shaw Mound gorget site.

The Tunacunnhee site consisted of four burial mounds with central submound pit burials as well as ancillary burials in various locations in the mounds. The mound fill consisted of quantities of rock as well as soil. The artifact inventory associated with the burials repeats many of the types regularly associated with the Hopewell mortuary complex including platform pipes, bi-cymbal copper earspools, copper panpipes, a copper celt, cut mica, and drilled bear canines, as well as rectangular copper plates. The copper plates were all within the size range of the Rockmart and Shaw Mound gorgets. They were respectively 15.25 x 10 centimeters (6 x 4 inches), 22.75 x 11.5 centimeters (9 x 4.5 inches), and 18.25 x 10.9 centimeters (7.2 x 4.3 inches) (ibid.:24). There can be little doubt but that the Tunacunnhee mounds were constructed during the Woodland Period and are representative of the generalized Woodland Period culture.

It is certainly stretching the data to their limits to attempt to compare the Rockmart gorget with copper gorgets from other sites in the area. The outline of the Rockmart specimen is without comparability to the gorget from the Shaw Mound or to those of Tunacunnhee although all these gorgets are roughly the same size. We know nothing of the context of the Rockmart gorget other than it came from a mound, as did the other gorgets. Because it has no counterpart in either the Archaic or the Mississippi periods, we are probably correct in assigning it to the Woodland Period on the basis of its being a large sheet copper gorget, from a mound in northwest Georgia, and because other Woodland Period mound sites in the area have produced similar large sheet copper gorgets.

Appendix

Moore Site Names, State Site File Numbers, and Findings of the Sites Investigated by Moore

Site Name as Given by Moore[1]	State Site File No.[2]	Burial Types, Selected Diagnostic Artifacts, and Cultural Period[3]
Georgia Coast		
CAMDEN COUNTY, GEORGIA		
Mound at Fairview	9Cm1	Primary burials of adults, children, and infants, burned human bone; copper plate fragment with repoussé decoration; complicated stamped sherds in fill; Mississippi Period.
Mound near Fairview	9Cm2	Bundle burials; sherds with incised cross-hatched decoration in fill; cultural affiliation indeterminate.

[1]The Moore sites are listed here by the state and county in which they occur and in the order in which they are discussed in Moore's text and in the introduction. In several instances the county name has changed since the time of Moore's investigation. In those cases the current county name is given in brackets following the county name used by Moore. In cases in which Moore investigated several mounds at or in the vicinity of a single named location, I have listed each mound separately in parentheses and have identified the mound by a name taken from a descriptive term used by Moore or I have numbered the mounds in the order in which they are discussed by Moore.

[2]In not a few instances no state site number has been assigned to a Moore site because the site has not been relocated or if it has been relocated the site has not been reported to the state site files. I suspect that many of Moore's sites will never be relocated because they have been destroyed.

[3]The cultural periods are given here only in the most general of terms. On the northern half of the Georgia coast, where thanks to Chester DePratter (Thomas and Larsen 1979:table 30) the ceramic sequence is most refined, the Historic Period would embrace the Altamaha Phase; the Mississippi Period would embrace the Savannah and Irene phases; the Woodland Period would embrace the Refuge, Deptford, Wilmington, and St. Catherines phases; and the Archaic Period would embrace the St. Simons phase. The southern half of the Georgia coast lacks the synthesis and detailed ceramic sequencing present for the northern half of the coast. Generally, the same periods are present and they repeat many of the same phases. The Historic Period on the southern coast is represented by what might be termed the Mocama (i.e., Timucua) Phase characterized by the San Pedro ceramic series (Ashley and Rolland 1997), replacing the northern Altamaha (i.e., Guale) Phase with the Altamaha ceramic series. On the southern coast the Irene and probably the Savannah phases of the Mississippi Period disappear. They are apparently replaced by an expansion of the St. Johns IIa ceramics into the Camden County area (Larson 1958b). During the Woodland Period, the area south of the Altamaha River delta experienced a significant intrusion of Swift Creek and probably Weeden Island ceramic types, which suggests that a phase reflecting this fact should be defined.

Site Name	File No.	Burial Types, Artifacts, Period
Mound near Woodbine	9Cm3	Primary burials, burned human bone; complicated stamped sherds in fill; perhaps Mississippi Period.
Mound at Owen's Ferry	9Cm4	Burial type indeterminate; checked stamped sherds in fill; cultural affiliation indeterminate.
GLYNN COUNTY, GEORGIA		
Two Mounds South of Brunswick		
(mound at South Brunswick)	9Gn24	Nothing found.
(mound near Fancy Bluff)		Nothing found.
MCINTOSH COUNTY, GEORGIA		
[Three] Mounds in Lawton's Field		
(Mound A)	9Mc1	Primary burials; checked and complicated stamped sherds in fill; probably Mississippi Period.
(Mound B)	9Mc2	Primary burials, some in log tombs, burned human bone; complicated stamped sherds in fill; Mississippi Period.
(Mound C)	9Mc3	Bark-covered primary burials; cultural affiliation indeterminate.
Townsend Mound	9Mc4	Primary and bundle burials, burned human bone; glass beads with one burial; complicated and checked stamped and incised sherds in fill; Mississippi and Historic periods.
Passbey Mound	9Mc5	Primary burials, burned human bone; checked stamped sherds in fill; Woodland or Mississippi Period.
[Five] Mounds near "The Thicket"		
(Mound No. 1, Mansfield property)	9Mc6	One primary burial, cremated bone; cultural affiliation indeterminate.
(Mound No. 2, Mansfield property)	9Mc6 (?)	Burial type indeterminate; cultural affiliation indeterminate.
(Mound No. 3, Mansfield property)	9Mc8	Primary and bundle burials, burned human bone; copper-covered wooden ear disks; cultural affiliation indeterminate.
(mound on Ravenel property)	9Mc7	Bundle burial, huge central mortuary deposit of bone including 27 crania; cultural affiliation indeterminate.

Site Name	File No.	Burial Types, Artifacts, Period
(mound on King property)	9Mc9	No burials; apparently a shell midden.
Mound at Shell Bluff	9Mc11	Primary and bundle burials, burned human bone, urn burials; probably Mississippi Period.
Creighton Island—North End	9Mc12	Six infant urn burials, 220 primary burials, 3 bundle burials, 10 pockets of burned human bone; Mississippi Period.
Creighton Island—Mound near Landing	9Mc13	Central mortuary deposit of burned and unburned human bone; Mississippi Period.
Hopkins Mound, Belleville	9Mc14	Primary burials, deposits of burned and unburned human bone; cultural affiliation indeterminate.
Mound near Crescent	9Mc15	Primary and bundle burials, burned human bone; cultural affiliation indeterminate.
Walker Mound	9Mc16	Primary, bundle, and urn burials, burned human bone; Mississippi Period.
Mound near Contentment	9Mc17	Primary and bundle burials, burned human bone; probably Mississippi Period.
[Two] Low Mounds near Broro Neck		
(mound on Thomas property)	9Mc18	Probable primary or bundle burials, burned human bone; cultural affiliation indeterminate.
(mound on Paris property)	9Mc19	Burned human bone; cultural affiliation indeterminate.
Sapelo Island		
[Large] Mound at Bourbon	9Mc20	Primary and urn burials, burned human bone; Mississippi Period.
Low Mound at Bourbon	9Mc21	Primary burials; cultural affiliation indeterminate, probably Woodland Period.
Mound in Dumoussay's Field	9Mc22	Primary, urn, and bundle burials, burned human bone; Mississippi Period.
Aboriginal Enclosure at Sapelo High Point [Sapelo Shell Ring]	9Mc24	No burials; Late Archaic Period.

Site Name	File No.	Burial Types, Artifacts, Period
[Two] Mounds at Bahama		
(Mound No. 1)	9Mc25	Central mortuary pit with unburned and burned human bone; cultural affiliation indeterminate, probably Woodland Period.
(Mound No. 2)	9Mc25	Central mortuary pit with unburned and burned human bone; cultural affiliation indeterminate, probably Woodland Period.
LIBERTY COUNTY, GEORGIA		
[Two] Mound[s] at Laurel View		
(large mound on McClosky property)		Pockets of burned human bone, isolated skulls; cultural affiliation indeterminate, probably Woodland Period.
(small mound on McClosky property)		Pockets of burned human bone, isolated skulls; cultural affiliation indeterminate, probably Woodland Period.
St. Catherines Island		
Mound near South-end Settlement	9Li3	Primary, bundle, and urn burials, burned human bone; Mississippi Period.
Mound near Middle Settlement	9Li12	Moore reported no burials, Thomas and Larsen (1979:81) reported one burial; Thomas and Larsen (ibid.) identified the mound as Early Woodland.
Mound in King's New Ground Field	9Li5	Primary and bundle burials, burned human bone; cultural affiliation indeterminate, probably Woodland Period.
Mound in the Greenseed Field	9Li6	Primary burials, burned human bone, central mortuary pit containing unburned human bone; cultural affiliation indeterminate, probably Woodland Period.
Mound near the Light-house	9Li7	Primary burials, pocket of burned human bone from several individuals; cultural affiliation indeterminate.
[Two] Low Mounds at the North-End		
(large mound)		No burials found; cultural affiliation indeterminate.
(small mound)		Fragmentary skull; cultural affiliation indeterminate.

Site Name	File No.	Burial Types, Artifacts, Period
BRYAN COUNTY [I.E., CHATHAM COUNTY], GEORGIA		
Ossabaw Island		
Middle Settlement, Mound A	9Ch24	Primary burials, urn burials with unburned and burned human bone, large deposits of burned human bone, dog burial; Mississippi Period.
Middle Settlement, Mound B	9Ch25	Primary and bundle burials, large deposit of unburned and burned human bone, dog burials; cultural affiliation indeterminate, probably Woodland Period.
Middle Settlement, Mound C	9Ch26	Primary burials, deposits of burned human bone, including one huge mortuary deposit of burned human bone; cultural affiliation indeterminate, probably Early Woodland Period.
Middle Settlement, Mound D	9Ch27	Primary burials, urn burials, burned human bone, dog burials; *Unio* shells; cultural affiliation indeterminate, probably Woodland Period.
Middle Settlement, Mound E	9Ch28	Primary burials; cultural affiliation indeterminate, probably Early Woodland Period.
Middle Settlement, Mound F	9Ch29	Primary burials; *Unio* shells; cultural affiliation indeterminate.
Bluff Field, Mound A	9Ch30	Primary burials, central mortuary pit with burned human bone, dog burial; cultural affiliation indeterminate.
Bluff Field, Mound B	9Ch31	Primary burials, burned human bone, central pit with burned human bone; Mississippi Period.
Bluff Field, Mound C	9Ch32	Burned human bone in a small pit; Mississippi Period.
CHATHAM COUNTY, GEORGIA		
Skiddaway Island		
Third Settlement, Mound A	9Ch21	Primary burials, burned human bone; cultural affiliation indeterminate.
Third Settlement, Mound B	9Ch22	Primary burials; cultural affiliation indeterminate.
North-end Settlement	9Ch23	Primary burials; cultural affiliation indeterminate.

Site Name	File No.	Burial Types, Artifacts, Period

South Carolina Coast

BEAUFORT COUNTY, SOUTH CAROLINA

Site Name	File No.	Burial Types, Artifacts, Period
Mound near Bluffton		Two small deposits of burned human bone; cultural affiliation indeterminate.
Mound on Callawassie Island	38Bu19	Primary burials, dog burials; reexcavation by University of South Carolina assigned mound to St. Catherines Phase of Woodland Period.
[Two] Mounds near Hasell Point		
(large mound)		Mound disturbed; no burials; cultural affiliation indeterminate.
(small mound)		Primary burials, burned human bone; cultural affiliation indeterminate.
Aboriginal Enclosure, Guerard Point		No burials; cultural affiliation indeterminate.
Mound at Indian Hill		Primary burials, central mortuary deposit of burned human bone; cultural affiliation indeterminate.
Larger Mound, Little Island	38Bu23	Primary infant burial under fireplace in buried structure; platform mound; Mississippi Period.
Smaller Mound, Little Island	38Bu23	Four deposits of burned human bone; cultural affiliation indeterminate, probably Mississippi Period.
[Four] Mounds near Button Hill		
(larger mound on Christianson property)		No burials found; cultural affiliation indeterminate.
(smaller mound on Christianson property)		No burials found; cultural affiliation indeterminate.
(mound on Carter/White property)		Four deposits of mixed burned and unburned human bone; cultural affiliation indeterminate.
(mound on Waterhouse/Carter property)		Four deposits of mixed burned and unburned human bone, one in a large central pit; cultural affiliation indeterminate.
Indian Hill, St. Helena Island		No burials; platform mound; Mississippi Period.
Mound on Polleewahnee Island		No burials; cultural affiliation indeterminate.

Site Name	File No.	Burial Types, Artifacts, Period

Savannah River

CHATHAM COUNTY, GEORGIA

[Two] Mounds near Pipemaker's Creek [Irene]	9Ch1	
(large mound)		No burials; platform mound; Mississippi Period.
(small mound, i.e., "burial mound")	9Ch1	Primary burials; Mississippi Period.

SCREVEN COUNTY, GEORGIA

[Two] Mounds near Hudson's Ferry		
(mound on the Prior property)		Primary burials; Mississippi Period.
(small sand mound)		Cremation of one individual; cultural affiliation indeterminate.
[Two] Mounds near Mill's Landing		
(large mound, on Mill's property)		No burials; probably platform mound; cultural affiliation indeterminate, probably Mississippi Period.
(smaller mound)		No burials; probably platform mound; cultural affiliation indeterminate, probably Mississippi Period.

BARNWELL COUNTY [I.E., ALLENDALE COUNTY], SOUTH CAROLINA

[Two] Mounds near Brook's Landing [Lawton mound group]	38Al11	
(northernmost mound)		Small deposit of burned human bone; probably a platform mound; Mississippi Period.
(second, contiguous, mound)		No excavation; Mississippi Period.

BURKE COUNTY, GEORGIA

Stony Bluff	9Bk6	No excavation; quarry site; used from Archaic through Mississippi periods.
[Two] Mounds near Demeries's Ferry		
(larger mound)		Primary or bundle burials; mound badly disturbed; cultural affiliation indeterminate.
(smaller mound)		No burials; cultural affiliation indeterminate.
[Three] Mounds near Shell Bluff		
(two mounds in cultivated field)		No burials; badly disturbed; cultural affiliation indeterminate.
(mound on hill)		Modern burials; probably platform

Site Name	File No.	Burial Types, Artifacts, Period
		mound; cultural affiliation indeterminate.

Altamaha River

WAYNE COUNTY, GEORGIA

Mound Opposite Fort Barrington		Human bone present; mound badly disturbed; cultural affiliation indeterminate.

LIBERTY COUNTY [I.E., LONG COUNTY], GEORGIA

Mound near wood landing		No burials; cultural affiliation indeterminate.
[Two] Mounds on Joiner's Island		
(small mound)	9Lg19	Deposit of burned human bone; mound badly disturbed; cultural affiliation indeterminate.
(large mound)	9Lg20	No burials; cultural affiliation indeterminate.
[Seven] Mounds near Lake Bluff		
(large mound)		Primary burials, burned human bone; probably Mississippi Period.
(six low mounds)		One mound contained an urn burial, another mound had a large central mortuary pit with unburned human bone; cultural affiliation indeterminate.
[Three] Mounds near Old River		
(smaller mound)		Mound disturbed; human bone in vandal's back dirt; cultural affiliation indeterminate.
(larger mound)		Central mortuary pit with unburned and burned human bone; cultural affiliation indeterminate.
(neighboring mound)		No burials; cultural affiliation indeterminate.

WAYNE COUNTY, GEORGIA

Mound near Oglethorpe Bluff		No burials; cultural affiliation indeterminate.
[Five] Mounds near Mitchell's Lake		
(first mound on Madry property)		Bundle burial, cremation, deposit of mixed unburned and burned human bone; cultural affiliation indeterminate.

Site Name	File No.	Burial Types, Artifacts, Period
(second mound)		One bundle burial; cultural affiliation indeterminate.
(third mound)		No burials; cultural affiliation indeterminate.
(fourth mound)		One bundle burial; cultural affiliation indeterminate.
(fifth mound in old field)		Six bundle burials; Mississippi Period.

LIBERTY COUNTY [I.E., LONG COUNTY], GEORGIA

[Two] Mounds near Beard's Bluff

(first mound on Jones property)		No burials; probably platform mound; cultural affiliation indeterminate.
(second mound on Jones property)		One deposit of burned human bone; cultural affiliation indeterminate.

WAYNE COUNTY, GEORGIA

Mound near Fort James		No burials; cultural affiliation indeterminate.
Mound near Reddish's Landing	9Wy2	Large mortuary deposit of mixed unburned and burned human bone; cultural affiliation indeterminate.

TATTNALL COUNTY [I.E., TOOMBS COUNTY], GEORGIA

[Two] Mounds near Matlock Water Road

(larger mound)		Large central mortuary deposit of mixed unburned and burned human bone; cultural affiliation indeterminate.
(small mound)		Unburned human bone disturbed by cultivation; cultural affiliation indeterminate.
[Two] Mounds near the Ohoopee River		No excavation of either mound; cultural affiliation indeterminate.

APPLING COUNTY, GEORGIA

Mound below Tilman's Ferry

Primary burials; probably Mississippi Period.

[Two] Mounds near Iron Mine Landing

(first mound)		Bundle burial of two individuals; cultural affiliation indeterminate.
(second mound)		Bundle burial and pieces of burned human bone; cultural affiliation indeterminate.

Site Name	File No.	Burial Types, Artifacts, Period
Mound near Hell's Shoal		Primary burial, burned human bone in urn; cultural affiliation indeterminate.
Mound near Buckhorn Bluff		Primary burials, deposit of burned human bone; cultural affiliation indeterminate.
TATTNAL COUNTY [I.E., TOOMBS COUNTY], GEORGIA		
Mound at Gray's Landing		No burials; cultural affiliation indeterminate.

References Cited

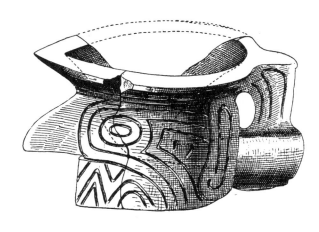 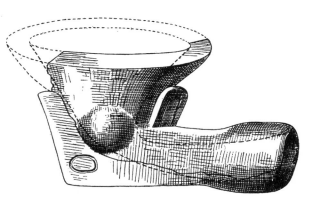

Adams, William H., editor

1985a   *Aboriginal Subsistence and Settlement Archaeology of the Kings Bay Locality: The Kings Bay and Devils Walkingstick Sites.* Department of Anthropology, University of Florida, Reports of Investigations 1. Gainesville.

1985b   *Aboriginal Subsistence and Settlement Archaeology of the Kings Bay Locality: The Kings Bay and Devils Walkingstick Sites.* Department of Anthropology, University of Florida, Reports of Investigations 2. Gainesville.

1986   *Archaeological Testing of Aboriginal and Historical Sites, Kings Bay, Georgia: The 1982–1983 Field Seasons.* Department of Anthropology, University of Florida, Reports of Investigations 4. Gainesville.

1987   *Historical Archaeology of Plantations at Kings Bay, Camden County, Georgia.* Department of Anthropology, University of Florida, Reports of Investigations 5. Gainesville.

Anderson, David G.

1994   *The Savannah River Chiefdoms: Political Change in the Late Prehistoric Southeast.* University of Alabama Press, Tuscaloosa.

Ashley, Keith H., and Vicki L. Rolland

1997   Grog Tempered Pottery in the Mocama Province. *Florida Anthropologist* 50(2):51–65.

Brain, Jeffrey P., and Philip Phillips

1996   *Shell Gorgets: Styles of the Late Prehistoric and Protohistoric Southeast.* Peabody Museum Press, Peabody Museum of Archaeology and Ethnology, Harvard University, Cambridge.

Braley, Chad O., editor

1986   *Archeological Investigations at 9McI41, Harris Neck National Wildlife Refuge, McIntosh County, Georgia.* Report submitted to U.S. Department of the Interior, Fish and Wildlife Service by Southeastern Archeological Services, Athens, Georgia.

Brooks, Mark J., Larry Lepionka, Ted A. Rathbun, and John Goldsborough
1982   *Preliminary Archaeological Investigations at the Callawassie Island Burial Mound (38Bu19), Beaufort County, South Carolina.* Institute of Archaeology and Anthropology, University of South Carolina, Research Manuscript Series 185. Columbia.

Bushnell, Amy T.
1994   *Situado and Sabana: Spain's Support System for the Mission Provinces of Florida.* American Museum of Natural History, Anthropological Papers 74. New York.

Caldwell, Joseph R.
1943   *Cultural Relations of Four Indian Sites of the Georgia Coast.* Unpublished M.A. thesis, Department of Anthropology, University of Chicago, Chicago.

Caldwell, Joseph R., and Catherine McCann
1941   *The Irene Mound Site, Chatham County, Georgia.* University of Georgia Press, Athens.

Caldwell, Joseph R., and Antonio J. Waring, Jr.
1939a   [The initial descriptions of Georgia coastal ceramic types]. *News Letter, Southeastern Archaeological Conference* 1(5):4–7.
1939b   [The initial descriptions of Georgia coastal ceramic types.] *News Letter, Southeastern Archaeological Conference* 1(6):1–12.

Crane, H. R.
1956   University of Michigan Radiocarbon Dates I. *Science* 124:664–72.

Crook, Morgan R., Jr.
1978a   *Mississippian Period Community Organizations on the Georgia Coast.* Ph.D. dissertation, Department of Anthropology, University of Florida, Gainesville. University Microfilms, Ann Arbor, Michigan.
1978b   Spatial Associations and Distribution of Aggregate Village Sites in a Southeastern Atlantic Coastal Area. *Florida Anthropologist* 31(1):21–34.
1980   Archaeological Indications of Community Structures at the Kenan Field Site. In *Sapelo Papers: Researches in the History and Prehistory of Sapelo Island, Georgia,* edited by Daniel P. Juengst, pp. 89–100. West Georgia College Studies in the Social Sciences 19. Carrollton.
1984   Evolving Community Organization on the Georgia Coast. *Journal of Field Archaeology* 11(3):247–63.
1985   Space, Time, and Subsistence at Bourbon Field. *National Geographic Society Research Reports* 21:95–100.
1987   *Lowe Site Report: A Contribution to Archaeology of the Georgia Coastal Plain.* Georgia Department of Transportation, Office of Environmental Analysis, Occasional Papers in Cultural Resource Management 3. Atlanta.

Davis, Mary B.
1987   *Field Notes of Clarence B. Moore's Southeastern Archaeological Expeditions, 1891–1918: A Guide to the Microfilm Edition.* Huntington Free Library, Bronx, New York.

DePratter, Chester B.
1974a   An Archaeological Survey of Ossabaw Island, Chatham County, Georgia: Preliminary Report. Report on file at the Antonio J. Waring, Jr. Archaeological Laboratory, State University of West Georgia, Carrollton.

1974b   Archaeological Survey of University of Georgia Property on Skidaway Island,
        Georgia. Report on file at the Georgia State Archaeological Site Files,
        Riverbend Research Laboratories, University of Georgia, Athens.

1975   *An Archaeological Survey of P. H. Lewis Property, Skidaway Island, Chatham
        County, Georgia.* Laboratory of Archaeology, University of Georgia, Athens.

1979   Ceramics. Chapter 5 in *The Anthropology of St. Catherines Island: 2. The
        Refuge-Deptford Mortuary Complex,* edited by David Hurst Thomas and Clark
        Spencer Larsen, pp. 109–32. American Museum of Natural History, Anthropo-
        logical Papers 56(1). New York.

Drucker, Lesley M.

1982   *Archaeological Testing and Data Recovery for a Proposed Road Realignment at
        9McI41, Harris Neck National Wildlife Refuge, McIntosh County, Georgia.*
        Carolina Archaeological Services, Resource Studies Series 46. Columbia.

Eubanks, Thomas H., and William H. Adams

1986   *Archaeological Resources Management Plan for the Kings Bay Archaeological
        Multiple Resource Area.* Department of Anthropology, University of Florida,
        Reports of Investigations 3. Gainesville.

Ford, James A.

1937   An Archaeological Report on the Elizafield Ruins. In *Georgia's Disputed Ruins,*
        edited by E. Merton Coulter. University of North Carolina Press, Chapel Hill.

Fryman, Mildred L., John Griffin, and James J. Miller

1979   *Archaeology and History of the Harris Neck National Wildlife Refuge, McIntosh
        County, Georgia.* Report prepared for U.S. Fish and Wildlife Services by Cul-
        tural Resource Management, Tallahassee, Florida, under contract with Inter-
        agency Archeological Services, Atlanta.

Goggin, John M.

1952   *Space and Time Perspective in Northern St. Johns Archeology, Florida.* Yale
        University Publications in Anthropology 47, Yale University Press, New
        Haven.

Harper, Francis, editor

1958   *The Travels of William Bartram: Naturalist's Edition.* Yale University Press,
        New Haven.

Holder, Preston

1936   Correspondence and field notes dealing with the St. Simons Island and Sea
        Island WPA archaeological excavations. Photocopies on file at the Antonio J.
        Waring, Jr. Archaeological Laboratory, State University of West Georgia,
        Carrollton.

1938   Excavations on St. Simons Island and Vicinity, Winter of 1936–1937. *Proceed-
        ings of the Society for Georgia Archaeology* 1:8–9.

Holmes, William H.

1903   *Aboriginal Pottery of the Eastern United States.* Twentieth Annual Report,
        Bureau of American Ethnology, 1898–1899, pp. 1–201. Washington.

Jefferies, Richard W.

1976   *The Tunacunnhee Site: Evidence of Hopewell Interaction in Northwest Georgia.*
        University of Georgia, Anthropological Papers 1. Athens.

Jones, Charles C.

1873   *Antiquities of the Southern Indians, Particularly of the Georgia Tribes.* D.
        Appleton, New York.

Juengst, Daniel P., editor
    1980   *Sapelo Papers: Researches in the History and Prehistory of Sapelo Island, Georgia.* West Georgia College Studies in the Social Sciences 19. Carrollton.

Knight, Vernon James, Jr.
    1996   *The Moundville Expeditions of Clarence Bloomfield Moore.* University of Alabama Press, Tuscaloosa.

Larsen, Clark Spencer
    1982   *The Anthropology of St. Catherines Island: 3. Prehistoric Human Biological Adaptation.* American Museum of Natural History, Anthropological Papers 57(3). New York.
    1990   *The Archaeology of Mission Santa Catalina de Guale: 2. Biocultural Interpretations of a Population in Transition.* American Museum of Natural History, Anthropological Papers 68. New York.

Larsen, Clark Spencer, and David Hurst Thomas
    1982   *The Anthropology of St. Catherines Island: 4. The St. Catherines Period Mortuary Complex.* American Museum of Natural History, Anthropological Papers 57(4). New York.
    1986   *The Archaeology of St. Catherines Island: 5. The South End Mound Complex.* American Museum of Natural History, Anthropological Papers 63(1). New York.

Larson, Lewis
n.d. Coastal Mission Survey [1953]. Manuscript on file at the Antonio J. Waring, Jr. Archaeological Laboratory, State University of West Georgia, Carrollton.
    1955   Unusual Figurine from the Georgia Coast. *Florida Anthropologist* 8(3):75–81.
    1957   The Norman Mound, McIntosh County, Georgia. *Florida Anthropologist* 10(1-2):37–52.
    1958a   Southern Cult Manifestations on the Georgia Coast. *American Antiquity* 23(4):426–30.
    1958b   Cultural Relationships between the Northern St. Johns Area and the Georgia Coast. *Florida Anthropologist* 11(1):11–22.
    1980   The Spanish on Sapelo. In *Sapelo Papers: Researches in the History and Prehistory of Sapelo Island, Georgia,* edited by Daniel P. Juengst, pp. 35–45. West Georgia College Studies in the Social Sciences 19. Carrollton.

Lyon, Edwin A.
    1996   *A New Deal for Southeastern Archaeology.* University of Alabama Press, Tuscaloosa.

McKinley, William
    1873   Mounds in Georgia. *Smithsonian Institution, Annual Report, 1872* 27:422–28.

Michie, James L.
    1980   *An Intensive Shoreline Survey of Archeological Sites in Port Royal Sound and the Broad River Estuary, Beaufort County, South Carolina.* Institute of Archaeology and Anthropology, University of South Carolina, Research Manuscript Series 167. Columbia.
    1982   *An Archeological Investigation of the Cultural Resources of Callawassie Island, Beaufort County, South Carolina.* Institute of Archaeology and Anthropology, University of South Carolina, Research Manuscript Series 176. Columbia.

Milanich, Jerald T.
    1977   A Chronology for the Aboriginal Cultures of Northern St. Simon's Island, Georgia. *Florida Anthropologist* 30(3):134–42.

Moore, Clarence B.

1896   Certain River Mounds of Duval County, Florida. *Journal of the Academy of Natural Sciences of Philadelphia, Second Series* 10(4):449–501.

1897   Certain Aboriginal Mounds of the Georgia Coast. *Journal of the Academy of Natural Sciences of Philadelphia, Second Series* 11(1):1–144.

1899a   Certain Aboriginal Mounds of the Coast of South Carolina. *Journal of the Academy of Natural Sciences of Philadelphia, Second Series* 11(2):146–66.

1899b   Certain Aboriginal Mounds of the Savannah River. *Journal of the Academy of Natural Sciences of Philadelphia, Second Series* 11(2):167–72.

1899c   Certain Aboriginal Mounds of the Altamaha River. *Journal of the Academy of Natural Sciences of Philadelphia, Second Series* 11(2):173–84.

1899d   Recent Acquisitions: A Copper Gorget. *Journal of the Academy of Natural Sciences of Philadelphia, Second Series* 11(2):185.

1903   Sheet-Copper from the Mounds Is not Necessarily of European Origin. *American Anthropologist* 5:27–49.

1905   Certain Aboriginal Remains of the Black Warrior River. *Journal of the Academy of Natural Sciences of Philadelphia, Second Series* 13(2):125–244.

1907a   Moundville Revisited. *Journal of the Academy of Natural Sciences of Philadelphia, Second Series,* 13(3):337–405.

1907b   Mounds of the Lower Chattahoochee and Lower Flint Rivers. *Journal of the Academy of Natural Sciences of Philadelphia, Second Series* 13(3):426–56.

1922   Additional Mounds of Duval and of Clay Counties, Florida. In *Indian Notes and Monographs.* Museum of the American Indian, Heye Foundation, New York.

Moorehead, Warren K.

1922   *The Hopewell Mound Group of Ohio.* Field Museum of Natural History Publication 211, Anthropological Series 6(5). Chicago.

Otto, John

1984   *Cannon's Point Plantation, 1794–1880: Living Conditions and Status in the Old South.* Academic Press, New York.

Phillips, Philip, James A. Ford, and James B. Griffin

1951   *Archaeological Survey in the Lower Mississippi Alluvial Valley, 1940–1947.* Papers of the Peabody Museum of Archaeology and Ethnology, Harvard University 25. Cambridge.

Putnam, Frederic Ward

1896   Review of Certain Sand Mounds of Florida: by Clarence B. Moore. *Science,* n.s. 3(58).

Shetrone, H. C.

1926   Exploration of the Hopewell Group. Vol. 4, pt. 4 of *Certain Mounds and Village Sites in Ohio,* edited by William C. Mills. Ohio State Archaeological and Historical Society, Columbus.

Simpkins, Daniel L.

1975   A Preliminary Report on Test Excavations at the Sapelo Island Shell Ring, 1975. *Early Georgia* 3(2):15–37.

1990   *A Phase II Archaeological and Historical Investigation of Springfield Plantation and a Civil War Earthwork at the North End of Skidaway Island State Park.* Report prepared for the Planning Section of the Georgia Department of Natural Resources by Archaeological Research Services of West Georgia College. Carrollton.

Singleton, Theresa Ann
    1980   *The Archaeology of Afro-American Slavery in Coastal Georgia: A Regional Perception of Slave Household and Community Patterns.* Ph.D. dissertation, Department of Anthropology, University of Florida. University Microfilms, Ann Arbor, Michigan.

Smith, Hale G.
    1948   Two Historical Archaeological Periods in Florida. *American Antiquity* 8(4 pt. 1):313–19.

Smith, Robin L.
    1986   *Prehistoric Camps and Villages: Testing at 9Cam171H and 9Cam188, Kings Bay, Georgia.* Jeffrey L. Brown Institute of Archaeology, University of Tennessee at Chattanooga.

Smith, Robin L., Bruce Council, and Rebecca Saunders
    1985   *Three Sites on Sandy Run: Phase II Evaluation of Sites 9Cam183, 184, and 185 at Kings Bay, Georgia.* Jeffrey L. Brown Institute of Archaeology, University of Tennessee at Chattanooga.

Snow, Frankie
    1977   *An Archeological Survey of the Ocmulgee Big Bend Region.* South Georgia College, Occasional Papers from South Georgia 3. Douglas.

Steponaitis, Vincas P.
    1983   *Ceramics, Chronology, and Community Patterns: An Archaeological Study of Moundville.* Academic Press, New York.

Thomas, Cyrus
    1887   *Burial Mounds of the Northern Sections of the United States.* Fifth Annual Report of the Bureau of Ethnology to the Secretary of the Smithsonian Institution, 1883–'84, pp. 3–119. Washington, D.C.
    1894   *Report on the Mound Explorations of the Bureau of Ethnology.* Twelfth Annual Report of the Bureau of Ethnology to the Secretary of the Smithsonian Institution, 1890–1891, pp. 17–742. Washington, D.C.

Thomas, David Hurst
    1987   *The Archaeology of Mission Santa Catalina de Guale: 1. Search and Discovery.* American Museum of Natural History, Anthropological Papers 63(2). New York.

Thomas, David Hurst, and Clark Spencer Larsen
    1979   *The Anthropology of St. Catherines Island: 2. The Refuge-Deptford Mortuary Complex.* American Museum of Natural History, Anthropological Papers 56(1). New York.

Thomas, David Hurst, Grant D. Jones, Roger S. Durham, and Clark Spencer Larsen
    1978   *The Anthropology of St. Catherines Island: 1. Natural and Cultural History.* American Museum of Natural History, Anthropological Papers 55(2). New York.

Thomas, David Hurst, Stanley South, and Clark Spencer Larsen
    1977   *Rich Man, Poor Men: Observations on Three Antebellum Burials from the Georgia Coast.* American Museum of Natural History, Anthropological Papers 54(3). New York.

Thomas, Kenneth H., Jr.
    1989   The Sapelo Company: Five Frenchmen on the Georgia Coast 1789–1794. *Proceedings and Papers of the Georgia Association of Historians* 10:37–64.

Trowell, Chris T.
    1992   Georgia Archaeology at the Turn of the Century: Newspaper Reports. In *The Profile Papers: Technical Papers from the First Seven Issues of the Society for Georgia Archaeology Newsletter: August, 1968–March, 1992.* Society for Georgia Archaeology Special Publication 1.

Waring, Antonio J., Jr.
    1945   "Hopewellian" Elements in Northern Georgia. *American Antiquity* 11(2):119–20.

Waring, Antonio J., Jr., and Lewis Larson
    1968   The Shell Ring on Sapelo Island. In *The Waring Papers: The Collected Works of Antonio J. Waring, Jr.,* edited by Stephen Williams, pp. 263–78. Papers of the Peabody Museum of Archaeology and Ethnology, Harvard University 58. Cambridge.

Webb, William S., and Raymond S. Baby
    1957   *The Adena People No. 2.* The Ohio Historical Society.

Webb, William S., and David L. DeJarnette
    1942   *An Archeological Survey of Pickwick Basin in the Adjacent Portions of the States of Alabama, Mississippi, and Tennessee.* Smithsonian Institution, Bureau of American Ethnology Bulletin 129. Washington, D.C.

Willoughby, Charles C.
    1922   *The Turner Group of Earthworks, Hamilton County, Ohio.* Papers of the Peabody Museum of Archaeology and Ethnology, Harvard University 8(3). Cambridge.

Worth, John E.
    1995   *The Struggle for the Georgia Coast.* American Museum of Natural History, Anthropological Papers 75. New York.

Certain Aboriginal Mounds
of the
Georgia Coast

BY

CLARENCE B. MOORE

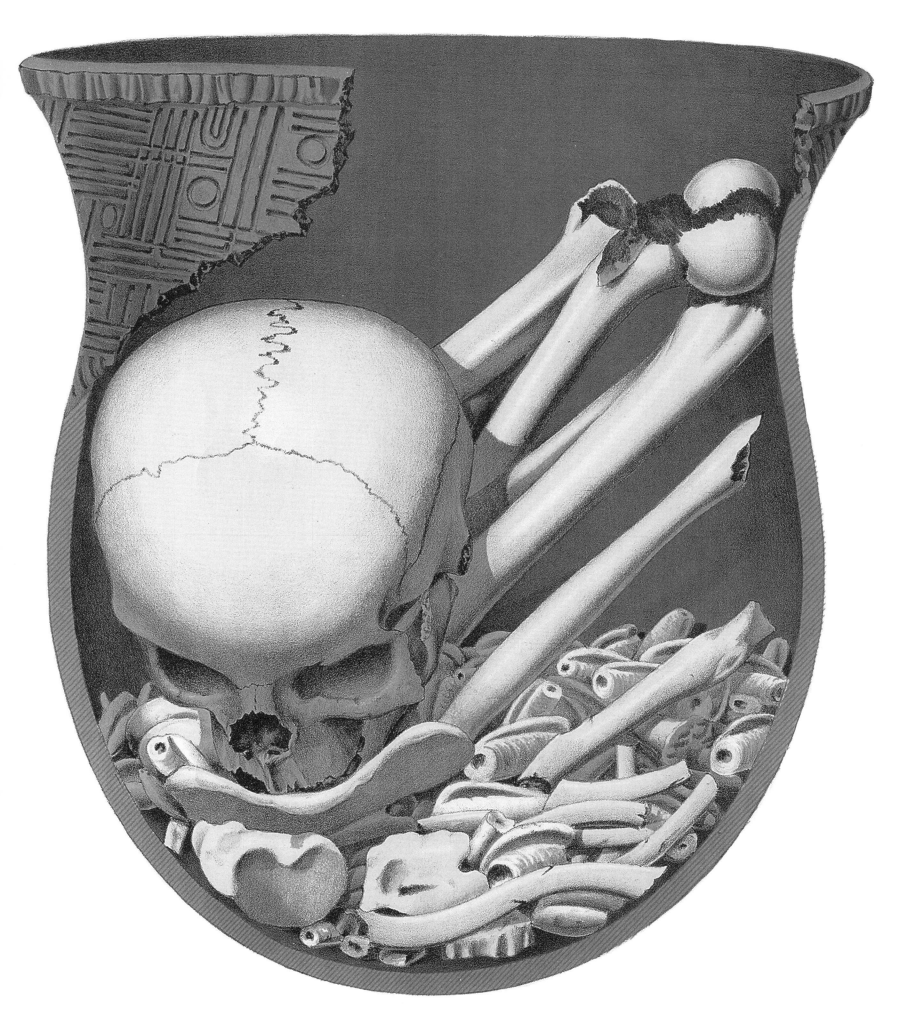

MOORE: GEORGIA COAST MOUNDS.

VESSEL A (BURIAL NO. 3).   MOUND ON ST. CATHERINE'S ISLAND.   (TWO-THIRDS SIZE.)

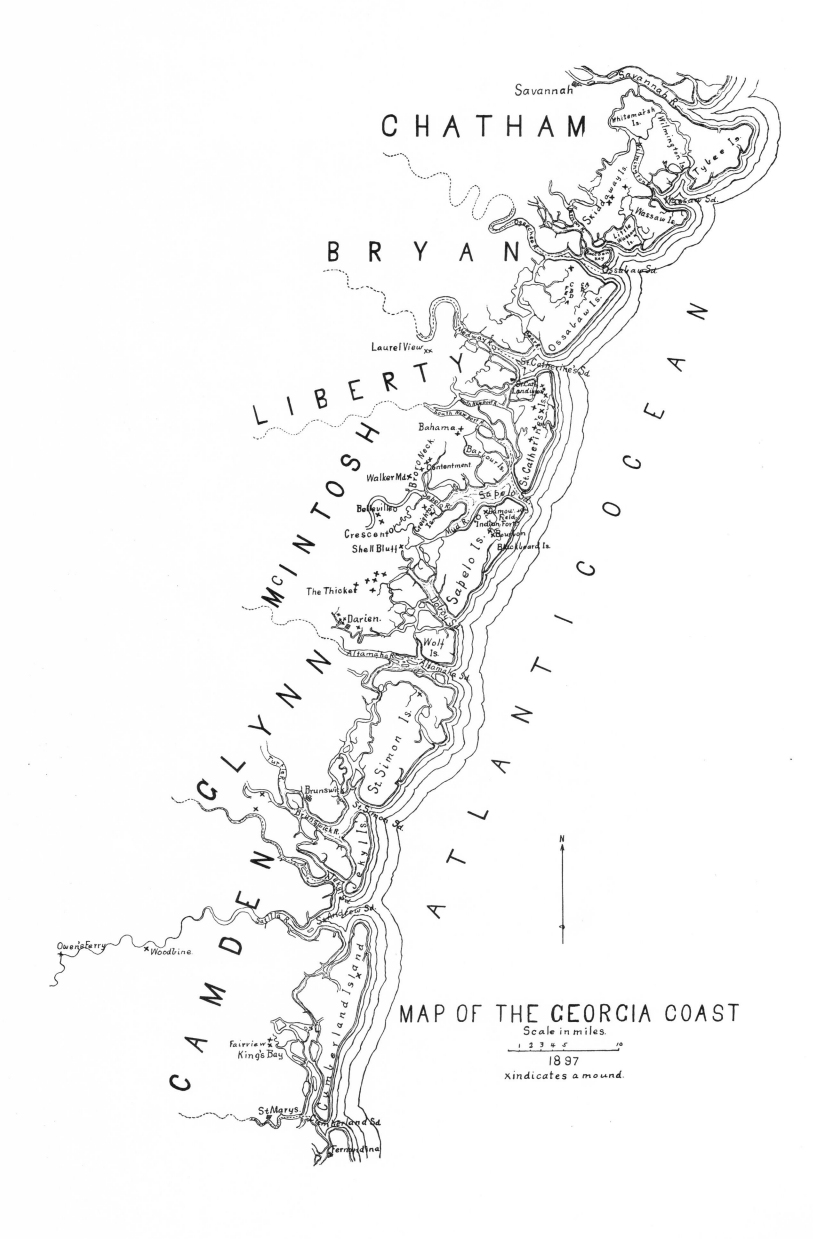

CHATHAM

BRYAN

LIBERTY

McINTOSH

GLYNN

CAMDEN

ATLANTIC OCEAN

Savannah

Savannah R.

Whitemarsh Is.

Wilmington Is.

Tybee Is.

Skidaway Is.

Wassaw Is.

Little Wassaw Is.

Wassaw Sd.

Ogeechee R.

Raccoon Key

Ossabaw Sd.

Ossabaw Is.

Laurel View XX

Medway R.

Bear R.

St. Catherine's Sd.

McCash Landing

St. Catherine's Is.

North Newport R.

Bahama

South Newport R.

Broro Neck

Contentment

Walker Md.

Barbour Is.

Sapelo Sd.

Belleville

Sapelo R.

Sapelo

Crescent

Crooked R.

Mud R.

Barnous' Field

Indian Fort

Bourbon

Shell Bluff

Sapelo Is.

Blackbeard Is.

The Thicket

Doboy

Darien

Wolf Is.

Altamaha R.

Altamaha Sd.

St. Simon Is.

Turtle R.

Brunswick

Brunswick R.

Jekyl Is.

St. Simon Sd.

St. Andrew Sd.

Satilla R.

Owen's Ferry

Woodbine

Cumberland Island

Fairview

King's Bay

St. Marys.

Cumberland Sd.

Fernandina

N

MAP OF THE GEORGIA COAST

Scale in miles.

1 2 3 4 5   10

1897

X indicates a mound.

JOURNAL

OF

THE ACADEMY OF NATURAL SCIENCES

OF PHILADELPHIA.

CERTAIN ABORIGINAL MOUNDS OF THE GEORGIA COAST.

By Clarence B. Moore.

Our thanks are tendered for material assistance in this work to the Marquis de Nadaillac, to Dr. E. Goldsmith, and to Professors Putnam, Holmes and Pilsbry. Our acknowledgments are due also for the aid extended by our lamented friend, the late Professor Cope.

Again we have to thank Dr. M. G. Miller for continuous assistance in the field and in the preparation of this report.

June, 1897.   C. B. M.

As the reader is aware, an inland passage by water, parallel to the ocean, enables vessels of light draft to traverse the entire coast of Georgia without venturing to sea or incurring risk greater than the minimum one of crossing certain sounds at a distance from the open water.

This marine highway, shown on ordinary maps, is connected with a net-work of waterways and tributary streams, many appearing on sectional charts alone,[1] enclosing considerable fertile territory suitable for living sites, and great tracts of low-lying marsh.

Fish and oysters are abundant in this region, and were doubtless still more so in early times, but great deposits[2] of oyster shells are not so numerous as on the

---

[1] U. S. Government Charts, Nos. 156, 157, 158.

[2] The circular enclosure on Sapelo Island and a great causeway on Barbour's Island are the only shell deposits of importance met with by us on the Georgia coast. A considerable shell deposit on St. Simon Island has been reported. We have not seen it.

Florida coast, nor do they compare in size with the great heaps of fresh-water shells so noticeable on the St. Johns River.

Before proceeding to a detailed description of certain coast mounds of Georgia, we wish to point out that it has not been our intention to investigate each mound included within the limits of the entire territory, as we have done on the St. Johns and the Ocklawaha Rivers, Florida, but rather, by demolishing a considerable number, to give a general idea of the aboriginal earth-works of the territory bordering the Georgia coast.

Five months of continual work have been devoted by us to the coast mounds of Georgia, during which time most of the territory has again and again been traversed by steam motive power, so that but little time has been consumed in transit. A few important mounds still remain unexamined, through no fault of ours, however, notably at the north end of Ossabaw Island and on the islands of St. Simon and Sapelo.

But little work has been previously done among the mounds of the Georgia coast. The late Col. C. C. Jones, whose interesting work[1] we have largely consulted, occasionally refers to certain objects as derived from coast mounds, but nowhere makes reference to any systematic explorations.[2] The territory is virtually a new one for the archæologist, though relic hunters have at times left traces of their work in the shape of comparatively small trenches or superficial excavations near the summits of certain mounds.

Before proceeding to a detailed description of our mound work it may be well to make clear to the lay reader certain terms frequently to be used by us.

The " bunched " burial, which we found to predominate in Florida when the condition of the bones made determination possible, is present also in the coast

Fig. 1.—A " bunched " burial. (Not on scale.)

mounds of Georgia, though to a much more limited extent. This method of interment consisted of bunching together a number of bones; sometimes the skull and long bones of one individual with perhaps some of the smaller bones, or in others, taking parts of the skeletons of two or three individuals and burying them in a heap together. The exposure of the dead body until deprived of flesh, prior to inhumation, was a common aboriginal custom. In Fig. 1 we give a representation of a typical bunched burial.

In the Georgia coast mounds the burial in anatomical order exceeded all others, though it is not unlikely that many at least of the skeletons had suffered exposure

[1] " Antiquities of the Southern Indians."
[2] See also " A Primitive Urn Burial," Smithsonian Report, 1890, p. 609 *et seq.*, by Dr. J. F. Snyder, in relation to Southern Georgia.

previous to inhumation but were held together by ligaments when placed in the sand. Occasionally, some bone or bones in a position not to be accounted for under the hypothesis of shifting sand, testifies to this.

Of the burials in anatomical order, the "flexed" burial predominates. This form consists in placing the remains usually on the right or on the left side and

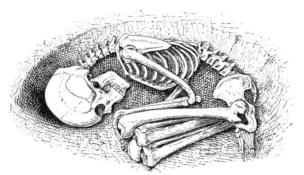

Fig. 2.—A "flexed" burial. (Not on scale.)

drawing the knees and chin well together with the legs drawn up almost parallel to the thighs. The arms occupy almost any position except an extended one. This form of burial doubtless recommended itself through economy of space,—a flexed skeleton calling for a grave not much over three feet in length. Fig. 2 shows a typical "flexed" burial.

In determination of sex there have been consulted the conformation of the forehead, the glabella, the superciliary ridges, the thickness of the outer upper

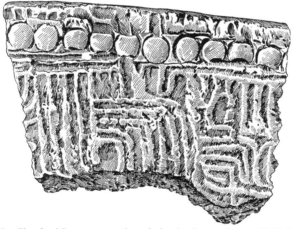

Fig. 3.—Sherd with ornamentation of circular impressions. (Full size.)

margin of the orbit, the character of the facial bones, the muscular marking of the temporal region, size of mastoid process, size of external occipital protuberance and muscular markings in its vicinity, character of lower jaw, size of mental prominences, form of clavicle, size and muscular markings of the bones in general.

Age, when stated, was based upon an examination of the teeth and sometimes of the epiphyses. When not otherwise stated in our descriptions, the skeleton is that of an adult.

All anatomical determinations have been made by Dr. M. G. Miller, who has been present during all our field work in Georgia and in Florida.

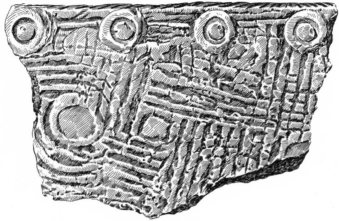

Fig. 4.—Sherd with button-like decoration.   (Full size.)

We shall see that burials of infants in some localities, of adults in others, were in large jars made of clay tempered with gravel,[1] almost invariably of the same type, consisting of a rounded base, an almost cylindrical body, a slightly constricted

Fig. 5.—Sherd showing loss of decoration.   (Full size.)

neck and a flaring rim, whose margin was exteriorly decorated with circular impressions, contiguous or nearly so, doubtless of a section of a reed (Fig. 3), or with button-like ornaments some distance apart, made separately and impressed before baking (Fig. 4), and which sometimes are seen to have fallen from their places, as

[1] Termed gritty ware. This ware forms the majority of that found on the Georgia coast.

shown in Fig. 5 ; or with an encircling band impressed at intervals (Fig. 6).   The decoration of the body and neck of these vessels is usually a complicated stamped pattern so well known in Georgia and in Carolina.

One of these burial jars (various forms were used for cremated remains) is shown in Plate IX.

The late Col. C. C. Jones describes four similar vessels, all containing infant

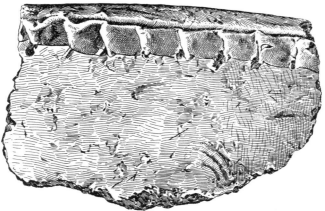

Fig. 6.—Sherd showing band with impressions.   (Full size.)

remains, as coming from mounds of the Georgia coast.[1]   We shall not again go into a detailed description of this form of vessel, but shall refer to it as the common, or ordinary type.

The reader will observe that considerable care has been taken in referring to, or in describing, vessels of shell or of earthenware, to note whether or not they were imperforate as to the base.   This, it may be well to explain to some, has been done in reference to a custom obtaining to a considerable extent in Florida where vessels placed with the dead often had the bottom knocked out, the base perforated, or a hole made in the base at the time of manufacture, presumably " to kill " the vessel to free its soul to accompany that of the dead person.   This curious custom has been regarded as peculiar to Florida, but it is interesting to note a possible observance of it to a limited extent in the mounds of the Georgia coast.   It is well to note, however, that in cinerary urns, perforation of base is never met with.

Mounds Investigated.

Fairview, Camden County (2).	Crescent, McIntosh County.
Woodbine, Camden County.	Walker Mound, McIntosh County.
Owen's Ferry, Camden County.	Contentment, McIntosh County.
Brunswick, Glynn County (2).	Broro Neck, McIntosh County (2).
Lawton's Field, Darien, McIntosh Co. (3).	Sapelo Island, McIntosh County (3).
Townsend Mound, Darien, McIntosh Co.	Bahama, McIntosh County (2).
Cat Head Creek, Darien, McIntosh Co.	Laurel View, McIntosh County (2).
"The Thicket," McIntosh County (6).	St. Catherine's Island, Liberty Co. (7).
Shell Bluff, McIntosh County.	Ossabaw Island, Bryan County (9).
Creighton Island, McIntosh County (2).	Skiddaway Island, Chatham County (3).
Hopkins Mound, Belleville, McIntosh Co.	

[1] " Antiquities of the Southern Indians," p. 456.

LOW MOUND AT FAIRVIEW, CAMDEN COUNTY.

Fairview, the property of Captain W. F. Bailey, to whom we are indebted for courteous permission to investigate, lies on the bank of Marianna Creek which empties into Kings Bay, Cumberland Sound.

The mound, in a cultivated field, had a diameter of base of 38 feet, a height of 2 feet 8 inches, though a large stump remaining on the mound gave evidence of a loss of about 1 foot additional height through the agency of the plow.

The mound was completely demolished.

The closest examination of the structure of this mound seemed to indicate that the usual pit, made previous to the erection of the mound, was wanting, and that the mound, composed of loamy brown sand and unstratified, had been erected upon the undisturbed level ground.

There were no marginal burials. In addition to fragmentary bones, thrown up by the plow, human remains were met with at seven points.

One and one-half feet from the surface and 10 feet from the northwestern margin of the mound was the flexed skeleton of a child, in anatomical order.

An adult skeleton, showing the same form of burial, lay 2 feet from the surface.

One foot down was a deposit of fragments of calcined human bones beneath a local layer of oyster shells. With the remains lay a sheet copper ornament with repoussé decoration.

A burial, well in toward the center, had seemingly its full quota of bones, and the lower portion of the skeleton lay in anatomical order. The cranium, however, was upside down; the mandible lay on its side, embracing one bone of the forearm and two ribs. In all probability ligaments held together a part of this skeleton at the time of its removal to the mound. Reference has already been made to the custom formerly obtaining with many of the southern Indians, namely, the exposure of the body for a certain time previous to interment. Juan Ortiz, a member of a former expedition, rescued by De Soto, had been accorded by his captors the task of keeping carnivorous wild animals from remains thus exposed.

About 2.5 feet down, just above a thin layer of calcined oyster shells extending several feet beyond, were the bones of a young infant. With them were many shell beads of various sizes.

At another point lay a deposit of calcined bits of bone, some certainly human, all probably so.

Almost in the center of the mound were parts of a skeleton, considerably scattered. A small hole apparently had been dug previously at this point, causing a disarrangement of the bones.

Sherds were limited in number, about one dozen being met with, the majority plain though several bore a complicated stamped decoration.

With the exception of two or three bits of chert the mound yielded nothing farther of interest.

Low Mound near Fairview, Camden County.

In pine woods, about one-quarter of a mile in a northerly direction from the preceding mound, on property of Mr. Robert H. Frohock, to whom our acknowledgements for permission to dig, are herewith tendered, was a mound 2 feet 5 inches in height and 34 feet across the base.

The northern half was completely dug through. Considerable charcoal and fireplaces lay seemingly on the base.

Several bunched burials and fragments of human bones were met with at various points. Nothing in the way of art relics was encountered with the exception of about one-half of a small and gracefully-shaped vessel of earthenware and several sherds, most of which bore an incised cross-hatched decoration.

Mound near Woodbine, Camden County.

About three-quarters of a mile in a westerly direction from the town of Woodbine near the Satilla river, is Bedell's Landing. About one-quarter of a mile south of the landing is a very symmetrical mound 4 feet 9 inches in height and 40 feet across the base. A number of large hickories are on the eastern side and these were left standing through a natural desire on the part of the owner of the large plantation on which the mound is situated to preserve the earthwork as a landmark. About two-thirds of the cubic contents of the mound were displaced and subsequently returned, leaving the mound in appearance as we found it.

Our thanks are tendered to Mr. J. K. Bedell, the owner, for full permission to investigate, a courtesy which, considering the proximity of the mound to his homestead, might have reasonably been declined.

The mound was composed of light-brownish sand with a slight admixture of clay. A vertical section of the mound from the summit plateau to where traces of human handiwork came to an end, had a height of 6 feet.

The usual fireplaces and admixture of charcoal with the sand were encountered. The mound had probably at an earlier period lost somewhat in height and had been considerably disturbed within recent years through use as a place for burial. In fact, at the present time, but 35 yards distant, are numerous graves dating from the last half of the present century, and several intrusive burials, doubtless of this period, were discovered in the mound. One skeleton, the bones of which still had a raw appearance, had, near the pelvis, two brass buttons apparently belonging to an old fashioned "dress coat," while another had iron nails, probably belonging to the coffin, in close proximity. The intrusive skeletons were buried at length and considerable care had been bestowed in the arrangement of the bodies, in one instance the hands being folded at the waist.

Original burials numbered about two dozen and were so badly decayed that in the case of some the method of interment was not determinable. When unmistakably identified as to position the bones were found in anatomical order. The bodies had been variously flexed. These interments were found from 1.5 feet from the surface to a depth of 6 feet. In some cases local layers of sand dyed with the red oxide of iron lay immediately above the bones.

At two points in the mound were pockets made up of fragments of calcined human bones. In the mounds of Florida such pockets are sometimes found though cremation was not, so far as our experience extends, largely practised there. We shall see later to how considerable an extent this form of burial was in vogue among the aborigines of the Georgia coast.

EARTHENWARE.

Sherds were very infrequent and probably of accidental introduction, none lying with human remains. They were, as a rule, undecorated, though the complicated form of stamp, so well known in Georgia, was present.

No vessels of earthenware were encountered.

In a central portion of the mound, 5 feet from the surface, near human remains, was an undecorated tobacco pipe of earthenware, of a type common to the mounds of the lower thirty miles of the St. Johns river and other sections, where the aperture for the stem rivals that of the bowl in size. We have figured [1] a pipe of this type in our account of the mound at Point La Vista, Duval County, Florida.

STONE.

A graceful lance-point of chert lay with a skeleton about 4 feet from the surface.

Two polished "celts" lay with burials 1 foot and 2.5 feet from the surface, respectively.

A small hammer-stone and a portion of a pebble were with the pipe to which reference has been made.

Loose in the sand was an arrowhead of chert.

SHELL.

Loose in the sand, throughout the mound, were several conchs (*Fulgur*) and fragments of conchs.

Upon a number of occasions shell beads lay with the burials.

A little over one foot below the surface, over the ribs of the skeleton of a child, was a gorget of shell, irregularly oval in form, 4.5 inches by 5.5 inches. Near the upper margin is a perforation for suspension. A companion to this perforation had apparently been destroyed by a blow from a spade, received at the time of discovery. The concave surface of this gorget shows traces of intricate incised decoration, the exact pattern of which is no longer apparent.

Less than one foot from the surface, with human remains, were two stopper-shaped objects of shell. This form (Fig. 7) so well known in certain sections, is not present in the mounds of the Georgia coast strictly speaking and has not been met with by us in shell in Florida though present in the great deposit of objects

[1] "Additional Mounds of Duval and of Clay Counties, Florida."

of earthenware found by us in the Thursby Mound, Volusia County.[1] These may have served as ear-plugs since we know it to have been an aboriginal custom to wear articles of considerable size thrust through the lobe of the ear.

About 3 feet from the surface, lying near the cranium of a skeleton, were beads of shell, some of considerable size; several stopper-shaped objects of shell;

an imperforate drinking cup wrought from *Fulgur perversum ;* and an undecorated gorget of shell, 3.75 inches by 4.5 inches, with double perforation for suspension. Almost immediately above these remains and relics was an intrusive burial of recent times, having fragments of clothing and buttons.

Other stopper-shaped objects were found associated with a finger-ring of copper, to which reference will be made later.

About 3 feet from the surface was a nest of oyster shells and charcoal.

Fig. 7.—Stopper-shaped object of shell. Mound near Woodbine. (Full size.)

COPPER.

Associated with human remains, 1.5 feet from the surface, was an ornament of sheet copper almost oblong in shape. The margin was beaded,[2] as is so commonly the case with similar ornaments in Florida, and a central concavo-convex boss had its origin in a great number of semi-perforations placed closely together with the aid of some pointed implement. The sheet copper is decidedly thicker than that met with in Florida, more resembling sheet copper we have seen from Ohio. Not far from the center of the margin of the smaller end is a perforation for suspension. Length, 3 inches; maximum breadth, 2.75 inches; minimum breadth, 2.25 inches.

About 1.5 feet from the surface, 2 feet from a skeleton lying at the same level, was a circular ornament of sheet copper, 3 inches in diameter. The usual concavo-convex boss at the center is present, as likewise is the beaded margin. There is one perforation for attachment or suspension.

In the northern slope of the mound, about 2 feet from the surface, with a skeleton, were shell beads, several stopper-shaped objects of shell and, in place on a finger bone, a finger-ring wrought from a band of thin sheet copper (Fig. 8).

Fig. 8.— Finger-ring of sheet copper. Mound near Woodbine. (Full size.)

Prehistoric finger-rings are of extreme rarity in this country. In the cemetery at Madisonville, Ohio, where are the famous ash-pits, Professor Putnam found on the fingers of one skeleton four rings made from bands of sheet copper, and speaks of such rings as " unique in American archæology."[3] Professor Putnam does not recall the discovery of similar rings from the date of publication of his report to the present time.

[1] " Certain Sand Mounds of the St. Johns River, Florida," Part I, Fig. 100.
[2] The same beaded margin, so frequently seen on ornaments of sheet copper in Florida, is represented as present on a sheet silver disc from Peru. " Necropolis of Ancon," Reiss and Stübell, Berlin. Part VIII, Plate LXXXI, Fig. 19.
[3] XVI and XVII Annual Reports, Peabody Museum, p. 166.

2 JOURN. A. N. S. PHILA., VOL. XI.

It is worthy of remark that similarly shaped finger-rings of metal bands have been found on Peruvian mummies, two such rings being figured[1] in Reiss and Stübel's magnificent plates. Unfortunately, the metal from which the rings are made is not specified, but as they are shown of a deep green shade presumably copper is represented. On ornaments of silver containing copper one is not likely to find so marked and so uniform a deposit of carbonate.

MISCELLANEOUS.

The tooth of a fossil shark, about 4 inches in length, apparently unassociated, lay 5 feet from the surface.

Another shark's tooth, 1 inch in length, lay in caved sand. At its base was a perforation possibly for suspension as an ornament, or just as probably for attachment to a wooden handle for use as a cutting tool, such implements having been found by Mr. Cushing in the mud near shell-heaps of the southwestern coast of Florida.

On or just beneath the surface, at a considerable distance from any burial, was a polychrome glass bead which we believe to have been dropped upon the mound subsequent to its completion.

REMARKS.

The interesting mound near Woodbine, which we have included here, has nothing in common with the mounds of the coast, being on fresh water and at a considerable distance from the sea. This fact should be borne in mind when the contents of the mound are taken into consideration.

MOUND AT OWEN'S FERRY, CAMDEN COUNTY.

At Owen's Ferry, on the left hand side of the Satilla river, going down, in full view from the water, on the property of George S. Owen, Esq., of Savannah, is a symmetrical mound apparently uninvestigated previous to our visit. It is picturesquely situated on a bluff sloping to the water's edge and on it grow a number of forest trees. The mound, considered a landmark, is in full view of the Owen house and we deem it an especial courtesy on the part of Mr. Owen to have placed it so readily at our disposition.

In shape the mound resembles an inverted bowl. Its height from the east, which may be considered a fair average, is 6 feet 4 inches; its diameter at base, 52 feet. Over one-half of the mound, the northernmost portion, was dug away and subsequently replaced. The mound was composed of light yellow sand without stratification.

Small fragments of human bone in the last stage of decay, were present at three points.

[1] "The Necropolis of Ancon," Berlin. Part III, Plate XXX, Fig. 14.

A few sherds, some plain and some ornamented with the usual diamond or square stamp, lay loose in the sand, as did three arrow-heads of chert, found separately. Well in toward the center was an irregular mass of oyster shells, about 6 feet from the surface.

The result of our examination of this mound surprised us greatly, since it strongly resembled the rich little mound at Woodbine a few miles below.

Two Mounds South of Brunswick, Glynn County.

At South Brunswick, opposite the town of Brunswick, about 200 yards in a southerly direction from the railroad wharf, was a mound 2 feet high and 26 feet across the base. It bore no marks of previous investigation. A total demolition of the mound was without result.

About 1.5 miles inland from Fancy Bluff, an abandoned plantation on a creek a short distance from South Brunswick, was a mound 2 feet 3 inches in height, and 28 feet across the base. This mound was investigated so far as a large tree upon its northern portion permitted. No discoveries of any sort were made.

Mounds in Lawton's Field, Darien, McIntosh County.

The town of Darien, on a branch of the Altamaha river, is about 10 miles distant from the sea in a straight line.

In the northern outskirt of the town is a large field, the property of Mr. P. C. Lawton, an intelligent colored man, who readily placed at our disposal three mounds included within the limits of his field.

Mound A. This mound, which had been plowed over for years, had, according to report, lost considerably in height which, at the time of its total demolition by us, was 4 feet 6 inches. Its diameter at base was 46 feet.

Previous investigation was limited to a narrow superficial trench through a portion of the mound.

The mound was composed of yellowish sand with local layers of oyster shells, calcined in one instance, and of sand, brownish in color, probably through presence of foreign material. A layer of brownish sand, about 1 foot in thickness, seemed to mark the lower portion of the mound, as immediately below it was bright yellow sand, undisturbed, and containing no object of artificial origin. At the center, from this bright yellow sand to the highest portion of the mound, vertically, was 6 feet.

A number of fragmentary and disconnected human bones were found in the neighborhood of the trench, left by previous investigators. Undisturbed human remains, which were almost entirely confined to the eastern side of the mound, were eleven in number. The form of burial was that in anatomical order. The skeletons were considerably flexed. Nearly, if not, all had been, to all appearance, wrapped in bark much of which, though badly decayed, still remained.

Sherds were comparatively of infrequent occurrence and were apparently of accidental introduction. The plain, the checked stamp, and the intricate stamp were represented.

The mound was unusually devoid of artifacts. Large shell beads were present with several skeletons, and some small ones with the skeleton of an infant.

With human remains, just beneath the present surface, were two stone hatchets, one very rude; one pebble and one bit of earthenware.

Loose in the sand were a bit of fossil wood, and, in another portion of the mound, a small mass of sandstone, pitted on one side. Unassociated, 5.5 feet from the surface was a very rude implement of stone.

Mound B. This mound, about 30 feet south of the preceding one, had a height of 4 feet, a diameter at base of 36 feet. A narrow trench, about 2 feet in depth, had previously been dug through a portion of it.

The mound was completely demolished.

Its composition was almost identical with that of Mound A.

HUMAN REMAINS.

Exclusive of certain loose bones, disturbed by previous investigators, 32 burials were noted in the mound. Of these, 30 were in anatomical order and flexed, while two consisted of deposits of charred and calcined fragments of human bones. Above certain skeletons lay small local layers of oyster shells. With one skeleton was a small amount of sand tinged pink with red oxide of iron—its sole occurrence in the mounds of Lawton's field.

With very few exceptions, skeletons were associated with wood or bark, in some cases included above and below and again apparently heaped over with bark or with slabs of wood, in the last stage of decay. Several skeletons were enclosed in cribs or pens of wood, as for instance, one 8.5 feet from the eastern margin of the mound and 4 feet from the surface. The bones lay in a pen composed of logs from 3 to 5 inches in diameter. The longitudinal logs had an average length of 3 feet, that of the transverse ones at the bottom was about 2 feet, at the top about 20 inches. The top was composed of parallel logs running longitudinally. There was no bottom to this pen or, more properly speaking, coop. Within it lay a skeleton flexed on its right side, heading south. The head and body were in line, the head at one end of the pen, the pelvis at the other. The thighs were flexed sharply on the body and the legs on the thighs. The right leg rested between the logs at the side of the pen, the foot projecting; while the left foot extended beyond the end of the pen. The arms lay along the body with the forearms lying between the thighs. We give a representation of this coop in Fig. 9, reproduced from a sketch made to a scale and on the spot. It has been found impossible to convey the decayed and crushed appearance of the wood, but the number and positions of the various pieces are exactly represented. The bones of the feet, held in place by the sand, fell apart when the sand was removed.

In this pen, with the bones, were four small bits of chert, one showing a certain amount of workmanship; one small cube of quartz and a small mass of clayey material.

With another skeleton in a somewhat similar coop, though less well preserved, was a small polished chisel of stone and a diminutive pebble.

Though, as stated, a great majority of the skeletons were buried with wood or bark, there were certain notable exceptions.   One burial in the eastern margin, 3.5 feet from the surface, showed no trace of woody material.   The cranium of this skeleton was preserved in good condition (A. N. S. Cat. No. 2,159).

Considerably below the level of the surrounding territory, beneath the extreme western margin of the mound, were two graves, distinguished by the dip of the artificially colored brown sand constituting the lowest stratum of the mound, into the undisturbed yellow sand of the field.   Neither grave showed any trace of wood or bark.

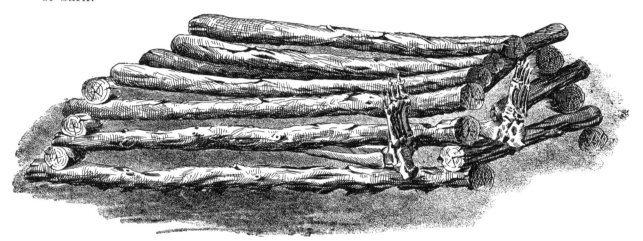

Fig. 9.—Burial pen.   Mounds in Lawton's Field, Mound B.   (About one-eighth size.) [1]

Grave No. 1 contained a skeleton 5 feet 3 inches from the surface of the mound and 2 feet 3 inches below the bottom of the basal layer of brown sand which at this point extended two feet below the level of the surrounding territory.   The mound at this point had a height of 1 foot.   No artifact lay with the skeletal remains though, in close association, was the right humerus of an adult bald-eagle [2] (*Haliæetus leucocephalus*).   The bone was in a subfossilized condition.   The bones of both forearms of this skeleton were anchylosed at the upper extremity in a position of pronation.   They were sent to the Army Medical Museum at Washington. No anchylosis was noted at other points of the skeleton.   The cranium, in fairly good condition, was preserved (A. N. S. Cat. No. 2,160).   In this skeleton the bones of one hand were missing while the axis rested against the sacrum and a first rib and atlas lay above the pelvis.   The lower jaw was back of, and turned from, the

[1] In the cut the feet are incorrectly represented as upright, their true position having been nearly parallel to the logs.
[2] Kindly determined by Dr. R. W. Shufeldt.

cranium and, moreover, gave every evidence of not belonging to the skull. The teeth of the lower jaw showed considerably more wear than those of the upper jaw. In the upper jaw one wisdom tooth showed little sign of wear, while the other had been but recently lost. On the other hand, there had been a loss of both wisdom teeth of the lower jaw with absorption of the alveolar process. Moreover, the teeth of the jaws do not seem to coincide. It is seen that these signs of disturbance can be accounted for only under the hypothesis of exposure of the body previous to interment—a very common practice in some sections—and that the parts not in anatomical order had fallen from the skeleton which otherwise was held together by ligaments. The lower jaw, probably lost or mixed, was intentionally or otherwise, substituted by another.

About 8 feet due south from grave No. 1, 4.25 feet from the surface of the mound, and about 3 feet below the level of the surrounding territory, was grave No. 2, 3.5 feet long, by 33 inches wide, by 1 foot deep. The skull was saved in good condition (A. N. S. Cat. No. 2,155). The tibiæ and fibulæ showed inflammatory swelling. With the cranium were three shell pins of familiar type.

EARTHENWARE.

Sherds were not numerous, a few undecorated or with variously stamped patterns being met with.

Two and one-half feet below the surface of the southern margin, with human

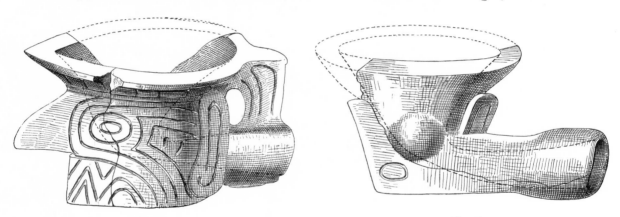

Fig. 10.   Fig. 11.
Tobacco pipes of earthenware. Mounds in Lawton's Field, Mound B. (Full size.)

remains was an inverted imperforate vessel with flaring rim and encircling band of complicated decoration. The ware is of excellent quality. Height, 4.75 inches; diameter of rim, 4.25 inches; of body, 5 inches (Plate I, Fig. 1).

Two undecorated vessels of poor material, of about 3 pints and 1 pint capacity respectively, lay together about 2 feet distant from a skeleton on the same level. The smaller vessel, irregularly oblong, unfortunately received a blow from a spade. The larger, a bowl of ordinary pattern, was broken by pressure of sand. Both have been completely restored.

Scattered fragments belonging to two earthenware tobacco pipes were recovered some little distance apart, and subsequently reunited as shown in Figs. 10 and 11. One is still coated interiorly with carbonized material, probably tobacco. Tobacco pipes of this type are figured by the late C. C. Jones as coming from a mound on Colonel's Island on the Georgia coast.[1]

SHELL.

With various burials were five drinking cups of shell (*Fulgur perversum*), two imperforate, three having round and even perforations in the base. These holes were much more carefully made than those made by roughly knocking out a portion, so frequently found in the Florida mounds. This perforation, the reader will recall was an aboriginal custom obtaining in Florida though not universally practised. It is supposed to have been done to " kill " the vessel, thus freeing its soul to accompany that of the departed into the other world. We have found no perforation of shell drinking cups north of Darien.

Shell beads were not numerous and were present in but two cases.

Near the margin, together, were seven fresh-water mussel shells (*Unio Cuvierianus*, Lea[2]) and nearby, a number of marine shells (*Littorina irrorata*[2]). These apparently, were not in the neighborhood of human remains.

STONE.

Ten inches below the present surface of the mound was a beautifully polished little hatchet of plutonic rock,[3] apparently unassociated. Another larger hatchet was found superficially. Several pebbles lay with burials or loose in the sand.

MISCELLANEOUS.

Beneath the base of the mound, with human remains, was the lower portion of the femur of a bear, evidently separated by a cutting tool.

In a portion of the trench made previous to our investigation, which had been partially filled, were various objects of recent manufacture : a rusty pocket knife ; a fragment of glass ; the head of an iron hammer ; an iron ring, etc. A hasty or unscrupulous investigator could easily refer these objects to the period of construction of the mound.

Mound C. In the same field, about 300 feet east of Mound A, was a mound 2 feet 9 inches in height. Its diameter of base was 34 feet.

A small and superficial trench had previously been made through a portion of it.

The mound was completely dug through.

Seven entire skeletons were met with in addition to a few loose bones disturbed by the makers of the previously mentioned trench. All skeletons were apparently lying flexed on the side, and all but one were buried with coverings of bark or wood

[1] C. C. Jones, " Antiquities of the Southern Indians."
[2] Identified by Prof. H. A. Pilsbry.
[3] We are indebted to Dr. E. Goldsmith for determinations of rock, included in this report.

which dropped into small pieces upon removal. In some cases the covering of wood was simply thrown over. In one instance, however, in the case of a child buried 2 feet deep beneath the extreme southern margin of the mound which at that point was about on a level with the surrounding territory, the skeleton was covered by a coop 26 inches in length, 14 to 16 inches in breadth, lying northeast and southwest. In this case the top consisted of flat pieces placed transversly and not of logs laid longitudinally as in the case of the coop in Mound B.

Beneath one burial was a thin layer of ashes, while another was surmounted by a layer of oyster shells, 6 to 8 inches in thickness.

No artifacts were present with the burials. A few sherds lay loose in the sand. Superficially and near no human remains was a copper bead apparently of European manufacture.

The curious burials present in Mounds B. and C. in Lawton's field, where skeletons were enclosed in pens, must not be considered as representative of the coast since nowhere else have they been met with by us. We have it on excellent authority that in mounds farther up the Altamaha this form of burial was in vogue.

TOWNSEND MOUND, McINTOSH COUNTY.

This mound, about one mile east of Darien, was placed at our disposal by Mr. J. S. Townsend, of Darien, the owner, to whom our cordial thanks are tendered.

The mound, which, it is believed, had sustained no previous investigation, is reported to have been under cultivation in ante-bellum days, and at that time, to have been ploughed over for considerable periods.

Its present height is 3 feet 8 inches; the diameter of its circular base, 42 feet.

With the exception of a few square feet surrounding two live oaks on extreme marginal portions, the mound was completely dug through.

The mound was composed of yellowish-brown sand, without stratification. In various parts were layers of oyster shells. In the central portion was an irregular layer of these shells, 3 feet in thickness at places. Occasionally, near human remains, were pockets of sand dyed pink or red, with hematite.

HUMAN REMAINS.

This mound, a perfect charnel house, teemed with skeletal remains from margin to center, human bones being met with at fifty-nine points, and it probable that these interments represented the remains of fully seventy-five individuals.

Interments varied as to depth from .5 of a foot to 4.5 feet from the surface.

Three forms of burial prevailed: cremation, the bunched burial and the burial in anatomical order. Deposits of portions of human bones, charred and calcined by fire, were noted at five points in the mound. Once charred remains lay associated with many bones unaffected by fire. We shall refer to this farther on.

In all, 18 bunched burials were present, some representing parts of but one individual, others being layers of bones in absolute confusion, one such having a length of 3.5 feet, a breadth of 22 inches, a thickness of 8 inches. In several of these layers five or six crania were present. With one layer was a mass of calcined human remains to which reference has been made.

In each case burials in anatomical order showed flexion to a certain extent—in certain cases to a much greater extent than in others. No uniformity of direction had been observed as to the positions of the skeletons—crania pointing to every point of the compass. Twenty-six skeletons lay upon the right side, eight upon the left. One lay upon the back with legs flexed to the left; another upon the back, had the face turned to the left. The position of one skeleton in caved sand was undetermined.

The bones in this mound, perhaps owing to the presence of shell, were unusually well preserved, offering a marked contrast to skeletal remains in many Florida mounds from which frequently all intermixture of shell is absent.

In no instance did the remains indicate individuals of unusual size. The linea aspera was not especially defined. One platycnemic tibia had an index of 54, which, as the reader will recall, means that the transverse diameter is .54 of that taken antero-posteriorly. No signs of injury or disease were present with the exception of alveolar abscesses. Three crania were preserved in fairly good condition. Two of these (Cat. Nos. 2,156 and 2,157) are in the collection of the Academy of Natural Sciences of Philadelphia. The remaining one was sent to the Army Medical Museum, Washington.

HUMERI.

	Male.		Female.		Uncertain.	
	Perforated.	Not Perforated.	Perforated.	Not Perforated.	Perforated.	Not Perforated.
Right	4	15	3	2	3	11
Left	6	11	3	1	5	8

Of the 10 male skeletons in which both humeri were recovered in a condition for determination, 7 showed no perforation in either humerus; two skeletons showed the right humerus perforated, the left imperforate; in one skeleton the condition was reversed.

Of the 2 female skeletons recovered, one had the right humerus perforated, the left imperforate; the other, perforation of both humeri.

Of the uncertain humeri but one pair, the left perforated, the right imperforate, belonged to the same skeleton.

ARTIFACTS.

Earthenware.—No earthenware vessels were present in the mound nor were sherds associated with human remains. A small number of sherds, probably

3 JOURN. A. N. S. PHILA., VOL. XI.

accidentally introduced, plain, with the ordinary square stamp, with intricate stamped decoration and in one case, incised, were present.

Eight tobacco pipes, whole or but slightly broken, of the same type as those from the mound at Darien, came from different points in the mound. They lay in immediate association with human remains, as in fact, did all artifacts discovered, save only the sherds. Of these tobacco pipes, two of which we show in Figs. 12 and 13, one had incised decoration while several had encircling bands upon the

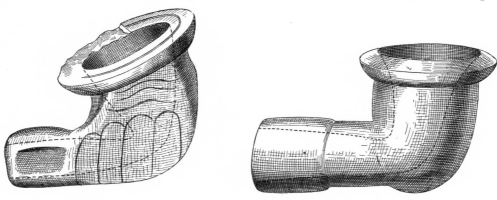

Fig. 12.   Fig. 13.
Tobacco pipes of earthenware. Townsend Mound. (Full size.)

bowl. All were moderate in size, differing markedly from the great tobacco pipes from the mounds of Duval Co., Florida. In the bowls of some remained carbonized material—doubtless tobacco.

Shell.—With numerous burials were shell beads, at times a few only and again in considerable numbers; some minute in size, others—sections of columellæ—over 1 inch in length. Nineteen of these longitudinally perforated sections were found with one burial.

Eleven pins of shell of the familiar type, none over 2.5 inches in length, were with various crania, often with shell drinking cups. These drinking cups were imperforate. One, with the skeleton of a child, was but four inches in length. We have not met with so diminutive a shell drinking cup before.

A number of fresh-water mussel shells (*Unio Shepardianus*),[1] perforated for suspension, lay with other objects near a skeleton.

With a bunched burial 2 feet from the surface, were five implements wrought from columellæ of *Fulgur carica*, ground at the beak doubtless to serve as chisels. In four the spire remained, from the fifth this portion had been removed.

Stone.—Three small polished "celts," each about 2 inches in length, two about double that size and a fine chisel 10 inches in length, with a maximum breadth of 3 inches, a maximum thickness of .9 of one inch, lay with human remains.

Two discoidal stones, each about 1.75 inches in diameter, one .75 of an inch in thickness, the other a little over 1 inch, were found separately with human remains. This is the southernmost occurrence of the discoidal stone in our investigations.

[1] Identified by Prof. H. A. Pilsbry.

But one arrowhead came from the mound.

Two bits of soapstone lay separately with burials.

A number of pebbles, each about 1 inch in diameter, were with several skeletons, and a considerable number, each about the size of a pea, doubtless formerly enclosed in a turtle shell to form a rattle, were met with together near a burial.

Several bits of chert, fragments of hatchets and one-half of a good-sized pebble of quartz were variously associated.

Glass.—A considerable number of glass beads lay with a burial two feet from the surface.

Miscellaneous.—A bit of plumbago, also a mass of bitumen, came from the mound, and ordinary piercing implements of bone were with two interments.

ASSOCIATION.

To give an idea of the association of various objects present in the mound we shall describe certain burials and the objects found with them.

One foot from the surface, with a skeleton, were the nineteen large shell beads already referred to; a saw apparently of a diminutive saw-fish and a bit of chert.

Another skeleton, with sand tinged red near the cranium, had five shell pins almost in contact with the skull, and eighteen large beads of shell.

A skeleton having a thin layer of oyster shells immediately above it, had associated several piercing implements of bone and one arrowhead of chert.

With a bunched burial, contiguous to a confused mass of human bones, around the skull, were a few shell beads, many beads of glass, and one minute piece of copper or of brass, of about the area of twice that of the head of a pin. It was carbonated through and through.

With a bunched burial, 2 feet from the surface, were three tobacco pipes, two slightly broken; four pebbles; three piercing implements of bone, and five cutting implements of shell.

The reader will bear in mind that these objects described as associated are not additional artifacts but have previously been referred to separately.

REMARKS.

We have noted the presence of glass beads at one point in the mound. The burial with which they lay had no appearance of being intrusive. Unfortunately, the height of the mound was such that one can draw no conclusion as to the period of the burial on account of its comparatively superficial character.

PASSBEY MOUND, McINTOSH COUNTY.

This mound, in the yard of Mr. Frank Passbey (colored) is in the suburbs of Darien, about 1 mile northwest of the town proper. It had been under cultivation but no previous investigation was apparent.

Its present height is 5.5 feet; the diameter of its base, 48 feet. The mound was about one-half dug through. It was composed of yellowish-brown sand with a band of sand about 3 inches thick running about 1 foot below the level of the surrounding territory.

Human remains were encountered at eleven points. In each case but one, where incineration had been practised, burials were in anatomical order, flexed and lying on the right side or on the left side with no uniformity of direction. Several marginal burials were considerably below the blackened stratum, to which reference has been made, and in each case the stratum was disturbed, showing the burials to have been made subsequent to the extinction of the fires.

Several burials in the mound showed partial disturbance, and at these points the sand was less solid than elsewhere, probably through removal of trees when the mound was cleared for cultivation.

With the interments were no artifacts whatever. Loose in the sand were four or five sherds, undecorated or with the usual square or diamond-shaped stamp. The only other object of human origin, present in that portion of the mound excavated by us, was an arrowhead of quartz. This, so far as our experience extends, is the southernmost occurrence of this material in use for a lance-head or for a projectile point.

MOUNDS NEAR "THE THICKET," McINTOSH COUNTY.

About 5 miles by land, or about 12 by water, in a northeasterly direction from the town of Darien, is a settlement on Peace Creek, having no general name, either locally or on the chart, but, with the exception of certain homes of colored people, it is composed of various estates, each having a name of its own, such as "The Forest," "The Thicket," etc. As the boat landing is situated on the estate known as "The Thicket," we shall, for convenience, give that name to the entire settlement.

About three-quarters of a mile in a westerly direction from the landing at "The Thicket," on the property of Mr. Mansfield, of Darien, are three mounds about one-quarter of a mile apart. All are symmetrical and vary in height from 5 to 7 feet. Two of these mounds were investigated, though not demolished. Their diameters of base are about 40 and 50 feet respectively. They are composed of yellow sand unstratified, and having that raw look indicative of absence of organic matter. The smaller mound yielded absolutely nothing, with the exception of a flexed skeleton near the surface at the margin, which we took to be intrusive, and some charred bones with several small shell beads, two or three inches below the surface.

The larger mound was not excavated in our presence though experienced persons were in charge. Fragmentary human remains were reported as present at two points and these also we take to have been intrusive. With the exception of a few small bits of earthenware and one arrowhead loose in the sand in the larger mound, no artifacts were met with.

Within sight of a road at " The Thicket," on the property of Mr. H. S. Ravenel, of Darien, was a symmetrical little mound of brownish sand, 3 feet 5 inches in height and 30 feet across the base.

It was totally demolished.

In the northwestern margin, 33 inches below the surface which was there just above the surrounding level, was a layer 4 feet by 3 feet by 10 inches thick, of oyster shells and sand completely blackened by an admixture of charcoal. With this blackened sand was considerable other sand dyed red with hematite. This curious layer formed the bottom of a pit as was clearly shown by undisturbed sand of a different color on either side. Closest scrutiny failed to reveal human remains or artifacts in this peculiar pit.

About the center of the mound, 2 feet from the surface, was a bunched burial with two crania and a variety of other bones. In association was a great quantity of powdered hematite scattered among many oyster shells.

Four feet down beneath the central plateau, directly beneath the burial already referred to, was a confused mass of human bones including 27 crania, about 5 feet by 6 feet by 10 inches thick. The oyster shells and hematite lying beneath the bunched burial formed a covering for this mass of bones. With the bones was a small discoidal shell bead and a tubular bead of shell about .75 of an inch in length.

A few sherds lay loose in the sand throughout the mound.

On Mr. Mansfield's property at " The Thicket," about one-half mile in a westerly direction from the landing, on the edge of the road and opposite the church, was a symmetrical mound 2 feet 9 inches in height and 30 feet across the base. No previous investigation was apparent.

It was totally demolished.

The mound, which was composed of yellowish-brown sand, contained no oyster shells. Scattered bits of charcoal and one local layer of charcoal were present.

Human remains were in the last stage of decay. Apparently in all but three cases the bunched burial was represented. One skeleton lay in anatomical order and two pockets of calcined human bones were centrally situated 4 feet from the surface, immediately on a layer of sand blackened by fire and by intermixture with charcoal. In all, fragments of 13 crania were noted in the mound.

Nine inches down apparently near no human remains, were, the shaft of a bone of a lower animal, longitudinally grooved; a number of fragments of columellæ of marine univalves, and a mass of stone of volcanic origin about 2 inches by 1.5 inches by .5 of an inch, deeply grooved on one side and grooved to a certain extent on the other. This stone had, in addition, been used as a hammer as a portion involving the groove, had been split off.

With a skeleton at length, to which reference has been made, near the cranium, was a portion of a disc of copper carbonated through and through. Immediately beneath the cranium were 246 small chips of chert. This skeleton lay 3 feet from the surface.

About nine inches down, with sand colored with hematite, which was presen. with certain other burials in the mound, were a few small bits of chert; several small shell beads and parts of two copper discs each about 2.3 inches in diameter and having three concavo-convex concentric circles by way of ornamentation. On one side of each was the usual wood or bark.

Reference has been made to a black band of sand running through the mound. This layer .75 of one foot in thickness, was, at the center of the mound, 4 feet from the summit, or 1 foot 3 inches beneath the surrounding level. In close proximity to one of the pockets of human bones which we have noted as lying in this blackened sand, was an imperforate vessel of very thick and heavy ware; length, 8 inches, maximum width, 3.1 inches, height, 1.8 inches, consisting of three compartments joined longitudinally very much in the same style as the vessel figured by us as coming from the Monroe Mound[1] in Florida. Vessels of this character are supposed by some to have been used for paint, the separate compartments holding different colors.

A sheet of mica about 3 by 2 inches was found in caved sand.

A few sherds, possibly half a dozen, were scattered throughout the mound.

An irregularly shaped mound about 5 feet in height, mainly composed of shells, on the property of a colored man named King, was dug into without result.

MOUND AT SHELL BLUFF, McINTOSH COUNTY.

Shell Bluff on Shell Bluff creek, approximately three miles by land and six miles by water, from Crescent, is the property of George E. Attwood, Esq., who kindly placed at our disposition a mound in a cultivated field near his residence.

This mound, reduced by years of ploughing, scarcely rose above the general level. It was distinguished by the paucity of oyster shells upon its surface, which lay more thickly on certain other portions of the field. It being impossible to arrive at any conclusion as to the exact area containing burials, a semicircle was taken with radii of 46 feet converging at a point seemingly the most prominent of the slight elevation. This semi-circle, including what we took to be the eastern half of the mound, was carefully dug through. The remaining portion of the mound apparently had not been used for interments beyond a few feet from the cross-section and after 26 feet of it had been dug through, without material result, the work was abandoned.

The mound was composed of yellowish-brown sand with the usual layer of surface loam above. There was no marked base line nor any stratum of oyster shells in the mound, though several pits containing burials, extending into undisturbed sand, were filled with them.

This mound, Mr. Attwood informed us, had been dug into by him at one spot, the result being a discovery of three vessels of earthenware filled with charred and

[1] Certain Sand Mounds of Duval County, Florida, Plate LXXIII, Fig. 2, Journ. Acad. Nat. Sci., Vol. X.

calcined fragments of human bones and covered with other vessels inverted. Owing to this previous investigation and the obvious reduction in height of the mound, a detailed description of the contents will not be given.

Sherds were not numerous and none with the complicated stamp was met with. Loose in the sand was a large pebble-hammer of circular outline.

The mound, not greatly above the water level, was unusually moist; and human remains, which were encountered 31 times, were, as a rule, when not calcined, in very poor condition. The usual diversity of form of burial was present, including that in anatomical order, the bunched burial, inhumation of parts of skeletons, pockets of calcined remains and cremated fragments in cinerary urns. We append certain burials seemingly worthy of record, including all associated with any artifacts.

Burial No. 8. Nineteen feet east of the point taken as the center, and about 1 foot 9 inches below the surface, was a layer of charcoal and charred wood about 3 inches thick. It was 4.5 feet across and extended in 28 inches. Above a portion of it was a thin layer of oyster shells. Beneath the center of the layer of charcoal, which was entirely unbroken, were the two bones of a forearm of a child, showing no signs of fire. With them was an imporforate drinking cup of shell, so carefully ground exteriorly that all prominent parts had been removed.

Burial No. 12 A. A comparatively small vessel of about two gallons capacity with a checked stamp decoration, crushed into small fragments. It had contained many pieces of calcined human bones. The record of its exact position was overlooked.

Burial No. 14. Sixteen feet E. by N., on the base of a pit containing numerous oyster shells, 16 inches from the surface, was the skeleton of a male flexed on the right side, heading S. by W. The cranium, an exception to the almost universal rule in this mound, was well preserved and showed a marked artificial flattening of the frontal bone. It was sent to the Army Medical Museum, Washington, D. C.

Burial No. 16. Twenty-one feet N. E. by N., 2 feet down, was a partially flexed skeleton of a male on the right side, heading N. W. by W. With it were two pebble-hammers, one, of quartz, about 3.5 inches in length, shows considerable use on one end as a hammer, while the other had been roughly chipped to a cutting edge, a feature new in our mound investigation.

Burial No. 20, B. C. D. E. Fourteen feet E. by N., on the same level, their bases 2 feet 9 inches from the surface, in line, were three vessels. The one to the left (C), imperforate, undecorated, somewhat resembling a bell-jar in shape, was almost intact, and contained to within 6 inches from the surface, a mass of fragments of calcined human bones (Plate II). This vessel, which had a diameter at mouth of about 8 inches, a maximum diameter of 10.5 inches and a height of 10.5 inches approximately, was completely covered by an undecorated jar (B), which fell into small fragments upon removal. In contact with C was a gracefully shaped vessel (D), imperforate, undecorated and entirely intact (Plate III). Approximately, it measured 7.5 inches in height, 7.5 inches across the mouth, and 9.5 inches maximum diameter. Within it were a certain number of calcined fragments of human bones. In contact with D was a bowl (E) in fragments. It bore the checked stamp decoration, and apparently contained no human remains, though immediately behind it was a small pocket of calcined fragments.

Burial No. 21. Ten feet S. E., skeletal remains disturbed by the plough. Below the chin were several large shell beads in line and a number of small ones.

CREIGHTON ISLAND, MCINTOSH COUNTY.—NORTH END.

Creighton Island, bounded on the north by the Sapelo river, a branch of Sapelo Sound, has on the northern portion, on such parts as were examined by us, great fields long under cultivation. Scattered through these fields are numerous shell-

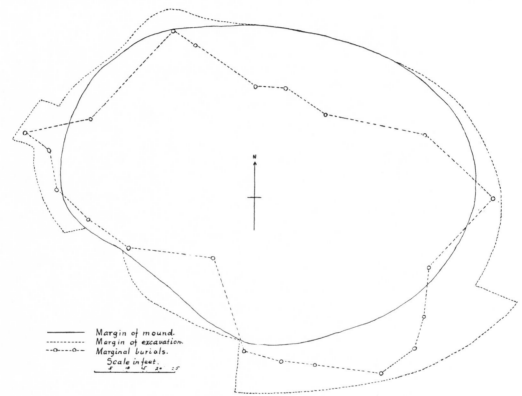

Fig. 14.—Diagram of mound at north end of Creighton Island.

heaps not greatly above the general level. Abundant sherds with incised decoration and with complicated stamp are scattered over the surface in every direction. All this interesting territory was cordially placed at our disposition by George E. Attwood, Esq., of Shell Bluff, near Crescent, Georgia, the owner, whose mound at Shell Bluff has already been described by us.

About one mile S. E. by E. from the landing was a mound, or rather an irregular ridge, extending about N. W. and S. E. a distance of 116 feet. Its maximum width at base was 100 feet approximately. Scattered oyster shells lay over the surface. Its height,[1] which attained its maximum at the central part, was 34 inches. Disturbed sand at this point extended 38 inches beneath the general level, as we afterwards learned on the total demolition of the mound, which was carefully sliced down and much adjacent level territory dug through. The diagram (Fig. 14) shows the outline of the mound, the outlying territory dug through and the area in which burials were met with, which included, we believe, all having any connection with the mound.

There had been no previous investigation, the nature of the mound being unknown even to the owner.

COMPOSITION OF MOUND.

The mound was composed of yellowish-brown sand lying upon undisturbed sand of a bright yellow color. The usual fire places and fragments of charcoal were present at various points. A dark band ran, off and on, through the mound at about the level of the surrounding territory. It presumably marked the base, but was so broken and so irregular that but little could be determined from it.

Oyster shells in layers and in pockets were locally present but so irregular were the deposits that none but a general description of them can be given. The southern half of the mound proper showed no shell save in small local pockets until at a distance of 23 feet from the center in a southerly direction, where a deposit of considerable extent began, continuing about to the center. This deposit was somewhat undulating in shape, at times almost reaching the surface, and again dipping one or two feet below it. Sixteen feet from the center the deposit divided abruptly leaving a space 8 feet broad filled with sand. Shell continued 18 feet to the west and 7 feet to the east of this interruption. The western deposit, reaching to just beneath the surface loam, was 3 feet thick. Its side adjoining the sand was perpendicular. The eastern deposit had an average thickness of 1.5 feet, its western margin, however, contained a considerable pocket of sand extending down from the surface. This division of the shell layer was doubtless caused by a pit dug through it, as several burials were present in the sand. A few feet farther in, the layer reunited, having then a total length of 34 feet. This layer, disappearing toward the center of the mound, gave place to two others in the eastern and western portion of the mound, each of considerable length, which ran out after continuing a few feet toward the north. Other layers of shell in the northern portion of the mound were local and restricted as to size.

About the center of the mound was a pit (see section, Fig. 15), about 5 feet 8 inches in diameter, of the type prevalent among the sea-islands and upon the neighboring mainland. Upon its base, 6 feet 10 inches from the surface (it may be as well to describe the burial in connection with the pit), was a layer of fragments of calcined human bones, 6 inches in thickness, with many large shell beads. Upon this layer were about 2 feet 8 inches of dark yellow sand surmounted by about 3 feet 8 inches of oyster shells. At the western upper extremity of the pit

---

[1] Long continued cultivation must have considerably impaired the original height.

4 JOURN. A. N. S. PHILA., VOL. XI.

was a layer of oyster shells, almost superficial, 2 feet in thickness. The eastern upper margin would have contained a similar deposit had it not been that a pit of sand, 2 feet 4 inches across had been let into the shell at that point.

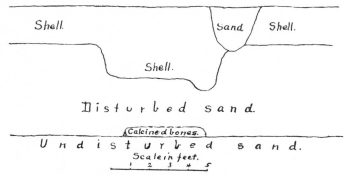

Fig. 15.—Diagram of central pit. Mound at north end of Creighton Island.

While various pits were present in this mound, in no mound investigated by us have they been so difficult to distinguish exactly. This arose partially from the considerable size of some, but mainly from the fact that but few extended into the bright yellow undisturbed sand beneath the base, and that the others in the disturbed sand, having been filled with homogeneous material, offered no distinct line of demarcation.

Beginning in the level ground and extending a considerable distance along the western marginal portion of the mound, was one of those great excavations filled with dark loam and refuse, and containing no burials, so often found in mounds of this type and for whose existence we have no explanation to offer save that possibly great pits made to furnish material for the mound were allowed slowly to fill during the occupation of the territory. The sand and loam filling pits of this class are always far darker than the sand of the mound which they adjoin.

HUMAN REMAINS.

In seven cases layers of decayed wood or bark, occasionally showing marks of fire, lay above human remains, and in two cases, above and below. Doubtless similar deposits in many other cases had disappeared through decay. It is interesting to note in this connection that a Yamacraw Indian (the Yamacraws lived near Savannah) dying in London during a visit in 1734, was interred by his companions, strapped between two boards [1]—a survival of an ancient custom.

Human remains were present at every depth in the mound proper, and in certain outlying territory, at 262 points as follows :

220 skeletons.

10 pockets of calcined fragments of human bones.

6 urn-burials of uncremated remains of infants.

3 bunched burials.

[1] " Antiquities of the Southern Indians," p. 185.

13 parts of skeletons disturbed by aboriginal pits.

7 fragmentary skeletons, in caved sand, disturbed by the plow, etc.

3 skeletons in the last stage of decay.

Skeletons.—Of the 220 skeletons the following subdivision as to sex may be made, prefacing it with the explanation that, under the head of uncertain sex are included such skeletons whose characteristics were not sufficiently marked for determination; and such others, mainly from pits in the damp sand, whose advanced state of decay made a definite conclusion impossible:

78 males.

64 females.

47 uncertain.

16 adolescents.

12 children.

3 infants.

These skeletons lay in the following positions:

166 flexed on the right side.

32 flexed on the left side.

7 partially flexed on the right side.

6 partially flexed on the left side.

2 with extremities flexed and trunk on back.

2 extended at full length.

1 semi-reclining.

1 body on back, thighs flexed to either side.

3 infants disturbed by our men in digging.

The two skeletons buried at full length on their backs were 2 feet and 2.5 feet from the surface, respectively. The condition of the bones of both was exceptionally good but one cannot base final conclusions upon the state of preservation of bones. The arms of one lay along the trunk, while those of the other were flexed to the pelvis. No aboriginal artifacts were present with either, nor, on the other hand, were buttons, coffin-nails, or any like object, discovered though specially careful search was made.

The direction in which the skeletons headed was as follows: 185 were included between the compass points S. E. and S. W., many being due S. Of the remaining 35—21 headed south of the E. and W. points; 4 headed due E.; 1, E. by N.; 1, E. N. E.; 1, N. E. by E.; 1, N. E. by N.; 2, W. N. W.; 1, W. by N.; while the positions of the 3 infant skeletons inadvertently scattered by our diggers, were not determined.

The bones were in fairly good condition though in nearly every case the crania were badly crushed. No fractures were present, a considerable number of diseased bones were met with. Caries of the teeth, practically absent in Florida from other than superficial skeletons, was met with upon a number of occasions. Muscular attachments indicated less powerful individuals than many interred in Florida mounds. No marked platycnemia or pilastered femurs were present with one marked exception. A pair of femurs from an undoubtedly original burial have indices of about 159, which is greater, we believe, than any ever before recorded.[1] This index is

[1] Dr. Topinard has contributed an interesting note on a femur found by us in the mound at Tick Island, Florida. "Certain Sand Mounds of the St. Johns River, Florida," Part I.

arrived at by dividing the lateral into the fore and aft diameter. A tibia of the same skeleton has an index of 51; that is, its lateral diameter is about half of its fore and aft diameter. One of these femurs and the tibia were sent to the Army Medical Museum, Washington. It may interest the lay reader to know that the lateral flattening of the tibia and marked development of the linea aspera of the femur are now known to be the result of muscular action as in walking, running, ascending slopes and the like and not racial characteristics.

Calcined Remains.—The majority of the 10 pockets of calcined human bones were of moderate size, representing in each instance the remains of one individual. Several, however, were considerable layers and contained in addition numbers of loose bones unaffected by fire.

Urn-burials.—Under perfectly level ground, a considerable distance from the slope of the mound, was a vessel of the ordinary type with base perforation (A), upright and capped by an imperforate vessel of the same type, inverted and without a rim (B). Within the upright vessel were the remains of the skeleton of an infant of about 2 years of age. These vessels, both badly crushed, were sent to the Peabody Museum, Cambridge, Mass., where they have been carefully pieced together.

Near the others was a vessel of the same type, a portion of whose bottom was broken, but held in place by sand. It was otherwise intact. In the sand, within the vessel, were particles of bone resembling sawdust, and a portion of the tooth of an infant. This vessel (C) was sent to the Field Columbian Museum, Chicago.

Forty-eight feet E. by S. from the point taken as the center of the mound, was a vessel (D) of the ordinary type, imperforate as to the base, 21.5 inches in height, the maximum ever reported for this type, and having a diameter of mouth of 18.5 inches and a maximum diameter of body of 15 inches. A portion of the rim had been ploughed away and lost. Near the base were certain bones of an infant, judging from the femur. No teeth were present.

Vessel E, of the ordinary type, badly broken by the plow, had a circular piece crushed in, but not removed from the base. It was capped by a decorated bowl (F) crushed to fragments, some of which were held in place by the sand. This vessel has not been included in our list of urn-burials, as the most careful search failed to reveal the slightest trace of skeletal remains; but beyond question, such remains had occupied the urn at an earlier period.

Vessel G had been a bowl of about 4 gallons capacity, with marginal incised decoration surmounting the complicated stamp. Parts had been crushed and carried away by the plow. Beneath it was charcoal. Within it were fragmentary bones of an infant.

Vessel H, imperforate, of the ordinary type, rested upon decayed wood. It contained fragments of bones of a very young infant. Above the body of the vessel, whose rim had been carried away by the plow, were large fragments of earthenware, perhaps the remainder of a surmounting vessel.

Vessel I was represented by the lower portion of the body of a vessel of the ordinary type with base perforation. It contained fragments of diminutive human bones.

Vessel J, of the ordinary type, also had suffered through the agency of the plow. No human remains were discovered though their former presence can hardly be questioned.

The method of urn-burial in this mound presented certain points of similarity to, and of divergence from, that of certain other coast mounds, as the reader later on may remark. All these burial urns lay in the southern and eastern parts of the mound, in which they followed the general custom. They contained the uncremated bones of infants in common with the urn-burials of Ossabaw Island (cremation apart), but differed from the mounds of Sapelo Island where skeletal remains of adults exclusively were in the urns and of St. Catherine's Island where, with but one exception, adult remains were present in the urns.

Aboriginal disturbances.—When parts of a skeleton or skeletons were discovered disarranged adjoining a grave it was inferred that the construction of the grave was the cause of the disarrangement. Great care was taken to distinguish these disturbances from bunched burials.

Canine remains.—The skeleton of a dog, in the last stage of decay, was found unassociated with any human remains. The interment of dogs in mounds of the sea-islands will receive special reference in our account of Mound D, Ossabaw Island.

STONE.

In the mounds of the Georgia coast stone is not abundant. The mound on Creighton Island proved somewhat of an exception to this rule.

Hatchets.—Nine hatchets, or "celts," always with skeletons, were present in the mound, the longest somewhat exceeding 7 inches. All were gracefully shaped and tapered into blunt points opposite the cutting edge, a feature characteristic of southern hatchets and still more pronounced in the "celts" of St. Domingo and neighboring islands. The material was mostly volcanic rock, but as mutilation of the specimen is necessary for exact determination, we have not thought it necessary to specify in each case.

Chisels.—Eighteen chisels from 1.75 to 5.3 inches in length, having a thin longitudinal section, somewhat convex on one side and usually flat on the other, lay at different points with burials. In addition, were five large chisels of graceful design, one a beautiful specimen, of slate, having a length of 12.6 inches, a breadth at the cutting edge of 2 inches, tapering to 1.1 inches at the opposite end. Its maximum thickness is .7 of one inch (Fig. 16). Another chisel, of banded slate, is 8.75 inches long; another, 9.8 inches; and two somewhat smaller.

Discoidal stones.[1]—Twelve discoidal stones, as a rule with burials, the largest 2.5 inches in diameter, came from the mound. Two were of quartz, ten of volcanic or of sedimentary rocks. One of these, unlike the rest, was a pebble, a portion of whose periphery had been pecked away to confer the circular outline. Certain discoidal stones, some of which are considerably larger than any found by us, are

---

[1] Discoidal stones are treated at length by the late Col. C. C. Jones.
The latest literature on the subject is to be found in Mr. Gerard Fowke's "Stone Art," Thirteenth Annual Report, Bureau of Ethnology.

34

supposed to have been used in the Indian game of *chungke* and to have been rolled down a level court. Discoidal stones of lava are used in the Hawaiian Islands in the game of *maika*. It is admitted that many discoidal stones, both on account of their size, which is too diminutive, and because their border slopes so as to interfere with rolling, must have served another purpose, probably in a different game. Those found by us show no wear and cannot have been used as smoothing stones or polishers. Discoidal stones have never been met with by us in Florida.

It is a curious fact that discs, roughly shaped from fragments of earthenware vessels, are frequently found in mounds of the Georgia coast [1] and these doubtless saw service in place of their prototypes in stone. It is interesting to note an aboriginal tendency to lighten labor or to supplement a deficient supply by the use of imitations. In neolithic Europe pendants made from canine teeth of large carnivores and pierced for suspension were imitated in horn and in bone,[2] while in

the great Shields Mound,[3] near the mouth of the St. Johns River, we found many canine teeth used as pendants and imitations of them made of shell. At the present time, the natives of Kings Island, Alaska, sew upon ceremonial gloves used in dancing, beaks of a bird, the puffin (*F. arctica*) and with them, reproductions in wood.[4]

[1] Their presence had been noted in other localities. "Stone Art," Thirteenth Annual Report, Bureau of Ethnology, p. 109.
[2] *L'Anthropologie*, July–August, 1896, p. 460.
[3] "Certain River Mounds of Duval County, Florida." Jour. Acad. Nat. Sci., Vol. X.
[4] Collection, Acad. Nat. Sci.

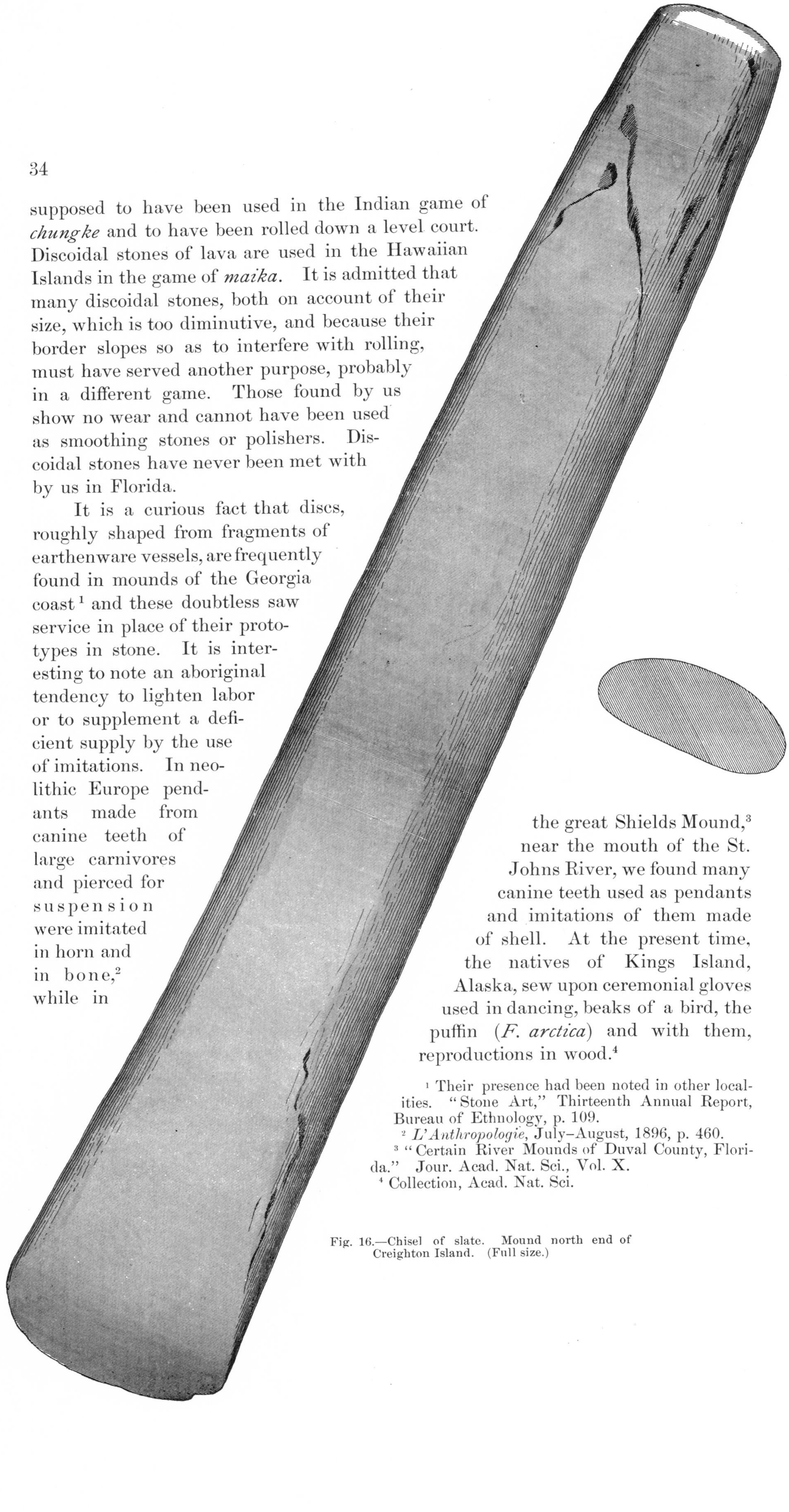

Fig. 16.—Chisel of slate. Mound north end of Creighton Island. (Full size.)

Arrow and lance points.—Fourteen lance heads and arrow points were found, of quartz, of chert, and of chalcedony. No lance head exceeded 4.5 inches in length. One had a breadth across the base of 2.7 inches. An interesting deposit of six spike-shaped arrowheads, ranging in length between 1.6 inches and 3.1 inches, were together with a burial.

Miscellaneous.—Throughout the mound were numerous pebble-hammers, 4 lying with one burial.

One pebble, about 3 inches in length, showed a considerable percentage of loss through use as a smoother or polisher. Several other smoothing stones were variously associated.

Several small fragments of soapstone vessels, without any particular shape, had been deposited with the dead. One had a cross hatch decoration.

Two nests of quartz pebbles each about the size of a pea, lay with human remains. These doubtless formed parts of rattles, the covering having disappeared through decay.

SHELL.

In no mound in Georgia or in Florida, investigated by us, have shell beads in any way approached in number those present in the Creighton Island mound, nor have we elsewhere found so large a percentage of burials associated with beads.

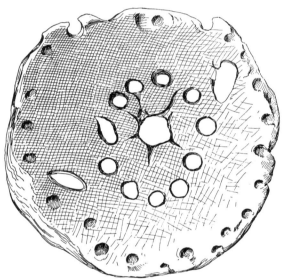

Fig. 17.—Gorget of shell. Mound north end of Creighton Island. (Full size.)

With thirty interments were large beads of shell, while small ones were present with twenty-eight. Certain burials, however, having large and small beads are included in both enumerations. Exclusive of great quantities of small beads of shell of the ordinary pattern, there were present in the mound many hundreds of massive beads having a length of nearly two inches or less. With one skeleton were 63 massive beads, while in a layer of calcined remains, in addition to almost innumerable small beads, were 267 having a diameter of half an inch and upwards.

None of these beads shows trace of fire. Many were large sections of columellæ probably belonging to *Fulgur*. Others were flat, circular or oval and pierced through their greatest diameter, sometimes a perforation 1.3 inches in length. Beads of this character were known as *runtees* and were highly esteemed by the aborigines.

Many skeletons in the mound had twenty or thirty massive beads each, often on the wrists and ankles, and some were so loaded that the mere weight must have been an inconvenience if thus worn in life.

Drinking cups.—Twenty-two shell drinking cups were present in the mound, some inverted, upon crania. All were imperforate. (The northernmost occurrence of base-perforation in the case of drinking cups, in our experience, was at Darien.) The largest cup had a length of 12.5 inches and bore an incised decora-

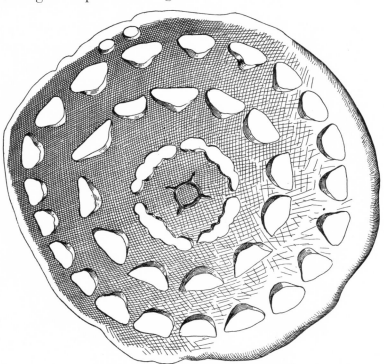

Fig. 18.—Gorget of shell. Mound north end of Creighton Island. (Full size.)

tion, unfortunately almost imperceptible, on a portion of the back. One cup, by the removal of the beak and by external grinding, greatly resembled Tennessee and Missouri vessels of earthenware having the conventional shell form.

Gorgets.—With the skeleton of an adolescent was a roughly made gorget of shell, irregularly circular, having a maximum diameter of 3 inches. It is decorated with perforations and semi-perforations as shown in Fig. 17.

With the skeleton of a male, having many objects in association, was a circular gorget, concavo-convex, a shape conferred by the form of the body whorl of the shell used in its manufacture, with a diameter of about 3.8 inches. Its decoration consists of three concentric circles of somewhat irregular incisions around a central four-pointed star. It has a double perforation for suspension (Fig. 18).

Another gorget, found with an infant and shown in Fig. 19, has a diameter of about 2.4 inches. Its decoration, carved and incised, is the rattlesnake. A part of the margin was broken by a blow from a spade.

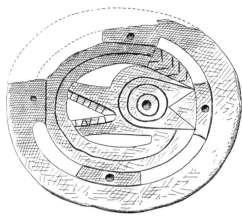

Fig. 19.—Gorget of shell. Mound north end of Creighton Island. (Full size.)

Chisels.—Two chisels, made by grinding beaks of *Fulgur* and removing the body whorl, were present in the mound.

Pins.—Shell pins, probably used in the hair, as they are invariably found near the skull, were met with to the number of sixteen. In length they ranged from 1 to 3.5 inches.

Mussel-shells.—Shells of various species of fresh water mussels were found with a number of interments. In some cases no perforation was present, in others the condition of the shell did not allow determination. In no instance was a perforation found.

Coral.—With the cranium of a skeleton was a mass of coral, 14 inches long, smoothed to the form of a " celt," the cutting edge being rudely formed, as also the blunt point of the opposite end.

PEARLS.

Nine pearls, some larger than a good sized buckshot, perforated for use as beads, were found with a burial, associated with beads of shell. Col. C. C. Jones[1] has written at length on pearls from southern mounds.

BONE.

Several small piercing implements of bone were met with.

With a skeleton was an implement 7.5 inches in length with a flat point, made from a longitudinal section of a long bone of a lower animal with the articular portion removed.

Together, also with a skeleton, were : an implement wrought from the ulna of a lower animal, 6.7 inches long, the articular portion remaining, and having its minor extremity ground to an oblique section, probably for use as a gouge; part of a wing bone of a large bird, with a length of 9.8 inches, the articular portions

[1] *Op. cit.*

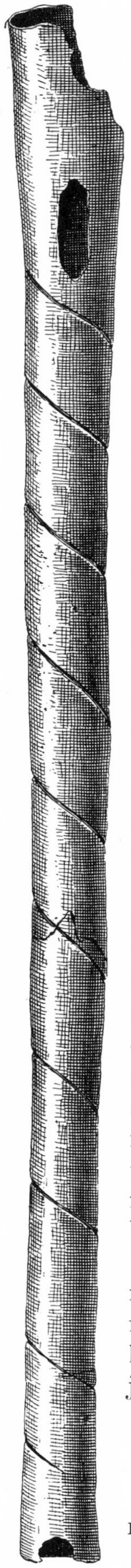

removed, having a perforation, through one-half its proximal extremity and around the bone an incised spiral line (Fig. 20); also the upper half of a similar object without decoration.

EARTHENWARE.

Sherds.—Sherds were not abundant in the mound. The complicated stamp and various patterns of incised decoration were represented. About 1 foot from a skeleton were numerous earthenware fragments representing parts of three vessels. One large fragment was decorated exteriorly with large squares, enclosing good-sized circular spots, in red pigment.

Smoothers.—A number of masses of roughly baked clay, one-half the area rounded, in size resembling a goose egg, were present in the mound. They had possibly been used to smooth clay in the manufacture of earthenware.

Hones.—A curious custom markedly prevalent along the Georgia coast, namely, the use of earthenware to sharpen pointed tools, was fairly represented in this mound. This custom, perhaps induced by a short supply of stone, was carried to such an extent that not sherds alone but certain entire vessels were secondarily used as hones.

Earthenware discs.—Certain discs made from fragments of earthenware vessels were found. We have spoken of these curious objects in treating of discoidal stones. They are referred to by the late Col. C. C. Jones.[1]

Tobacco pipes.—Nine tobacco pipes, with one exception undecorated, in shape of the type common to the coast were found, usually with burials, but upon several occasions apparently unassociated. Several are fragmentary to a certain extent and a number bear upon the stem or upon the bowl, and sometimes upon both, curious depressions caused by chipping, and equalling in size about one-half the area of one surface of the first joint of a finger. These chippings on pipes, found all along the coast, have, perhaps, some ceremonial significance, or were made to allow a firmer grasp with the fingers. In a number of bowls was a carbonized coating—doubtless tobacco. At first thought one might consider this a proof of recent inhumation, but the indestructibility of carbon is well known.

Near the surface, and unassociated, was a pipe having approximately a height of bowl of 2 inches and a diameter of bowl at the mouth of 2.2 to 2.4 inches. The bowl is strikingly ornamented with knobs, while from the proximal upper margin is a perforated projection. On the opposite side are traces of a similar one (Fig. 21).

[1] *Op. cit.* p. 348.

Fig. 20.—Object of bone. Mound north end of Creighton Island. (Full size.)

Colonel Jones figures [1] a somewhat similar pipe and describes it as coming from a mound near Macon, Ga.

We show (Fig. 22) another neat little tobacco pipe from this mound.

Vessels.—A detailed description of vessels used, or probably used, for interments has been given. Excluding these, there were present in the mound seven vessels of earthenware. With two exceptions, all these, and all the burial jars, were found in the southernmost half of the mound.

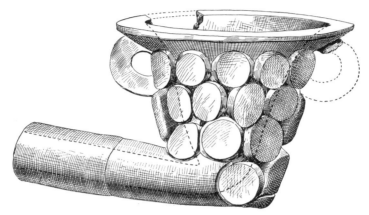

Fig. 21.—Tobacco pipe of earthenware. Mound north end of Creighton Island. (Full size.)

An undecorated bowl, of about one quart capacity with a kidney-shaped section, lay with the body of an infant. It was imperforate as to the base, as were all the seven under description.

With human remains, on the bottom of a grave-pit extending below the base of the mound, were two vessels. The larger, of black ware, had an ovoid body

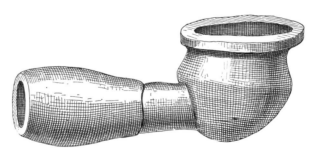

Fig. 22.—Tobacco pipe of earthenware. Mound north end of Creighton Island. (Full size.)

flattened at the base, with an upright neck rising from a slight depression in the body and flaring somewhat toward the margin. This vessel, which fell into many fragments upon removal, was successfully pieced together. Approximate measurements: maximum diameter of body, 5.6 inches; maximum diameter of mouth, 4 inches; height, 6.4 inches; height of neck, 2 inches. A cinerary urn of this type, though much larger, is figured in this Report as from the Walker mound.

[1] *Op. Cit.*

The second vessel, somewhat smaller, of yellow ware, was of the same type, but hopelessly disintegrated.

With human remains was an urn having a globular body, a constricted neck and flaring rim. It was decorated with two encircling rows of button-like prominences. Height, 5 inches; diameter of body, 5.3 inches; diameter of mouth, 5.6

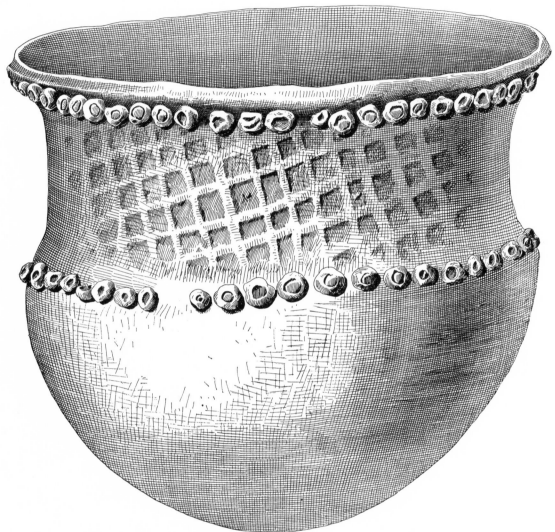

Fig. 23.—Vessel of earthenware. Mound north end of Creighton Island. (Full size.)

inches (Fig. 23). An almost similar vessel, in fragments, came from another portion of the mound.

With human remains was a vessel of black ware, undecorated, having a bowl-shaped body flattened at the base, a wide cylindrical neck with a slight flare at the margin, rising perpendicularly. Diameter of body, 6.1 inches; diameter of mouth, 5.2 inches; height of neck, 3.7 inches (Plate IV).

A very rude bowl, faintly decorated with a complicated stamp, lay inverted with the skeleton of a child. Diameter of mouth, 8 inches; height, 3.8 inches.

Several considerable fragments of medium sized, undecorated bowls were met with. It is possible that these, interred whole, were subsequently crushed and portions lost.

Miscellaneous.—An earthenware sphere, about .5 of one inch in diameter, lay loose in the sand.

COPPER.

In the eastern slope of the mound, 35 feet N. E. by E. from the center, on the base of a pit, 5 feet 8 inches from the surface, on which was an unbroken layer of oyster shells 2 feet in thickness, lay a skeleton in the last stage of decay. With it were various objects, including a chisel of copper (Fig. 24), 7.9 inches in length, with a breadth across the shank of 1.2 inches and 2 inches across the flaring cutting edge. Its thickness is .27 of an inch. It lay between wood or bark thoroughly decayed. Toward the end opposite the cutting edge on either side was a black band about 1 inch in breadth, where, apparently, it had been attached to a handle. A longer chisel of the same type, though much thinner, is figured [1] by the late Colonel Jones as coming from a mound of the Nacoochee Valley, Georgia. This chisel is the only copper found by us among the sea-islands of Georgia. The reader interested in aboriginal copper is referred to our memoir in Part II of "Certain Sand Mounds of the St. Johns River, Florida,"[2] where it is shown that the copper of the mounds is native copper, and far purer than the article produced in Europe during the mound building period.

MISCELLANEOUS.

With four skeletons were masses of plumbago, perhaps used as a black pigment.

[1] *Op. Cit.* Plate VI, fig. 2.
[2] Jour. Acad. Nat. Sci., Vol. X.

Fig. 24.—Chisel of copper. Mound north end of Creighton Island. (Full size.)

Small sheets of mica were met with seven times. They bore no particular shape when found, and the chipped and broken edges left any determination doubtful. Certain of these sheets were peculiarly flexible, resembling tin foil, a characteristic, we are informed, conferred by fire.

With numerous burials were masses of red hematite in powder.

ASSOCIATION OF ARTIFACTS.

We now proceed to give several typical associations of artifacts, the objects composing which have mostly been individually described.

With a bunched mass of bones were: a large shell drinking cup; small shell beads; sixty-three massive shell beads; nine pearls.

With a skeleton having a layer of fine charcoal covering pelvis and thighs were: fifteen massive shell beads at the neck, small shell beads at the wrist and two pebbles near the thigh.

By the skeleton of an adolescent were: two masses of plumbago; powdered hematite; two shell cups; three discoidal stones; some delicate tubular shell beads; a wedge-shaped arrow point of chalcedony; one pebble; one small sheet of mica.

With the skeleton of a male were: ten cores, spalls and chips of chert; two rude arrowheads, one of quartz, one of chert; a bit of quartz; a number of pebbles;

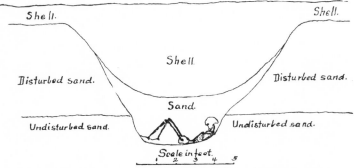

Fig. 25.—Diagram of grave-pit. Mound north end of Creighton Island.

several sherds; small fragments belonging to a soapstone vessel; a rude tobacco pipe of earthenware.

With a male skeleton were: three "celts;" a long chisel of slate; another somewhat smaller; five small chisels; one arrowhead; one smoothing stone; one nest of small pebbles; seventy-seven massive shell beads; small shell beads; a shell gorget; a bone pin, much decayed; an earthenware polisher; mica; hematite.

Let into undisturbed sand, upon the base of an interesting pit, was a skeleton of a male in a semi-reclining position. With the remains were: large and small shell beads; a deposit of small pebbles; a small stone chisel; a "celt;" powdered hematite. From the top of the pit containing this body to the level of the undisturbed sand was 5 feet 10 inches, including 1 foot of shell, there almost superficial. The exact width of the pit could not be determined, as the sand filling it resembled that of the mound. The pit had been filled with sand to the depth of 2.5 feet at the bottom, and considerably higher around it.   Oyster shells had then been poured in, forming a mass 3 feet 10 inches in depth, and 6 feet across where the pit was covered by the layer of shell belonging to that portion of the mound.   This interesting grave is shown in section in Fig. 25.

REMARKS.

The mound on Creighton Island, the largest of its type investigated by us, is full of interest to the student of archæology.   Absolutely nothing in any way indicating white contact was discovered, and we fail to see how, knowing the wide distribution of objects through aboriginal barter, it could have been in use after the coming of the whites and yet contain no object derived from them.

Within view of the landing at Creighton Island was a low mound containing irregular strata of shell, which, though not thoroughly demolished, had a number of trenches dug into it by us, and a portion of the center excavated.   Human remains in a layer, some cremated and some unaffected by fire, were encountered at the center of the mound.   No artifacts were found with them.   In other parts of the mound were many sherds with incised and with complicated decoration.   In addition was what remained of a curious little earthenware effigy of a woman, without head, arms or legs (Fig. 26).

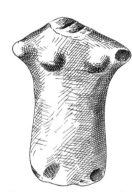

Fig. 26.—Earthenware effigy of female. Low mound at Creighton Island. (Full size.)

Another effigy of a woman, in a like state of mutilation, was shown us by a gentleman living on the mainland a few miles from Creighton Island, who stated it had been washed from a shell bluff on Cedar creek, fronting his residence. This figure tapered gracefully at the waist and bore incised ornamentation front and back.

HOPKINS MOUND, BELLEVILLE, McINTOSH COUNTY.

Belleville, on the south side of the Sapelo river, is the landing of the settlement of Crescent about 1.5 miles inland.

In woods, though formerly cultivated land, about 1 mile in a westerly direction from Belleville, is a mound on the property of C. H. Hopkins, Esq., of Meridian, near Darien, Ga., who cordially placed it at our disposition.

The mound had been considerably dug into previously, but no sustained investigation had been carried on.   Its height was 13 feet 2 inches; its diameter of base, 76 feet.   The ascent of the most uniform side was at an angle of 26°.   Investigation showed the mound to begin at about the commencement of its upward slope. A section 50 feet in breadth at the margin of the base, including the S. by W. to the S. E. by E. portion, with fairly oblique sides converging toward the center, was dug into along the base.   The mound was made of yellow sand of a lightish color with but little discoloration from organic or foreign matter of any sort.   In the central portion were five or six layers of oyster shells each about 4 inches thick, and separated by a little over one foot of sand. A well-marked black band at about the level of the surrounding territory extended to the center. No great central pit was present in the mound, nor were sub-basal graves encountered. Practically no sherds were met with. Interments, encountered at but ten points, began about 8 feet in from the margin. Flexed burials, masses of bones of various individuals together, an isolated cranium and pockets of fragments of calcined human bones were present. With certain burials was hematite and, with two or three of them, a few shell beads.

MOUND NEAR CRESCENT, McINTOSH COUNTY.

In territory covered with trees of considerable size, though evidently formerly cultivated ground, about one-half mile in a southerly direction from the Hopkins Mound, and about 1 mile from Crescent, was a mound also the property of C. H. Hopkins, Esq., to whom we again acknowledge our indebtedness for permission to investigate.

This mound, which had been dug into to a comparatively small extent, had a height of 7 feet and a diameter of base of 70 feet. The eastern half was completely dug through with the exception of a small portion surrounding a large forest tree.

The mound, so far as our investigation extended, was without stratification and was composed of yellowish-brown sand. A dark layer, from 6 inches to 1 foot in thickness, ran along the base. No oyster shells were discovered, nor were outlying pits met with. The mound did not extend into level territory beyond the commencement of the slope. Sherds were very infrequent and none bore the complicated stamp. One chert arrowhead and a rough mass of chert, resembling an uncompleted spear head, lay loose in the sand.

Human remains were met with at sixteen points, as follows: 6 small pockets of fragments of calcined human bones; 3 layers of calcined fragments and parts of human bones unmarked by fire; 1 skeleton; 6 isolated bones and bunched burials.

We append in detail the most noteworthy of the above.

A skull and portion of humerus, very badly decayed, were about 18 inches from the surface. Near these on the same level was a pendant of plutonic rock, considerably disintegrated, having an elongated oval, longitudinal section, about 3.25 inches in length. At the base were small nicks or tally marks.

Near the surface were fragments of bones badly decayed, indicating a burial at full length.

On the base, 6 feet 10 inches from the surface, was a layer of calcined and uncremated bones intermingled. In association was hematite and with one skull were six pearls perforated for use as beads.

Five feet from the surface was an isolated cranium. Toward the center of the mound, about 6 feet below the surface, was a considerable mass, mainly of long bones, imbedded in a quantity of powdered hematite.

Occupying a central position in the mound, 5 feet 9 inches down, was a layer of calcined fragments of human bones mingled with others showing no trace of fire. The dimensions of this layer were 2 feet 6 inches by 1 foot 8 inches by 2 to 3 inches thick.

In line below the above, on or in the base layer, was a layer similar in composition to the one above it, 2.5 feet by 4 feet by 5 inches thick.

The bones in this mound were badly decayed. None was encountered within 15 feet of the margin of the base.

WALKER MOUND, McINTOSH COUNTY.

This mound, in "Cooper's Field," may be reached from Sutherland Bluff on the Sapelo river, from which it is about two miles distant, but is more conveniently got at from Contentment, a small settlement on the west side of Broro river, about three quarters of a mile from its union with the Sapelo river. Broro river is a salt water channel joining the Sapelo river and Julianton creek.

The mound, about 1.5 miles in a westerly direction from Contentment, had a height of 5 feet 9 inches. Its diameter of base was 46 feet. It was the property of Mr. James Walker, of Darien, who kindly placed the mound at our disposal, without condition, to do with as we saw fit.

The mound had previously been dug into to an inconsiderable extent. On its northern margin grew a live-oak 5 feet in diameter, 3 feet from the ground. This tree was not removed, though otherwise the mound was totally demolished, being dug through at a depth considerably below the level of the surrounding territory.

The mound was composed of rich, loamy, brown sand with many local layers of oyster shells. The usual charcoal and fireplaces were present. A black layer from 3 inches to 1 foot in thickness, made up of sand mingled with charcoal in minute particles, ran through the mound at about the level of the surrounding territory. At the center of the mound, measurements showed this layer to be 5 feet 9 inches below the surface.

Although of very uneven distribution, human remains were numerous in the Walker mound, being encountered at thirty-six points (see diagram, Fig. 27), to which should be added a certain number presumably beneath the oak tree and probably a few disturbed by previous investigation.

As will be noted from the detailed account which follows, a deposit of human remains was by no means always limited to those of one individual, and it is not unlikely that the mound originally contained the complement of at least seventy-five skeletons, and probably considerably more. In reading the detailed description of the human remains present in the Walker mound, the reader is referred to the accompanying diagram, where burials are shown with numbers corresponding to those in the text.

1. Skeleton of child about 8 years of age, on back, knees to the right. A considerable amount of charcoal lay above the cranium.

2. Remains of skeleton of male. A fire had been built immediately on the pelvis, which, with some other bones, had been partially consumed. Considerable

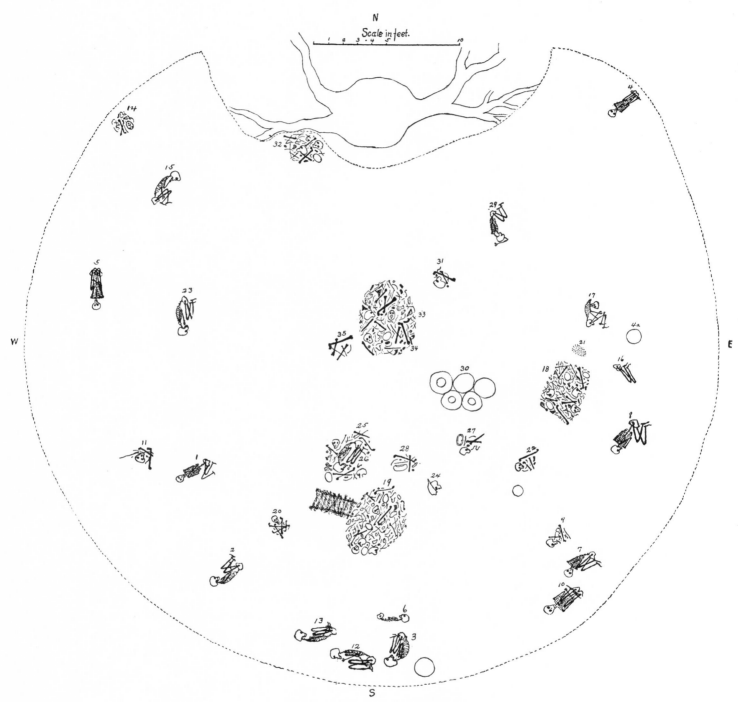

Fig. 27.—Diagram of Walker Mound.

charcoal remained. The skeleton lay on the left side. In association was sand, pink from hematite. The remains lay at a depth of 2 feet below the surface of the mound which was here but little above the surrounding level.

3. Skeleton of female on left side. Depth 2 feet 4 inches.

4. Skeleton of male on back. Remains of a fire along the left side. Face-bones and others in contact with the flames, considerably burnt. This skeleton, at the extreme margin, was 3 feet from the surface, or about that depth below the level of the field. It was doubtless a grave, as unquestionably, we think, were the other deep marginal burials in anatomical order.

4a. Twenty-one inches from the surface was an undecorated vessel with inverted rim, intact. Its height is 4.1 inches; its maximum diameter, 10.2 inches; its diameter of opening, 7.5 inches. Within it were the remains or a portion of the remains of the skeleton of an infant, in minute fragments, burnt and calcined.

Fig. 28.—Section of vessels with calcined bones. Walker Mound. (One-quarter size.)

With these burnt fragments were a number of shell beads showing no trace of fire —evidently added subsequent to the cremation. This bowl had apparently been placed upright on a small heap of sand in such a manner that a larger undecorated vessel inverted and placed over it, the inside of the bottom of the larger vessel in contact with the top of the small one, prevented all ingress of sand as shown in the section (Fig. 28). The dimensions of this larger vessel are : height 6.8 inches; diameter 13.5 inches. In shape the vessel is about square with rounded corners.

5. Skeleton of female on back. Depth 3 feet.

6. Skeleton of undetermined sex. Depth 22 inches. The position of this skeleton, disturbed by the digger, was not determined. About 2 feet distant were many fragments of a large vessel with stamped decoration.

7. Skeleton of uncertain sex, 31 inches down. Trunk on the back, legs to the

right. On this skeleton was a covering of wood or bark .25 of one inch thick, in the last stage of decay.

8. Skeleton of male, on back, head and knees to the right, 3 feet from surface.

Although the human remains in the Walker mound were, comparatively speaking, in good condition yet the cranium of this skeleton (A. N. S. Cat. No. 2,158) was the only one recovered in fair condition.

9. Skeleton of female, fell with caved sand. Probably lay originally about 3 feet from the surface.

10. Skeleton of female on back, 2 feet down.

11. Skeleton of female, 3 feet from surface, disturbed by workmen, position not determined.

12. Skeleton of uncertain sex, somewhat on the right side. This skeleton, coming from a portion of the mound but little above the level of the surrounding field, was nevertheless 4 feet from the surface and lay at the base of a grave dug into the yellowish sand of the field, and filled with the brownish sand of the mound.

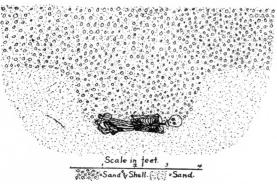

Fig. 29.—Grave containing skeleton 13. Walker Mound.

13. Another grave containing a skeleton of a male on left side. This grave, at the margin of the mound, showed a distinct line of demarcation from the surrounding soil to a height of 26 inches from its base. Above this was a mass of material 2 feet in thickness, similar to the contents of the mound at that place and to that present in the grave. Through this material the line of the grave could not be traced. The surface of the mound at this point was about level with the surface of the field (Fig. 29).

14. Another marginal grave containing a skeleton 4 feet from the surface. This skeleton was too much affected by a fire which had been placed immediately above it to permit determination of sex or position. With the bones were charcoal and fifteen shell beads .5 to 1 inch in length.

15. Skeleton of male with legs to the left and head pushed over on the chest, 3 feet from the surface.

16. Portion of skeleton 1.5 feet down. The body, from the pelvis up, had been removed by a previous investigation.

17. Skeleton of adolescent of about 14 years of age, 3 feet down. It lay on the left side. The skull had rolled on to the chest. Certain epiphyses were separated about 6 inches from their respective shafts.

18. Beginning at one foot below the surface and extending to a depth of from 8 to 10 inches was a confused mass of human remains about 4 feet in length and 3 feet in breadth. At one end were eleven crania together. Immediately above this deposit were four imperforate shell drinking cups and three polished stone chisels having a much flatter section than the ordinary "celt." With the remains were two pins of shell, the larger 4 inches in length.

The entire surface of the mound was covered with oyster shells to an average depth of 6 inches, but above this deposit the shells dipped down into the sand coming in contact with the upper surface of the layer of bones. It was evident that this was a species of grave made after the completion of the mound, though, likely enough, of about the same period, since, as we shall see, similar confused masses of bones were present in the mound at depths clearly showing their original deposit (see section of grave, Fig. 30).

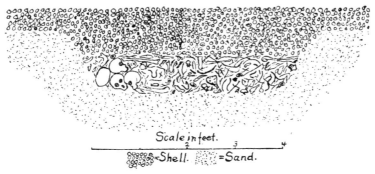

Fig. 30.—Section of grave 18. Walker Mound.

19. A grave similar in style of construction to the preceding. Its depth from the surface was 26 inches. It extended in on the same plane a distance of 5 feet with a breadth at first of 2 feet, broadening to 4 feet and narrowing to 2 feet at the end. It contained a mass of human bones, some calcined, and a few bones of a lower animal unaffected by fire. With the human bones were numbers of shell beads of various sizes.

With the bones was an interesting pathological specimen[1] consisting of a human femur showing material shortening through fracture. This example of bone-setting—or rather the lack of it—by the aborigines is shown in Fig. 31.

This deposit of bones had, on the same plane, contiguous to it a pen or pyre, constructed of logs 3 to 8 inches in diameter, which were charred through and through. The depth of this curious pen was 9 inches; its length, 32 inches; its width was not exactly determined owing to caving of sand. Within this pyre were calcined human remains in fragments.

[1] Now at the Army Medical Museum, Washington, D. C.

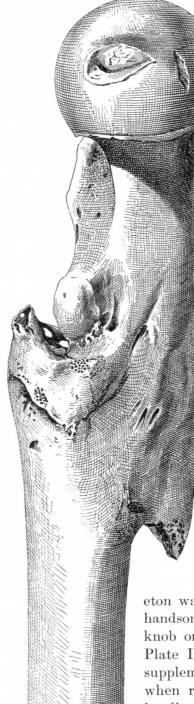

20. Certain human remains, buried in oyster shells at a depth of about 1 foot, fell with caved material before exact data were obtained. Two pairs of femurs were present and the deposit probably included the remains of several persons.

The reader's attention is called to the the fact that it is next to impossible to slice down a mound of sand as can so readily be done with a mound of clay. Mishaps through caving sand are of occasional occurrence even in the case of the most careful workers.

21. A deposit of calcined human remains about 1 foot from the surface. In association were the columella of a marine univalve and eight shell beads, each about 1 inch in length.

22. Bones of male in caved sand.

23. Skeleton of male on right side, face to the right. Nine inches down.

24. A cranium unassociated with other bones. Capping it was a handsome drinking cup of shell having on its outer side three incised lines forming a parallelogram with a portion of the margin of the opening as one of the shorter sides.

25. Four crania with other bones and a few shell beads.

26. Flexed skeleton of a female lying on the right side, 10 inches down, immediately above number 25.

27. A bunched burial including approximately the skeletal complement of a male, 18 inches from the surface. With this skeleton was a vessel of good material, scaphoid in shape and handsomely decorated with a variety of incised designs and a knob on either side, to which justice has not been done in Plate I, Fig. 2. Within the lines, the decoration had been supplemented by red pigment bright and fresh in appearance when removed from the mound in a state of moisture but hardly apparent when dry. A small portion at one end, broken from the vessel, was present with it, permitting complete restoration. Approximate measurements: length, 9.4 inches; height, 5.75 inches; maximum breadth, 7 inches; breadth of aperture, 5.75 inches.

Fig. 31.—Fracture of femur. Walker Mound. (Full size.)

28. A bunched burial 2 feet from the surface, a short distance from 27. With it was a vessel almost the exact counterpart of the one just described, save that the decoration, though on the same lines, is much more elaborate, considerably exceeding in pretension anything met with by us in Florida or elsewhere in Georgia. This decoration is shown diagrammatically in Plate XVI. Certain portions of this vessel, lying with it, were recovered, and were successfully fitted into place.

29. Another grave, 26 inches in depth from the surface. It was filled with oyster shells and contained the skeleton of a male lying on the right side, the right arm under the head.

30. Beneath the roots of a good sized tree, their tops 8 inches beneath the surface, together in a group, all upright, were five cinerary urns each filled almost to the top with a closely packed mass of charred and calcined fragments of human bones. With these bones were a few shell beads showing no trace of fire. The tops of the vessels were covered with large fragments of earthenware belonging to other vessels, which had prevented any entrance of sand. These vessels were of poor material, some especially so, being of slight consistency and held together only by the surrounding roots of the tree above them. Three of the vessels, when the matted mass of roots was removed, fell into pieces so small in size that all hope of restoration was abandoned. The remaining two, though broken into many pieces, were successfully restored. The larger of these two vessels has a height of about 15 inches, a maximum diameter of 15.5 inches and a diameter of aperture of 13.5 inches, approximately. It is ornamented beneath the rim with deep lines incised before baking (Plate V).

The smaller vessel has a globular body with a neck rising from a depression. The ornamentation is of a complicated stamp variety. Approximate measurements : height, 15 inches; maximum diameter, 14.5 inches; diameter of aperture, 6.25 inches (Plate VI). In immediate association with these cinerary urns were eight imperforate drinking cups of shell.

31. Fourteen inches down, in caved sand were the bones of a male.

32. Sixteen inches from the surface, with sand tinged with hematite, was a bunched burial of numerous bones, surmounted by a mass of oyster shells. A large number of shell beads were in association.

33. This interesting grave occupied an almost central position in the mound. Its shape was that of an inverted truncated cone supposing the truncated end to be slightly rounded. The top of the grave, forming a portion of the summit plateau, had a diameter of 8 feet; the depth of the grave, vertically from the surface to the bottom, was 5 feet 9 inches. This grave, after completion, had been lined with a layer of oyster shells about 6 inches in thickness. The bones, present in considerable numbers, had apparently been poured in from the northern side and distributed in a fairly even layer over the bottom and up the northern side to within 2 feet of the top (Fig. 32). On the eastern and western sides were occasional loose bones, but none was present on the southern side, except immediately on the base (Fig. 33). The horizontal distance from the southern margin of the bones on the bottom of the

grave to the northern margin along the side of the pit was 5 feet. The grave was filled with oyster shells and sand distinctly darker than the sand of the mound.

Fifteen crania, more or less imperfect, were present with the other bones, as were certain calcined fragments of human bone. Among the long bones was a

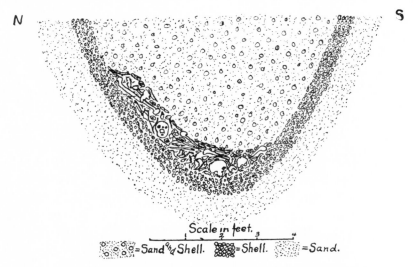

Fig. 32.—North and south section of grave 33. Walker Mound.

femur 19.75 inches in length, indicating a male about 6 feet in height—a stature we believe, greater than indicated by any bones discovered by us in Florida mounds.

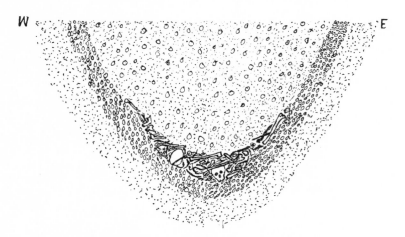

Fig. 33.—East and west section of grave 33. Walker Mound.

34. Immediately beneath the grave just described was a layer of oyster shells, which merged with, and took the place of, the black band running through the mound to which reference has been made. Particles of charcoal were abundantly present in the oyster shells and it would seem that these shells, at this point, 5 feet 9 inches from the surface, were there at the time when the fire was made which caused the black layer running through the mound. Just below the layer of shell,

which was 1 foot in thickness, in dark brown sand totally dissimilar to the yellow sand of the field, which enclosed the grave on either side, was a circular deposit of human bones, having a diameter of about 5 feet.   These bones included five crania and with them were numerous shell beads, many tubular; one being over 1 inch in length.   In one of the crania was a bright yellow sand differing in shade from any in the mound.   Small quantities of this sand were scattered here and there among the bones.

35.   A few bones of a male from superficial caved sand.

HUMERI.

	Male.		Female.		Uncertain.	
	Perforated.	Not Perforated.	Perforated.	Not Perforated.	Perforated.	Not Perforated.
Right	6	15	7	6	3	6
Left	8	9	5	5	7	10

Throughout the mound were the usual loose sherds of accidental introduction. At several points were large vessels of poor material crushed beyond repair.   None of these vessels contained human remains.

One small chisel of stone was found loose in the sand.

REMARKS.

In no one mound investigated by us has there been so well exemplified the various forms of aboriginal disposition of the dead—the burial in anatomical order; the burial of portions of the skeleton; the interment of great masses of human bones; the pyre; the loose deposit of incinerated remains; the burial of cinerary urns.

To a marked extent in this mound are noted, side by side, inhumation and incineration.

MOUND NEAR CONTENTMENT, McINTOSH COUNTY.

Contentment, a small settlement of colored persons, is on the bank of the Broro river, a water-way joining Sapelo river and Julianton creek.

In woods on ground probably formerly under cultivation, about one-half mile in a northerly direction from Contentment, was a symmetrical mound in the form of a truncated cone.   Its sides, by their steepness, gave evidence that no cultivation on the mound proper had ever been attempted.   A comparatively small and shallow excavation was the only trace of digging previous to our own.   The mound was kindly placed at our disposal by R. H. Knox, Esq., of Darien, under whose control the property is.

The mound had a height of 9 feet 9 inches, a base-diameter of 76 feet.   The southern half of the mound was dug away leaving a cross-section E. and W. No pits, outlying or in the body of the mound, were met with. A short distance in from the margin, a black band 6 to 10 inches in thickness was noticed extending through the part investigated by us, at the level of the surrounding territory. Apparently there had been considerable general disturbance beneath this band but as the sand of the mound resembled that of the surrounding territory, any exact line of demarcation was difficult to determine. No oyster shells in quantity were present, though the usual fire-places and pockets of charcoal sometimes contained a few scattering shells.

Human remains were encountered 45 times, at all depths, and extending in from the margin. Bones, in the last stage of decay, at times hardly indicated the form of burial. Occasionally burial of skeletons was indicated, while again, isolated skulls or skulls with a few other bones were met with. With some burials were masses of hematite in powder, sometimes extending the entire length of the skeleton. With one were three pebbles, all showing use as smoothing stones. Near human remains was a chert lance-head and with another interment was an undecorated bowl, broken by caving sand. A pebble and certain fresh-water mussel, and clam-shells lay near an interment.

Seven pockets of calcined bones, some including fragments entirely unaffected by fire, were met with. Centrally in the mound, 7 feet from the surface, with no pit apparent, was a layer of calcined and uncremated human bones, about 6 inches thick. With it were a graceful barbed arrowhead and a flat mass of gneissic rock about 4.5 inches by 2.5 inches with two parallel longitudinal grooves, probably made by sharpening pointed implements or by grinding shell beads into shape.

A considerable number of vessels, all imperforate, so far as could be determined, and undecorated or with an ordinary check stamp, were present in the portion of the mound investigated by us.

Just beneath the surface was a pot with checked stamp decoration, a rounded base and a somewhat cylindrical body—a common cooking vessel. Its height, and its maximum diameter, which was at its mouth, were 11.75 inches. In common with all the stamped pots encountered in this mound, its body was covered with soot showing its use to have been but a secondary one. It contained the calcined remains of not more than one individual and was surmounted by a considerable number of small and large fragments belonging to an undecorated bowl. It fell into pieces upon removal from the sand.

Eighteen feet east of the center, just beneath the surface and about one foot apart, were two interments in vessels, in all respects similar to the one just described.

Near these was an inverted, undecorated pot somewhat resembling in shape a reversed cone with rounded apex. It covered a few fragments of calcined human bones deposited on the sand. Approximate measurements: height, 7.75 inches; maximum diameter and width of mouth, 10.5 inches.

Closely associated with the foregoing bowl was an inverted, checked stamped vessel similar to those first described, covering calcined remains lying on the sand.

Another vessel also bearing the check stamp, half filled with calcined remains, had been capped by a vessel or a large part of a vessel represented by small fragments when found.

In another portion of the mound were the remains of two undecorated vessels in small fragments. One had presumably capped the other, judging by the position. A number of incinerated fragments of human bone were present.

In caved sand from the surface were several other broken vessels with incinerated bone, similar to the foregoing.

Specimens of the earthenware from the mound at Contentment were sent to the Peabody Museum, Cambridge Mass., and to the Davenport Academy of Science, Davenport, Iowa.

Low Mounds near Broro Neck, McIntosh County.

Broro Neck, a settlement of colored people, is about 1 mile northeast of Contentment. A mound on the outskirts of the settlement is on the property of Mr. Thomas Grant (colored). Its height is 3 feet 4 inches. It is 55 feet across the base. It was about one-half dug through. At places were great quantities of charcoal and pockets of hematite. A number of deposits of fragments of calcined bones were met with and a few portions of long bones showing no mark of fire. With skeletal remains were: two hammer-stones, one cockle-shell (*Cardium*), one good-sized shell bead.

About one hundred yards from the preceding mound, on the property of Mr. E. W. Paris (colored), is another mound, which has evidently been ploughed over for a number of years. Its present height is 1 foot 8 inches; its diameter of base, 44 feet. The mound was trenched to the center. About 19 inches from the surface was a deposit of calcined human bones with a small, coarse, undecorated earthenware bowl. The surrounding sand was scarlet from admixture of hematite. Nothing else of interest was met with.

Sapelo Island, McIntosh County. Bourbon.

Sapelo Island, which, with St. Catherine's and Ossabaw, was reserved for their individual use by the Indians, when much of the coast was ceded away,[1] has a settlement at the northern end reached by turning into a small creek from Sapelo sound and continuing up this creek a distance of about 2 miles. This settlement, called "Boobone" by the colored inhabitants, is said originally to have received the name Bourbon from French settlers.

Extending back from the landing is an extensive tract of rich land, undulating with shell deposits, long under cultivation, the property of Amos Sawyer, Esq., of Arlington, R. I., to whom we are indebted for cordial permission to make complete archæological investigation.

About one quarter of a mile S. E. by S. from the landing was a mound, the

[1] "The History of Georgia," Captain Hugh McCall, 2 vols., Savannah, 1811, Vol. I, page 37.

usual truncated cone in shape and still symmetrical, though rather considerable superficial digging had been attempted.

Its height was 8 feet; its diameter at base, 72 feet. The surface of the mound was covered with shell. With a beginning on the level ground 12 feet beyond the margin of the base, to ascertain the presence of outlying burials, none of which were met with, the entire southern half of the mound was sliced down, leaving an E. and W. cross-section. Next the remaining half was dug away with equal care.

The mound presented no uniform stratification. It was composed of local layers of bright yellow sand dug from beneath the surface loam of the field; of dark sand containing occasional shells, mostly belonging to the oyster; of shells with admixture of dark sand and, at the surface, of a layer of midden refuse made up of crushed shell and loam, varying from 8 inches to 2 feet in thickness and occasionally extending still farther down over burials let in from above. All the shell layers of the mound, some of oyster shells, some of shells of the salt-water mussel, seemed dis-

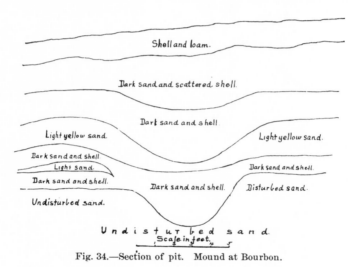

Fig. 34.—Section of pit. Mound at Bourbon.

tinctly to be crushed and packed together as though trampled upon for a considerable period of time which seemed to indicate that the mound had slowly grown for a period of years, during which it was treated as a place of abode.

There was present in the mound no central pit such as is usually found in mounds of the coast, though, beginning a little north of the center was a general dip in the lower layers of the mound over a pit extending 2 feet into undisturbed sand, containing a skeleton at length. This pit had at the base a breadth of 3 feet, its exact length we were unable to determine owing to frequent caving of sand though it must have exceeded 6 feet. The layers above this pit, when of shell, in common with all shell layers of the mound, were compact through tread of feet and seemed to indicate that the pit had been dug at an early stage of the building of the mound and but partially filled and that layers forming afterwards shared in the depression. Fig. 34 gives a lateral section of this pit and of the mound above it.

Though certain other pits were unmistakably present, with two or three exceptions in the marginal portion, we noticed none extending into undisturbed sand below the base, and though, owing to a rainy season, the base of the mound was just above water-level which induced the caving of sand and made exact scrutiny difficult, we believe few, if any, graves escaped us. In such parts of the body of the mound as were made up of yellow sand, burials were not present though many, apparently not in pits, lay in the dark sand. Many more seemed to be just beneath a thickening in the superficial layer of midden refuse while, in numerous cases, grave-pits extending into the dark sand were filled with shell debris from the surface layer.

HUMAN REMAINS.

In the mound, human remains were encountered at 192 points and others, it must be borne in mind, must have been removed by previous digging and by the use of the plow on the lower portions of the mound.

The 192 burials present in the mound, at the time of its demolition by us, may be classified as follows:

115 Skeletons.
11 Aboriginal disturbances.
15 Late disturbances.
31 Decayed and crushed remains.
2 Layers of uncremated bones.

8 Calcined deposits.
3 Skeletons in urns.
3 Calcined remains in urns.
4 Not noted.

Skeletons.—Of those successfully removed there were:

43 Males.
40 Females.
12 Uncertain.

5 Adolescents.
11 Children.[1]
4 Infants.[1]

Many of the skeletons lay between decayed wood or bark. Skeletons were as to position as follows:

	Flexed on right side.	Flexed on left side.	At length.	Special.
Male	27	5	6	5
Female [2]	28	4	2	5
Uncertain	8	1	1	2
Adolescent	3			2
Children [2]	8			2
Infants	3			1

The skeletons at length were face down and all were below the base, on it, or well down in the body of the mound.

Special positions were as follows:

Burial No. 10, child of about 10 years, flexed with trunk on back.

[1] Eight additional skeletons, badly crushed and decayed, two certainly of children and six of infants, are included with the crushed and decayed remains.
[2] Data as to the side of one flexed female skeleton and of one child are omitted in the field notes.

Burial No. 38, skeleton of infant, crushed and partly calcined.   Exact position not determined.

Burial No. 43, skeleton of male in semi-reclining position, head forward on chest.

Burial No. 90, skeleton of male, face down, and extended as far as the knees, with legs drawn back and foot bones almost in contact with the pelvis.

Burials Nos. 99 and 100, skeletons of child and of adolescent, crossing at hips, the child on top.   Both skeletons were extended to the knees with legs flexed back.

Burial No. 101, skeleton of female with trunk on back, thighs drawn up toward body but spread apart, with legs drawn back on thighs.

Burial No. 139, skeleton of female on back with lower extremities flexed up on body.

Burial No. 153, female, same position as 101.

Burial No. 154, skeleton of a male at full length, in water, 10 feet below surface, the upper part crushed but showing no trace of fire.   The thighs and lower part of the arms with the hands were calcined.   This burial might be included among skeletons at length.

Burial No. 158, skeleton of adolescent on back, the thighs partly flexed and separated.

Burial No. 160, a skeleton of uncertain sex in a semi-sitting position, head over on chest.   The cranium was saved (Acad. Nat. Sci., Cat. No. 2,163).[1]

Burial No. 168, skeleton of male on back as far down as could be determined, the legs having fallen with caving sand.   This skeleton was surrounded by a thin layer of sand, colored red with powdered hematite.

Burials Nos. 173 and 174, part of a skeleton of uncertain sex, face down including the pelvis.   At this point another skeleton, beginning with the cranium and including about one-half of the thigh bones, continued in the same direction. Then came thighs, legs and foot bones in anatomical order, probably belonging to the first skeleton.   These remains lay at a depth of 4 feet from the surface and were unquestionably an aboriginal disturbance.

Burial No. 177, a skeleton of a female, lying on back to the knees, with legs flexed back on thighs.

Burial No. 186, skeleton of female, trunk on back, thighs and legs flexed to the right.

Not included under the head of special positions, since both were flexed, were burials Nos. 58 and 59, consisting of the skeleton of a female holding between its arms the fragile remains of a very young infant.   The crania were in contact.

Of the 115 skeletons, 71 headed between S. E. and S. W., many crania pointing due S.

The remaining 44, with the exception of a woman, a child and an infant which are omitted from our field notes, headed as follows: E. S. E., 3; E. by S., 2;

---

[1] But one other cranium was in condition to preserve in this mound, namely that from Burial No. 73, a male (Acad. Nat. Sci., Cat. 2,162).

E., 11; E. by N., 1; E. N. E., 1; N. E., 4; N. N. E., 3; N., 5; N. N. W., 1; N. W., 1; W., 4; W. by S., 2; S. W. by W., 2; W. S. W., 1.

Aboriginal disturbance.—Aboriginal disturbance includes burials cut through by subsequent interments and possibly parts of skeletons accorded independent burial.

Late disturbance.—Under this head we include bones scattered by the plow, by superficial digging previous to our investigation, by caving sand and inadvertent disturbance by our men.

Decayed and crushed remains.—We have thus designated all such as seemed to be single skeletons which, through decay and through pressure were past determination as to sex, position and direction. It is not only possible but probable, however, that fragmentary aboriginal burials and small layers of bones of various individuals, badly decayed, have been included.

Layers of uncremated bones.—Two such layers unconnected with cremated remains were distinctly present in the mound. With one layer were five crania; with the other, six.

Calcined deposits.—Of the eight calcined deposits, the majority had fragments of human bones showing no trace of fire, associated with them. Some contained the remains, or parts of the remains of at least three individuals, while others probably represented but one skeleton.

Burial No. 117 was confined to the cremated remains of a child, a few remnants of whose bones were unburnt.

A small pocket of calcined bones lay upon decayed wood.

We have elsewhere referred to two partially cremated skeletons.

Skeletons in urns.—Vessel C, Burial No. 134, 15 feet N. E. by N. from the center of the mound, with its base 20 inches from the surface, its top just beneath the superficial shell layer, there 7 inches thick, was a vessel with incised decoration below the margin and a faint complicated stamp on the body. Decayed wood was above and below it. The vessel, crushed to fragments, was partly held together by sand and shells. It contained the long bones of an adult skeleton, parallel to each other and perpendicular to the base on which lay various smaller bones capped by the skull.

Near the preceding, forming a cluster with it and two other vessels, was a pot, Burial No. 135, Vessel D, on its side, having complicated stamp ornamentation. Decayed wood lay above and below it. Its condition was, if possible, worse than that of the preceding. It contained bones of an adult arranged similarly to those in Vessel C, and two polished stone hatchets, one rude quartz arrowhead, one undecorated earthenware tobacco pipe, and one fresh-water mussel shell, fragmentary through decay.

Vessel F, Burial No. 137, one of the group, had a complicated stamped decoration, but, unfortunately, was as fragmentary as its neighbors. It contained the remains of an adult arranged as in the other vessels and a circular piece of soapstone with incised decoration, to be described under another heading.

Calcined remains in urns.—Vessel A, Burial No. 25, 20 feet S. W. by W. from the center, was a flat-bottomed, undecorated, globular, imperforate vessel of about two gallons capacity, slightly constricted at the neck. It was crushed to fragments. Within were the calcined remains of an adolescent.

Vessel E, Burial No. 136, made the fourth of the group to which reference has been made. It appeared to be of the ordinary type but was crushed to small pieces. It seemed to have been about half full of incinerated human remains.

Vessel G, Burial No. 163, 9 feet N. N. W. from the center, lay in fragments over part of a layer of calcined remains. Its decoration was red bands running laterally. The arrangement of the fragments seemed to indicate a former inverted position for the vessel.

Not noted.—Four burials included under this head were interments where full data, though obtainable, are omitted from our field notes.

EARTHENWARE.

Sherds.—Sherds were of infrequent occurrence, the majority undecorated or cord-marked, though a few had incised decoration. Excluding the burial jars and

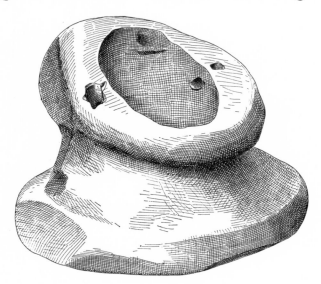

Fig. 35.—Vessel of earthenware. Mound at Bourbon. (Full size.)

one or two sherds believed to be superficial, the complicated stamp was not noted in the mound.

Vessels.—We have described certain vessels used for burial purposes.

With Burial No. 26, that of a child about eight years old, was an urn of about three pints capacity with globular body, constricted neck and flaring rim. Beneath the rim on the outside was an encircling row of button-like protuberances which had been modeled and pressed on to the clay before baking. Certain of these had dropped off.

Vessel B, an undecorated bowl with rounded base and slightly inverted rim, has a diameter at mouth of 10 inches; a maximum diameter of body of 11.75 inches; a height of 8 inches.   It contained a certain amount of decayed wood and a small quantity of material resembling sawdust—perhaps the last vestige of human remains.

With Burial No. 92, a child about seven years old, was a globular, undecorated pot of about one quart capacity.

With Burial No. 93, probably an aboriginal disturbance, was a curious vessel of earthenware, perforated for suspension at either side of the opening (Fig. 35), having a height of 2.5 inches; a maximum diameter of 3 inches.   Its use is not apparent though it strongly recalls that numerous class of fantastically shaped mortuary vessels of earthenware found in many tumuli of Florida.   A hole had been knocked through its base, the only case of base-perforation noted by us in the mound though certain of the burial jars were too fragmentary for determination as to this point.

In caved sand were several fragments of an oblong vessel having upright sides and inverted margin.   The vessel, or rather such parts as were recovered, have on the base and sides—an unusual occurrence—an intricate incised decoration.   Its height must have been 1.1 inches; its breadth of body, 2

 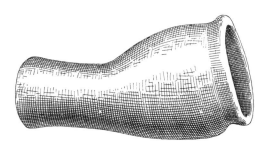

Fig. 36.   Fig. 37.
Tobacco pipes of earthenware.   Mound at Bourbon.   (Full size.)

inches; of opening, 1.5 inches.   Its original length is not obtainable as a part is missing.

With Burial No. 113, a male, was a cord-marked bowl of about one quart capacity.

Burial No. 154 had with it a small bowl in fragments bearing the checked, stamped decoration.

One of the most interesting pieces of earthenware ever met with by us lay with Burial No. 33, a mass of mingled calcined and unburnt bones, and consisted of a dish 12.2 inches in length, 7.7 inches across and 4.5 inches in height.   Beneath the rim, exteriorly, is a row of large protuberances and, in addition, the dish bears traces of ornamentation by the use of red pigment.   From either end project handles, one horizontal the other perpendicular—a curious feature.   This interesting piece is intact (Plate VII).

8 JOURN. A. N. S. PHILA., VOL. XI.

Tobacco pipes.—Thirteen tobacco pipes were present in the mound—several somewhat fragmentary. But two showed any serious attempt at ornamentation. One of these (Fig. 36) has a height of 2 inches, a diameter of bowl of 1.5 inches and a diagonal length of 2.8 inches, approximately. The bowl is supported by a figure probably representing a bird. Part of the body and tail served for the

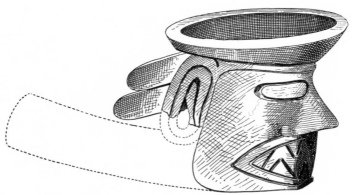

Fig. 38.—Tobacco pipe of earthenware. Mound at Bourbon. (Full size.)

reception of the stem. Found with this pipe was a small undecorated one shown in Fig. 37. The bowl forms an unusually obtuse angle with the remainder of the pipe.

In caved sand was a pipe representing a human head. The mouth is open showing the teeth and a curious head dress projects from the back of the head. A

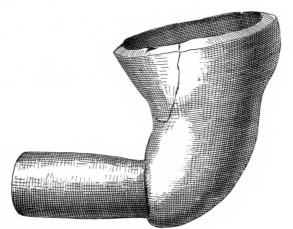

Fig. 39.—Tobacco pipe of earthenware. Mound at Bourbon. (Full size.)

portion of this pipe is wanting. Height and diameter of bowl, each 1.9 inches (Fig. 38).

An undecorated but rather gracefully shaped tobacco pipe (Fig. 39) lay with a burial.

A tobacco pipe of the poorest material and rude in form, apparently sun-dried, was recovered in pieces of hardly any consistency, though after drying it was fairly well put together. Diagonal length, 5.5 inches; diameter of bowl and height, each 3.3 inches; diameter of stem, 2 inches; orifice for stem, 1 inch.

SHELL.

Cups.—Thirty-four shell drinking cups, none remarkable for size or finish, were taken from the mound, ten forming one deposit. All were imperforate and three

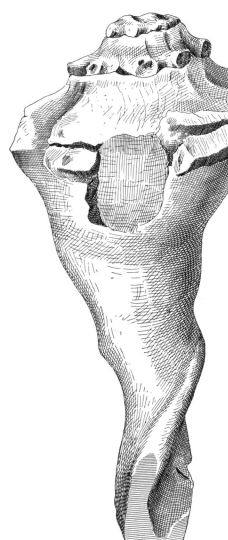

Fig. 40.—Chisel of shell. Mound at Bourbon. (Full size.)

varied from any yet found by us in Florida or in Georgia, we believe, in that they were wrought, not from *Fulgur perversum*, whose opening is to the left, but from a right handed *Fulgur* (*canaliculatum*).

Chisels.—Eighteen shell chisels were associated with human remains. These rather rough-looking implements, one of which we show in Fig. 40, made by grinding the beak to a cutting edge and removing the body whorl from the axis, must not be confounded with certain beautiful shell chisels found in Florida but not, so far as we know, on the Georgia coast, which are made from the lip of the great marine univalve, *Strombus gigas.*

Agricultural implements.—Two specimens of the right handed, heavy form of the conch (*Fulgur carica*), with perforation in the body whorl opposite the aperture and with the beak worn or chipped down, came from the mound.

Pins.—Twelve pins, the largest about 4.5 inches, lay with skeletal remains practically always near the head.

Gorgets.—In midden refuse composing a shell layer was a circular gorget of shell of about 2 inches diameter, having carved in the center a rough diamond-shaped figure (Fig. 41).

With Burial No. 92, a child of about 7 years, was a gorget near the head. This gorget, nearly circular, with a diameter of about 1.7 inches, bore the well-known design of the rattlesnake.

Beads.—Beads of shell were fairly numerous though in no wise comparable in size, number or state of preservation to those in the Creighton Island mound, with the exception of a fine tubular bead, 4 inches in length, having a diameter of .6 of one inch. To drill a bead of this sort longitudinally must have required considerable time. We are told by Adair,[1] " Formerly four doe-skins was the price of a large conch-shell bead, about the length and thickness of a man's fore-finger; which they fixed to the crown of their head as an high ornament—so greatly they valued them."

With one burial were a number of discoidal beads, each about one inch in diameter, perforated in the center through the minor axis. These beads must not be confounded with *runtees,* which have their perforation edgewise.

Mussel shells.—Great numbers of fresh-water mussel shells, all Georgia species, some perforated for suspension, others not, were present with human remains. With one burial were many shells (*Unio Shepardianus*), some decayed and broken, though 33, all perforated, were recovered in fairly good condition.

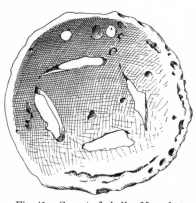

Fig. 41.—Gorget of shell. Mound at Bourbon. (Full size.)

PEARLS.

One pearl, perforated as usual, was met with.

STONE.

" *Celts.*"—Eleven polished " celts," most of them of volcanic rock, from 3 to 6.5 inches in length, were present in the mound. It has not been thought necessary to mutilate them for exact determination as to material. Several, probably of green-stone, were badly decayed through contact with water.

Pebble-hammers, hammer-stones, etc.—The mound was rich in these objects. One hammer-stone was apparently a portion of a celt. One pebble-hammer, with a length of 6.25 inches, had also seen use as a smoothing-stone. Certain ones, smoothed on four sides, presented an interesting appearance.

Arrow and Lance points.—Five arrow and lance points of chert, of chalcedony and of quartz, all of ordinary type, were found during the investigation.

Discoidal stones.—Four small discoidal stones were met with. One of micaceous sandstone was in a friable condition.

Fig. 42.—Ornament of soapstone. Mound at Bourbon. (Full size.)

Soapstone objects.—With caved sand, near human remains, was a portion of a vessel of soapstone—a large vessel, as shown by the slight concavity of the inner surface. It is about 4 inches square and has on the margins a rude and irregular decoration.

With Burial No. 50, a male, was a bit of a soapstone vessel, rudely decorated with incised lines on either side and on two of its three margins. With it was a circular ornament of soapstone having the margin divided by five incisions. Height, .5 of an inch; diameter, 1.2 inches (Fig. 42).

[1] " History of the American Indians," page 170. Cited by C. C. Jones.

With Burial No. 137, in vessel F, was an imperforate, irregularly circular piece of soapstone 2.3 inches by 2 inches by .5 of one inch thick. On one side was a rough incised design representing the serpent (Fig. 43); on the other a cross-hatch decoration (Fig. 44).

With Burial No. 45, was a curious little piece of soapstone 1.8 inches in height roughly wrought into the semblance of the upper portion of the human figure.

Fig. 43. Fig. 44.
Engraved tablet of soapstone. Mound at Bourbon. (Full size.)

The arms are plainly apparent, as is the mouth. The upper portion of the head seems to be wanting through breakage or through omission (Fig. 45).

Several unworked bits of soapstone pots were present with burials.

Miscellaneous.—A number of flakes of chert, probably used as cutting implements, lay with burials or loose in the sand. With a skeleton was a small nodule of black jasper.

Fig. 45.—Effigy of soapstone. Mound at Bourbon. (Full size.)

BONE.

Piercing implements.—Piercing implements, some probably hair pins, were fairly numerous. Many were decayed and broken. Some piercing implements retain the articular portion of the bone at the blunt end.

A curious feature, not before noticed by us, was the presence in this mound of sections of bone pins with burials, not broken but apparently intentionally divided by cutting. With one burial were no less than seven of these fragments. A less number were found at several other points in the mound.

Miscellaneous.—With human remains were the jaws of a small carnivore and part of a lower jaw of a much larger one with the lower portion, including the roots of the teeth, ground away, leaving a flat surface. We shall again refer to this curious aboriginal custom in connection with jaws similarly treated from mounds on St. Catherine's and Ossabaw Islands.

The carapace of a tortoise, somewhat fragmentary, with two perforations, was found with a burial. The lower part of the shell was probably absent through decay. In the mound at Bourbon were several tortoise shells in the last stage of decay, usually surrounding nests of small pebbles; once or twice, flakes of chert; once, small square pieces of shell, probably originally destined for beads, and a number of the teeth of the drum-fish. We have, in other mounds, met with deposits of drum-fish teeth which doubtless had remained after the enclosing tortoise shells had decayed.

Plumbago, perhaps used as black paint, was present with one burial.

Many burials throughout the mound were associated with the red oxide of iron in powder.

A small bead of blue glass was found by a digger engaged on the surface layer. This bead, in view of the absence of glass beads with burials in the body of the mound, we took to be a relic of later Indians who, we know, inhabited Sapelo Island until a comparatively recent period.

ASSOCIATION OF OBJECTS.

With Burial No. 31 were: two pebbles; a flat mass of undetermined stone; two fragments belonging to a pot or pots of soapstone; a pebble worn down as a smoothing implement; a shell chisel; three badly-decayed bone piercing implements; a flat fragmentary smoothing-stone and one large pebble-hammer.

With Burial No. 33, a mass of calcined and unburnt bones, were two stone hatchets; two earthenware tobacco pipes and the earthenware dish already described.

There lay with Burial No. 73, a male, shell beads at the wrist; five tobacco pipes, some with portions missing; two pebble-hammers; one pebble; two fresh-water mussel shells; one shell chisel; one discoidal stone with a concavity on one side; one small quartz arrowhead; one portion of a columella of some large marine univalve; one decayed turtle shell containing drum-fish teeth, etc.; one shell drinking cup; one bone pin; one discoidal stone.

SAPELO ISLAND, McINTOSH COUNTY. LOW MOUND AT BOURBON.

About 150 yards in a southerly direction from the large mound at Bourbon, was one having a diameter of base of 38 feet, a height of 3 feet 4 inches. Upon it lay the trunk of a large oak tree, which, with the root, interfered with complete investigation. Somewhat over one-half the mound was dug away, with the courteous permission of Amos Sawyer, Esq.

The mound at marginal portions was thickly covered with oyster shells, the layer gradually decreasing in thickness toward the center. The body of the mound was composed of black loamy sand. The presence of water near the base impeded investigation.

Human remains were met with at twelve points. Three skeletons lay at full length, two on the back and one face down in sub-basal graves under water. Other remains, all inhumations of single bodies, were in various positions, flexed, semi-sitting, reclining. There was no uniformity of direction nor any preponderance of a southern direction as a choice for the head. With one skeleton was hematite; with another, a few shell beads.

SAPELO ISLAND, McINTOSH COUNTY. MOUND IN DUMOUSSAY'S FIELD.

Dumoussay's Field, taking its name from a French owner, deceased on the island in 1794, as his headstone sets forth, is a considerable tract formerly under cultivation but now overgrown with underbrush and small trees. It is studded with shell-heaps. It is distant somewhat over one mile in a straight line from Bourbon—N. N. W.—and may also be reached by water through a branch of the creek on which Bourbon is situated.

About one-quarter of one mile in a northwesterly direction from the landing, which is only a harder portion of the marsh, was an irregular rise in the ground much reduced in height and spread out by cultivation. Its maximum height was 18 inches; its exact diameter was difficult to determine. Probably a circumference with a diameter of 50 feet would have included all portions above the general level of the field. It was dug through by us by permission of Amos Sawyer, Esq., to whom we are indebted for the privilege of opening the neighboring mounds at Bourbon.

Through what we took to be the center of the elevated part of the mound, a line 90 feet in length was drawn running east and west. Taking this line as a chord, a semi-circle with radii of 45 feet, including the southern portion of the mound, was marked out and completely dug through. Evidences of disturbance in the soil were met with about 29 feet from the central point, the first interment, however, being 23 feet S. E. by S.

Next, the northern half of the mound was dug through starting with a diameter of 53 feet and gradually converging to a line 32 feet N. of the central point where all disturbance in the sand seemed to cease, and a considerable number of feet beyond an interment. On the limits of the mound were the pits so often found with coast mounds, in this case about 3.5 feet deep and covering a considerable area. As usual, they were filled with sand black with organic matter much darker than the sand of the mound, but contained no burials.

The mound, which had evidently lost much of its original altitude through cultivation, had upon its surface but a few scattered oyster shells and contained practically none. There was no central grave, unless a broad area of disturbed sand near the middle, extending into the bright yellow sand beneath the base and containing a number of burials may be so regarded. Pits similar to this, though smaller, were present elsewhere in the mound.

Skeletal remains were met with at fifty-one points in the mound, excluding scattered fragments from near the surface. These burials were distributed as follows as to form: skeletons, 42; late disturbance, 1; bunched burials, 2; isolated cranium, 1; uncremated remains in vessels, 3; cinerary urn with calcined remains, 1.

Of the skeletons : 20, were of males ; 12, of females ; 6, of uncertain sex ; 3, of adolescents ; 1, of a child.

Of these 42 skeletons all but one were flexed [1] on the right side and all but the same one headed in a southerly direction, 17 being due south.   The one exception lay flexed on the left side with the head pointing E. N. E.

We append all burials of interest and all associated with any artifacts.

Burial No. 2, 23 feet S. E. by S. from the center, at the bottom of a pit, 3 feet 6 inches from the surface, extending 1 foot 3 inches into undisturbed sand, was a skeleton of uncertain sex flexed on the right side, head S.

Burial No. 5, 21 feet S. E. by S., 2 feet 4 inches down, was a skeleton of a male, flexed on the right side, head S.   With it was a tobacco pipe with portions of the rim missing, representing a human face and differing somewhat from the one from Bourbon, where the teeth are shown continuously, while in this specimen, which recalls the one from Darien, they are represented on either side only (Fig. 46).

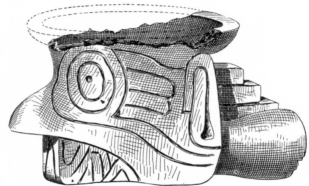

Fig. 46.—Tobacco pipe of earthenware.   Mound at Dumoussay's Field.   (Full size.)

Burial No. 8, 16 feet S. E. by E., 1 foot down, a skeleton of an adolescent, flexed on the right side, head S. by E.   Above the skeleton was a layer of charcoal about 6 inches thick, with burnt shells and sand.   In this layer were fragments of calcined human bones having no connection with the skeleton below, and a calcined shell pin.

Burial No. 13, 12 feet E., 2 feet 10 inches down—a bunched burial, the skull face up, the lower jaw under it and turned from it, one humerus above and one beneath, the cranium.   Ribs heaped over upper humerus.   No other bones except two vertebræ.

Burial No. 14, Vessel A, 11 feet S. E. by S., a vessel in fragments, probably broken by the plow.   With it were scattered fragments of calcined human bones and a discoidal stone.

Burial No. 16, 7 feet E. by S., skeleton of female, flexed on the right, head S., on the bottom of a pit, 4 feet 7 inches from the surface.   The pit extended 1 foot 9 inches into undisturbed sand.   Diameter of pit as it entered undisturbed sand, 4 feet 3 inches.   In the upper part of the pit was powdered hematite.

[1] One of these was a partial flexion.

Burial No. 26, male, flexed on the right side, head S. by W. Associated, were: two undecorated tobacco pipes, with parts missing; the lower half of a chert arrowhead; a bit of soapstone pot; two bone pins badly decayed.

Burial No. 30, 3 feet W. S. W., 3 feet down, a skeleton of an aged female, flexed on the right side, heading S. by E. At the neck were small beads and near by were: six imperforate marine shells (*Dosinia discus*)[1]; three pebbles used as smoothing stones; one attractive pebble-hammer of quartz; and two rectangular dishes, the smaller inverted within the larger, each with rounded corners and slightly converging sides, having, in addition, an inward slope toward the middle of the longer sides. On the base of the smaller vessel and extending somewhat over on one side, is a curious incised decoration shown diagrammatically in Fig. 47.

Professor Holmes considers it to be "most certainly representative of some life form or forms."

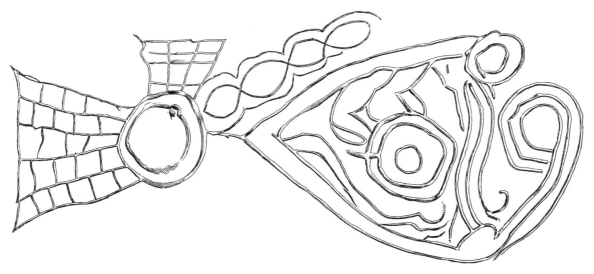

Fig. 47.—Incised decoration on dish. Mound at Dumoussay's Field. (Full size.)

Professor Putnam thus writes of it:—"As to the figure carved on the oblong dish from the Sapelo Island mound, both Mr. Willoughby and I find ourselves unable to reduce it to its elements. It is probably a conventionalized figure, which in time will be traced back to its realistic form."

The approximate measurements of the larger vessel, in which we noticed hematite, are as follows: length, 9 inches; breadth, 4.5 inches; height, 1.5 inches. The smaller dish was approximately 7 inches long, 3.25 inches wide, and 1.5 inches high.

Burial No. 32, Vessel B, 4 feet W. Just below the surface, was an undecorated imperforate bowl in fragments containing bits of uncremated bones of a young infant. Nearby were: an undecorated imperforate vessel with globular body, constricted neck and flaring rim, of about 3 pints capacity; one shell drinking cup and one conch shell.

Burial No. 34, 13 feet E. by N., a skeleton of a male, flexed on the right side, head S., having in association a mass of powdered hematite.

[1] Determined by Professor Pilsbry.

9 JOURN. A. N. S. PHILA., VOL. XI.

Burial No. 35, 6 feet N. W., 3.5 feet down, skeleton of a child, flexed on the right side, head S. W. by S. At the neck were eight massive beads of shell, the largest 2 inches in length, and a number of small beads. On the chest was a rattle made from the shell of a tortoise, very badly decayed, having within many little pebbles; a gorget of shell with part of the rim missing, having a diameter of 2.6 inches, bearing the design of a rattlesnake.

Burial No. 36, Vessel C, 7 feet N. W. by W. A few inches below the surface was a badly crushed, undecorated, imperforate vessel held in place by sand, 17.75 inches long with a maximum width of 12 inches. The orifice is 14 inches in length and 9.5 inches wide. The height varies from 6 inches at the middle of the side to 7 inches at the end. In shape the vessel resembles the larger one described with Burial No. 30. At the bottom of the vessel were small shell beads in numbers, while powdered hematite was present in it in places. The top was covered or partly covered by fragments of earthenware, not representing any entire vessel. This oblong vessel, which, pieced together, is shown in Plate VIII, enclosed a lower jaw; arm bones on either side and in the middle, ribs; part of the sternum and a few vertebræ. These bones were not in anatomical order.

In the sand immediately below the vessel were the skull without the mandible; the pelvis with the left lower extremity in anatomical order and flexed. The bones of the right leg were parallel to, and alongside of, those of the left leg, while the right thigh was about one foot away. Scattered phalanges and vertebræ lay about and the portion of the sternum not contained in the vessel was present. With these bones were massive shell beads and a shell drinking cup. This burial we consider the most interesting of any it has been our fortune to encounter.

Burial No. 41, 10 feet N. W. by N., 1 foot 2 inches below the present surface, was a bunched burial, having: the bones of the lower extremities with one tibia reversed from its femur, the long bones parallel; the pelvis on top; the ribs mingled; one humerus; no forearm bones; no cranium and but one vertebra.

Burial No. 46, 17 feet N. N. E., 2.5 feet down, a skeleton of uncertain sex, flexed on the right, heading S. With it was a shell drinking cup and one pebble.

Burial No. 48, 16 feet N. N. E., 2 feet 3 inches down, was the skeleton of a male, on right side, head S. by E. In the grave with the skeleton, 2 feet west of it, were two vessels, each of about 2 quarts capacity, of the type described as found near Burial No. 32, each on its base but tilting toward the other, so that a part of the rim of one lay in the aperture of the other. The interior of one was coated with red pigment. Near the knee of the skeleton were fragments of a cord-marked bowl of about three quarts capacity, not together, but spread out at some distance one from the other. This bowl, when pieced together, showed a base-perforation. Below the upper margin, on either side of a crack, were two perforations placed to permit the passing through of a cord or sinew to hold together the parts on either side. Below the skeleton and the two vessels first described was a continuous layer of decayed wood or bark.

Burial No. 49, 22 feet N., just beneath the surface was the skeleton of a male, partly flexed on the right side, heading S. With it were hematite and a rude pendant wrought from a section of the columella of a marine univalve, grooved at one end for suspension.

Burial No. 50, Vessels D and E, 24 feet N., just beneath the surface, was a badly broken vessel of the ordinary type with a perforated base. The rim had been ploughed away. Within were fragments of bones of an infant so young that the milk teeth had not erupted. Above this vessel was an inverted bowl in fragments, undecorated save for a row of small knobs beneath the exterior margin.

Burial No. 51, 25 feet N. by W., nine inches down, a skeleton of a male, flexed on the right side, head S. by E. Associated was a nest of small pebbles, doubtless formerly included within a tortoise shell.

With a number of burials not especially noted was decayed wood or bark. In the mound, loose in the sand, was a somewhat fragmentary undecorated tobacco pipe. Sherds, undecorated, cord-marked and with check and complicated stamp, were present. A portion of an undecorated vessel which, while whole, had also seen service as a hone, showed five grooves, a part of one of which had been on the missing portion.

Aboriginal Enclosure at Sapelo High Point, Sapelo Island, McIntosh County.

On Sapelo High Point, near the northwest end of Sapelo Island, overlooking Sapelo Sound and, at periods of storm, washed by the waters of Big Mud river (the southernmost fork of the sound) which had laid bare a section of the walls, is an almost circular aboriginal fortification or ceremonial enclosure. This enclosure (see plan, Fig. 48), which we examined by permission of Amos Sawyer, Esq., upon whose property it is, has a diameter, including the walls, of somewhat over 300 feet. The walls have an average height of from 5 to 7 feet, and a thickness of about 50 feet at the base. They are flattened on top where at present they have an average width of from 10 to 15 feet. They are covered with forest trees, and are composed exclusively of shells, mainly those of the oyster, with the usual midden refuse intermingled, such as fragments of bone, bits of earthenware, and the like.

Those most familiar with the history of Southern Georgia have failed to find any allusion to this work in chronicles or histories, nor does any local tradition attach to it.

That the work is aboriginal is, in our opinion, beyond the shadow of a doubt since a fortification made by Europeans would be of sand found on the spot and not from shells gathered here and there from small deposits at a distance. On one side of the mound only are shells within sight, and these consist of circular deposits not over 18 inches in height, from which no shells have been taken. There is no question then but this is one of those symmetrical works of the aborigines made by piling shell through a period of time to form some definite shape such as a great ridge on Barbour's Island not far from Sapelo, or at Enterprise, Florida, or the great oblong mound of shell lying in the swamp near Volusia, Florida, with no shell surrounding it, a full description of which we have given in the American Naturalist.[1]

[1] "Certain Shell Heaps of the St. Johns River, Florida," January, 1893.

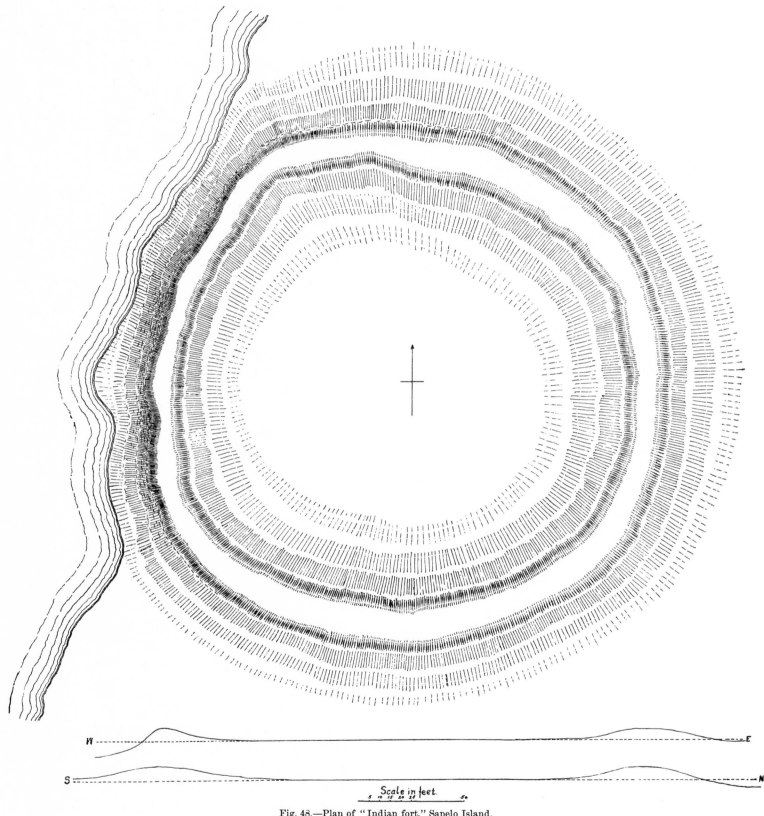

Fig. 48.—Plan of "Indian fort," Sapelo Island.

Excavations made within the enclosure gave varying results. At one point yellow, undisturbed sand was reached about 1 foot beneath the surface. Another excavation went through loam and midden refuse to a depth of 2.5 feet. Earthenware in fragments, shattered bones of the deer and a fragment of a temporal bone from a human skull were met with.

In a description of this enclosure, appearing in a report of the Smithsonian Institution,[1] reference is made to two circular enclosures in the vicinity. One is at present indistinct and has by no means the height assigned to it. The other escaped our attention.

Near the center of Sapelo Island is a mound of considerable size, the property of a Mr. Keenan, or Kennon, with whom we were unable to come to terms.

The Island of Blackbeard, called after the famous pirate of that name, lies to the northeast of Sapelo. We are indebted to the courtesy of Dr. Edward Giddings for permission to make any investigation we saw fit upon the island. Unfortunately, we were unable to locate any aboriginal works upon it though " Money Old Field," a tract formerly under cultivation, seemed to offer a likely situation. This field has been fairly riddled by seekers after mythical treasure, and it is owing to this foolish idea of buried gold that scientific investigators meet with hindrance from the ignorant.

MOUNDS AT BAHAMA, McINTOSH COUNTY.

Bahama,[2] situate at the union of Barbour's Island river and South Newport river, has a wide expanse of cultivated fields, many of which, by the presence of numerous low shell heaps, give evidence of aboriginal occupation. A careful search upon two occasions was accorded to this promising site with but meagre result. Two small mounds, each but little above the general level, were met with. These mounds were not completely demolished, though the central parts were dug out, with considerable additional trenching. In each case no interments were discovered save in a central pit.

In one mound the pit, filled to the surface with oyster shells, contained a confused mass of human remains, including three crania unaffected by fire. With these bones were fragments of calcined human remains and one piercing implement of bone.

In the second mound, upon which only scattered oyster shells were visible, was a pit about 3.5 feet deep, roughly circular and about 7 feet across at the top. The sides of the pit, which converged, were coated with a layer of oyster shells, about 6 inches thick. On the base was a deposit of remains similar in character to those in the other mound, including six crania. A certain amount of hematite was in association.

[1] 1872, page 422 *et seq.* "Mounds in Georgia," William McKinley.
[2] The post-office at this point has, we believe, lately been given the name Lacey.

MOUNDS AT LAUREL VIEW, LIBERTY COUNTY.

Laurel View is a high bluff on the south side of the Medway river. About 1 mile south of the bluff was a very symmetrical mound of white sand, 7 feet high and 38 feet across the base. It was on the property of Mr. McClosky of Augusta, Georgia. Prior to our visit a large trench had been dug completely through the mound and a portion of one side had been dug away. The remainder of the mound was totally demolished by us. A number of pockets of calcined human bones—

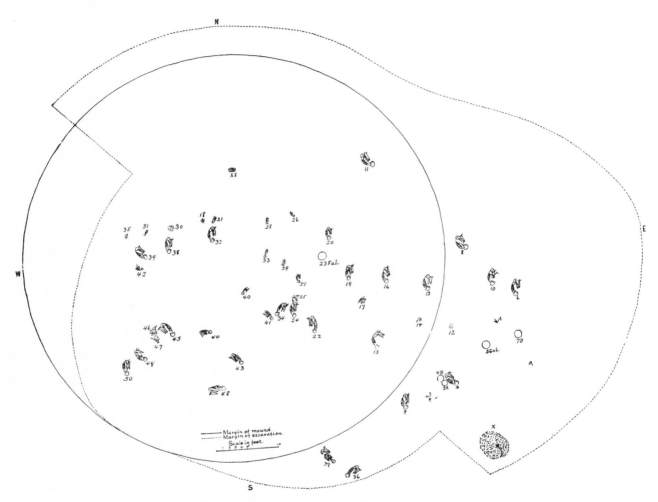

Fig. 49.—Diagram of mound near South-end Settlement.

about twenty—some associated with pink sand, were met with, also several solitary skulls very badly decayed.

A chert arrowhead lay loose in the sand and another was found unassociated with a cranium. A piercing implement of bone, of the ordinary type, lay with calcined remains.

About 100 yards northwest of the mound just described was a small one, intact as to previous investigation but much reduced in height by the plow. Its altitude was 22 inches; its diameter of base, 30 feet. It was totally demolished, being dug through at a depth considerably lower than the level of the surrounding territory.

Human remains were met with at eight points, some at a depth of 3 feet. At one point was a solitary skull unaffected by fire. Seven pockets of calcined bones comprised the remainder of the human remains in the mound, with the exception of one femur showing no trace of fire, which lay immediately beneath one of the masses of calcined bones.

Several local streaks of bright sand colored with hematite were present in the mound and scarlet sand was occasionally with human remains.

Five or six sheets of mica, with one of the pockets of burnt bones, were the only artifacts present in the mound.

St. Catherine's Island, Liberty County. Mound near South-end Settlement.

About three-quarters of one mile in a northerly direction from the South-end Settlement, in a field long under cultivation in former times but fallow at the time of our visit, was a rather symmetrical rounded mound 3 feet in height and 68 feet across the base, the outline of which was almost exactly circular, though, as the reader may see by consulting the diagram (Fig. 49), burials and artifacts were by no means included beneath the slope of the mound but extended to the east and south-east in perfectly level ground.

There had been no previous investigation.

The mound was dug through, including considerable outlying territory. Throughout the mound proper there ran, commencing at the beginning of what we took to be the original slope (for the external lower portions of the rise seemed to have been ploughed down from above), a dark band not on one level, as in many mounds we have investigated, but extremely irregular, often continuing a considerable distance into the pits which were numerous in certain portions of the mound. In default of a better theory, we believe that these pits were dug and but partly filled previous to the erection of the mound; that the field continued to be a dwelling site, and that the deposit of offal, debris, charcoal and the like, created a black surface layer in the depressions as well as on the level ground.

The mound was composed of dark loamy sand resting upon undisturbed yellow sand. Local layers of oyster shells were present, and the central portion of the mound was made up of a deposit of oyster shells about 2 feet thick—not midden refuse but loose as though brought there at one time and deposited. This deposit extended in some directions about 10 feet from the center, in others 20 feet, while to the N. W. it continued, tapering off in thickness, to the very verge of the mound. From the highest point of the mound to the level of the black base-line, was a perpendicular distance of just 3 feet.

The following is a detailed description of burials to be used in connection with the diagram.

Burial No. 1, 51 feet, E. S. E., from the center of the mound proper, beneath perfectly level ground, lying at the bottom of a pit, 2.5 feet from the surface, were fragments of a human skull badly decayed.

Burial No. 2, 42 feet, S. E. by E., on undisturbed sand, at the bottom of a pit of undetermined limits, 32 inches from the surface, was the skeleton of an adult, much decayed, apparently flexed on the right side, heading S. E.   With the bones were: a pebble-hammer; a lot of red paint made from red oxide of iron, as was shown by chemical determination; a flake of chert; a small bit of a soapstone pot and twenty-three quartz pebbles each about the size of a pea, lying closely together —the remains of a rattle.

Burial No. 3, Vessel A.   To the S. W. of Burial No. 2, in contact with its base, resting on undisturbed sand, 36 inches from the surface, entirely intact, was a vessel of the ordinary type (see introductory remarks as to this type at the commencement of this Report).   Height, 15.5 inches; maximum diameter of body, 11.5 inches; diameter of mouth, 13.5 inches.   Within this vessel, which was unprotected by an imposed vessel or by fragments, were a number of human bones of an adult, probably representing an entire skeleton.   Long bones together were upright against the side, while the cranium lay face down with ribs and other bones beneath, as shown sectionally in the frontispiece, in which, however, all the long bones are not distinguishable, certain ones being in rear of others.   The skull and long bones are represented exactly as found, never, in fact, having been removed from the vessel, but treated in place with numerous coats of shellac to impart durability.   The fragmentary smaller bones and the beads were removed with the sand and subsequently replaced, but not exactly in their former position.   Most of the beads lay on top of the mass of bones at the base of the vessel.

Burial No. 4, Vessel B.   To the north of, and in contact with, Vessel A, was an imperforate one of similar type somewhat crushed.   Within it were the bones of an adult, not in anatomical order and very much decayed.   The vessel was sent to the Ontario Archæological Museum.

Burial No. 5, Vessels Ca., b., 44 feet E. S. E., in a pit of uncertain limits, having its base 3.5 feet from the surface and extending 22 inches into undisturbed sand, was a vessel of the ordinary type, imperforate as to the base, having the rim badly crushed.   It contained the much decayed bones of an adult, probably male, not in anatomical order, with 34 large shell beads.   Capping this vessel, inverted, was an imperforate bowl, undecorated save for an encircling row of knobs some distance apart, about 1.5 inches below the rim.   The material, gritty ware, was fairly good in this case and had resisted pressure with the exception of a part of the rim and a portion below it, which were recovered.   Diameter of body, 16 inches; of mouth, 14.5 inches; height, 9.5 inches.   Ca. and Cb. were sent to the Peabody Museum, Cambridge, Mass., where they have been carefully put together.

Burial No. 6, 46 feet E. by S. was a pit 4.5 feet long, having its base 38 inches from the surface.   It extended 17 inches into undisturbed sand and was filled with oyster shells and black loam apparently from a local superficial layer.   On the base was a skeleton, flexed on the right side, head S.

Burial No. 7; Vessel D., 48 feet E. S. E., just beneath the surface, upright, with the rim and upper portion broken by the plow, was a vessel of the ordinary type, having a large intentional perforation of the base. The vessel was partly filled with oyster shells, though none was present on the surface at that part of the mound. On the base of the vessel was the skeleton of a child three or four years of age, flexed to such an extent that the head was almost in contact with the legs.

X. 55 feet S. E., a layer of charcoal and sand, the upper margin 6 inches below the surface, 4 inches thick at the start and 4 feet 2 inches across. It extended inward 5 feet 3 inches, tapering off somewhat in thickness.

Burial No. 8, 38 feet E., in the bottom of a small pit, 26 inches from the surface and extending into undisturbed sand, was the skeleton of an aged female, flexed on the right side, head S. E.

Vessel E, 39 feet S. E. by E., 2.5 feet from the surface, was an imperforate undecorated boat-shaped vessel, entirely intact. At either end was a small perforation for suspension. This vessel apparently contained no remains of any sort, nor did it seem to be in the vicinity of a burial. Maximum diameter of mouth and length, each 7 inches; maximum diameter of body, 9 inches; minimum diameter of mouth, 4.1 inches; minimum diameter of body, 5.3 inches; height, 4 inches.

Burial No. 9, 38 feet S. E., on undisturbed sand, on the side of a large pit of undetermined limits, was a skeleton of uncertain sex, much decayed, flexed on the right side, head S.

Burial No. 10, 42 feet E. by S. This skeleton of a female, flexed on the right side, head S., lay on undisturbed sand, 1.5 feet down. Oyster shells from the surface lay with the loam around it. Beneath the chin was a shell pin of ordinary type.

Burial No. 11, 27 feet N. E. by E., on the bottom of a pit, 3 feet 9 inches from the surface, 2 feet of which was into undisturbed sand, and having a diameter of 5.5 feet where it entered the undisturbed sand, was a badly decayed skeleton, probably male, flexed on the right side, head S. E.

Burial No. 12, 37 feet E. S. E., 2 feet 8 inches down, just above the bottom of the pit, were traces of bones in powder. Three bits of chert and several small flakes of mica lay with them.

XX. 15 feet N., a pocket of charcoal in the sand, 15 inches across at the start and 3 inches thick, tapering into the mound 9 inches.

Burial No. 13, 32 feet E. by S., a flexed skeleton of a female, on the right side, head S., let into undisturbed sand, 2 feet from the surface.

Burial No. 14, 32 feet E. S. E., 1 foot 6 inches from the surface, were a few crumbling fragments of bone, having with them two small polished chisels of stone; one graceful arrow point of chert and a nest of small pebbles formerly belonging to a rattle.

Burial No. 15, 27 feet S. E. by E., 2.5 feet from the surface, on the bottom of a pit let 8 inches into undisturbed sand, was the skeleton of a male, on the right side, partly flexed, the knees being at right angles to the body, head S. With the remains were: a nest of small pebbles, several small fragments of a soapstone vessel and three undecorated earthenware tobacco pipes of ordinary type, one against the skull, the others loose in the sand, 13 inches and 15 inches, respectively, above the

10 JOURN. A. N. S. PHILA., VOL. XI.

bones. One was partly filled with carbonized tobacco. These two pipes may have been contributions from bystanders during the filling of the grave.

Burial No. 16, 25 feet E. by S., a grave 5.5 feet long, extending 2 feet to undisturbed sand. On the bottom, 3 feet 9 inches from the surface, was a skeleton of a male, on the right side, head S. With it were: a small undecorated tobacco pipe of earthenware; a discoidal stone about 2 inches in diameter and 1 inch in thickness and a small ball of resinous material.

Burial No. 17, 22 feet E. S. E., 28 inches down, lying on the line of undisturbed sand, with no especial grave discernible but in generally disturbed material, was a pile of human bones in disorder with long bones on top of, and along side, the skull.

Burial No. 18, 8 feet N. W. by N., 4 feet down, in a small pocket were the greatly decayed remains of a very young infant, so crushed together that no determination as to position was possible. Associated were a number of shell beads.

Burial No. 19, 19 feet E. by S. A grave extending 1 foot 10 inches into undisturbed sand, the base 3 feet 7 inches from the surface, with a maximum diameter of 6.5 feet. On the bottom was the skeleton of a female, flexed on the right side, head S. On the trunk was hematite. Under the arm was a number of beads roughly wrought from sections of columellæ, each about 1 inch in length.

Burial No. 20, 16 feet E. by N., 4 feet 10 inches from the surface, on the bottom of a grave 6 feet across where it entered undisturbed sand into which it extended 2 feet 8 inches, was the skeleton of a child about 6 years of age, flexed on the right side, head S.

Burial No. 21, 7 feet N. N. W. A grave having its base 2.feet 3 inches from the surface, the lower 1 foot extending into a layer of oyster shells. On the bottom of the grave, which had a length of 22 inches, was the skeleton of an infant, badly crushed, with the head S. W. Shell beads were in association.

Burial No. 22, 17 feet S. E., on the base of a grave, 2.5 feet from the surface and extending about 1 foot 9 inches into undisturbed sand, was the skeleton of a male, flexed on the left side, head S. With it were large shell beads and an undecorated earthenware tobacco pipe of ordinary type lying near the skull.

Burial No. 23, Vessel Fa., b. Let into the yellow sand, with its base 3 feet 4 inches from the surface, was a burial jar (Fa.) of the usual type, imperforate, upright and very badly crushed. Within it were bones, probably belonging to a female, the long bones on end, side by side, near the skull, the other bones beneath. This jar, about 18 inches high, had been capped by an inverted bowl (Fb.) of black ware, with a decoration of small knobs, similar to the one previously referred to. This bowl, also crushed, was sent with the other vessel to the Museum of Natural History, New York.

Burial No. 24, 13 feet S. E., 3 feet from the surface, in a pit of undetermined limits, was a skeleton of a female, flexed on the right side, head S.

Burial No. 25, disturbed by the burial of No. 24, a little to the north of it on the same level, was the skeleton of a child, interred with an imperforate shell drinking cup, into which certain of the bones had been crushed.

Burial No. 26, 12 feet N. E. by E., was the skeleton of an infant, 1 foot 9 inches down, head S. E. The bones were too badly crushed for determination as to position, etc.

Burial No. 27, 11 feet E. S. E., on the bottom of a pit having a diameter of 2.5 feet where it entered the clear yellow sand into which it extended 1 foot 2 inches, and 3 feet 10 inches from the surface, was the skeleton of a child about three years of age, flexed on the right side, head S.

Burial No. 28, 8 feet N. E., 4 feet 10 inches down, let 14 inches into undisturbed sand, was an infant's skeleton somewhat disturbed, probably by the digger.

Burial No. 29, 8 feet E. by S. was another badly-decayed skeleton of an infant, disturbed in excavation. It lay 5 feet 3 inches from the surface in a deep pit.

Burial No. 30, 12 feet W. N. W., in the superficial layer of oyster shells, somewhat disturbed by the plow, was a deposit of calcined fragments of human bones, the only evidence of the practice of cremation present in the mound. Scattered throughout the deposit were numerous shell beads of different sizes, including thirteen fine specimens some over 1.5 inches in length, probably wrought from columellæ of the conch (*Fulgur*). These beads were in a much better state of preservation than others in the mound, which we attribute to their being among oyster shells. Above the deposit was an inverted, imperforate drinking cup of shell (*Fulgur perversum*) and on the outer edge a discoidal stone of about 2 inches diameter.

Burial No. 31, 15 feet W. N. W., an infant's skeleton much decayed, 3 feet 3 inches from the surface in a small pit extending 1 foot 3 inches below the base of the mound.

Burial No. 32, N. W. by N., 5 feet, lying on the undisturbed sand, 5 feet from the surface, at one end of a large pit running 26 inches beneath the base, was the skeleton of a male, flexed on the right side, head S.

Burial No. 33, 5 feet E, in a pit, 5 feet from the surface, were the badly-decayed remnants of the skeleton of a child. Lumps of charcoal lay near by.

Burial No. 34, 12 feet S. E., a skeleton of a female, flexed on right side, heading S. W., in a pit, 3.5 feet from the surface.

Burial No. 35, 18 feet W. N. W., a skeleton of an infant, just beneath the surface, disturbed by the plow. A shell pin was in association.

Burial No. 36, 41 feet S. S. E., on the bottom of a small pit, 32 inches from the surface, were the remnants of a skeleton in the last stage of decay. Apparently it was flexed on the right side, head S. W.

Burial No. 37, 38 feet S. S. E., a skeleton of a female, with trunk on the back, knees flexed to the right, head S. E.

Burial No. 38, 11 feet W. N. W., a skeleton of a male, on bottom of a pit extending into yellow sand, flexed on the right side, head S.

Burial No. 39, 16 feet W. by N., 3.5 feet down, in a small pit was the skeleton of a female, flexed on the right side, head S. E.

Burial No. 40, 6 feet S. by E., in a pit, 4 feet 10 inches down, was the skeleton of a child, head S. W., too much decayed for exact determination as to position, but a flexed burial on the right side was indicated. At the neck were beads of shell.

Burial No. 41, 12 feet S. E. by S., 3.5 feet down, with the skull resting on the mouth of an imperforate shell drinking cup, was the skeleton of a child from six to seven years of age, flexed on the left side, the head S. E. Small shell beads were at the neck and larger ones at the wrist.

Burial No. 42, 16 feet W., on the base, flexed on the right side, heading E., was the skeleton of an infant about 2 years old. Shell beads were on the legs and neck, a shell pin at the back of the head and a shell drinking cup nearby.

Burial No. 43, 18 feet S, 2 feet 8 inches down, in a large pit was the skeleton of a female, flexed on the left side, head S. E.

Fig. 50.—Pendant of soapstone. Mound near South-end Settlement. (Full size.)

Burial No. 44, 13 feet S. S. W., in a pit extending 1 foot into undisturbed sand, 3.5 feet from the surface, was the skeleton of a child about 5 years of age, flexed on the left side, head E. In association were: shell beads; two fragments of soapstone, from a pot or pots, one wrought into a rude pendant, roughly incised and grooved (Fig. 50); lumps of hematite; a rough arrowpoint; a bone piercing implement, badly decayed.

Burial No. 45, 16 feet S. W., in a pit, 4.5 feet from the surface, was the skeleton of a male, flexed on the left side, head S. E. This pit was filled with a mixture of oyster shells and surface loam.

Burial No. 46, in the same pit, southwest of, and in contact with, No. 45, on the same plane, was a number of bones not in anatomical order, probably belonging to a female. A femur lay partly on the skull, while some of the long bones were out of position and reversed.

Burial No. 47. In contact with No. 46 were a cranium, a femur and a humerus, belonging to a male.

Burial No. 48, 22 feet S. by W., a skeleton badly decayed on the bottom of a pit, 4.5 feet from the surface, heading E. As nearly as could be made out, the skeleton was flexed on the left side.

Burial No. 49, 22 feet S. W., a skeleton of a female on the bottom of a large pit, 3 feet 8 inches down, flexed on the right side, head S. E. Immediately above the bones was a thin local layer of oyster shells.

Burial No. 50, 26 feet S. W., a skeleton of a female, flexed on the right side, head S., on the bottom of a pit, 3 feet 3 inches from the surface.

A number of sherds, undecorated, cord-marked, and adorned with a complicated stamp, were met with throughout the mound.

Among the oyster shells was a piercing implement of bone.

Loose in the sand were several fragments of pebble-hammers and one rude arrowhead of quartz.

In caved sand, probably from a skeleton, were three small polished stone chisels.

In the mound near the South-end Settlement we note the absence of a great central pit and the presence of cremation at but one point; also that the great majority of burials were flexed on the right side and headed in a southerly direction, quite in keeping with the usual custom. All urn-burials of uncremated remains, with but one exception, were of adults, coinciding with the custom as practised on Sapelo Island. On the other hand, the reader will recall that infants alone were thus buried at Creighton Island, and will see further on the urn-burial of infants at Ossabaw Island.

St. Catherine's Island, Liberty County. Mound near Middle Settlement.

In a large field formerly under cultivation, but at present covered with scrub and timber of small size, about one-half mile in a southwesterly direction from the Middle Settlement, is a mound which has been ploughed over in former times and has been dug into to a considerable extent. Its height is 5 feet; the diameter of its base, 54 feet. It was trenched in various directions, and portions of the center were dug out without result. It was composed of yellowish-brown sand, unstratified, and may have been used for domiciliary purposes.

St. Catherine's Island, Liberty County. Mound in King's New Ground Field.

This mound, or what remained of it after years of cultivation, lay in a field within sight of the ocean, about one mile and three-quarters in a southeasterly direction from the main landing at St. Catherine's Island. Numerous low shell deposits were in the vicinity, though on the surface of the mound were scattered oyster shells only.

The mound had a height of 22 inches above the general level, which altitude agreed with observations taken at the completion of a cross-section.

Beginning far out in the level ground, trenches were run in, in all directions, until evidence of disturbance in the sand was met with. The usual great outlying pits, filled with rich, black loam, were present, but containing no burials, so far as our excavations went.

Through a point taken as the center of the mound proper, a straight line was drawn extending 51 feet to the northwest and 45 feet to the southeast. Connecting these two terminal points an irregular semi-circumference was taken, having a maximum distance from the center of 57 feet, as shown in diagram (Fig. 51), which included, it is believed, all the outlying pits and burials belonging to the southern and western half of the mound. This portion was carefully dug through to a depth at times of over 6 feet. The eastern and northern parts of the mound were not investigated. Throughout portions of the mound ran a black band from 6 inches to 1 foot in thickness, whose upper surface, as a rule, agreed with the general level of the field. But this band was sometimes absent over undisturbed sand, while, on the other hand, it often seemed thicker and darker over pits and graves. We have no solution to offer for this.

Though the usual great central pit was represented in this mound by a very moderate deposit of bones, yet in no other mound have we found so many grave-pits of such size as in this one.

Beginning 40 feet W. S. W., from the center, was a pit extending in 15 feet and having a breadth of 25 feet[1] and a maximum depth of about 6 feet. In this grave-pit were Burials Nos. 1, 7, 8, 12, 13, 15 and 22. The black band of which we have spoken was distinctly present above this entire pit at a depth of about 2 feet below the surface of the mound, while at either side at the same level, over undisturbed sand, it was entirely wanting for some distance.

There were present a few local layers of oyster shells and one mainly of fresh-water mussel shells (X), 13 inches by 20 inches by 10 inches thick. Its upper margin was 9 inches below the surface.

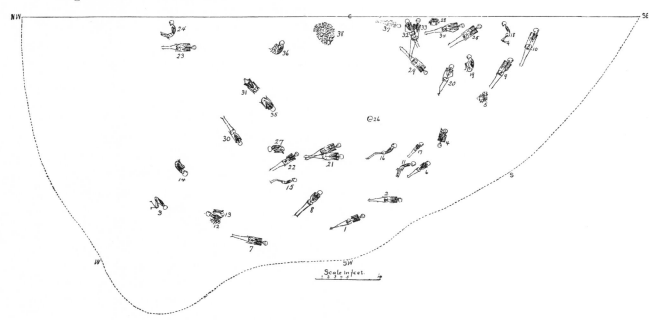

Fig. 51.—Diagram of one-half of mound in King's New Ground Field.

Sherds found by us were coarse and either undecorated or cord-marked. The complicated stamp was absent.

We give detailed descriptions of burials in connection with the diagram, omitting, as a rule, the size of pits :—

Burial No. 1, 33 feet S. W. from the center, 2.5 feet down, skeleton of female, head E. S. E., at full length on back, 5 feet 10 inches as it lay with feet partly extended.[2] Right humerus parallel to body, with forearm up and across chest. Left humerus along trunk, with left forearm flexed upward with hand to shoulder. Right ankle crossing left.

[1] These and kindred measurements are, of course, approximate.
[2] These measurements of skeletons at length do not indicate individuals of unusual size. The bones were not so closely in contact as in life, the shifting of the sand causing more or less separation.

Burial No. 2, 30 feet S. W. by S., 2 feet 8 inches down, skeleton of female at full length on back, head S. E., face to the right, 5 feet 4 inches as it lay with feet partly extended. Right arm and forearm parallel to body. Left upper arm along body with forearm crossing to pelvis. A few long bones lay loose in the sand about 1 foot above this burial.

Burial No. 3, 42 feet W., 2 feet 9 inches down, skeleton of aged male, head S., in semi-reclining position on left side. Incisor stumps only remaining in lower jaw. Alveolar process of other teeth absorbed. This especially marked in upper jaw. Signs of inflammatory disease in tibia, fibula and clavicle.

Burial No. 4, 25 feet S. by W., 2 feet down, head W. S. W., trunk on back, legs drawn up, knees somewhat to the left. A few bits of earthenware, perhaps by accident, lay with the bones.

Burial No. 5, 25 feet S. by E., 4 feet 4 inches to the bottom of a pit filled with black loam and oyster shells, extending 2 feet 6 inches into undisturbed yellow sand. Over this pit the black band continued, though dipping somewhat. Three feet 8 inches down in this grave was a bunched burial, probably of a male. Long bones were on either side of the skull, while two clavicles, together, lay somewhat apart from it. Certain bones were missing. The spinal column and ribs were in order, indicating partial union by ligaments. One ulna and one clavicle sent to Army Medical Museum, Washington, D. C., had false joints, results of former fractures.

Burial No. 6, 27 feet S. S. W., 3 feet 10 inches down, skeleton of a child between 8 and 10 years old, at length on face, chin toward left shoulder, 4 feet 4 inches as it lay, with feet extended, head E. by S. Both upper arms parallel to body; right forearm crossing under pelvis; left forearm not found, probably thrown back by digger.

Burial No. 7, 39 feet W. S. W., 4 feet 2 inches down, skeleton of female at full length on back, head S. E. by S., 5 feet 8 inches from head to heel as it lay. Upper extremities parallel to body.

Burial No. 8, 33 feet S. W. by W., 3 feet 10 inches down, skeleton of male at full length, face down, head E., 5 feet 6 inches from head to foot. Right and left arms parallel to body, forearms passing under pelvis.

Burial No. 9, 25 feet S. S. E., 4 feet 8 inches down, skeleton of male at full length on back, 5 feet 10 inches long with feet extended, head E. by N., chin to left shoulder. Right upper extremity along side of body. Left upper arm along thorax with forearm crossing to pelvis.

Loose in the sand, about 6 inches above No. 9, was the femur of an adult.

Burial No. 10, 28 feet S. E. by S., 6.5 feet down, on the bottom of a pit, 7 feet by 10 feet and extending 2 feet 10 inches into undisturbed sand, was a skeleton of a male at full length on the back, measuring 6 feet 6 inches as it lay, with feet extended, head E. N. E., chin turned toward left shoulder. Arms parallel to body. Sand colored with hematite lay near the skull. The black basal band lay above this pit.

Burial No. 11, at the same level, but a little farther in than skeleton No. 6, was a female skeleton on the left side, with the thighs partially, and the legs completely, flexed. The right upper extremity was parallel to the body, the left was down and under. The skeleton measured 3 feet 10 inches as it lay.

Burial No. 12, 38 feet W. by S., 5 feet down, a number of human bones not in anatomical order.

Burial No. 13, just below No. 12, on the bottom of the great pit, lying on undisturbed sand, was an ordinary flexed burial of uncertain sex, on the left side, head N. W., 5 feet 9 inches down.

Burial No. 14, 36 feet W., 2 feet 4 inches down, on the bottom of a well-defined pit apparently dug from the surface and filled with black loam and oyster shells, though oyster shells on the surface at the time of opening the mound were few and scattering, was a flexed burial of a male on the right side, head S. S. W.

Burial No. 15, 29 feet W. S. W., 4 feet 5 inches down, the skeleton of a child, about 10 or 11 years old, measuring 4 feet 1 inch as it lay, on the right side, the thighs somewhat drawn up, the knees bent, head E. S. E. Right upper extremity along body, the left crossing to pelvis.

Burial No. 16, 23 feet S. W. by S., 2 feet 9 inches down, measuring 5 feet 3 inches as it lay, with feet partly extended, was the skeleton of a woman on the right side with thighs bent slightly forward, legs down from thighs. Right upper arm a little out from body, with forearm returning to trunk. Left upper arm parallel to body, with forearm crossing the pelvis. Head E. by S.

Burial No. 17, 24 feet S. S. W., 5 feet down, skeleton of a child about 5 years old, full length on back, chin toward left shoulder, measuring 3 feet 4 inches as it lay, with feet somewhat extended. Right upper arm along chest, forearm removed by digger. Left humerus along chest, forearm crossing to pelvis.

Burial No. 18, 25 feet S. E. by S., 4 feet down, skeleton of female on right side, partly flexed, head N. E. by N. Right upper arm out a little with forearm returning toward pelvis. Left upper arm parallel to body, with forearm crossing to pelvis.

Burial No. 19, 20 feet S. S. E., 3 feet 10 inches down, female flexed on right side, head N. E.

Burial No. 20, 18 feet S. by E., 4 feet down, skeleton of female, full length, face down, measuring 5 feet 3 inches from head to heel, head E. N. E. Right arm akimbo. Left arm parallel to body. Left heel resting on right ankle.

Burial No. 21. 23 feet S. W. by S., 3 feet 8 inches down, were two burials on the same plane, diverging from the knees with the heads 2 feet apart. One, a male, lay at full length on face, and measured 6 feet 3 inches as it lay with feet extended, head S. E. Upper extremities parallel to body. The other, a female, head E. S. E., at full length on back, measured 5 feet 11 inches, with outstretched feet.

Burial No. 22, 28 feet W. S. W., 4 feet 9 inches down, skeleton probably female, full length on back, 5.5 feet long with feet extended, head E. by S. Right upper arm along body with forearm crossing pelvis. Left upper extremity parallel to trunk.

Burial No. 23, 30 feet N. W. by W., 4 feet 9 inches down, skeleton of male, at full length on back, head S. E., 5 feet 4 inches from head to heel. Upper extremities parallel to body.

Burial No. 24, 23 feet N. W., 3 feet 9 inches down, skeleton of female, partially flexed on the right side, with head N. E. by E.; thighs at right angle to body, legs flexed sharply back on them.

Burial No. 25, 19 feet S. E. by S., 5 feet down, skeleton of female, at full length on back, 5 feet 10 inches long with feet outstretched, head E. by S. Upper extremities parallel to body.

Burial No. 26, 17 feet S. W. by S., 2 feet down, beneath the outer margin of a local shell layer, was a skull with the inferior maxilary wanting and a portion of one rib. The local shell layer was 7 inches thick, and extended inward a number of feet.

Burial No. 27, 24 feet W. S. W., 3 feet 4 inches down, skeleton of male, flexed on the right side, measuring 2 feet 10 inches as it lay, the head pushed up at right angle to the body by lack of space in a pit. Head N. W. On the glabella was the mark of a severe blow.

Burial No. 28, 13 feet S. E. by S., skeleton of uncertain sex, 2.5 feet down, in a sort of sitting position, facing S. W.

Burial No. 29, 15 feet S. by E., 4 feet down, skeleton of female, at full length on back, head S., arms parallel with body, measuring 6 feet as it lay, the feet fully extended.

Burial No. 30, 26 feet W., 4 feet down, skeleton of female, at full length on face, 5 feet 2 inches from head to heel; head S. by W. Right upper extremity parallel to body. Left humerus parallel, forearm crossing to pelvis.

Burial No. 31, 19 feet W. by N., 1 foot 6 inches down, flexed skeleton of female, in crouching position, head N., face looking upward.

Burial No. 32, 11 feet S. S. E., skeleton of female, at full length, face down, head N. N. E. Legs and feet cut off by digger. Right upper extremity along body. Left humerus a little out with forearm crossing under pelvis.

Burial No. 33, 3 feet below No. 32. Skeleton of female, full length on back, head N. E. by E., 6 feet 6 inches as it lay. Arms parallel to body.

Burial No. 34, 15 feet S. E. by S. Skeleton of female, at full length on back head E. S. E., measuring 6 feet 2 inches, slanting into a pit with the head 1 foot 9 inches below the feet.

Burial No. 35, 19 feet W. Skeleton of male, in crouching position, head S., 1 foot 9 inches down.

Burial No. 36, 18 feet W. N. W., 1 foot 6 inches down, skeleton of adolescent, much flexed on right side, head E. On the skull were eight parallel rows of small shell beads, in close contact. Under the chin were small perforated marine shells (*Olivella*). The epiphyses of this skeleton were unattached. Both humeri showed considerable perforation.

Burial No. 37, 8 feet S. E. by S., skeleton of very young child, at full length, head S. E., too badly crushed for farther determination.   With it was the base of a cord-marked vessel of clay.

Burial No. 38, 6 feet W. by N., at the start just beneath the surface and slanting down to a depth of 1 foot 5 inches, was a confused mass of human bones about 7 inches thick, 4 feet wide and tapering inward a distance of 2 feet 9 inches. At one extremity of this deposit were a few fragments of calcined human bones, so near the surface that probably the major portion had been scattered by cultivation. With this deposit were: hematite; a few shell beads; two small, imperforate clay bowls, the smaller inverted within the larger; and a marine shell (*Pecten nodosus*) in two fragments.

In this mound, so far as investigated, though burials at length predominated, we note a considerable diversity of forms, a contrast to a neighboring mound in the Greenseed Field.

The paucity of artifacts is notable.

ST. CATHERINE'S ISLAND, LIBERTY COUNTY.   MOUND IN THE GREENSEED FIELD.

This mound, in a field long under cultivation, about 1.5 miles in a southerly direction from the main landing, was but little, if any, above the general level.   A few scattered oyster shells were lying upon the surface.   In order to include any possible pit or outlying burial, a circle with a diameter of 84 feet was dug through which included considerably more than that part of the territory devoted to inter ments, the most remote of which proving to be 31 feet from the center.   Evidence of human handiwork was apparent at a considerably greater distance.   As in the case of certain other mounds, a black band, apparently a basal line, was present at places, occasionally cut through by pits, and again following the line of excavation down almost to the upper margin of the bones.

In this mound, which extended some distance below the surface, were no grave-pits let into undisturbed sand and, with two or three exceptions, separate graves in the body of the mound were not determinable.

The mound was composed of yellowish-brown sand with practically no shell except in a central pit, roughly bowl-shaped, having a maximum diameter of about 9 feet.   This shell deposit, beginning less than one foot below the surface, with a thickness of about 18 inches, attained a depth of nearly two feet in the center of the pit, measured from its upper surface to the surface of the mound.   The thickness of the deposit at this point was about 2.5 feet.   Beneath this mass of shell was Burial No. 28, which, with other interments, is shown on the diagram (Fig. 52).

The usual outlying pits, in this case two in number, were present in this mound.   Both were filled with black loam and scattering oyster shells.   One began 42 feet from the center, was 21 feet across and extended inward 18 feet.   Its maximum depth was 3 feet 7 inches.   The second pit began 47 feet out, was 23 feet across and extended inward 15 feet.   Its average depth coincided with that of the other.   As usual, no burials were present in them.

In the sand of the mound were two arrow heads and a number of rude sherds.

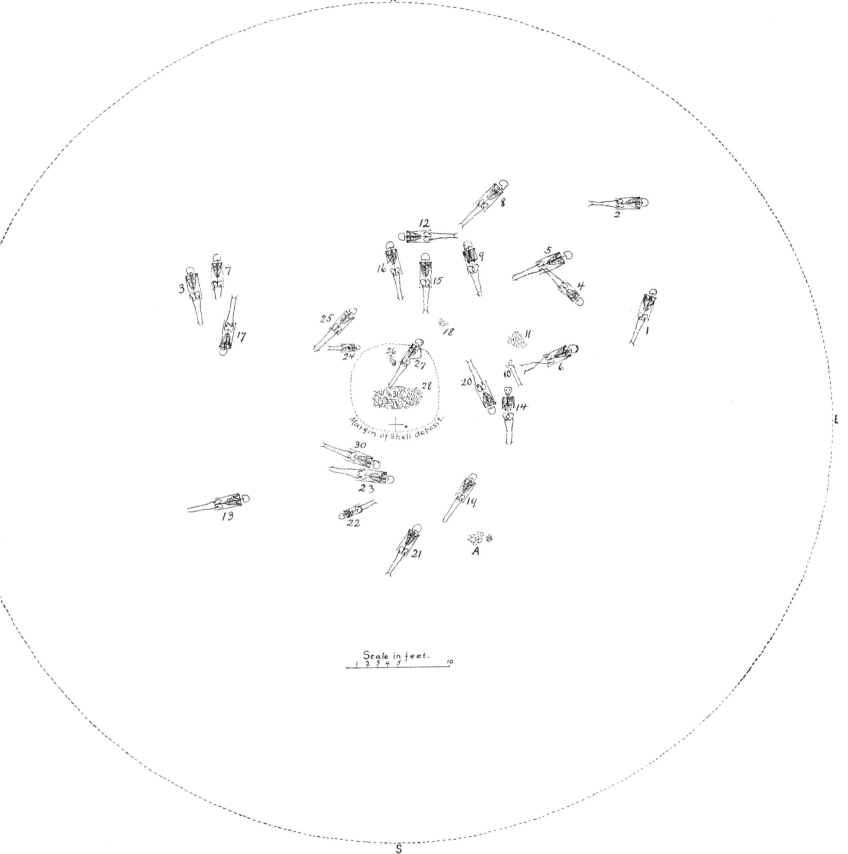

Fig. 52.—Diagram of mound in Greenseed Field.

Two, from one vessel, however, were of good quality. No example of the complicated stamp was met with.

Human remains were encountered at 31 points. Of these, 25 were skeletons from which comparatively full data were obtained. The bones of four infants, badly crushed, were present in addition, and two layers of bones, some calcined, others unaffected by fire.

Of the 25 skeletons: 7 were of males; 5 were of females; 8 were uncertain; 2 were of adolescents; 2 were of children; while the skeleton of one adult was not determined owing to decay.

Twenty-three lay full length, face down, while two lay at full length on the back. The faces of the prone skeletons occasionally were turned to the side. As a rule the upper extremities were parallel to the body.

There seems to be no uniformity of direction in which the skeletons lay. The upper portion of one skeleton was missing through aboriginal disturbance. The other 24 headed as follows: E., 2; E. by N., 1; E. N. E., 2; N. E. by E., 1; N. E., 2; N. E. by N., 2; N. N. E., 1; N., 3; N. by W., 3; W., 1; W. S. W., 1; S. by W., 1; S. S. E., 1; S. E., 1; E. S. E., 1; E. by S., 1.

Burial No. 11, 15 feet N. E. by E., 3 feet 3 inches down, was a layer of calcined fragments of human bones, 23 inches across at the start and 6 inches thick. Eight inches in it had tapered to a width of 16 inches, though keeping the same thickness. It converged and disappeared 15 inches from the start. Uncremated bones were mingled throughout.

Burial No. 28. On the undisturbed yellow sand beneath the central shell deposit was a layer of bones of numerous individuals, inextricably mixed, having a thickness of about 8 inches. It extended in 4 feet 9 inches, and was about 28 inches across. At the western extremity were a few fragments of calcined bones and numbers of tubular shell beads, the largest 2 inches in length. In addition, were a piercing implement of bone, and several considerable portions of lower jaws of large carnivores, having their lower parts, including much of the roots of the teeth, ground away, thus widening and squaring the bases, as we have already described in this Report, and shall have occasion to refer to again in relation to specimens from a mound on Ossabaw Island. Professor Putnam informs us that jaws similarly treated—human and of lower animals—from the mounds of Ohio are in the Peabody Museum, Cambridge, Mass.[1]

It has been suggested that this method of treatment originated in a desire to loosen the teeth to facilitate extraction, but this seems hardly likely, for, as a rule, teeth treated this way are present in the jaws when found, and we have never seen single teeth pierced for suspension, whose bases showed evidence of grinding. Jaws treated in this way have been considered by some to have been used as ornaments.

There is in the collection of the Academy of Natural Sciences a rough wooden effigy or mask, from Alaska, representing the head of a dog or of a wolf. Set in this mask are jaws imitated in bone, squared off at the base somewhat like the

[1] See also "Primitive Man in Ohio," Moorehead, page 227, et seq.

jaws from the mounds, and, as the wide-spread prevalence of aboriginal customs is well known, we think it not unlikely that the jaws from the mounds, in former times, saw service in masks of wood, which have disappeared through decay. Professor Cushing lately found in Florida numbers of wooden masks with other aboriginal articles of wood preserved beneath mud, and it is our opinion that the aborigines of the sand mounds inhumed numbers of articles of wood which have not lasted until the present time. In fact, our own researches in Florida mounds have brought to light wood preserved by contact with copper.

A few beads, hematite and fragments of uninteresting vessels, represented all additional articles met with in the mound.

St. Catherine's Island, Liberty County. Mound near the Light-house.

In the border of the woods, in view of the sea, about one-half mile in a southeasterly direction from the landing, near the site of the projected light-house, was a fairly symmetrical mound entirely of sand, having a height of 3 feet, a diameter at base of 56 feet.

Much of the mound was dug through. At places were bits of decayed human bones near the surface, and, near the center, just below the surface, a pocket of calcined fragments of human bones belonging to at least two adults and one adolescent.

About 6 feet from the center, in a grave beneath the base, was a badly-decayed skeleton on its back with knees flexed against the thighs. Near it lay another.

One arrowhead of chert lay loose in the sand.

St. Catherine's Island, Liberty County. Low Mounds at the North-end.

In pine woods, about 1 mile in an easterly direction from the main landing are two mounds about 50 yards apart, the larger having a diameter of 42 feet, a height of 3 feet; the smaller, a diameter of 36 feet, a height of 14 inches. There had been no previous examination. Each of these mounds was excavated as to the central portions and was thoroughly trenched. A few fragments of a decaying human cranium were met with in the smaller mound, while the investigation of the larger was without result.

In the vicinity of these mounds was a somewhat larger one which, being a valued land mark, we did not touch.

Careful attention was paid to numerous low shell-heaps studding the island of St. Catherine's. In some, results were negative, while from others came sherds incised and with the complicated stamped decoration in use in the best class of the burial mounds of the coast.

Ossabaw Island, Bryan County. Middle Settlement. Mound A.

About half way from either extremity of the western side of Ossabaw Island, on a small creek about five miles from the main channel, are a few cabins tenanted exclusively by colored people, and known as the Middle Settlement.

Near this settlement are a number of aboriginal mounds on property controlled by Mr. C. H. Harper of Rome, Georgia.

In a field long under cultivation, at the southern outskirt of the settlement, was a low mound, probably much reduced in height by the plow, which, in addition, had been impaired for complete archæological investigation by the hauling away of a considerable quantity of oyster shells from the central portion. The depression thus made was clearly apparent, and nowhere extended through the layer of oyster shells with which all but the marginal portion of the mound was covered. However, as no artifacts or burials were found by us entirely in the shell layer, and as the marginal portion of the mound seemed to be intact, it would appear that no material injury had been done. Nevertheless, the colored man who had superintended the removal of the shell previous to our work, referred to skeletons and earthenware pots containing bones, found by him, so the result of our investigation must not be regarded as complete.

The mound was dug through at a depth much below the general level, during the latter part of November, 1896.

The mound, with a height of 18 inches and a diameter of base of about 45 feet, was composed of a rich loamy sand of a dark brown color, extending much below the level of the surrounding territory to undisturbed bright yellow sand. There was no mistaking the artificial portion of the mound. The thickness of the highest remaining part was 28 inches, or 18 inches above the general level and 10 inches below it. The deposit of oyster shells, to which reference has been made, was of irregular thickness, averaging, perhaps, 16 inches. Throughout this interesting mound were great numbers of sherds and many vessels of earthenware of poor material—clay mixed with coarse sand—gritty ware, as it is called. Owing to the inferiority of the material comparatively few were recovered in good condition though nearly all had been interred apparently intact—save perforation of the base in some cases—and not broken or with essential portions missing, as they were often buried by the thrifty Florida Indians. The ordinary form of mortuary ware encountered in this mound had the rounded base and almost cylindrical body contracted slightly at the neck beneath a flaring rim, often with a beaded margin, to which we have often referred as the ordinary type.

Besides numerous sherds there were found in the mound, loose in the sand, two large beads of shell, one pebble-hammer and a mass of stone about two-thirds the size of a clenched fist, probably a portion of a hammer-stone.

We proceed to a detailed description in conjunction with the diagram (Fig. 53).

Burial No. 1, 24 feet S. of a point supposed to occupy a central position on the surface of the mound, 1 foot from the surface, was the skeleton of a child about 5 years of age, head E.

Burial No. 2, 22 feet S. by E., skeleton of a female, head S., cranial sutures open, well defined Inca bone. Cranium preserved in good condition (A. N. S. Cat. No. 2,164). Body on back with lower extremities flexed to the right. A small layer of charcoal, with minute fragments of calcined bones intermingled, lay over the lower portion of the trunk. This skeleton was 1 foot 10 inches from the surface.

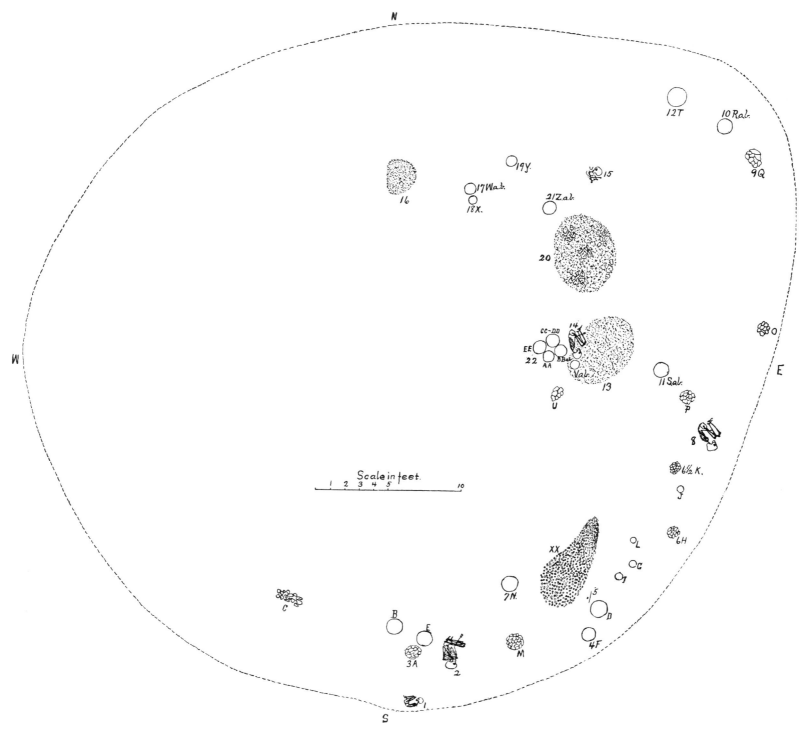

Fig. 53.—Diagram of Mound A.

Burial No. 3, Vessel A, 21 feet S., 1 foot from the surface to its upper margin, upright, as were all the mortuary vessels in this mound, was a bowl of about four gallons capacity, crushed into fragments. The vessel, imperforate, was filled with sand. On its base was the skeleton, or parts of the skeleton, of a child about six years of age, unaffected by fire, which apparently had been doubled and thrust in. The pelvis and bones of one leg were not discovered.

Vessel B, 19 feet S. Just below the surface was a vessel of the ordinary type, having an intentionally-made perforation in the base. No covering protected the vessel and no bones or remnants of bone were discovered, though beyond question, in our opinion, the skeletal remains of a small infant had disappeared through decay.

Vessel C, 18 feet W. of S.[1] About 1 foot from the surface was a layer about 2 feet long, composed of scattered fragments of large vessels.

Vessel D, 23 feet S. E., 19 inches down (all measurements of depth in our account of this mound are given to the upper margin of objects), was a vessel of the ordinary type though with unusually distinct decoration. Its base had been intentionally perforated. Portions crushed from the rim have been, with one small exception, recovered and fastened in place. No skeletal remains were found in the sand with which this vessel was filled, and doubtless here again the work of decay had been complete. Approximate measurements: height, 17 inches; diameter of mouth, 14 inches; maximum diameter of body, 12 inches (Plate IX).

Vessel E, 20 feet S., 20 inches from the surface. This vessel is not farther referred to in our notes and was probably in a very fragmentary condition.

Burial No. 4, Vessel F, 24 feet S. E., vessel of the ordinary type, 12 inches from the surface, containing on the bottom, which was perforated, the bones of a child, in no apparent order and greatly decayed. This vessel was badly broken. Nearby in the sand was a small chisel of polished volcanic rock—*Dolerite* or *Diorite*.

Burial No. 5, just north of Vessel D, loose in the sand, were a patella and a fibula of an adult.

Vessel G, 22 feet S. E. A globular vessel of about 1 gallon capacity, having the bottom knocked out. Incised decoration surrounds the upper portion. Parts of the rim are missing.

Burial No. 6, Vessel H, 23 feet E. S. E. A large vessel 16 inches down, crushed into small fragments. With it were a few bits of calcined human remains.

Vessel I, 22 feet S. E. Two feet from the surface was a globular vessel with flaring rim and incised decoration (Plate XIII, Fig. 2). An attempt to knock out the base had involved a part of the side and of the rim. Many portions were missing. Approximate measurements: diameter at mouth, 5.5 inches; maximum diameter, 7 inches; height, 6.5 inches.

Vessel J, 22 feet E. by S., a globular, undecorated, imperforate vessel, 2 feet down. Rim broken off and missing. Maximum diameter, 5 inches.

---

[1] West of south and corresponding terms, though not points of the compass, are used by us to allow a somewhat wide latitude in indicating position on the diagram.

Burial No. 6½, Vessel K, 21 feet E. by S., 2 feet 5 inches down, a vessel crushed to small fragments, among which lay bits of calcined human bones.

Vessel L, 21 feet S. E., 2 feet down, just below a local layer of oyster shells, was an imperforate, undecorated dish, with a maximum diameter of 4.5 inches, a height of 2.1 inches. This little vessel, a flattened cone in shape, was entirely unassociated.

Vessel M, 22 feet S. by E., a large undecorated vessel in small fragments.

Burial No. 7, Vessel N, 18 feet S. by E., a somewhat broken vessel of the usual type, with perforated base, containing the bones of an infant, unaffected by fire, apparently in anatomical order. Just above the skull (the bones lay at the bottom of the vessel) was a large fragment of earthenware not sufficient in size, however, to prevent the entrance of sand. This vessel was sent to the Museum of the University of Pennsylvania.

XX, 21 feet S. E., a layer of oyster shells calcined to a white powder, 3 feet by 7 feet and 4 to 5 inches thick. At one point were bits of charcoal. The outer margin of this layer was 20 inches from the surface. A gradual slope carried its terminal margin to a level 1 foot higher.

Burial No. 8, 23 feet S. of E., skeleton of a young person, flexed on the right side, head S.

Vessel O, 26 feet E., a vessel of the ordinary type, extremely rotten and fragmentary.

Vessel P, 21 feet S. of E., an imperforate vessel of the common type, but of rather better and thicker material than usual, though crushed to fragments. This vessel, which had doubtless held an infant's skeleton (though no remnants were apparent) was capped by a number of large fragments which had formed parts of an undecorated bowl. These, with the fragments of Vessel P, were sent to the Peabody Museum, Cambridge, Mass., where they have been carefully put together.

Burial No. 9, Vessel Q, 29 feet N. E. by E., 1 foot 4 inches from the surface, a vessel of the usual type, imperforate, containing decaying remnants of an infant's skull. The body of the vessel was crushed to small fragments.

Burial No. 10, Vessel Ra, 29 feet N. E. by E., a vessel of the usual type, 18 inches from the surface, 17 inches of which was the unbroken layer of oyster shells. It ran 14 inches into the undisturbed yellow sand (the reader will recall that the depth given is taken from the upper margin), where an excavation had been made to receive it. Its base contained a small, neatly cut perforation large enough to admit the first joint of the little finger. In the sand at the bottom there remained one deciduous tooth.

Above Ra, inverted, was a bowl of black ware (Rb) somewhat broken, the upper part having incised decoration; the lower, intricate stamped decoration (Plate X). Approximate measurements: diameter, 12.75 inches; diameter of opening, 12 inches; height, 5.75 inches.

Burial No. 11, Vessel Sa, 19 feet E., a vessel of the usual type, badly crushed and broken. At the bottom were fragments of human bone so decayed as to

12 JOURN. A. N. S. PHILA., VOL. XI.

resemble sawdust. Two bits, larger than the rest, belonged to a child of tender years. No fire had been used in connection with these remains, and the reader will bear in mind that when cremation had been employed, the fact will be distinctly stated. This vessel, lacking certain portions, was sent to the Davenport Academy of Natural Science, Davenport, Iowa.

Sa was capped by a bowl of black ware (Sb) undecorated, save for an encircling row of projections somewhat below the margin (Plate XI). It was practically intact. Approximate measurements: maximum diameter, 13.75 inches; diameter of aperture, 12.75 inches; height, 6.25 inches. From the upturned base of this bowl to the surface of the mound was a distance of 2 feet 2 inches.

Burial No. 12, Vessel T, 28 feet N. E., 1 foot 5 inches from surface, a vessel of the usual type, almost intact. In the sand at the bottom were minute fragments of bone with two deciduous teeth and the cap of another. A small hole had been knocked through the base. Approximate measurements: height, 18.5 inches; maximum diameter of body, 13.5 inches; diameter at aperture, 16 inches.

Burial No. 13, beginning 14 feet E., just below the surface was a layer of calcined human remains, at first 22 inches wide, gradually increasing to 5 feet. Its thickness, 2 inches at first, was 6 inches at its terminal limit. It extended in toward the center of the mound, a distance of 4.5 feet, where it was 2 feet below the surface. With the fragmentary bones were found two shell pins and one small bead of shell.

Vessel U, 12 feet E., portions of a vessel of black ware, 3 feet from the surface. Its only decoration was a row of knobs around and below the margin.

Vessel Va, 13 feet E., a vessel of the common type, was intact save for two small pieces missing from the rim. In the base was a small perforation, above which was the bottom of a pot tightly fitted in. Upper portions of this pot, which was incomplete, lay within it. Va was capped by large sherds seemingly belonging to one vessel, perhaps placed there in a less fragmentary condition and subsequently crushed by weight of sand. No human remains were found in Va, though there can be but little doubt as to their former presence.

Burial No. 14, in a grave, 3 feet from the surface, 3.5 feet in length, dipping 1 foot into the yellow sand, almost in contact with the vessel Va, which, however, was not within the limits of the grave, was the skeleton of a person about eighteen years of age, with epiphyses of femurs and tibiæ unattached and one wisdom tooth showing. The skeleton lay on the right side, the legs flexed, head S. The cranium (A. N. S. Cat. No. 2,165) was preserved in good condition. Above this grave the layer of oyster shells on the surface was intact.

Burial No. 15, 20 feet N. E., a bunched burial of the bones of a child about 6 years of age, 2 feet from the surface.

Burial No. 16, 12 feet N., a layer of calcined fragments of human bones, 16 inches from the surface. Its maximum thickness was 2 inches; its length, 2.5 feet; its breadth, 2 feet.

Burial No. 17, Vessel Wa, 14 feet N. by E., 1 foot 6 inches from the surface, in the brown sand and just beneath the layer of oyster shells, was a gourd-shaped, undecorated vessel of black ware, intact save for a small crack on the side. This vessel was filled almost to the top with fragments of calcined human bones some of which at least had belonged to adults, and, in common with all we have encountered containing calcined bones, was imperforate as to the base. Approximate measurements: height, 8.5 inches; maximum diameter, 10 inches; diameter of orifice, 5 inches.

Superimposed upon the orifice of Wa, inverted, was a small vessel (Wb), with everted rim somewhat broken, though capable of almost complete restoration.

Burial No. 18, Vessel X, immediately behind Wa, 15 inches from the surface was a vessel of the ordinary type in use for infant inhumation, imperforate, filled to the top with calcined fragments of human bones. Approximate measurements: height, 15 inches; diameter of body, 11 inches; diameter of aperture, 13 inches. This vessel was sent to the Carnegie Museum, Pittsburgh.

Twenty feet E. of N. E., the brown sand of the mound made a dip into the undisturbed yellow sand to a depth of 21 inches. From the level of the yellow sand to the surface of the mound was 27 inches, so that the bottom of this excavation, which was beneath an unbroken layer of oyster shells on the surface, was 4 feet deep. At the very base of the excavation were several good-sized fragments of earthenware but no human remains or anything to suggest a reason for its construction.

Burial No. 19, Vessel Y, 17 feet N. by E., 14 inches from the surface was an imperforate vessel of the usual form with stamped ornamentation on the body but having the constricted portion and the rim undecorated. This vessel, which was filled with fragments of calcined human bones, was crushed to pieces though held in place by sand. It was pieced together with the exception of a few small bits. Approximate measurements: diameter of orifice, 9 inches; of neck, 7 inches; of body, 8 inches; height, 9.5 inches.

Burial No. 20, 13 feet E. N. E., a pocket of fragments of calcined human bones, 5 feet 9 inches by 4 feet 6 inches, from 2 to 5 inches in thickness. With the remains at several points were large pieces of earthenware representing perhaps a fourth of a vessel. They were distinctly not fragments of an entire vessel crushed through pressure.

Burial No. 21, Vessel Za, 16 feet N. E., an imperforate vessel of the common type having a height of about 1 foot, with rim and portions of the body crushed but lying beside it. It was filled with fragments of calcined human bones. Across the opening were large fragments of a portion of another vessel. Za was sent to the Peabody Museum, Cambridge, where it has been almost entirely pieced together.

Burial No. 22. Together, practically in contact, were four cinerary vases each filled to the top with fragments of charred and calcined human bones, with which were numerous shell beads showing no trace of fire, placed in an excavation made in the yellow sand (CC), and filled around with brown sand (BB) to the level of the rims, or rather to where the rims had been previous to breakage, and covered from the tops up with oyster shells (AA), which dipped to the upper margin of the vessels as shown in Fig. 54. These vessels are represented by the following:

Vessel AA (Plate XII), of red ware, imperforate, with upright neck and slightly flaring rim. The usual complicated stamped decoration is present. This

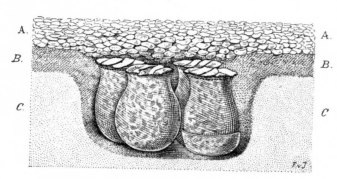

Fig. 54.—Deposit of cinerary urns. Mound A. (Not on scale.)

vessel has been pieced together from a very fragmentary condition, with several portions wanting. Approximate measurements: height, 16 inches; maximum diameter, 14 inches; diameter of mouth, 10.5 inches. Over its mouth was part of the bottom of an earthenware vessel.

Vessel BBa, of the usual model, though of black ware, was capped with a dish of red ware (BBb). Both, though held in place, were in fragments.

Vessel CC was a large undecorated bowl of earthenware holding within it, in an upright position, a vessel (DD) of the usual type, covered as to its orifice with pieces of earthenware. Both vessels, though held in place, were very badly crushed.

Vessel EE, a vessel of the usual type, its mouth covered with fragments of earthenware. The rim was badly crushed and portions of it were not recovered. This vessel was sent to the Ontario Archæological Museum, Toronto, Ontario.

Under perfectly level ground, adjacent to the mound and beginning at that portion of the margin included between N. E. and S. W. ½ W., were outlying burials as shown in diagram Fig. 55. The ground seemed to have suffered a general disturbance at the period of the inhumations and individual pits were difficult to determine though several were unquestionably met with.

Vessel FF, 27 feet S., a vessel of the ordinary type, upright, its base 31 inches below the surface. It was badly crushed. Though no trace of human remains was present it had doubtless contained the skeleton of a very young infant. The fragments were sent to the Peabody Museum, Cambridge, Mass.

Burial No. 23, Vessel GG, 27 feet S. S. E., a vessel of the ordinary type, imperforate, with the entire upper portion crushed away. Minute fragments of bone were present.

Burial No. 24, 28 feet S. by W., 30 inches from surface,[1] extending somewhat into undisturbed sand, was the skeleton of a child three to five years of age, flexed on the right side, head S.

Vessel HH, 33 feet E. by N., an imperforate, undecorated vessel, globular as to its body, with constricted neck and flaring rim, apparently unassociated and intact

[1] Depths of vessels and of skeletons in the outlying part of Mound A, were taken from the under margins.

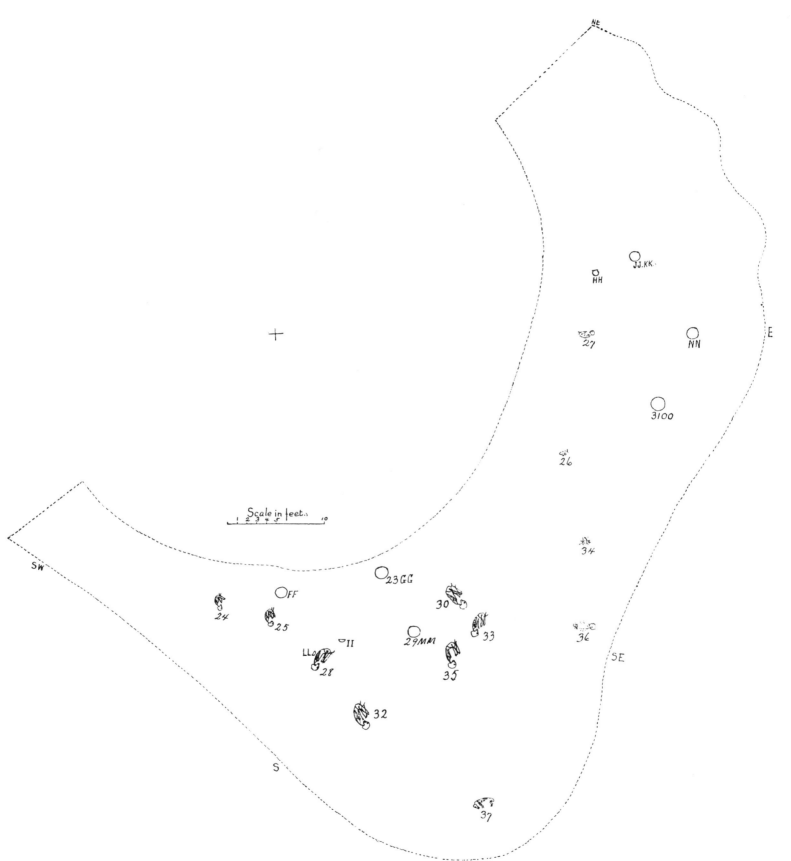

Fig. 55.—Diagram of outlying portion of Mound A.

but for a small breakage of the rim. Approximate measurements: diameter of mouth, 5.5 inches; of body, the same; height, 4.5 inches.

Burial No. 25, 29 feet S., 25 inches down, skeleton of child about five years of age, flexed on right side, head S.

Burial No. 26, 32 feet E. S. E., part of a skull and of a clavicle, near the surface.

Burial No. 27, 31 feet E., 2 feet 6 inches down. Remains of a child, very much decayed, apparently flexed on the right side, head E.

Vessel II, 33 feet S. by E., an imperforate bowl, apparently unassociated, with a maximum diameter at its mouth of 7.2 inches and a height of 3 inches, decorated with incised lines below the exterior margin (Plate XIII, Fig. 1). No trace of human remains was discovered.

Burial No. 27½, Vessels JJ and KK. Vessel JJ, a bowl with a faint stamped decoration, imperforate, in fragments but held in place by sand. Its outline was somewhat that of an inverted, truncated cone. Approximately it measured 12.5 inches maximum diameter and diameter of mouth. Its height was 7 inches. This bowl had been placed over the mouth of a vessel of the ordinary type (KK), but was not inverted as usual but let into the opening in an upright position. From the upper margin of JJ to the surface was 11 inches. KK, a vessel of ordinary type, 14 inches in height, was badly crushed. Its base, which had a perforation, was below the water level, 27 inches down. It contained deciduous human teeth.

Burial No. 28, 34 feet S. by E., a skeleton of a female, flexed on the right side, head S. W., 2 feet from the surface. With it was an imperforate bowl (LL) with handle projecting from upper margin at one side, and interestingly decorated, as shown in Plate XIV, Fig 1. Approximate measurements: diameter of mouth, 6 inches; maximum diameter of body, 6.2 inches; height, 2.8 inches.

Burial No. 29, Vessel MM, 34 feet S. S. E., a vessel of the ordinary type, with base-perforation, the rim and part of the body ploughed away and lost. Human remains were represented by one deciduous molar.

Burial No. 30, 32 feet S. E. by S., skeleton of female, flexed on right side, head S. E. by S., 2 feet 10 inches down.

Vessel NN, 42 feet E., a vessel of the ordinary type, with base perforation, rim and part of body ploughed away. The infant's bones, which this vessel at one time doubtless contained, had disappeared.

Burial No. 31, Vessel OO, 39 feet E. by S., a vessel of the ordinary type with the upper portion ploughed away. On the base were bones in powder and the lower jaw of an infant. The base proper showed no perforation, but on one side vertically about 2 inches above the base, was a hole, carefully made, somewhat over 1 inch in diameter. This is a departure from the general rule.

Burial No. 32, 40 feet S. by E., in all probability the skeleton of a female. The glabella was practically wanting and the supra-orbital ridges were but slightly developed. The general frame, however, indicated a fairly muscular person— probably a powerful female. A number of small shell beads, one shell pin, and part of another, lay near the head.

Burial No. 33, 36 feet S. E. by S., 13 inches down, skeleton of adolescent, flexed on right side, head S. S. W.

Burial No. 34, 38 feet S. E. by E., human bones disturbed by plow.

Burial No. 35, 37 feet S. E. by S., 2 feet 11 inches down, skeleton of adolescent, flexed on right side, head S.

Burial No. 36, 43 feet S. E., at the bottom of a distinct pit, 2 feet 5 inches from the surface, were the remains of a skeleton too much decayed for determination.

Burial No. 37, 54 feet S. S. E., 20 inches down, skeleton of a dog.

An interesting feature in Mound A was the discovery of portions of a vessel of red ware of aboriginal type and decoration, interiorly glazed in places. Earthenware regularly glazed would indicate European contact. Professor Putnam writes as follows of these fragments:

" After consultation with Professors Jackson and Hill of the Chemical Department [Harvard], I am more than ever convinced that the glazing on a portion of the jar from the Georgia mound is entirely accidental. When you come to study the pieces you will find that the whole interior of the jar has apparently been coated with ashes mixed with water. Now suppose such a jar was heated on the inside by putting in hot coals of wood; the potash in the coating of ashes and the potash contained in the wood, mixed with the slight silicious matter in the clay, would make an accidental glazing.

" It does not seem possible that this glazing is formed by lead or salt, for the slight burning of the pottery is not sufficient to form a glazing of either of these substances; much more heat would be required.

" Professors Jackson and Hill were sure that it would be useless to analyze the glazing, as we should have to scrape off nearly all there is to get enough to make a good analysis, and we should probably get only negative results. I therefore consider that this was simply an accidental case of partial glazing caused by some special burning of the pottery. The fact that the glazing is confined to one portion of the lip of the jar and to a part just below the lip on the bulge indicates that the hot coals were in contact with that portion only. If the jar was inverted over hot coals for the purpose of heating the inside (as was evidently common in ancient times), it might easily have fallen over in the fire and the coals have tumbled into this portion of the jar."

The various forms of burial and their distribution in Mound A are worthy of attention. It will be noticed that in no part of the mound, outside of calcined remains, among which were parts of adult skeletons seemingly belonging to males, were skeletal remains of adult males—the skeletons being exclusively those of women, adolescents, children and infants—and that in one portion of the mound burial vases exclusively contained skeletons of infants, unaffected by fire, while in other portions cinerary urns were present filled with fragments of calcined human skeletons. Again we see pockets of calcined human remains and skeletal remains of woman and of children unaffected by fire and not included in vessels of earthenware.

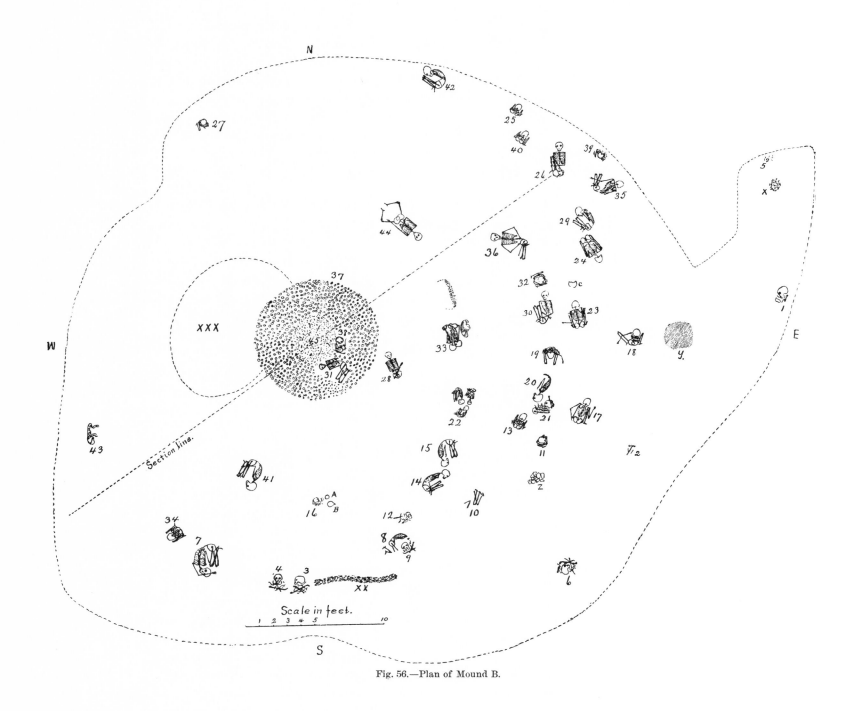

Fig. 56.—Plan of Mound B.

About 68 yards in a N. E. direction from Mound A is the remnant of a shell heap nearly all of which, above the general level, has been carted away for lime. A small portion still remaining shows the height of the heap to have been somewhat over 2 feet. The diameter, difficult to determine at present, was probably about 50 feet.

This shell heap was trenched around the margin and in several directions toward the center. No human remains were encountered nor any indication that the heap had been used for sepulchral purposes. Sherds were abundant. One, with an average diameter of 4 inches, showed a number of grooves made by sharpening pointed tools. From different parts of the mound came three discs of earthenware cut from fragments of vessels, each about 1.5 inches in diameter.

OSSABAW ISLAND, BRYAN COUNTY. MIDDLE SETTLEMENT, MOUND B.

This mound, in a cultivated field, lay somewhat over one-half mile in a N. E. direction from the Middle Settlement.

Its height above the level of the field was a trifle over 7 feet, and a measurement taken from the surface at the center of the mound to the base-line, when the mound was half dug through, showed a corresponding altitude. The diameter of the mound at the base, we took to be about 46 feet, but as portions of the margin were covered with a thick deposit of oyster shells, it is not unlikely that in places the extreme outlying portions escaped us.

The mound, covered with undergrowth and small live-oaks, showed no sign of previous investigation, although a considerable excavation made into the shells of the margin, to obtain material for lime, was apparent.

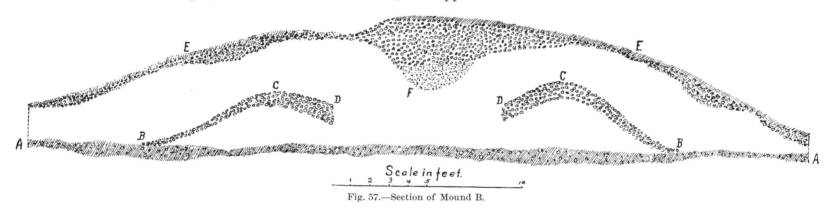

Fig. 57.—Section of Mound B.

The mound, with the exception of certain marginal portions, was dug through as shown in the diagram (Fig. 56) at a level much below that of the surrounding field that no grave or pit might pass unnoticed. At the level of the field there ran through the mound a dark layer, AA (see section, Fig. 57), varying from a few inches to one foot in thickness, composed of crushed oyster shells, small bits of charcoal, and earth blackened by admixture of organic matter. This we took to be the original surface of the ground upon which the aborigines were living previous to the inception of the mound. Beneath, and sometimes through, this layer there ran down at places into the clear yellow sand, masses of dark disturbed sand filled with organic matter and bits of charcoal, of which portions of the mound were composed. These evidently had been pits, and while the purpose of those containing human remains was evident, the cause for the digging of others containing no skeletal remains is unexplained.

Rising from the base-line at BB was a layer of oyster shells (CC) varying in thickness from 2 or 3 inches to 1 foot. This layer, after a downward slope, terminated abruptly at DD, when within 4.5 feet of the center of the mound, up to which point, however, it had been a continuous layer. The shells of this layer lay loosely together and were not crushed and packed, leading to the belief that they had been placed there intentionally at one period and were not midden refuse due to surface habitation. Beneath this layer (CC) the sand reaching to the base-line was of a yellow color much resembling that below the base though it contained in addition occasional oyster shells and particles of charcoal, not present in the sub-basal sand. Above the layer CC, and dipping to the base-line between the terminal points of the layer, was sand of a dark brown color extending to the superficial layer of oyster shells (EE) which covered the entire mound. This layer (EE) varied greatly as to thickness, at some places disappearing almost entirely, at others attaining a thickness of from 1 to 2 feet. It was filled with midden refuse, bones of lower animals, sherds, charcoal, etc., and was unquestionably a gradual deposit made by the use of the mound as a dwelling site. Around certain portions of the margin of the mound, where doubtless the shell had been carried and thrown, the deposits had a thickness of almost 4 feet and extended below the surface of the field, which we accounted for under the hypothesis that sand removed for the construction of the mound had left hollows subsequently filled by shell. Above the upper layer of oyster shells was a deposit of black surface loam, several inches in thickness. The pocket of shell (F) shown in the diagram, is referred to in our detailed description as Burial No. 37.

From a careful study of the mound it was suggested to us that its original construction had been a circular ridge of light sand, about 3 feet in height, sloping up on all sides from the level of the field, and enclosing a sort of basin, and that this ridge had been intentionally coated with oyster shells. That the central portion corresponding to the area between the terminal points of the stratum (CC) had been subsequently dug out, thus accounting for the abrupt termination of the shell stratum, and that later the entire ridge and basin had been covered with sand, brown in color or made so through percolation, extending on all sides considerably beyond the surface of the ridge, and that the mound thus formed had for a period been used as a place of abode. The reader, however, must bear in mind that conclusions of this sort are by no means final.

Several small local layers of hematite were present near the base.

Throughout the mound, but principally in the midden refuse, were fragments of earthenware vessels. These, with several exceptions found at the base, were of gritty ware, while all were either undecorated, cord-marked, basket-marked, or stamped with the well-known square impression. To the best of our knowledge, none bore any variety of the complicated stamped decoration present in the low neighboring mounds.

In various parts of the mound were pebbles of different sizes, and from the midden refuse of the base, unassociated, came a bone pin with incised decoration around the head. A disc of earthenware, irregularly circular, with a diameter of about 3.5 inches and a thickness of .5 of 1 inch, lay by itself 7 feet from the surface. This disc had been fashioned and baked and not cut from part of a vessel as were certain earthenware discs present in other mounds of the coast. Though, owing to the considerable quantity of oyster shells in the mound, one might have looked for human remains in a fairly good state of preservation, their condition was not such as to warrant their removal, the crania in particular being decayed and crushed. No fractures were noticed in the bones or any pathological condition of importance.

We shall now proceed to a detailed description of certain features present in the mound and of the interments. Unless otherwise stated, depths of skeletons are given from the surface to the uppermost portion of the skeleton, a measurement of which we disapprove, preferring the vertical distance to the plane upon which the remains were deposited, a method which we have followed in most of our other descriptions in this Report.

1.—34 feet E. from center, 6 inches from the surface, in the shell debris, which at that part covered the slope of the mound to a considerable depth, were the skull of an adult, part of a clavicle, and portions of a pelvis and of a humerus.

2.—24 feet E. by S., just below the surface, in the shell, were a portion of a femur and two fragments of smaller long bones. With these was a bit of chert, while near by, though perhaps having no connection with them, lay a tobacco pipe of soapstone, absolutely intact, still bearing marks of the maker's tools (Fig. 58).

3.—18 feet W. of S., bunched burial of adult male, 22 inches from the surface.

4.—1.5 feet W. of No. 3, bunched burial of adult male, 3.5 feet down.

5.—35 feet E. by N., 3.5 feet down, just beneath the marginal shell layer, were a fragment of scapula and six phalanges scattered over a small area. The mound had suffered no disturbance at this point.

6.—24 feet S. E., a grave dug through the superficial shell layer into the yellow sand of of the field at a point where the upward slope had just begun. From the surface of the shell layer to the bottom of the grave-pit was 4 feet. The pit proper, whose depth was

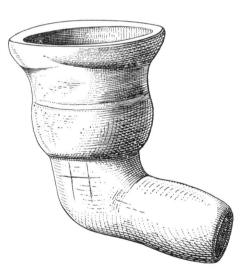

Fig. 58.—Tobacco pipe of soapstone. Mound B. (Full size.)

23 inches, was filled with brown sand mixed with oyster shells showing that at least a certain portion of the superficial shell deposit was present when it was dug. Above the pit were 17 inches of shell deposit surmounted by 8 inches of black surface loam. At the bottom of the grave was a bunched burial of an adult, probably female.

X.—35 feet E. by N., a fireplace 2 feet 4 inches down.

XX.—18 feet S., a fireplace 10 inches from surface—a narrow band of charcoal 6 feet in length.

7.—19 feet S. by W., 2 feet from surface, skeleton in anatomical order, probably female, head S., body on right side and badly twisted, knees drawn up toward side of head, legs flexed on thighs, left arm over head, right arm down along body with forearm flexed upward. With this skeleton was a bit of chert. The black base-layer at this point was 5 inches thick and 3 feet 3 inches from the surface.

8.—17 feet S. by E., 2 feet down, below the unbroken surface of loam and of oyster shells was a portion of a flexed skeleton, the skull, with the exception of half of the mandible, being absent. Upper part of trunk to the east on left side. Upper portion of each humerus absent, but remaining portions of upper extremities in anatomical order and in proper relation to remainder of skeleton present. Fragments of clavicle and ribs in sand near upper part of trunk. Vertebræ of trunk in order, also pelvis and bones of lower extremities, with exception of parts adjacent to, and comprising, knees, which were absent. About 1.5 feet distant were half of a lower jaw, a piece of a rib, and of a clavicle, doubtless belonging to the skeleton which had been dug through at a period prior to the formation of the shell deposit for the burial of No. 9.

9.—1 foot immediately below No. 8 was a bunched burial of an adolescent, lying on the black base-line.

Y.—27 feet E., a layer of sand, cherry colored through admixture with hematite, 3 feet 10 inches from the surface. This layer was about 3 inches above the black band marking the base of the mound, was from .5 of 1 inch to 1 inch in thickness, had a length of 1 foot 10 inches, and extended inward 2 feet.

10.—16 feet S. E., 10 inches down, lower extremities flexed in anatomical order, part of one humerus and two-thirds of the bones of its lower arm. All other portions of the skeleton absent, doubtless a comparatively recent disturbance.

Z.—19 feet E. S. E., 3.5 feet down, just below the black base-line, was a nest of fragments of various vessels, filling a little pocket.

11.—18 feet E. by S., 2 feet from surface, lying on the black base-line, with surface layer of oyster shells unbroken, was a skeleton of a female in a sitting position, facing S. of E. The head was forced down between the thighs and legs as shown in Fig. 59. Behind the skeleton was a marine mussel shell filled with powdered hematite.

12.—15 feet S. S. E., bones probably belonging to a female, in caved sand.

13.—16 feet E. by S., a grave containing an adult skeleton of uncertain sex, in a crouching position, trunk bending forward on thighs, and supported by the lower extremities of legs and heels. Above the bones were 18 inches, vertically, of oyster shells and around them 25 inches, vertically, of brown sand mingled with oyster shells.

14.—14 feet S. E., a grave extending through the black line of the base and

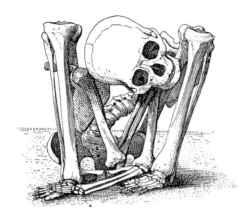

Fig. 59.—Burial No. 11. Mound B. (Not on scale.)

filled with brown sand. Surface to bottom of grave, 7 feet; to bones, 6 feet; to broken line of base, 4 feet; diameter of grave, 4 feet. A flexed burial on left side, head N. E., as nearly as could be determined. Unusual decay. Sex undetermined.

15.—13. 5 feet S. E., flexed skeleton of male on right side, 6 inches from surface, head S.

16.—12 feet S., just below the upper layer of oyster shells and immediately above the second layer to which reference has been made, 2 feet from the surface, were the crushed bones of an infant. With them were an imperforate, undecorated vessel of about one pint capacity, having a portion missing from the side and rim (A), and an undecorated imperforate cup (B), elongated at one end and terminating in an extension for a handle, resembling in shape and size a type found in Florida. Its capacity is somewhat less than one pint.

17.—20 feet E. by S., a grave having its base 5 feet 4 inches from the surface and extending 1 foot 4 inches into undisturbed sand below the base. The mouth of this grave was impossible to determine. The superficial shell layer above it was intact and there was no unusual admixture of oyster shells. It was therefore of a period prior to the making of the shell layer. At base of grave was the skeleton of a male, head N., flexed, with body facing down. Thighs flexed up along body with legs flexed back upon them. Right elbow in toward body; left, somewhat extended.

18.—23 feet E., a grave, from surface to bones, 5 feet 4 inches; to bottom of grave, 6 feet 3 inches; depth below broken base of mound, 2 feet 3 inches. Thickness of unbroken surface layer of shell at this point, 2 feet. In the grave, in a semi-sitting position, facing S. W., was the skeleton of an adult male with right arm extended from the side; left arm along side, forearm crossing body. Right thigh, with leg flexed against it, at right angle to body; left thigh, with leg bent against it, flexed upon body.

19.—17 feet E. of S., skeleton of male in sitting position, head S. and pressed forward, chin on chest. Thighs at right angle to body, with legs flexed back parallel to them. Feet against pelvis. Right arm along chest, forearm across body; left arm out from side with forearm crooked from body. This skeleton lay in a pocket filled with oyster shells, 15 inches down.

20.—1 foot S. of No. 19, upper portion of skeleton of male, about 1 foot below the surface, head S. Trunk above pelvis and cranium alone remained, the rest having been cut away by Burial No. 19.

21.—A burial, 3 feet below No. 20, lying on the black basal layer, was much massed together, the greater part of the bones being in anatomical order, others, however, being out of place. An astragalus and its os calcis, separated, lay on the skull. The left humerus was across the skull with no forearm bones in connection. The mandible was separated from the cranium. This burial (sex not determined) had evidently been partially held together by ligaments when, after previous exposure, it was interred in the mound.

22.—12 feet E. by S., crushed skeletons of three children with shell beads and a few small shells (*Olivella*) longitudinally perforated. The remains lay in the surface shell layer 1 foot down.

23.—19 feet N. of E., 3 feet down on the black base-layer, a skeleton of a male in the position of one who, crouching, had fallen forward. Right arm along side, forearm across and under body; left arm along side, forearm extending from body. Thighs flexed sharply along side of trunk, with legs flexed back along thighs, throwing feet under pelvis.

C.—1 foot N. of No. 23, on same level was a large portion of a cord-marked bowl filled with black loam many shades darker than the surrounding black sand, and containing the bottom of a vessel stamped in small squares. This base had a sort of projection at one end, possibly made intentionally and may have served as a dish.

24.—21 feet N. of E., skeleton of adult male, 3 feet from surface, practically in the same position as No. 23, head S. E., 3 feet from surface.

25.—23 feet N. E., a grave filled with oyster shells, running through the brown sand to base of mound, a vertical distance of 3 feet. This grave may have been dug while the shell layer was in process of formation. The surface showed no depression. Resting on the base of the grave was the skeleton of an adult male, in a sitting position, facing N. E.

26.—A grave 23 feet N. E., 4 feet in depth from the surface and 2 feet 6 inches from the bottom of the shell layer. The grave went through and extended beyond the black line of the base, a distance of 14 inches. On the bottom was a skeleton of uncertain sex, head N., an ordinary flexed burial.

27.—19 feet N. by W., a grave two feet across. Surface of mound to bottom of grave which extended 10 inches below the base line, 4 feet 9 inches. This grave, filled with brown sand without oyster shells, contained skeleton, probably female of about 20 years of age, in a sitting position, facing S. W.

28.—6 feet S. of E., skeleton of uncertain sex, 1 foot down in shell, head N. A portion of this skeleton fell in caved sand.

29.—22 feet E. by N., skeleton of female, head N.; an ordinary flexed burial, 4 feet beneath surface on the base of a grave composed of dark brown sand, which ran into the yellow sand 9 inches below the bottom of the black base layer, which, at this place, was 9 inches thick.

30.—17 feet E., a skeleton of an adult male, 3 feet from the surface, on back, head N., arms along side, forearms across body, thighs flexed up to right, legs parallel to thighs. In association were a core of chert, and part of a *Fulgur*, filled with sand dyed a bright red with hematite.

31.—3 feet S. E., 1 foot down, in shell, flexed skeleton of a male on back, head W.

32.—17 feet N. of E., 2 feet 3 inches down, skeleton of adult male, seated, leaning back, head facing W. and forced over on chest, legs drawn up, right humerus extended from side at right angles to body, forearm flexed and parallel to side of body, left humerus against body with forearm across trunk.

33.—10 feet E., 9 inches down, 2 skeletons: female below, on face, head S.; male on plane above. Caving sand interfered with detailed examination. Beneath these skeletons, which were covered by an unbroken layer of shell, was the skeleton of a dog. Not far distant from No. 33, was a layer of charcoal and oyster shells showing marks of fire, 4 to 5 inches in thickness, covered by fragments of calcined human bones. This layer, 28 inches in length, caved previous to a complete examination.

34.—18 feet S. S. W., 2 feet down, skeleton of youth facing S. S. W., in a kneeling position, leaning forward.

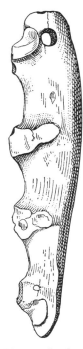

Fig. 60.—Pendant of shell. Mound B. (Full size.)

35.—25 feet E. by N., 2 feet 9 inches down, skeleton of female, on face, head E., thighs turned to left side, projecting from body, legs flexed sharply on thighs, right arm along body, forearm crossed on body, left arm extended out, running between thighs.

36.—A grave, 17 feet E. by N., 16 inches below upper margin of base-line, at that point about 9 inches thick. Surface to skeleton, 5 feet. Skeleton of male on back, head W., arms akimbo, the thighs flexed to right angle to body and turned to right, legs sharply flexed back on thighs.

37.—A grave at center of mound having the shape of an inverted cone with rounded apex, 4 feet in height. Diameter of opening 9 feet. At the bottom a layer of calcined human bones having a maximum thickness of 1 foot 6 inches. Among the calcined bones were a great number of shell beads of various sizes and shapes and a curious pendant of shell (Fig. 60), which, unlike the beads, showed exposure to fire. In addition, were many imperforate teeth of a dog or of a wolf and a number of human phalanges unaffected by fire. This grave was filled with oyster shells and it was impossible to say at what stage of the shell deposit above it was constructed. It is shown on the cross section.

38.—At the center of the mound, 1 foot 8 inches down, in the shell covering grave 37, was the skeleton of an adult male disarranged by caving of surrounding oyster shells.

39.—25 feet E. by N., 4 feet 8 inches down, in a semi-sitting position much resembling that of skeleton No. 11, was a male skeleton facing S With it were: a cannon bone of a deer; a bit of chert; a few shell beads; a portion of a pebble and a tooth of a fossil shark, 4.25 inches in length with portions cut from either side of the base for convenience in hafting (Fig. 61). Portions were split from either side of the point showing hard usage. We have before met with large fossil teeth of sharks in mounds of Florida and of Georgia, but none bore marks of service or of workmanship of any kind. We have seen also small teeth of fossil sharks, which came from mounds of the St. Johns River, Florida.

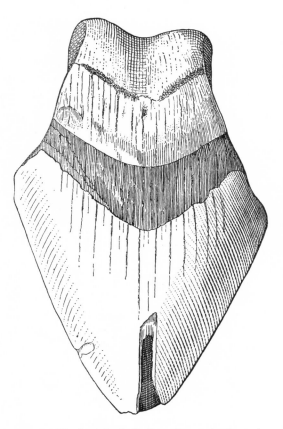

Fig. 61.—Tooth of fossil shark, used as an implement. Mound B. (Full size.)

These teeth had a perforation at the base and were used either as pendants or as knives, like sharks teeth of the present geological period—found by Mr. Cushing during his recent investigations—which were pierced and fastened to small handles.

40.—22 feet N. E., a grave, in which was a skeleton sitting in about the same position as No. 13, facing N. E. Right humerus along body, right forearm flexed on humerus, left humerus along body with forearm across and outside of legs. Back of the skeleton, on the pelvis, with the spinal column directly in front, was a cord-marked bowl or a large part of one, crushed to fragments. This grave, the bottom of which was 4 feet from the surface, extended through the black base-layer of the mound, there 8 inches thick, and continued 1 foot beyond. The grave was filled with brown sand containing some oyster shells, and it is probable that it was made at a time when the surface layer of oyster shells was in process of formation.

41.—12 feet S. by W., skeleton of male on left side, head S. Right humerus across body, forearm extended. Left humerus under body, forearm partly flexed. Thighs flexed on body, legs back and parallel to thighs.

42.—22 feet N. by E., 3 feet down, skeleton probably male, much flexed on right side, head N. W.

43.—18 feet W. by S , 4.5 feet down including 1 foot 3 inches below the line of the base of the mound, was the skeleton of a dog.

44.—11 feet N. E., 6 feet from the surface, was the skeleton of a woman, lying on back in an unusually extended position for this mound. Head S. E. Thighs out from body and raised to an angle of 45 degrees. Legs down at same angle. Right humerus along body, forearm across trunk; left humerus and forearm parallel with body. This skeleton measured 3 feet 9 inches as it lay.

45.—In the center of the mound, on the base, was a fire place approximately 3.5 feet by 3 feet, with a mass of calcined human bones and bones unaffected by fire, having an average thickness of about 7 inches. Much of the material, at least, had not been calcined on the spot, as bones showing no trace of fire, lying on the fire place, had above them a layer of calcined fragments. A great number of shell beads showing no trace of fire lay scattered through the remains. Numerous fragments of earthenware were present.

XXX.—A little W. of the center was a layer of calcined earth and lime presumably from oyster shells, showing intense and prolonged heat. Its length was 11 feet; its breadth about 6 feet. It had an average thickness of about 1 foot. This curious layer, whose upper surface was 6 feet from the surface of the mound, upon careful examination seemed not to have been subjected to fire upon the spot, since oyster shells, bits of deer horn, bones of lower animals, etc., showing no trace of fire, were scattered through it.

This mound differed considerably in shape and in contents from a number of neighboring mounds which were lower and which contained various forms of urn-burial. In it moreover, as we have stated, earthenware with complicated, stamped decoration was absent. It is possible that Mound B was of a different period from that of some of its neighbors.

OSSABAW ISLAND, BRYAN COUNTY. MIDDLE SETTLEMENT, MOUND C.

In the verge of the woods bordering the field to which reference has been made, about 300 yards in a northerly direction from Mound B, was one of much the same type as Mound B, having a height of 8 feet. It had undergone but little previous investigation. The center of the mound, a peak of shell, was easily discernible.

The diameter of the mound was difficult to determine, as it did not rise directly from a general level but in a series of irregular slopes caused by occupation of the surrounding territory as a dwelling site, resulting in a deposit of oyster shells and debris. Portions of the outlying territory were thickly covered with oyster shells while other parts, consisting of dark loamy sand, had oyster shells and sherds to a depth of several feet.

The lower portions of the mound had been under cultivation in former times as deep furrows were plainly visible, though at the time of our investigation (1897) the mound was thickly covered with undergrowth and with small trees. It being impossible to determine just where the mound proper merged with midden refuse, a diameter of 68 feet was selected, which, on the side where oyster shells were absent, brought the circumference somewhat beyond the apparent base of the mound. We are of opinion, however, that in the case of this mound, certain outlying burials escaped us.

At the base of the northern portion of the mound was a thick deposit of oyster shells presumably having no direct connection with the mound but thrown there during the period of occupation of the territory as a dwelling site. Much of this was not included in our investigation.

14 JOURN. A. N. S. PHILA., VOL. XI.

The entire northern half of the mound was dug down leaving a cross-section almost E. and W. Subsequently the central portion of the remaining half was dug out. The remainder of the mound was not investigated.

Upon the light yellow undisturbed sand beneath the mound, but below the outer portions only, was a dark band, averaging 1 foot in thickness, composed of black loam, fragments of oyster shells and bits of charcoal. Farther in, this band was replaced by a layer of oyster shells from 6 inches to 1 foot in thickness which continued through the mound. This black band and shell deposit we regarded as marking the original level of the ground. The deposit of oyster shells, however, divided in places and, coming together again, enclosed masses of dark yellow sand, about 1 foot in thickness and 3 to 4 feet in length. Supposing the layer of shells to be the base line, we are at a loss to account for the presence of the sand.

While the height of the mound was but 8 feet above the immediately surrounding level, the perpendicular distance from its apex to the upper margin of the black band was 10 feet. This apparent discrepancy, we suppose, may be accounted for under the hypothesis that a deposit of midden refuse, made subsequent to the completion of the mound, had surrounded it to a height of 2 feet and over.

The body of the mound was composed of yellow sand darkened by the presence of much organic matter. This sand was irregularly streaked in places and contained here and there local layers of shell, and of sand reddened with admixture of the oxide of iron.

Though there was no general deposit of oyster shells covering the surface, as was the case with Mound B, a great central pit, filled with oyster shells was present with an out-cropping through the immediately central parts of the mound. The dark yellow sand of the body of the mound was covered with an irregular layer of rich black surface loam.

We have referred to a deposit of shell contiguous to the mound. This deposit joined the mound and included that part of the margin lying between E. by N. and N. N. E., and had a breadth of 27 feet converging from a small beginning at either end to a depth of 7 feet 10 inches. Four and one-half feet in from the margin of the mound as taken by us, the deposit had a breadth of 12 feet, and, instead of solid shell, as before, was from the surface down :

Shell	3 feet 7 inches	Dark sand	3 inches
Brown sand. .	1 foot 2 inches	Light brown sand . .	6 inches
Shell	1 foot 6 inches	Undisturbed sand.	

The black band, to which we have referred, cut through by this curious combination, was visible at either side, its upper margin being 2 feet 6 inches below the surface. The deposit disappeared a few feet farther in from the point where the measurement was taken.

Sherds were of frequent occurrence. With the exception of 2 or 3 from the immediate surface, all were undecorated or cord-marked—the latter predominating. The reader will recall that in Mound B also no ware with the complicated stamp was discovered.

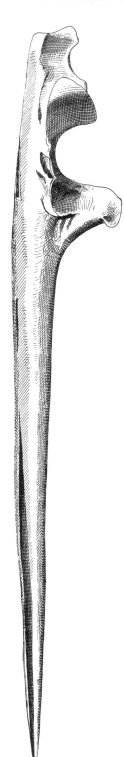

Fig. 62.—Piercing implement
of bone. Mound C.
(Full size.)

Several sherds were singly or doubly grooved, showing use as hones.

One fragment of earthenware from a large vessel had a thickness of .9 of 1 inch.

An imperforate vessel of about 1 quart capacity with a rough checked-stamp decoration came from caved sand.

In caved sand was an undecorated vessel in shape somewhat like a modern gravy-boat. The bottom had been intentionally knocked out. Length, 7.3 inches; width, 4.7 inches; height, 3 inches.

A globular, undecorated vessel lay in caved sand. Diameter at mouth, 4.3 inches; maximum diameter, 5.5 inches; height, 4.3 inches.

Two bowls, one badly crushed, were in caved sand.

Throughout the mound were several deposits of fragments of pots, placed upon each other. As usual, these nests were composed of pieces belonging to different vessels.

A number of pebble-hammers and fragments of pebble-hammers were found separately in midden refuse and unassociated with human remains.

From the basal layer came a silicified astragalus of a large mammal, which had seemingly been in use as a hammer as portions from one end were split off, as by blows.

Mostly from the midden refuse came numerous fragments of bone pins, while at a considerable depth in the sand was found an ulna of a lower animal, fashioned into a highly polished piercing implement 7.8 inches in length (Fig. 62).

In the surface loam was a section of a long bone .7 of 1 inch in height, with diameters of .6 of 1 inch and .8 of 1 inch respectively. On either side, between the upper and lower margins is a groove. The bone is polished, and at one place slightly stained with copper. This object may be of a period later than that of the mound.

Apparently not in immediate association with remains, together, were ten agricultural implements of shell (*Fulgur carica*).

Though human remains in Mound C were, as a rule, fairly well preserved, no unbroken crania were met with. No evidence of disease was present on the bones and but one fracture was found, that of an ulna which had united with much less deformity than has been the case with some fractures we have met with. Though careful notes of all burials were taken, yet, owing to similarity of form to interments in Mound B, we deem it unnecessary to go into detail.

Mound C, like Mound B, was riddled with pits in which lay a majority of the skeletons. Burials were noted to the number of 92, though this figure conveys no idea of the exact number of individuals represented, since at times only portions of the skeleton were present, while on the other hand, several skeletons, buried in conjunction, have been included as one interment. Pockets of calcined human bones were five times encountered, two being met with south of the cross-section while digging out central portions of the mound.

As was the case in Mound B, no urn-burials of any sort were present.

With thirteen burials were artifacts: pierced *Olivella* shells; bone pins; shell beads; fresh-water mussel shells; pebble-hammers; sandstone hone; shell drinking cup; small imperforate bowl; two conchs (*Fulgur carica*), pierced for use as implements.

Occupying a central position in the mound was a pit, roughly circular, clearly dug down from the surface where it had a diameter of about 13 feet. Eight feet below the surface it had converged to a base about 3 feet across. The pit had been filled with sand mingled with midden refuse and had been capped with a solid

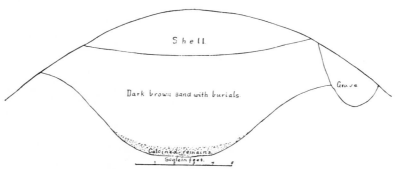

Fig. 63.—Section of central pit. Mound C.

deposit of oyster shells having a maximum thickness of 2.5 feet. The upper eastern portion of the pit had been cut through by a grave (see diagram of pit Fig. 63), and at different points the pit itself contained skeletal remains placed there at the time of the filling. On the bottom of this pit and extending up on the sides, was an irregular deposit of fragments of calcined human bones, having an average thickness of about 5 inches and a diameter of 7 feet measured across between the margins extending upward (Burial 82). Mingled with the calcined fragments was a curious medley as follows: a great number of shell beads of various shapes, some tubular, one having a length of about 3 inches, mostly unaffected by fire but some showing calcination; 8 pearls, pierced, one showing traces of fire; 8 chert spalls together; 14 chips of chert together; 53 quartz pebbles, intimately associated, each about the size of a pea; great numbers of sherds, including one circular in shape, with a central perforation; a considerable number of bone pins, one 7.5 inches long with a perforation (Fig. 64). In addition to this diverse collection was the body of the lower jaw of some carnivore, and parts of other jaws, with the lower portions ground away as we have described in the account of the mound at Greenseed Field.

OSSABAW ISLAND, BRYAN COUNTY.   MIDDLE SETTLEMENT, MOUND D.

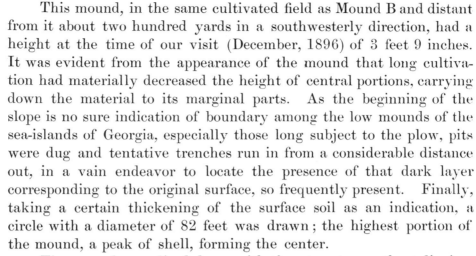

Fig. 64.—Piercing implement of bone. Mound C. (Full size.)

This mound, in the same cultivated field as Mound B and distant from it about two hundred yards in a southwesterly direction, had a height at the time of our visit (December, 1896) of 3 feet 9 inches. It was evident from the appearance of the mound that long cultivation had materially decreased the height of central portions, carrying down the material to its marginal parts.   As the beginning of the slope is no sure indication of boundary among the low mounds of the sea-islands of Georgia, especially those long subject to the plow, pits were dug and tentative trenches run in from a considerable distance out, in a vain endeavor to locate the presence of that dark layer corresponding to the original surface, so frequently present.   Finally, taking a certain thickening of the surface soil as an indication, a circle with a diameter of 82 feet was drawn; the highest portion of the mound, a peak of shell, forming the center.

The mound was sliced down with the utmost care, those digging, where it seemed necessary, going as much as 8 feet below its surface. Of the many mounds it has been our fortune to investigate, none has offered more difficulty in the description of the limits of its component parts.   The undisturbed sub-sand was light yellow, at times almost white.   Above this came darker yellow sand somewhat discolored by the presence of organic matter and showing a certain amount of disturbance discernible by the presence of streaks, bits of charcoal, etc., but no distinct dark line marking the base was anywhere apparent.   Over this layer came a final one of dark brown sand, which, like the disturbed yellow layer, locally varied in thickness so that no general data were obtainable.   Moreover, the dark brown layer and the yellow layer below it, so merged together that a line of division was indistinguishable even to the most careful and most experienced observers.   At the central portion of the mound was a layer of shell at first beneath the surface and having at the beginning but the thickness of a single shell, increasing gradually toward the center and merging with a second layer of shell which made its appearance several feet farther in, all around, until, at the immediate center of the mound, it appeared at the surface and extended to a considerable depth below the base, forming the great shell pit shown in the cross-section (Fig. 65).   This shell layer had probably an average diameter of 30 feet.   The portion exposed at the surface was about 15 feet in diameter as shown in the cross-section.   The shells comprising these layers, while mainly of the oyster, included also those of the clam, the conch (*Fulgur*), various marine mussels, the "cockle" (*Cardium*) and numerous smaller salt water shell-fish.

The mound, as the detailed description will show, was riddled with pits, the lower parts of which were clearly distinguishable when extending into undisturbed sand. The parts of the pits in the body of the mound, having been filled with the sand removed during their excavation, resembled so closely the sand surrounding them, that the exact limits were impossible to define. These pits, it was quite evident, were of the period of the mound, many showing no admixture with the dark sand of the upper layer or of shell, though a layer or layers of shell often lay above them. Some, however, showed dark sand in places, but these also at times were underneath undisturbed shell and were doubtless made prior to the completion of the mound. In almost no case could we distinguish the exact beginning of a pit.

Skeletal remains, so numerous in this mound (we have reference to those outside the mortuary vessels), were in a fairly good state of preservation compared to many we have encountered elsewhere, though with one exception, which is particularly noted in the detailed description, no crania were saved, owing to their crushed condition.

In following the detailed description, whose numbering corresponds with that of the diagram (Fig. 66), the lay reader must not confuse the three forms of urn-

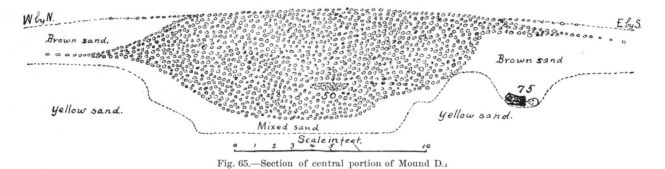

Fig. 65.—Section of central portion of Mound D.[1]

burial present in this mound; namely, skeletal remains of infants, unaffected by fire; the remains of single individuals, which had undergone cremation, and urns filled with a confused mass of fragments of calcined human bones belonging to individuals of all ages. Where fire had been employed it is distinctly stated.

Two arrowheads or knives of chert, several bits of chert and pebble-hammers, some fragmentary, lay loose in the sand, as also the lower part of a broad chisel of ferruginous shale, having a thin section and a sharp cutting edge.

Burial No. 1, a pit, or grave, located 24 feet W. by N. from the point taken as the center of the surface of the mound, as are all other similar measurements of superficial distance in our detailed account, was in a portion of the mound where the central shell layer had not begun, the shell layer X shown in the diagram and in Fig. 67, which gives an accurate idea of the grave, being of a purely local character. In the bottom of this grave, which extended into the undisturbed

[1] The "yellow sand" in the section is undisturbed sand.

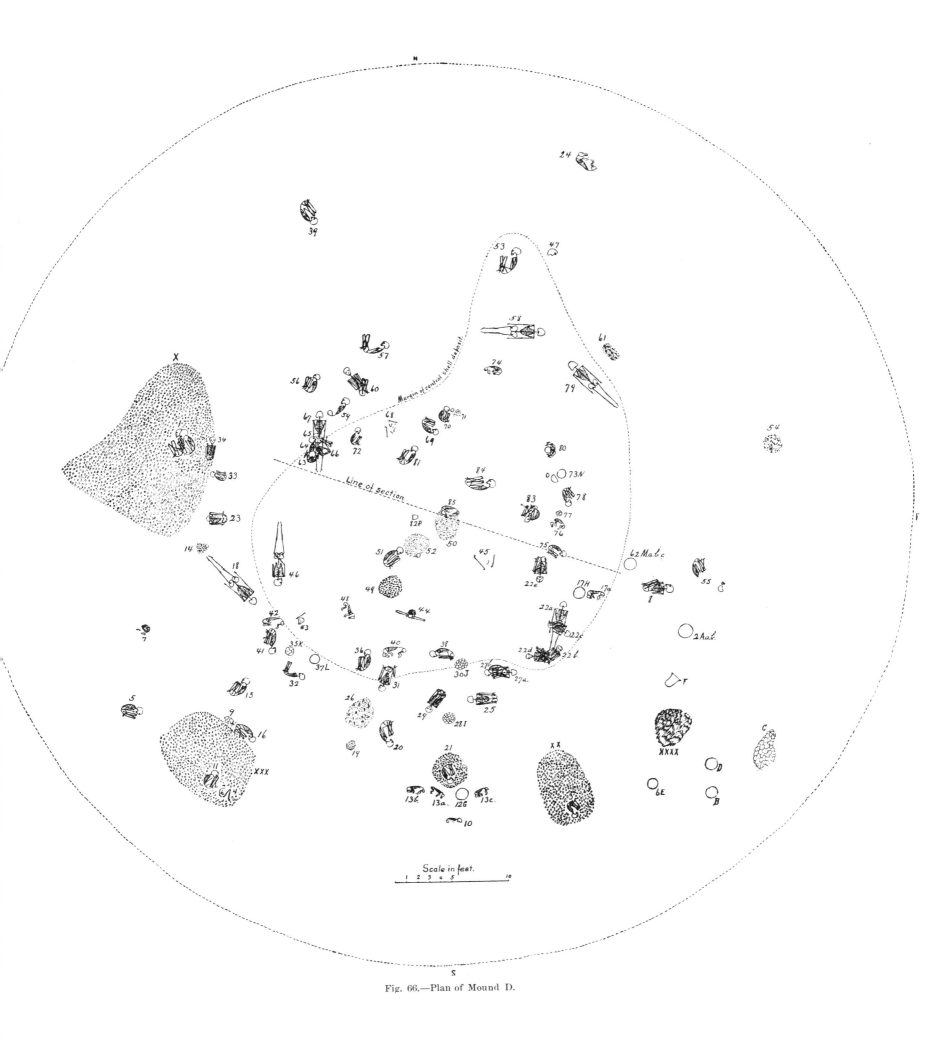

Fig. 66.—Plan of Mound D.

yellow sand, one immediately above the other, were the skeletons of two males, similarly interred, heads N., flexed on right side. With one was an undecorated bone pin or piercing implement which fell to pieces during removal.

X.—A local shell layer extending above these burials. It began 34 feet a little N. of W. and extended inward 13 feet. Its thickness at the outside margin was 2 feet (all such measurements are approximate) increasing to 28 inches above the grave from where it tapered sharply to 2.5 inches at its inner limit.

Burial No. 2, Vessel Aa, 24 feet E. by S., a practically intact vessel of the common type, with base perforation, upright as usual. Its base was 12 inches above the undisturbed yellow sand which, at this point, was 3 feet 4 inches from the surface. The height of the vessel is 16 inches, its upper margin therefore was 1 foot from the surface.

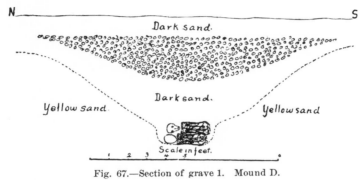

Fig. 67.—Section of grave 1. Mound D.

About half-way down, inside of Aa, was an inverted, imperforate bowl of black ware having stamped complicated decoration (Ab). Portions of the rim were broken and missing. On the bottom of Aa, were the skull of an infant in fragments and other bones, including several ribs. These vessels were sent to the National Museum, Washington, D. C.

Burial No. 3, upon a local shell layer (XX) 30 feet S. by E., 22 inches down, was the flexed skeleton of a child just starting on its second dentition. Head S.

XX.—A shell layer beginning immediately under No. 2, extending inward 6 feet 10 inches. Breadth at outer margin, 4 feet, 3 feet at termination; 1 foot 8 inches thick at the beginning, decreasing to 6 inches, increasing to 1 foot and then tapering away.

Vessel B, 35 feet S. E., a vessel of the ordinary type, 14 inches in height, resting on undisturbed yellow sand 2 feet 10 inches from the surface. The base had a portion intentionally knocked out. The entire side was crushed in and broken into small fragments. Over the opening had been placed several large pieces of earthenware, but with that lack of care distinguishing the makers of the mounds at Ossabaw from those of the Walker mound, these pieces had been allowed to slide over somewhat during the filling in of the pit, thus permitting the entrance of sand. No bones were noted in this vessel, but beyond question the remains of an infant had disappeared through decay.

Vessel C, 36 feet S. E., a layer of fragments of earthenware vessels, 22 inches by 3 feet 8 inches, 18 inches below the surface. It was made up of overlapping sherds of large size, at times single, and again double, and not of several vessels placed on their sides and crushed by the weight of sand, since cord-marked pottery lay with that having the complicated stamp, and when a fragment was imposed upon another, it often occurred that the convex portion of an upper sherd fitted into the concave portion of a lower, which could not be the case were two sides of a previously entire vessel brought into apposition through breakage. No remains or artifacts lay in the neighborhood of this layer.

Vessel D, 33 feet S. E., the lower portion of a vessel of the ordinary type, with perforated base, having the rim and upper part of the body crushed into small fragments. The vessel had been let down somewhat into the undisturbed yellow sand. From base of vessel to surface, 3 feet.

Burial No. 4, 33 feet S. W., portions of a skeleton with unattached epiphyses, partly in anatomical order, 3 feet 9 inches from the surface, below a local shell layer. A considerable portion of this skeleton was missing, presumably through a later burial (No. 11) placed below it, which was, however, aboriginal and contemporary with the mound, as shown by the undisturbed shell layer above. A diseased humerus from this burial was sent to the Army Medical Museum, Washington. With the bones was a mass of red pigment, which chemical tests showed to be an iron paint ore, probably hematite, and not cinnabar, which would have indicated European contact.

XXX.—A layer of oyster shells having its S. E. corner over Burial No. 4. In thickness it varied from 10 inches to 7 inches to 4 inches. Its outer margin was 8 feet 10 inches across. It extended into the mound a distance of 6 feet 8 inches, where it had a terminal breadth of 5 feet. The upper surface of this layer was 1 foot 10 inches from the surface of the mound.

Burial No. 5, a grave 33 feet W. of S. W. This grave, 3 feet from the surface to the base, 26 inches in diameter, ran 9 inches into the clear yellow sand on which the skeleton lay. The burial was that of an adult female, head E., on left side and so flexed that its major diameter was but 25 inches. Decay was noted in several of the molars, a condition not infrequent in this mound.

Burial No. 6, Vessel E, 31 feet S. S. E., a vessel of the usual type, inverted. The body and base so badly fractured that it was impossible to arrive at any conclusion as to a perforation in the base. Within the vessel were a few fragments of the bones of a child, including two phalanges of the toe, unaffected by fire. In addition, were some calcined shells and a fragment of a calcined shell with a central perforation. This vessel had been placed in a pit, the base of which, 3 feet 4 inches from the surface, was 8 inches below the line of the clear yellow sand, and was 3 feet 6 inches across at the point of entrance into the yellow sand.

XXXX.—29 feet S. E., a layer of decayed or fire-blackened wood, 1 foot in thickness, 3 feet 9 inches across, extending inward about 3 feet where it had a breadth of about 1 foot. It lay at the bottom of a pit filled with brownish sand. No human remains or artifacts were in association.

Burial No. 7, 29 feet W. by S., a circular pit, with a diameter of about 30 inches, whose base was 36 inches from the surface, the upper 22 inches being surrounded by disturbed brownish sand, the lower 14 inches extending into undisturbed yellow sand. About 6 inches from the base was a portion of a thorax, one scapula and the head of a humerus.

Vessel F, 25 feet S. E., a vessel of the ordinary type, lying on its side on undisturbed yellow sand, there 2 feet from the surface. No bones were discovered and the vessel was too much crushed to furnish exact data of any sort.

In the outer S. E. portion of the mound, unassociated with human remains, were six fresh-water mussel shells, one within the other, four badly crushed. The remaining two showed no perforation.

Burial No. 8, 21 feet E. by S., probably a grave, but the line of demarcation impossible to determine. On the base, 2 feet 4 inches down, was a skeleton, head E., and turned to the left, trunk on face, knees to left, legs flexed back on thighs. Arms parallel to sides of body, forearms flexed up. This skeleton, of an individual about 5 feet 5 inches in height, was of a slender male or of a strongly built woman.

Burial No. 9, 27 feet S. W., in a pit, 2 feet 6 inches from the surface, above No. 16, were a few scattered bones including phalanges, two bits of radius, one patella, two ossa innominata.

Burial No. 10, 28 feet S., a skeleton of a child lying on undisturbed yellow sand, there 3 feet 9 inches from the surface. The bones were inadvertently dug into and disarranged. No pit was apparent—by no means conclusive proof of its non-existence in the case of this mound.

Burial No. 11, 32 feet S. W., a grave beneath Burial No. 4 and under the shell layer XXX, having its base 5 feet 4 inches from the surface. The most careful endeavor failed to define the limits of this grave which contained a skeleton of a male on left side, head N. E. with one knee under the head and one against the forehead.

Burial No. 12, Vessel G, 26 feet S., a bell-jar shaped vessel, imperforate, with faint checked stamp, inverted on the yellow sand, there 3 feet 6 inches from the surface. A small section of the rim was missing. Several cracks were filled with a quick-setting cement which was allowed to dry while the vessel was in place. The vessel contained the calcined bones of a child lying on sand which extended up inside about two-fifths of the height of the vessel, which is 12.5 inches. Its diameter of mouth, which is also its maximum diameter, is 12.5 inches.

Burial No. 13a, b, c, 26 feet S., three skeletons of dogs buried singly within a few feet of each other.

Burial No. 14, 22 feet W., a pocket of calcined human remains and charcoal, 31 inches down, 9 inches across at the start, and about 3 inches thick. It tapered inward a distance of about 13 inches. Among the fragmentary bones were a number of shell beads, some calcined and others unaffected by fire.

Burial No. 15, 25 feet S. W., a grave, surface to bottom of pit, on which skeleton lay, 4 feet 6 inches. It extended 1 foot 6 inches into clear yellow sand. Its limits in the disturbed sand above were not distinguishable. It contained a flexed skeleton of male on right side, head N. E.

Burial No. 16, 2 feet 9 inches directly below No. 9, or 4 feet 10 inches from the surface to the bottom of the pit on which the bones lay, a flexed burial of a female on left side, head S. E.

Burial No. 17, Vessel H, 14 feet S. E. by E., the lower portion of an imperforate vessel of the ordinary type, just below the surface. Portions had been broken off and scattered by the plow. It had been filled with a mass of calcined human remains, some of which from the upper part, lay scattered about.

Burial No. 17a, a skeleton of a dog some distance below Vessel H.

Burial No. 18, 21 feet S. of W., on the line of the clear yellow sand, there 4 feet 3 inches down, lay a skeleton of uncertain sex at full length, face down, head S. by E. The skeleton measured 6 feet and .5 of an inch as it lay, but the parts were not in immediate contact. No grave was noticeable.

Burial No. 19, 23 feet S. by W., a pocket of calcined fragmentary human bones on the line of the clear yellow sand just 3 feet from the surface, about 6 inches across at the start and 4 inches thick, broadening to 10 inches and tapering to a point 10 inches from the start. With the calcined fragments were shell beads unaffected by fire.

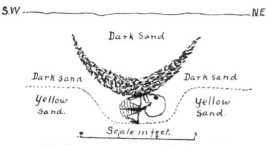

Fig. 68.—Section of grave 21. Mound D.

Burial No. 20, 3 feet E. of No. 19, apparently a grave extending 12 inches into the clear yellow sand and having its base 3 feet 6 inches from the surface. It contained the skeleton of a male, an ordinary flexed burial on the right side, head S.

Burial No. 21, 25 feet S., a pit extending 1 foot into the yellow sand, its base 3 feet from the surface (Fig. 68). At the bottom lay a skeleton of a young person about 10 years of age, flexed on the right side, head S. Above the skeleton was a layer of charcoal about 6 inches thick, mixed in places with burnt sand and shell, extending up the sides of the pit to a level about 1 foot 6 inches above. The diameter of the pit which was apparently circular, was, where the charcoal terminated, 3 feet 4 inches. The jaw and other parts of the skeleton lying in contact with the charcoal were charred or calcined, while other portions lying away from it showed no mark of fire.

Burial No. 22a, 14 feet S. E., a grave 7.5 feet long by 2 feet wide, running 17 inches into the undisturbed yellow sand, its base 4 feet 3 inches from the surface, containing skeleton of a woman at full length, face down, head N. by E., arms along side, measuring 5.5 feet as it lay.

Burial No. 22b, over the feet of Burial No. 22a, in disturbed sand, 3 feet 2 inches from the surface, a flexed burial of a young adult female, head N. E. Right knee up at right angle to the body, leg parallel to the thigh; left knee in contact with the head. Right arm and forearm down along body; left arm along body, with forearm across body.

Burial No. 22c, 30 inches from the surface, above pelvic portion of Burial No. 22a. Male, face down, head S. E. Knees and legs to the left. Arms along body with forearms under it.

Burial No. 22d, above Burial No. 22b, but just beneath surface, skeleton of an adult male, disturbed by the plow, lying on back, head W., knees to the left.

Burial No. 22e, 10 feet E. by S., on the line of undisturbed sand, a flexed skeleton of a female, face down, head S. A pebble-hammer lay in association.

Above these burials, with the exception of No. 22d, the central shell layer first made its appearance, at first but an inch or two in thickness, increasing over the burials to 14 inches where its upper margin was 8 inches below the upper surface of the mound.

Burial No. 23, 21 feet W., 2 feet 8 inches down on clear yellow sand with a thin layer of oyster shells above it, was the skeleton of a female, face down and under the body, head W., a knee on either side of the head with arms between body and thighs.

Burial No. 24, 35 feet N. by E., skeleton of a dog, 2 feet 7 inches down.

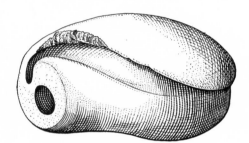

Fig. 69.—Massive bead of shell. Mound D. (Full size.)

Burial No. 25, 17 feet E. of S., flexed skeleton of female, face down, head W., 2 feet 10 inches from the surface on the line of the undisturbed yellow sand. No grave was apparent.

Burial No. 26, 21 feet W. of S., a pocket of calcined fragments of human bones and charcoal, 3 inches thick at the start, lying on the line of undisturbed sand, 3 feet 8 inches down. This layer at the start was 1 foot 10 inches across, broadening 18 inches inward to 27 inches, with a maximum thickness of 8 inches and tapering from that point to its end, 2 feet 11 inches from the start.

Burial No. 27a, 16 feet S. by E., a pit with charcoal, much resembling No. 21, having its base 4 feet 2 inches from the surface. At its base was a skeleton of uncertain sex, flexed, trunk face down, head E. Though the skull lay in the charcoal, it bore no marks of fire.

Burial No. 27b, about 10 inches above No. 27a, was a flexed skeleton of a male, on right side, head W.

Burial No. 28, Vessel I, 19 feet S., just beneath the surface was a vessel crushed to fragments by the plow, with calcined pieces of human bones which the vessel had contained.

Burial No. 29, 18 feet S., flexed skeleton of male on back, on undisturbed sand, 3 feet 3 inches from surface, head S. W.

Burial No. 30, Vessel J, 14 feet S., undecorated vessel broken into fragments by the plow, containing calcined bones of a child and many small shell beads with 33 massive beads,[1] some at least wrought from the columella of *Fulgur carica* and still showing traces of the attractive natural carnelian color, the largest having a length of 2.25 inches and a diameter of 1.4 inches (Fig. 69). Two similar beads lay in the sand near by. With the shell beads were 16 pearls,[2] perforated, but otherwise in good condition, the largest having a diameter of 10.7 mm. by 9.6 mm.

Burial No. 31, 17 feet S. by W., skeleton of female on line of clear yellow sand, there 3 feet 6 inches from surface, head S. Trunk much twisted. Pelvic portion on back, upper trunk twisted to left. Left shoulder under and toward opposite side. Left arm and forearm along body. Right arm and forearm under body. Right thigh at right angle to body and projecting upward, leg flexed back against it. Left thigh along body with leg against thigh.

Burial No. 32, 20 feet S. W., skeleton of young person on yellow sand 3 feet 9 inches from surface, on right side, head E., body partially flexed, knees at right angles to body with legs flexed back on thighs.

Burial No. 33, 21 feet W. by N., skeleton of a child, flexed on left side, head W., lying on clear yellow sand in a grave the boundaries of which were not exactly distinguishable.

Burial No. 34, 22 feet W. by N., skeleton of an adolescent, lying on yellow sand 6 feet from surface, flexed on back, head N., next to Burial No. 1 and probably in same pit.

Burial No. 35, Vessel K, 19 feet S. W., an undecorated bowl of black ware, crushed by the plow, but partially held together by sand. Nearby were human bones and fragments of bone unaffected by fire, probably scattered by the plow. Their connection with the bowl, which apparently contained no human remains, could not be established.

Burial No. 36, 16 feet S. by W., skeleton of male, on undisturbed sand 4 feet from surface, flexed on right side, head N.

Burial No. 37, Vessel L, 18 feet S. W., a vessel of the ordinary type with top and upper body crushed by the plow, half filled with calcined human remains and imperforate, as are all vessels we have found holding calcined remains.

Burial No. 38, 13 feet S., skeleton of female, flexed on right side, head W., lying on the level, 2 feet below the surface.

Burial No. 39, 31 feet N. by W., a grave having its base 6 feet 2 inches from the surface, and extending about 4 feet into undisturbed sand. Its diameter at the line of the yellow sand was 8 feet 8 inches, lessening to 2 feet 9 inches, one foot above the base upon which lay a skeleton of a male, flexed on right side, head S. E. A bit of cord-marked pottery—possibly of accidental introduction—lay near the foot.

Burial No. 40, 14 feet S. by W., skeleton of a dog, 3 feet from surface.

Burial No. 41, 20 feet S. W., a pit extending 14 inches into yellow sand and having its base 4 feet 4 inches from the surface. On the base lay a skeleton of a female, flexed on left side, facing back, head S.

[1] See " Art in Shell," Plate XXXIV, Report Bureau of Ethnology, 1880-1881.
[2] As to pearls in Southern mounds see Antiquities of the Southern Indians, C. C. Jones, Chapter XXI.

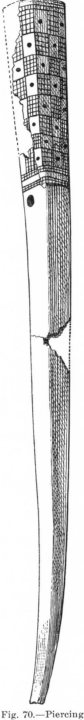

Fig. 70.—Piercing implement of bone. Mound D. (Two-thirds size.)

Burial No. 42, skeleton of a dog, immediately above No. 41.

Burial No. 43, 18 feet S. W., 3 feet 6 inches from surface in same pit as No. 41, were a single skull and one tibia, about 3 feet distant. These bones had probably been disturbed by the introduction of the burial below.

Burial No. 44, 10 feet S. by W., skeleton of a female lying on a shell layer 2 feet 10 inches from the surface. The head, which would have been N. E., was bent over and crushed on the pelvis. The lower trunk lay on the back, the upper was bent over. The right arm lay along body with forearm flexed along thigh. The left arm was alongside of body with forearm across pelvis. The thighs extended laterally at right angles to opposite sides of the body. Legs were flexed back against them.

Burial No. 45, 6 feet S. E., several scattered human bones in the great central shell pocket. Other bones were scattered at various points throughout.

Burial No. 46, 16 feet W. by S., on the line of the yellow sand, there 3 feet 10 inches from the surface, was a skeleton of a female, at full length, measuring 5 feet 8 inches as it lay, on back, head S., face E., right arm along side, forearm crossing to pelvis; left arm along body, forearm flexed back with hand to shoulder.

Burial No. 47, 26 feet N. by E., on the yellow sand, there 2 feet from the surface, isolated cranium wanting face bones and lower jaw.

Burial No. 48, 13 feet S. W., 3 feet 6 inches down, skeleton of animal, probably dog, which fell into small bits upon removal.

Burial No. 49, 9 feet S. W., a fireplace composed of a layer of charcoal and blackened sand, 4 inches thick at start and 1 foot 8 inches across. One foot inward it was 25 inches across and 5 inches thick, lessening from that point to its termination 26 inches from its outer margin. It was 18 inches below the surface of the mound.

Burial No. 50, 2 feet S., in the great central shell pocket, 4 feet from the surface, was a deposit of calcined human bones, 3 inches thick at the beginning and 13 inches in breadth. Sixteen inches inward it was 25 inches across and about 4 inches thick. It extended inward 2 feet 9 inches. With the calcined bones was no charcoal, and fragments of bones of lower animals lying among them showed no trace of fire. The cremation, therefore, had not been carried into effect on the spot. With the remains was an interesting pointed implement 11.3 inches in length (Fig. 70), wrought from a split bone of a lower animal, with a carefully incised decoration on the handle, a part of which is missing. An interesting feature is a former fracture repaired by the use of bitumen. With the piercing implement was what may have been a portion of a neatly carved handle of another bone implement; a small bone implement that crumbled to pieces, and half a rude chert arrowhead or knife.

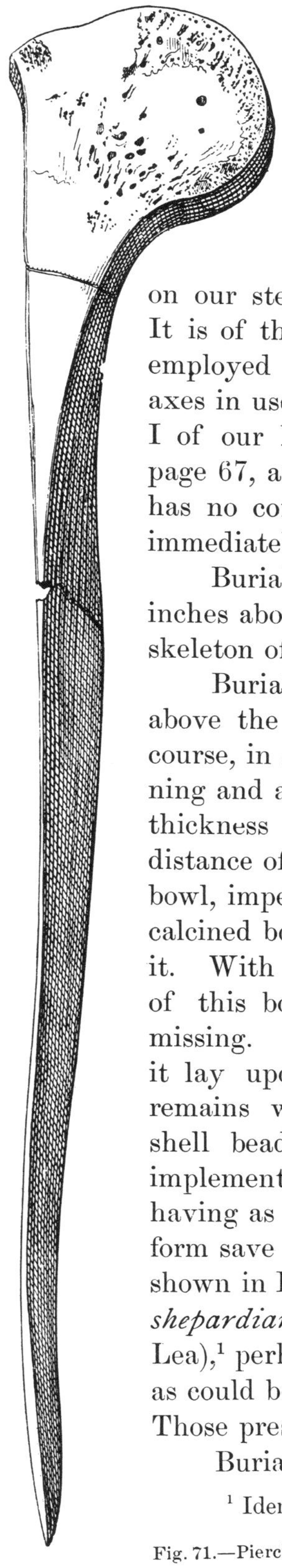

Twenty-five feet N. by E., and 2 feet from the surface, which at this part had no layer of oyster shells and seemed encumbered to a considerable extent with sand plowed from higher portions of the mound, was an axe of steel. This axe, which was not greatly rusted and is now doing duty on our steamer, had a certain amount of wood remaining in the eye. It is of the form at present known as the " turpentine axe " and is employed for " boxing " pine trees. It bears no resemblance to those axes in use among later Indians, one of which is figured by us in Part I of our Report on the " Mounds of the St. Johns River, Florida," page 67, and, in our opinion, was a recent addition to the mound, and has no connection with the period of its construction. It was not immediately associated with human remains.

Burial No. 51, 7 feet S. W., 6 feet 8 inches from the surface, or 4 inches above the base of the great central pit, beneath the shell, was a skeleton of a male, flexed on left side, head N. E.

Burial No. 52, just E. of the head of Burial No. 51, about 10 inches above the bottom of the pit, was a layer of calcined human bones (of course, in small fragments) having a thickness of 4 inches at the beginning and a breadth of 1 foot 7 inches. One foot from the beginning its thickness was 5 inches, its breadth 2 feet. It extended inward a distance of 26 inches. At the eastern outer corner was an undecorated bowl, imperforate, of about one pint capacity, filled with fragmentary calcined bones which possibly had entered from the layer contiguous to it. With these was a molar of a bear. Partially covering the opening of this bowl was a somewhat larger one from which a portion was missing. On either side of the bowls was hematite and a thin layer of it lay upon the upper surface of the layer of bones. With the remains was a small cord-marked bowl in pieces, containing a few shell beads. In addition, unaffected by fire, were three piercing implements of bone, two of ordinary type, the other, 8.3 inches long, having as a head the articular portion of the bone—a common enough form save that a certain portion had been removed from either side as shown in Fig. 71. Near these was a mass of fresh-water mussels (*Unio shepardianus*, Lea; *Unio dolabriformis*, Lea; *Unio roanokensis*, Lea),[1] perhaps fifty, nearly all hopelessly decayed and crushed. So far as could be determined each one bore a double perforation for suspension. Those preserved show no variation from living forms.

Burial No. 53, 25 feet E. of N., a grave having its base 4 feet 9

[1] Identified by Professor Pilsbry.

Fig. 71.—Piercing implement of bone. Mound D. (Full size.)

inches from the surface and extending 2 feet 8 inches into the yellow undisturbed sand. The diameter of this grave, 2 feet 1 inch beneath the surface, where it first became apparent upon entering the clear sand, was 8 feet. It converged to a base upon which lay a skeleton of a male, flexed on right side, head N. E. The superficial layer of shell began at this point.

Burial No. 54, 30 feet N. of E., a layer of charcoal, blackened sand and calcined shells, 8 inches thick, 20 inches long, extending inward 18 inches. The upper margin of this layer was 3.5 feet from the surface.

Burial No. 55, 25 feet E. by S., a part of a skull and a sacrum, 2 feet 4 inches from the surface. One foot 2 inches lower and about 2 feet farther inward was a skeleton flexed on its right side, lacking the skull but having the sacrum in place.

Burial No. 56, 17 feet N. W., 3 feet 9 inches from the surface, skeleton of young person with epiphyses unattached, flexed on right side, head N. E.

Burial No. 57, 17 feet N. by W., 3 feet from the surface on undisturbed sand lay a skeleton of a male, on the right side, flexed, the knees out, head E. This skeleton showed a fairly well-united fracture of the lower end of the fibula.

Burial No. 58, 19 feet N. by E., in a pit having its base 5 feet from the surface, beneath a superficial layer of 2 feet 4 inches of shell, which began over No. 53, was a skeleton of uncertain sex, at full length, face down, measuring 5 feet 6 inches as it lay, head E., arms parallel to body. Above the skeleton, beginning at the surface, were :

Dark sand . . . . . . 1 foot 3 inches
Shell layer . . . . . . 2 feet 4 inches

The pit beginning immediately under the shell was filled with 1 foot 5 inches of disturbed yellow sand. As no oyster shells were mingled with the sand filling the grave, it is evident that the grave was completed before the beginning of the layer above it, and not dug through it.

Burial No. 59, 14 feet N. W., 3 feet 4 inches from surface, skeleton of male with bones disarranged through inadvertence of diggers.

Burial No. 60, 16 feet N. W., a grave filled with brown sand, having disturbed yellow sand on either side. From surface of mound to base of pit, 3 feet 3 inches. On undisturbed sand, flexed skeleton of female, head N. W., shoulders on back, lower trunk turned to the left, knees to the left.

Burial No. 61, 21 feet N. E., a pocket of calcined human bones and charcoal, 3 feet 4 inches from the surface to its lower margin, 10 inches thick, 20 inches across and extending inward 10 inches. Near this fireplace was the lower articular portion of the femur of a bear, neatly severed by a cutting tool. A similar specimen was taken from Mound B, Darien.

Burial No. 62, Vessel Ma, 17 feet E. by S., a vessel of the ordinary type, having its upper margin 9 inches below the surface, crushed to fragments by the plow, which, however, were subsequently recovered and pieced together. Height, 18 inches; diameter of mouth, 13.5 inches; diameter of body, 11.5 inches. Upright, within vessel Ma, was an undecorated bowl of black ware, slightly flaring (Mb). Approximate measurements: maximum diameter, which was at the mouth, 8.5 inches; height, 5 inches. Within Mb, was a third vase (Mc) of black ware, having a globular body and flaring rim with decoration around the margin consisting of raised circles enclosing projections. Diameter at mouth, 5 inches; of body, 5.1 inches; height, 6 inches. Within Mc were a few calcined fragments of the bones of an infant. Both Mb and Mc, though badly broken, have been pieced together with practically no missing parts. Above and around Ma were pieces of earthenware belonging to at least two vessels, which may have served as a covering before the advent of the plow.

Burial No. 63, 13 feet W. by N., 2 feet 6 inches from the surface, in a grave which had its base on the undisturbed sand 4 feet 6 inches down, was a seated skeleton, facing N., with head crushed down on the pelvis. Both arms were parallel with the body, the forearms crossing on the pelvis. The thighs, with legs flexed back on them, projected up on either side. Sex uncertain.

Burial No. 64, immediately beneath No. 63, flexed skeleton of female, trunk to the left, head N. and facing in that direction.

Burial No. 65, isolated skull of a child in contact with the cranium of No. 64.

Burial No. 66, with the pelvis against No. 65 and the cranium of No. 64 was a skeleton of a young person, head S., upper trunk on back, head over on chest, legs flexed and turned to the right. Right arm along body with forearm beneath thighs. Left arm a little out and down, with forearm across pelvis.

Burial No. 67, along the bottom of the grave in which were Nos. 63, 64, 65 and 66, was the skeleton of a woman, face down, at full length, 5 feet 8 inches long as it lay; head N., arms and forearms parallel to trunk.

Burial No. 68, 10 feet N. by W., scattered human bones, 4 feet from surface.

Burial No. 69, 9 feet W. of N., skeleton of young person, flexed on right side, head S. E., 3 feet down. In association were a number of *Olivella* shells pierced for stringing.

Burial No. 70, on the same plane, and about 1 foot N. of No. 69, was the skeleton of a child about 5 years of age, flexed on the left side, head N. With it was a cord-marked bowl imposed upon a basket-marked cup, each of somewhat less than one pint capacity and imperforate as to its base. At the bottom of the cup were traces of red pigment.

Burial No. 71, just E. of the cranium of No. 70 were parts of the skull of an infant and a few fragmentary bones.

Burial No. 72, 11 feet N. W., 3 feet down, flexed skeleton of child from three to five years of age, badly crushed, head N.

Burial No. 73, Vessel N, 11 feet E. by N., just beneath the surface, an upright urn-shaped vessel with a faint diamond-stamped decoration, of poor material and completely rotten. It contained the calcined remains of a child. Though in such bad condition this vessel was cemented in place, pieced together and allowed to dry before removal and was thus recovered in fairly good condition. Approximate

16 JOURN. A. N. S. PHILA., VOL. XI.

measurements: height, 11 inches; diameter of mouth and maximum diameter of body, each about 8.75 inches (Plate XV).

Vessel O. Immediately behind Vessel N, on its side, facing it, was an imperforate bowl intact, with complicated, stamped decoration (Plate XIV, Fig. 2). Approximate measurements: diameter of mouth, and maximum diameter of body, each, 8.2 inches; height, 6 inches. No human remains were found in association, within or without.

Burial No. 74, 14 feet E. of N., skeleton of a dog.

Burial No. 75, 11 feet S. of E., 4 feet 9 inches down in a pit shown in the cross-section of the mound, a flexed skeleton of a child, head E.

Burial No. 76, 10 feet E., skeleton of a dog, 3 feet from the surface, at the bottom of a small pocket, beneath a local shell layer. This small pit had been dug through the shell layer, or through part of it, during its formation, as the pit had been filled with shells from the layer. However, a layer of calcined human bones (Burial No. 77) entirely intact, lay above the pit containing the dog, which was therefore not an intrusive burial.

Burial No. 77, 10 feet E., 6 inches from surface, a pocket of calcined human bones, 5 inches thick, circular, with a diameter of about 7 inches.

Burial No. 78, 11 feet E., 3 feet 8 inches from surface, in disturbed sand, skeleton of a child, flexed on right side, head S.

Burial No. 79, 18 feet N. E., 6 feet 9 inches from the surface, at the bottom of a pit and let into the clear yellow sand, was the skeleton of a male, at full length, face down, head N. W., with arms and forearms parallel to body. The cranium was saved (A. N. S., Cat. No. 2,166).

Burial No. 80, 11 feet E. by N., on the clear yellow sand on the slope of the pit ending with Burial No. 79 was a skeleton in a sitting position leaning forward, facing W., head forced down to pelvis, right arm along body, forearm crossing above pelvis, left arm along body, forearm forward at right angle. Thighs with legs against them, parallel to body.

Burial No. 81, 7 feet N. by W., 3 feet 8 inches down, just beneath the shell layer, in disturbed yellow sand, probably part of a large grave, the exact boundaries of which were not traceable, was a skeleton on right side, head N. W. A few scattered bones of another body, probably disturbed by the burial of No. 81, lay about.

Burial No. 82, Vessel P, in the central shell pocket, 3 feet W., 3 feet 6 inches down, crushed but held together by the shell, on its side, with a certain portion missing, was an imperforate cord-marked pot of poor material, approximately measuring 5.5 inches in height and 6 inches across its opening, where it had its maximum diameter. In it were the bones of an infant, unaffected by fire.

Burial No. 83, 8 feet E., nearly on the bottom of a pit, 3 feet from the surface, was the skeleton of a female on left side, head S. W., very much twisted as shown in Fig. 72. Beneath the cranium was the shell of a fresh-water mussel.

Burial No. 84, 5 feet N. E., 3 feet 4 inches down in a pit the limits of which were not determined, was the skeleton of a male, on the right side, head E.

Burial No. 85, 1 foot N., skeleton of a dog.

Mound D furnishes a good example of the curious forms of burial prevalent on the Georgia coast. We do not think all the skeletons were intentionally arranged as found, believing some, at least, were forced into pits comparatively small in size (for shovels in those early days were not so convenient as now, and digging was more onerous), and were twisted into positions more or less the result of chance. The burials at full length, usually at a great comparative depth from the surface, were unquestionably intentional as to their form, though the placing of the skeleton on its back or on its face may have been a matter of accident. In addition, we have layers of calcined human bones; uncremated infant skeletons buried in jars; incinerated remains of single infants in urns; and jars filled with incinerated remains, the result of a general cremation.

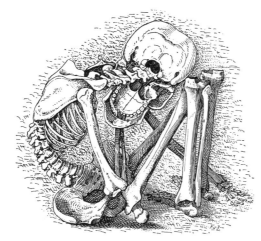

Fig. 72.—Burial No. 83. (Not on scale.)

One curious feature was the presence of numerous skeletons of dogs, which were not found in fragments, here and there a scattered bone, but interred in their entirety. These dogs, therefore, evidently had not served as food. Curiously enough, however, the dogs did not lie with or near human skeletons, as one would expect had they been slain and buried with their masters, but were accorded interment by themselves.

In no mound of the coast of Georgia have burials of dogs approached in number those in Mound D, though occasional ones—always represented by the entire skeleton—have been met with.

In Florida we found in a shell-heap on the Econlockhatchee creek, Orange County, a part of a canine jaw of considerable interest, which the late Professor Cope described and figured in the American Naturalist, July, 1893, in connection with certain references to prehistoric dogs in that number.[1]

Later, another fragmentary canine jaw was discovered by us in a Florida shell-heap.

On the base of the Tick Island mound, Volusia County, Florida, we found the skeleton of a dog, the skull of which is now in the collection of the late Professor Cope and was described by him in a note in our "Certain Sand Mounds of the St. Johns River, Florida," Part II.

On the base of the Light-house mound near Fernandina, Florida, were two skeletons of dogs, one in very poor condition. The skull of the better preserved one is in the possession of Professor Putnam and references to it by Professors Cope

[1] "Certain Shell Heaps of the St. Johns River, Florida, Hitherto Unexplored," by C. B. Moore. Third paper.

and Putnam may be found in our "Certain Florida Coast Mounds north of the St. Johns River,"[1] page 25 *et seq.*

Professor Putnam, in whose possession all our Georgia canine skulls now are (1897), after an extended comparative study, is convinced that there can be no doubt that a prehistoric dog existed, in type resembling the collie but with slightly broader jaws.

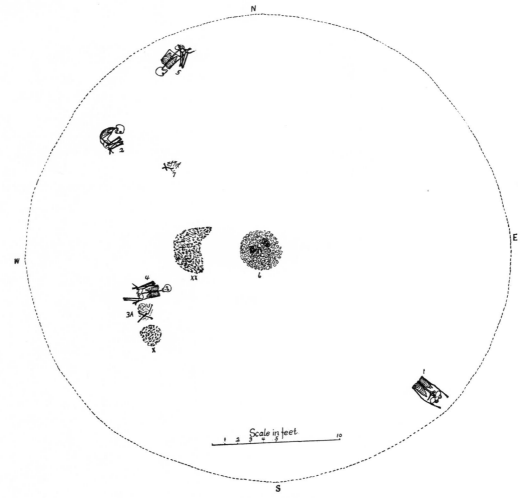

Fig. 73.—Diagram of Mound E.

Mr. Mercer has lately described a portion of a canine jaw found by him in a Maine shell-heap, with a note by Professor Cope.[2]

OSSABAW ISLAND, BRYAN COUNTY. MIDDLE SETTLEMENT, MOUND E.

This mound, in the same field and about 300 yards W. of Mound D, had been plowed over for so long a period that little could be determined as to its original

[1] Privately printed, Philadelphia, 1896.
[2] "An Exploration of Aboriginal Shell Heaps." Publications of the University of Pennsylvania, Vol. VI, page 123 *et seq.*

height. Its altitude at the time of the demolition of the mound by us was 14 inches; its diameter we judged to be about 38 feet.

Like many other mounds of its class it was composed of dark sand over undisturbed yellow sand, separated by a dark band, probably the original surface of the field. The line of the base showed marked irregularities, with several curious pits similar to those already referred to in other mounds. Oyster shells covered the central portion of the mound to a depth of about 1 foot 6 inches.

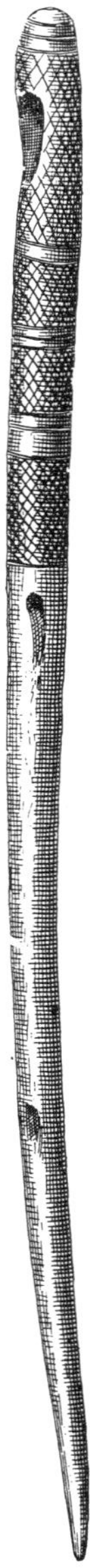

We give a detailed description of the skeletal remains in conjunction with the diagram (Fig. 73).

1.—16 feet S. E., a grave with the base 34 inches from the surface and 22 inches below the base line of the mound. In it was part of a skeleton in anatomical order, trunk on back and upper extremities in order, arms down along body, cranium missing but a few teeth lying on ribs, lower extremities missing with the exception of left foot which lay on trunk immediately above pelvis.

2.—15 feet N. W., a female skeleton, head N. E., flexed on left side, 10 inches down.

X.—12 feet S. of W., a fire-place 1 foot beneath surface, 20 inches long, with a maximum thickness of 2 inches, and extending inward 1 foot 7 inches.

3.—11 feet W. by S., 8 inches down, a number of loose human bones having in association fragments of a vessel of about 2 quarts capacity, crushed flat. The cranium was missing. This disturbance probably owed its origin to the plow.

4.—8 feet W. by S., a skeleton of uncertain sex, head E., trunk on back, left thigh extended, leg flexed back upon it, right thigh flexed toward body, leg drawn down upon thigh, arms and forearms parallel to body. This skeleton, one humerus of which showed an imperfectly united fracture,[1] was 15 inches from the surface.

5.—12 feet N. by W., a grave with base 37 inches from the surface, containing a skeleton with trunk on back, head S. W., thighs flexed on body and turned to the right, legs flexed against thighs, right arm and forearm parallel with body, left arm along body with forearm flexed at a right angle across body. From the bottom of the grave to the top of the black base-line was 25 inches. The pit was 3 feet 3 inches across at the top.

Fig. 74.—Bone pin with incised decoration. Mound E. (Full size.)

XX.—7 feet W., a fire-place about 2 inches thick, 1 foot 4 inches below the surface. Its outer margin had a length of 30 inches, broadening to 3 feet 9 inches about 1 foot 11 inches inward. From the left corner a small spur projected 9 inches farther in.

6.—2 feet W., a curious grave, 5 feet 6 inches in diameter at its apparent

[1] Sent to the Army Medical Museum, Washington, D. C.

starting point beneath the black base layer of the mound and 3.5 feet across its base, extended toward the center a distance of 3.5 feet. The black basal layer of the mound continued unbroken above it, showing its completion previous to the inception of the mound. From the surface of the mound to the bottom of the grave was 5 feet 4 inches. From the bottom of the black band to the bottom of the grave was 3 feet 6 inches. In the grave, 4 feet 10 inches from the surface, were three skeletons of children all about five or six years of age. With them were many fragments of pots in layers and one small undecorated cup with a curious knob on the outside at the bottom. This cup, somewhat crushed, has been almost completely restored.

7.—Just beneath the surface were certain human bones, doubtless remains of a skeleton disturbed by a plow.

In the shell debris covering the mound was a bone pin 6 inches in length, encircled as to the upper part with incised decoration extending 2 inches down (Fig. 74).

OSSABAW ISLAND, BRYAN COUNTY. MIDDLE SETTLEMENT, MOUND F.

This low elevation, in the same field as Mound B and about 200 yards in a westerly direction from it, had long been under cultivation. Its highest portion, where superficial shell had a somewhat greater upward slope, was about 20 inches above the general level. The limits of the mound were not definitely fixed. A diameter of 76 feet was taken and the southernmost half of the circumference was carefully dug through.

The mound, which had absolutely no dark band running through it, was composed of black loam mixed with oyster shells. The usual grave-pits were present, the majority being filled with midden refuse, though several contained dark sand only.

Human remains, in an excellent state of preservation, were met with to the number of twenty. No urn-burials of any sort or pockets of calcined remains were found.

One skeleton of a dog was found, interred alone, as usual.

Cord-marked ware in the form of sherds, was present through the body of the mound but the complicated stamp was unrepresented save by two or three fragments from near the surface. One undecorated sherd had a thickness of 1.1 inches.

Four pebble-hammers lay separately in the sand. Three others, two of quartz and one of *Granulite*,[1] lay together, away from human remains. One had a length of about 6 inches.

Four rude piercing implements of bone came separately from the midden refuse in which also was found the tine of a stag-horn, severed by a cutting tool.

Burials were of the flexed variety; the majority of skeletons on the left side. The direction of the heads of eighteen was noted. Ten were to the E., two to the N. E., two to the S. E., two to the W., one to the N. and one to the S. W.

A little hematite lay with one burial. With another were two fresh-water mussel shells and a mass of rock, somewhat worked.

[1] All determinations of rock are by Dr. Goldsmith.

OSSABAW ISLAND, BRYAN COUNTY. BLUFF FIELD, MOUND A.

The Bluff Field is a cultivated tract about 2.5 miles by land in a northeasterly direction from the Middle Settlement, and is under the same control.

Mound A, about midway between the extremities of the field, and perhaps 75 yards from the bluff, had a height of 2 feet 3 inches above the surrounding level. We gave to it a diameter of about 56 feet, which probably included more than the mound. The mound had been much plowed away but bore no trace of previous investigation, save several small holes dug by colored men.

The mound was completely dug through. It was composed of black loam with oyster shells scattered here and there and contained several local layers of shell. The central portion of the mound, with an average diameter of 24 feet, was a solid mass of oyster shells from the surface down to a thin stratum of black loam from 6 to 12 inches in thickness. Beneath was undisturbed grayish-white sand. At the center of the mound this mass of shell was 2 feet thick. Marginal pits filled with black midden refuse and containing no burials, were present.

Human remains in fairly good condition were met with at fourteen points —one deposit of calcined remains and thirteen skeletons. The skeletons, heading in all directions, were flexed on the right, on the left, or with trunk on back and lower extremities to the right or to the left. The calcined remains were a layer at the bottom of a pit extending 18 inches into undisturbed sand with fragments of charcoal above it. Completely covering the area where the pit entered the undisturbed sand, was a layer of four thicknesses of large cord-marked sherds.

Away from human remains was the skeleton of a dog, the principal parts of which were forwarded by us to Professor Putnam.

By the cranium of a child was a practically undecorated pot, imperforate, with inverted rim, in the shape of an inverted cone with rounded apex, or of an acorn with blunted point. Diameter of aperture, 4 inches; maximum diameter, 5 inches; height, 4.3 inches (Fig. 75).

Scattered sherds were practically unrepresented in the mound. A mass of stone, probably amphibolic gneiss, pitted, and used as a smoothing stone, lay loose in the sand.

On the surface, near Mound A, lay a rude implement, probably of amphibolic gneiss, about 4 inches in length, somewhat resembling in form a hoe-shaped implement, or spud. It is much chipped at the edge, having probably seen service as a hoe. It bears a longitudinal groove showing secondary use as a hone.

OSSABAW ISLAND, BRYAN COUNTY. BLUFF FIELD, MOUND B.

This mound, in the extreme S. W. part of the field, had a height of 19 inches. A certain amount had been ploughed away. No previous investigation was reported or noted.

A diameter of 40 feet was taken, and the circumference dug through, including we believe, considerably more than the mound. It was composed of black loamy sand with oyster shells scattered throughout. Toward the center the shells became more numerous but were not in a compact mass. From what seemed to be the center of the surface of the mound to undisturbed sand was 26 inches.

Sherds were of very infrequent occurrence, none bearing the complicated stamp.

The mound, in swampy ground, contained human remains at six points, all badly decayed.

Burial No. 1, 3 feet W. of center, just beneath the surface, was a small pocket of scattered fragments of calcined human bones with charcoal at either extremity.

Fig. 75.—Vessel of earthenware. Mound A, Bluff Field. (Full size.)

Burial No. 2, in a central position in the mound, on the bottom of a pit 29 inches deep and extending 10 inches into undisturbed sand, was a deposit of calcined fragments of human bones, 14 by 18 inches, and 4 to 6 inches in thickness. At either side, and above this deposit, was charcoal. At its outer margin was a pebble-hammer of quartz and a small chisel of greenstone. A little farther in, resting on its imperforate base, was an undecorated bowl, with a slightly inverted rim, having a diameter at mouth of 5.3 inches, a maximum diameter of 6 inches and a height of 2.8 inches. Upright within this was a curious little imperforate, undecorated vessel. Diameter of mouth, 2.3 inches; maximum diameter, 3 inches; height, 2.4

inches (Fig. 76). Beneath the larger vessel was a tobacco pipe of earthenware, having the usual curious chipping on the stem, 3.4 inches in length ; diameter of bowl, 1.3 inches (Fig. 77). On the upper surface of the deposit lay a neatly shaped arrowhead of chert.

Burial No. 3, 3 feet N. E., 3 feet from the surface, on the bottom of a pit extending 16 inches into undisturbed sand and having a diameter of 3 feet 4 inches at its line of junction with the body of the mound, consisted of the bones of a small child in fragments through decay. Surrounding sand was tinged with hematite.

Fig. 76.—Vessel of earthenware. Mound B, Bluff Field. (Full size.)

In contact with this skeleton was another, also of a young child, equally fragmentary, the legs extending up along the side of the pit. Above this skeleton was a layer of sherds three and four thick. Beneath both skeletons was charcoal.

Burial No. 4, 2 feet N., in a grave with its base 33 inches from the surface, and 2 feet in diameter where it entered the undisturbed sand, into which it ran 14 inches, was the skeleton of a child about 5 years of age, flexed on the right side, heading W.

Directly N. on the same plane, were the skeletal remains of a child about 3 years of age, flexed on the back, heading W.

Burial No. 5, 6 feet N. W., 30 inches down, just let into undisturbed sand, was a skeleton of an adult female, flexed on the right side, head N. W.

Burial No. 6, 5 feet N. by W., 2 feet from the surface, was the skeleton of a young infant, unfortunately disturbed by one of our men in digging.

This mound calls to mind Mound A, of the Middle Settlement, in that the skeletons of adult males were

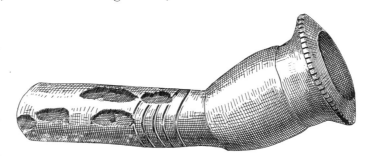

Fig. 77.—Tobacco pipe of earthenware. Mound B. Bluff Field. (Full size.)

excluded, and, as in Mound A, calcined remains were present. These remains included adult skeletons, but whether male or female we are unable to state. Another curious feature of this mound was the central position of burials.

17 JOURN. A. N. S. PHILA., VOL. XI.

OSSABAW ISLAND, BRYAN COUNTY. BLUFF FIELD, MOUND C.

This mound, in a portion of the field used for the cultivation of rice, lay in low ground which was drained by us before proceeding to investigate, and even then the presence of water was a hindrance. The mound, which had been much dug into by negroes living on the island, was about 150 yards N. of Mound B and had a height of 30 inches, which in no wise represented its original altitude. A diameter of 50 feet, which more than included the mound, was taken, and the circumference dug through with the exception of where a former trench had been excavated.

The mound offered no structural feature of interest. Sherds were fairly abundant, the majority decorated with the complicated stamp.

A mass of coral, about thrice the size of a clenched hand, lay unassociated.

With no interment, but doubtless belonging to one previously removed, were a number of shell beads.

A grooved pebble-hammer and one-half of a sandstone hone lay separately, loose in the sand. A portion of a tobacco pipe, with projecting knobs upon the bowl, came from midden refuse.

In the entire mound human remains were met with at but three points.

Burial No. 1, Vessel A, the lower portion of a large imperforate vessel with complicated stamp, the upper part plowed away, filled with calcined human bones. With them were: a chert nodule; an oblong piece of chert, showing a certain amount of chipping; a fragment of chert; and part of a lance head of the same material.

Burial No. 2, 5 feet W., 1 foot down, on the bottom of a small pit was a deposit of fragments of calcined human bones, 1.5 inches thick at the start, 18 inches across and extending inward 17 inches where it attained a thickness of 3 inches. Above a portion of this deposit were a number of good sized fragments from several vessels. The decoration on two sherds was of interest. On one (Fig. 78), in relief, was an encircled point, sometimes an emblem of the sun-god, also a symbol of the Mayas and found in Europe on the painted pebbles of Mas d'Azil.[1] The other is shown in Fig. 79.

Professor Holmes, "considering the locality," is "inclined to regard them as merely ornaments or parts of patterns."

Thomas Wilson, Esq., writes of them as follows:

"The signs or marks which you have found on the pottery in * * * * * Georgia, and about which you wrote me, have been noticed by me during my investigations of the Swastika sign. But I have never been able to find any connection between them and the Swastika, nor to find them in such association as to induce me to believe that they had either a symbolic or ideographic character, or were other than the mere decoration or ornamentation which we find in so many hundreds of other forms on the respective implements and objects of prehistoric times."

Professor Putnam takes a different view. He says:

---

[1] Of, and after, the period of the reindeer. "*Les Galets Coloriés du Mas d'Azil.*" *L'Anthropologie* (supplément). *Juillet-Août*, 1896. Pl. XI, Fig. 9.

"As to the circle with the dot, there can hardly be a doubt that it is a sun symbol. Of course in the minds of some persons this would simply be a circle with a dot in it, a mere decoration without any particular meaning; but I have long been convinced that in the development of American art, after passing through the realistic stage, conventionalized forms were used, and at this period of development, symbolism became a marked feature in certain regions. Finally the spaces around the essential figure or symbol were sometimes filled up at the fancy of the artist; the main point in all higher decoration *being the expression of a thought* by a conventionalized form or sacred symbol.

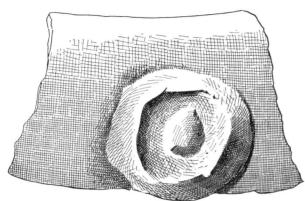

Fig. 78.—Sherd, Mound B, Bluff Field. (Full size.)

"The sun symbol, we may say, is cosmopolitan. It is widely expressed by a simple circle or a circle with a central dot. In this connection I call your attention to the paper by Mr. Willoughby and myself entitled 'Symbolism in Ancient American Art,' and a more recent paper following out the same line of thought, written by Mr. Willoughby and entitled: 'An Analysis of Decorations Upon Pottery from the Mississippi Valley.' The perusal of this paper will, I think, convince you that the decorations consisting of circles, crosses and scrolls are really the more or less conventionalized rendering of certain symbols. You will notice this circle and dot combined with the swastika-like figure of the four winds in Fig. 11 of Mr. Willoughby's paper, and you will find the sun symbol in various connections shown in many of the figures; also in some of the figures in our joint paper on 'Symbolism.'

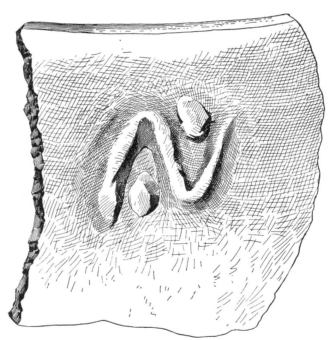

Fig. 79.—Sherd, Mound B, Bluff Field. (Full size.)

"The peculiar Z-shaped figure with the two dots probably has the same meaning as the swastika, or being a half swastika as Mr. Willoughby says, it probably indicates a gentle wind or breath, in other words, life. This is the actual meaning of the symbol as used among some of the Pueblo tribes. You will find this same Z-shaped figure in the center of a design, representing a woman, drawn by the Mokis, in Mallory's paper, page 705 of the Report of the Bureau of Ethnology, 1888-89. In this, however, the two dots are not represented. I know of only one other example like yours, and that is shown on a small human figure carved in ivory from a mound in Ohio. This figure is represented with some sort of decoration over the chest and on that decoration is carved the Z-shaped design with the two dots as shown on your potsherd."

Burial No. 3, Vessel B, 4 feet W. N. W., approximately the lower third of a large imperforate vessel, the remainder of which had been ploughed away. Within were fragments of calcined human bones and 26 barrel-shaped beads of shell, remarkably well preserved, the largest about .75 of one inch in length.

The Cabbage-Garden and the Long-Field, neighboring tracts, were carefully searched for mounds without success, though shell heaps were abundant. A number of these were investigated without results of especial interest.

SKIDDAWAY ISLAND, CHATHAM COUNTY. THIRD SETTLEMENT, MOUND A.

This mound, in a field long under cultivation, leased by Fanny Johnston, colored, in the Third Settlement, scarcely rose above the general level. Its diameter was estimated at 74 feet; a section line extending E. S. E. and W. N. W. was run through what seemed to be the center of the mound and the half to the south was dug through. There was no sign of previous investigation. The usual pits and graves were present.

In the half of the mound investigated, human remains were met with at twenty-seven points as follows: four pockets of calcined remains; four late disturbances; one not determined; eighteen skeletons.

Of the 18 skeletons: two were at full length on back; nine at full length on face; four were flexed on the left side; one flexed, face down; while one, with the trunk on back, had the legs partly flexed; one was in a sitting position, with the head crushed down on the pelvis.

Excluding the burial in a sitting position the skeletons headed: E., 1; E. by N., 2; N. E. by E., 1; N. E., 3; N. N. W., 2; N. W., 1; W. S. W., 2; S. W., 1; S. E. by S., 1; S. E., 2; E. S. E., 1.

The five flexed burials, however, headed between S. E. and W. S. W.

Sherds were rarely met with in the mound. None of complicated stamp was present.

Near a burial was part of a gracefully shaped hammer of quartzite and a pebble-hammer.

With another burial were six pebble-hammers of quartz, one smoothing stone and hematite.

Several fragmentary implements of stone and one bone piercing implement were met with.

A fact carefully noted by us, all through our investigation of the Georgia Coast, but not referred to until its close, namely, the utter absence of artifacts with burials at length, was again emphasized in this mound. Though as a rule, extended burials lay near the base, on it or below it, and often great pits had been made for their accommodation, yet associated artifacts were always wanting. As a rule, calcined deposits not enclosed in cinerary urns and masses of bones not in anatomical order were the most favored in respect to art-relics, though flexed burials were not entirely neglected.

SKIDDAWAY ISLAND, CHATHAM COUNTY. THIRD SETTLEMENT, MOUND B.

What the plow had spared of this mound lay in a cultivated field about 300 yards N. of Mound A. Its height was about 18 inches. Oyster shells were scattered on its surface and throughout the adjacent field. A diameter of 60 feet was taken and the eastern half completely dug through. Marginal pits filled with refuse were present. Local layers of oyster shells and the usual grave-pits were met with. One grave extended 4 feet below the surface.

Human remains, encountered at eleven points, included one aboriginal disturbance and three inadvertently dug into by men in our employ. The remaining seven are given in detail.

Burial No. 1, female in kneeling position, leaning forward, head N. E.

Burial No. 3, male in sitting position, facing N. Head crushed almost to pelvis.

Burial No. 5, 13 feet N. E., child from 3 to 5 years of age, in sitting position, facing E.

Burial No. 6, child about six years old, apparently flexed on right side, head S.

Burial No. 7, skeleton of uncertain sex in a sitting position, facing about S. S. W., tilted against one side of the pit.

Burial No. 8, skeleton of male, kneeling and crooked forward, head N. W.

Burial No. 11, skeleton of adolescent flexed on left side, head S. E.

Several pebble-hammers were met with.

Earthenware of the complicated stamp was wanting.

SKIDDAWAY ISLAND, CHATHAM COUNTY. NORTH-END SETTLEMENT.

This mound, in a field formerly under cultivation, about 1.25 miles in a S. S. W. direction from the northern end of the island, had sustained a certain amount of previous investigation. Its height was 2 feet; its diameter, apparently about 45 feet. The mound was completely dug down by us.

Several skeletons offering no points of especial interest and the lower part of a vessel of the ordinary type were met with. The upper part of this vessel had been ploughed away and lost. Near by lay one fragment of a calcined bone.

No artifacts of interest were found.

REMARKS.

The mounds of the Georgia coast, as judged by their contents, lead us to believe them to have been relics of a race ill supplied with stone, almost without copper, but given to the manufacture of earthenware, which, however, lacked diversity of type.

The builders of these tumuli differed markedly from the aborigines of Florida in their method of constructing many of their mounds, in possessing a totally different type of tobacco pipe, in the absence of mortuary earthenware with ready-made perforation in the base.

They coincided, however, in the absence of the grooved axe and of the mortar made of stone. In both sections this utensil was probably of wood, as are some along the Georgia coast at the present time.

In mortuary methods we note a striking difference between the mound-makers of the Georgia coast and their neighbors to the south. In Florida, cremation, though practised, was by no means carried to so great an extent as on the coast of Georgia, while, to the best of our belief, placing of cremated remains in cinerary urns and uncremated skeletal remains in jars was unknown in Florida.[1]

A point of interest, as illustrating diversity of custom in neighboring localities, is that when jars were used for uncremated remains, infants exclusively were selected in some localities, as at Creighton Island, and at Ossabaw Island, and adults in others, as at Sapelo Island, and at St. Catherine's Island with one exception.

Another feature of interest was the occasional occurrence of mounds in which the skeletal burials were those of women and children exclusively. But the most striking feature of all and one for which we vainly seek a solution is the use in the same mound of forms of burial so varied, varieties of inhumation and of cremation lying side by side.

We are told by Cabeça de Vaca,[2] who, as the reader recalls, crossed from Florida to Mexico comparatively early in the sixteenth century, that certain aborigines of northwest Florida burned the remains of their doctors while burying those of all others. Here we see a distinction in form of burial, which, however, cannot apply to the Georgia coast, for even had physicians been proportionately as numerous in former times as they are at present, still the percentage of cremations in the coast mounds is too great to consider these cremations the remains of medicine-men alone. Besides, as we have seen, cremated remains of infants are met with on the Georgia coast.

In conclusion, we call the attention of the reader to mortuary customs across the sea in former times, so ably presented by the Marquis de Nadaillac in the succeeding paper, "Inhumation and Incineration in Europe."

---

[1] Colonel C. C. Jones (*op. cit.* page 456), refers to urn-burial in Florida. We think this accomplished writer, who did little work in that State, must have accepted erroneous information. Vessels buried beside skeletons often receive a certain number of bones from them, a fact which may have misled investigators as to urn-burial in Florida.

[2] "It is their custom to bury the dead, unless it be those among them who have been physicians, and those they burn." The Narrative of Alvar Nuñez Cabeça de Vaca, translated by Buckingham Smith. Washington, 1851, page 49.

MOORE: GEORGIA COAST MOUNDS.

1. VESSEL OF EARTHENWARE, MOUND B, DARIEN.　　2. VESSEL OF EARTHENWARE, WALKER MOUND.　　(BOTH FULL SIZE.)

PLATE II.

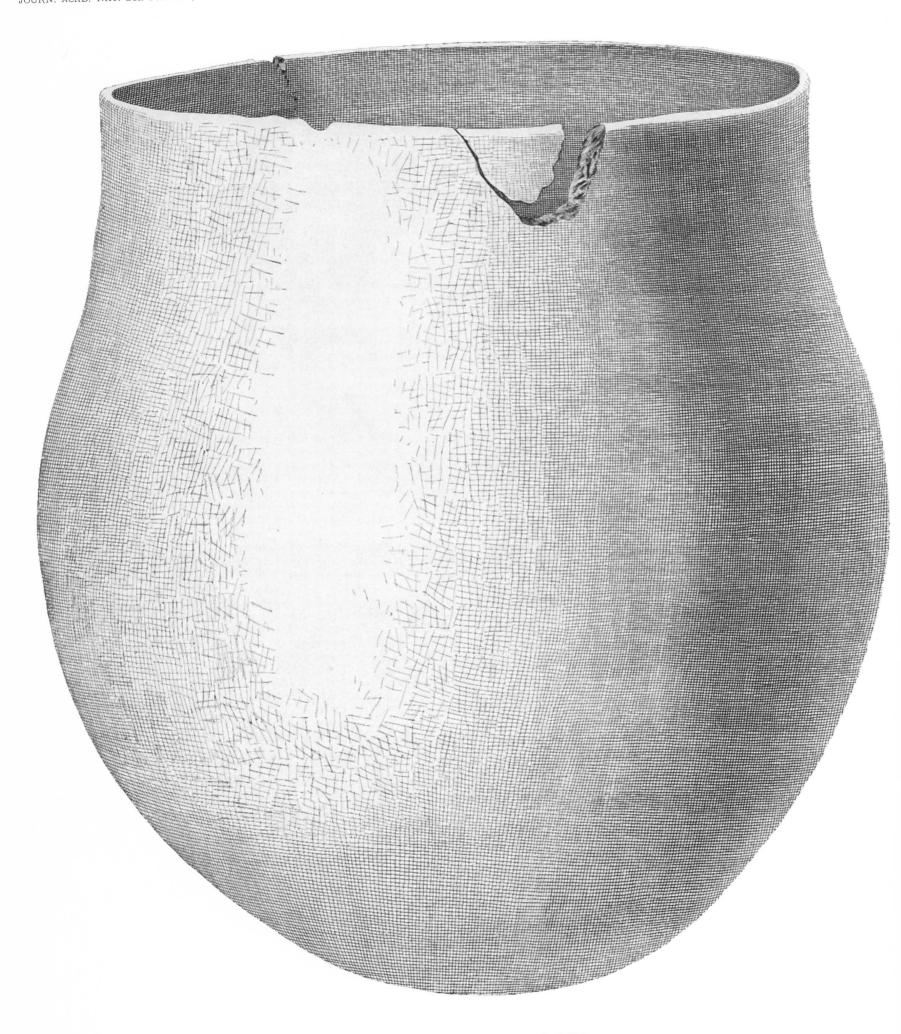

MOORE: GEORGIA COAST MOUNDS.

VESSEL C (BURIAL 20).   MOUND AT SHELL BLUFF.   (SEVEN-EIGHTHS SIZE.)

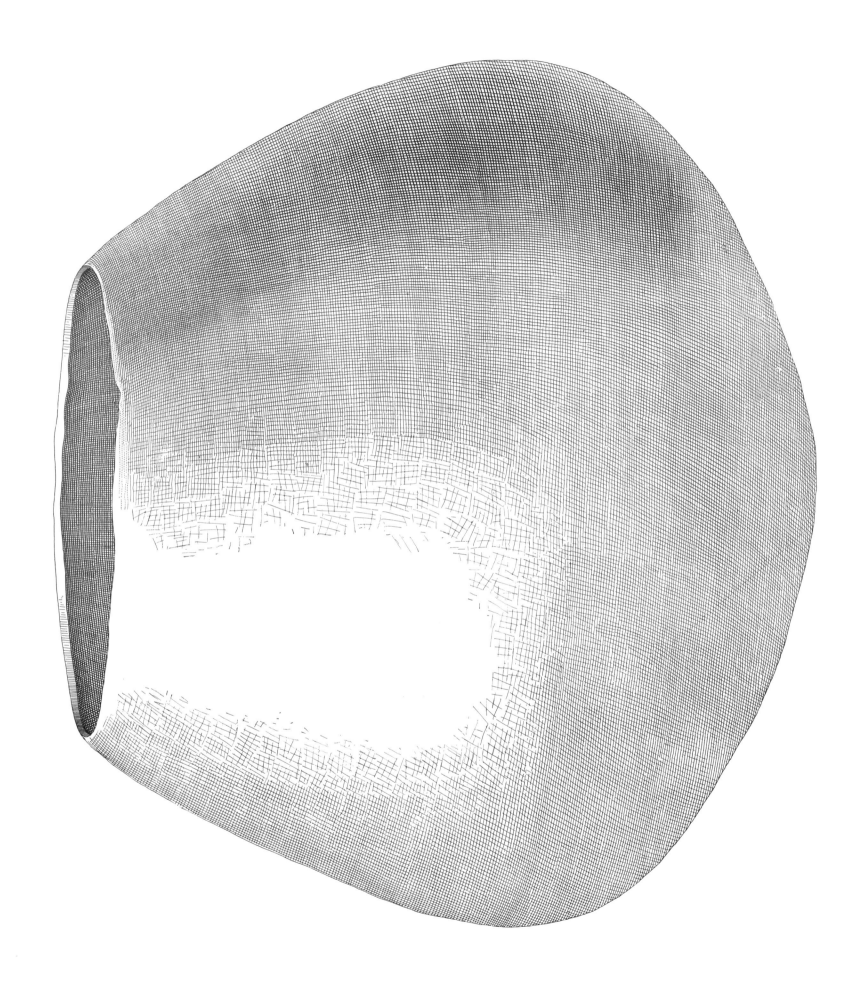

MOORE: GEORGIA COAST MOUNDS.

VESSEL D (BURIAL 20A).   MOUND AT SHELL BLUFF.   (FULL SIZE.)

PLATE IV.

MOORE: GEORGIA COAST MOUNDS.

VESSEL OF EARTHENWARE.   MOUND NORTH END OF CREIGHTON ISLAND.   (FULL SIZE.)

MOORE: GEORGIA COAST MOUNDS.

CINERARY URN, WALKER MOUND.   (HALF SIZE.)

PLATE VI.

MOORE: GEORGIA COAST MOUNDS.

CINERARY URN, WALKER MOUND.   (THREE-FIFTHS SIZE.)

PLATE VII.

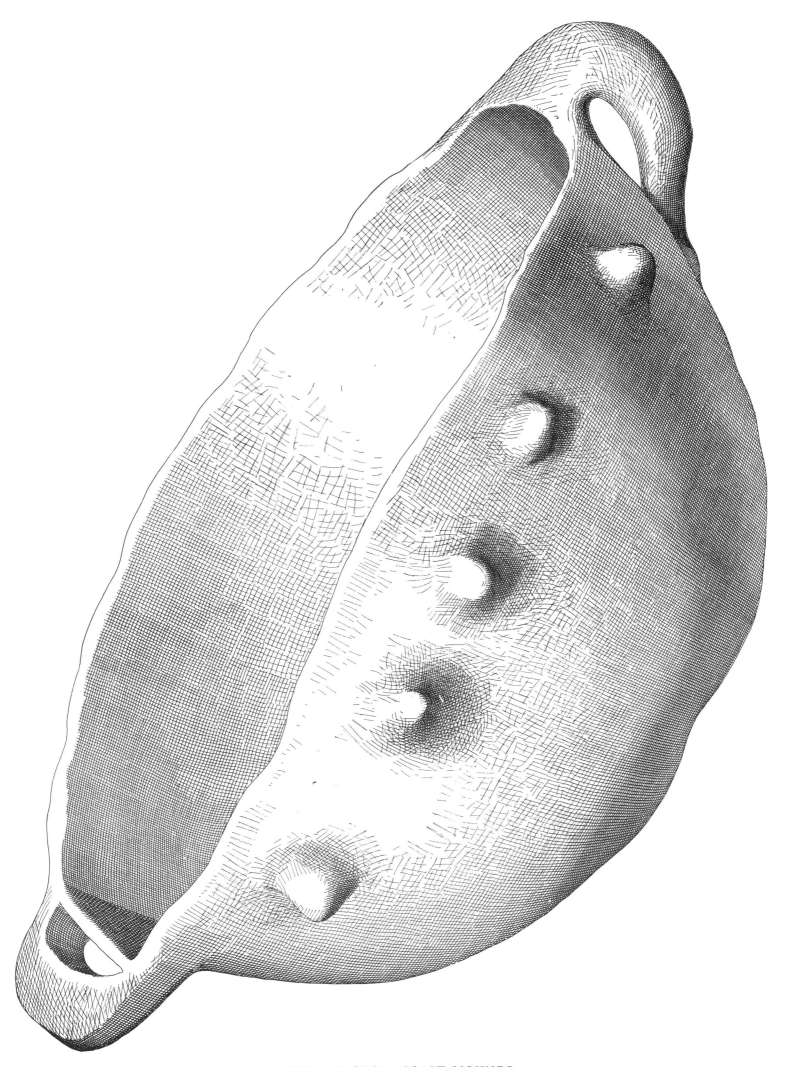

MOORE: GEORGIA COAST MOUNDS.

DISH OF EARTHENWARE.   MOUND AT BOURBON, SAPELO ISLAND.   (FULL SIZE.)

PLATE VIII.

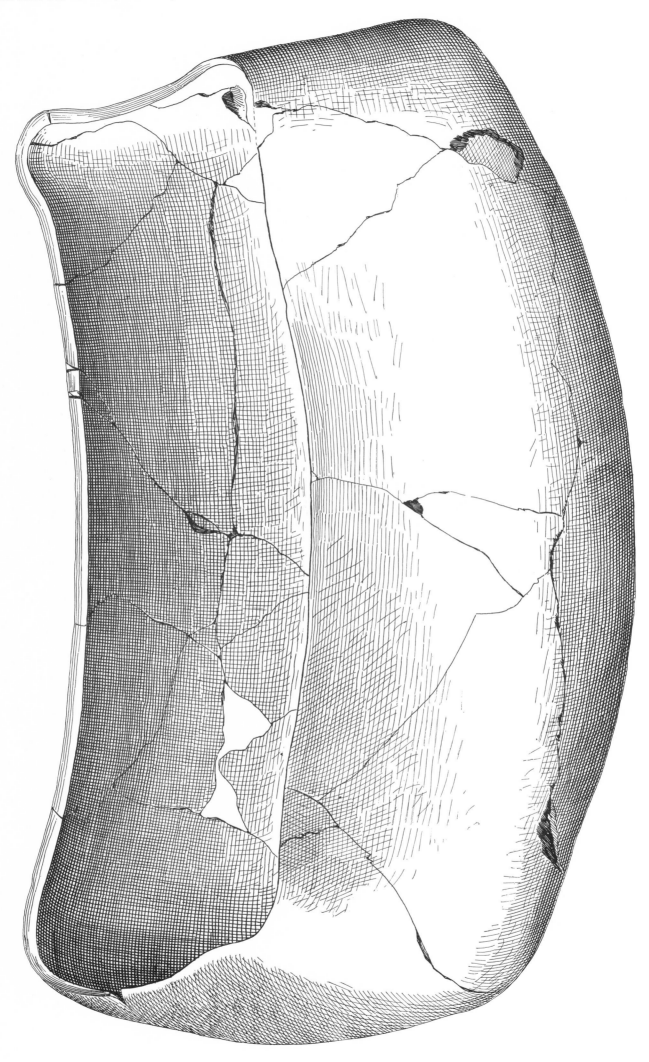

MOORE: GEORGIA COAST MOUNDS.

VESSEL C (BURIAL 36).   MOUND IN DUMOUSSAY'S FIELD, SAPELO ISLAND.   (THREE-FIFTHS SIZE.)

PLATE IX.

MOORE: GEORGIA COAST MOUNDS.

VESSEL D.   MOUND A, MIDDLE SETTLEMENT, OSSABAW ISLAND.   (ABOUT FIVE-EIGHTS SIZE.)

PLATE X.

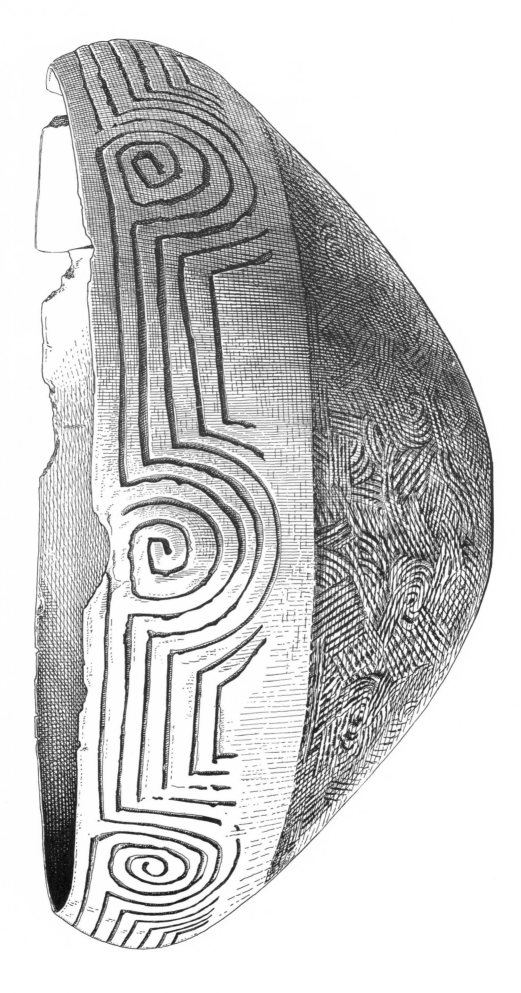

MOORE: GEORGIA COAST MOUNDS.

VESSEL R8.   MOUND A, MIDDLE SETTLEMENT, OSSABAW ISLAND.   (ABOUT FOUR-FIFTHS SIZE.)

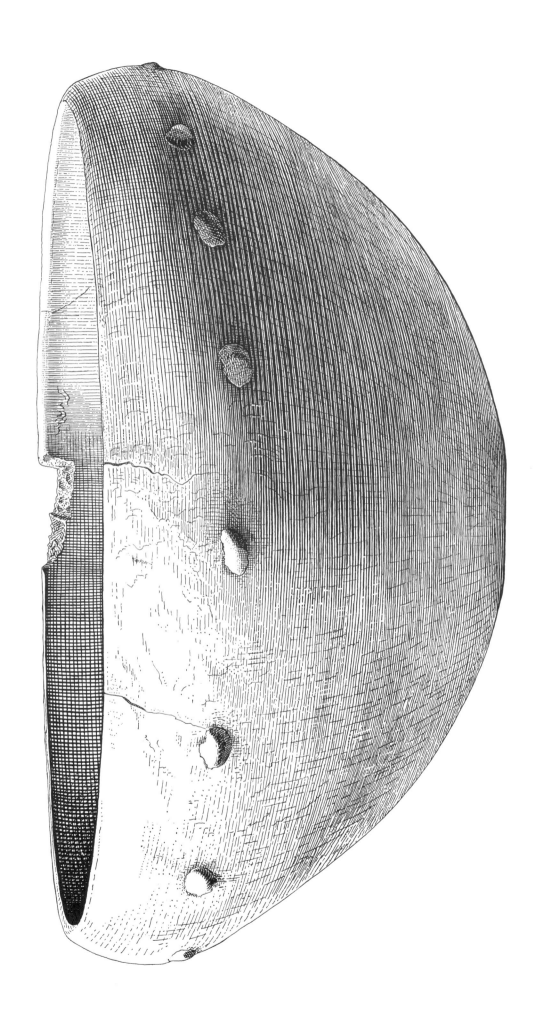

MOORE: GEORGIA COAST MOUNDS.

VESSEL 58.   MOUND A, MIDDLE SETTLEMENT, OSSABAW ISLAND.   (ABOUT FIVE-SEVENTHS SIZE.)

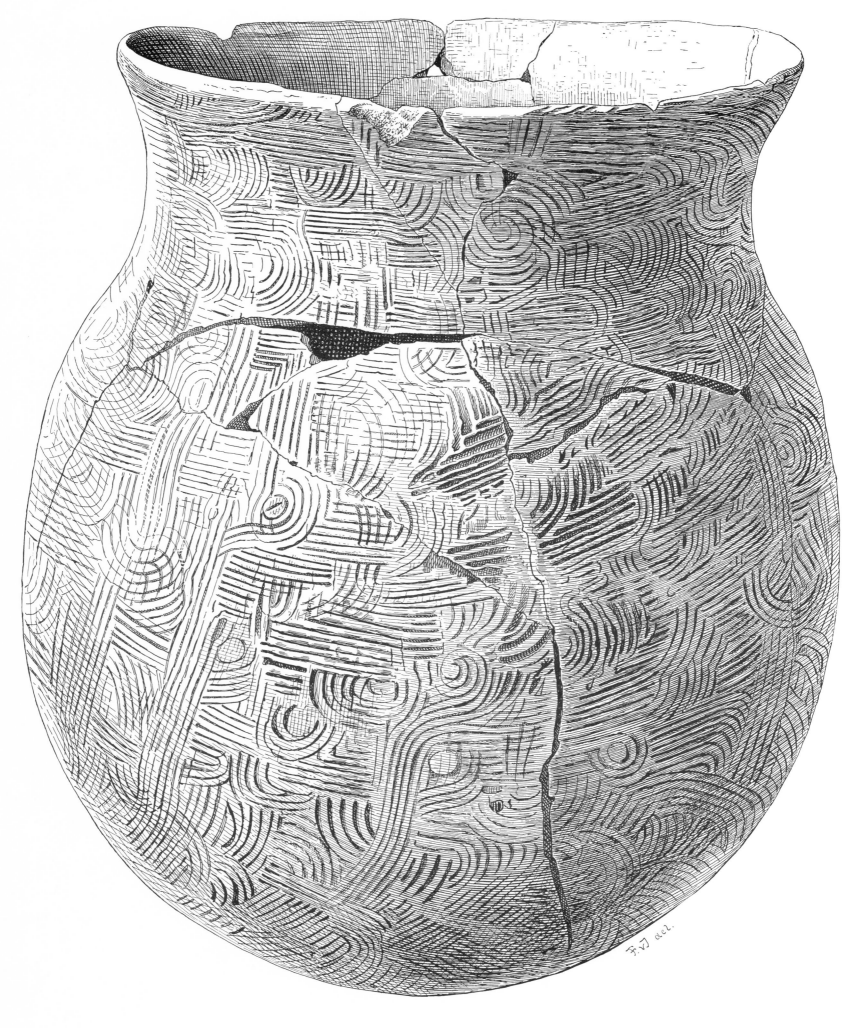

MOORE: GEORGIA COAST MOUNDS.

VESSEL AA.   MOUND A, MIDDLE SETTLEMENT, OSSABAW ISLAND.   (ABOUT TWO-THIRDS SIZE.)

MOORE: GEORGIA COAST MOUNDS.

1. VESSEL II.   2. VESSEL I.   BOTH MOUND A, MIDDLE SETTLEMENT, OSSABAW ISLAND.   (FULL SIZE.)

1

2

MOORE: GEORGIA COAST MOUNDS.

1. VESSEL LL.   MOUND A, MIDDLE SETTLEMENT, OSSABAW ISLAND.   (FULL SIZE.)
2. VESSEL O.   MOUND D, MIDDLE SETTLEMENT, OSSABAW ISLAND.   (FULL SIZE.)

PLATE XV.

MOORE: GEORGIA COAST MOUNDS.

VESSEL N.   MOUND D, MIDDLE SETTLEMENT, OSSABAW ISLAND.   (TEN-ELEVENTHS SIZE.)

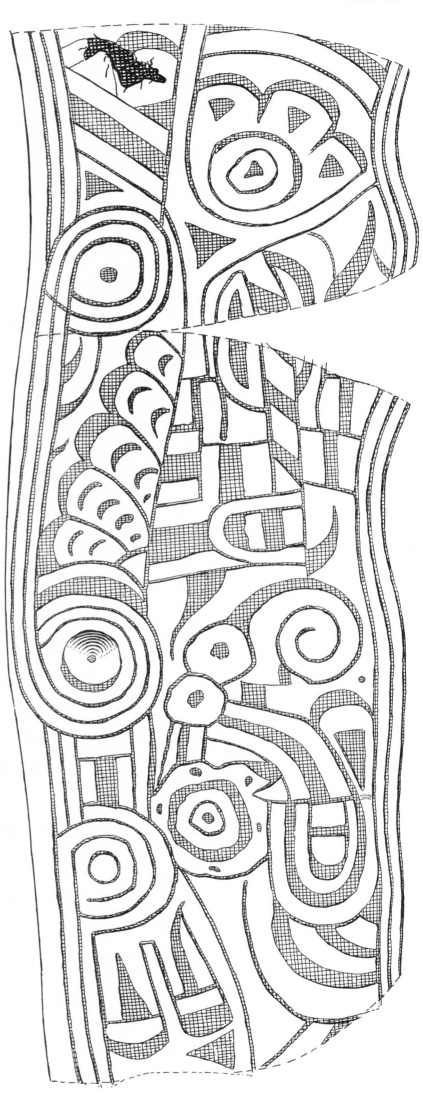

MOORE: GEORGIA COAST MOUNDS.

DIAGRAM OF INCISED DECORATION ON VESSEL OF EARTHENWARE.   WALKER MOUND.   (NINE-TENTHS SIZE.)

Certain Aboriginal Mounds
of the
Coast of South Carolina

Certain Aboriginal Mounds
of the
Savannah River

Certain Aboriginal Mounds
of the
Altamaha River

Recent Acquisitions

BY

CLARENCE B. MOORE

PLATE XVII. FRONTISPIECE.

MOORE: SOUTH CAROLINA COAST MOUNDS.

ABORIGINAL STRUCTURE.   MOUND ON LITTLE ISLAND.

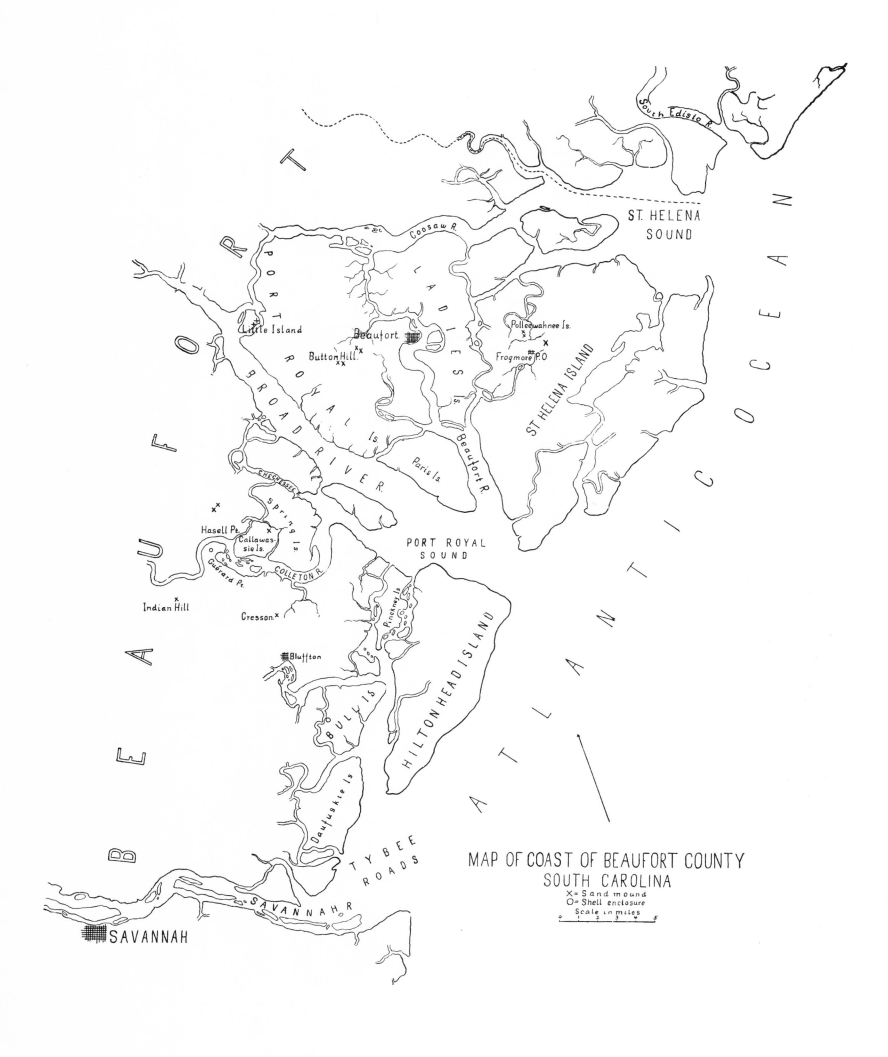

ST. HELENA
SOUND

South Edisto R.

Coosaw R.

PORT ROYAL

LADIES Is.

Little Island

Button Hill

Beaufort

Polleewahnee Is.

Frogmore P.O.

St. HELENA ISLAND

BROAD RIVER

Paris Is.

Beaufort R.

CHECHESSEE

Spring Is.

Hasell Pt.

Callawas-
sie Is.

PORT ROYAL
SOUND

Guerard Pt.

COLLETON R.

Indian Hill

Cresson

Pinckney Is.

Bluffton

HILTON HEAD ISLAND

BULL Is.

Daufuskie Is.

TYBEE
ROADS

SAVANNAH R.

SAVANNAH

B E A U F O R T

A T L A N T I C   O C E A N

MAP OF COAST OF BEAUFORT COUNTY
SOUTH CAROLINA

X = Sand mound
O = Shell enclosure

Scale in miles
0   1   2   3   4   5

CERTAIN ABORIGINAL MOUNDS OF THE COAST OF SOUTH CAROLINA.

By Clarence B. Moore.

At the conclusion of our work on the Georgia coast, the results of which we have published in this Journal,[1] it seemed advisable, for the purpose of comparison, to continue our labors northward along the coast of South Carolina, or rather as much of it as affords an inland passage by water, sheltered by sea-islands, as is the case along the entire coast of Georgia. The portion of the South Carolina littoral permitting inland navigation lies between the Savannah river on the south and Georgetown on the north, about 125 miles in a straight line. A very extended amount of territory, however, much of it low lying marsh, is included between the sounds; the rivers, which are often only arms of the sea, the creeks and waterways of this portion of the coast.

That part of the coast lying between the Savannah river and St. Helena sound (see map) was many times gone over by us, and the inhabitants carefully questioned. In addition, we received material aid from a number of gentlemen of South Carolina and Mr. Clarence U. V. Benton, of near Beaufort, in particular, who made careful inquiries over an extended period of time, and afforded us much valuable information as to the locality of mounds. In this district, the coast of Beaufort county, in addition to the localities particularly referred to as having mounds, we searched Daufuskie island, Bull island, Hilton Head island, Jenkins island, Pinckney island, Spring island, Ladies island, and part of the mainland without finding mounds used for burial, though dwelling sites marked by the presence of oyster-shells were often met with, and on Bull island an interesting circular enclosure of oyster-shells of the same type as the great enclosure on Sapelo island, Georgia, though smaller.

The coast district lying between St. Helena sound and Charleston was less thoroughly searched. Inquiries were made along the inland route, and, in addition, parts of the North Edisto river, Bohicket creek, Steamboat creek, and the Stono river were gone over in a fruitless search, which yielded to our inquiries nothing but tar kilns and comparatively modern fortifications. Furthermore, there seemed to be, on the part of the inhabitants, a total ignorance of the existence of mounds on this part of the coast.

[1] "Certain Aboriginal Mounds of the Georgia Coast." Vol. XI.

From Charleston to Georgetown the inland route runs largely through marsh, and it is possible at but few places to effect a landing on solid ground. Pilots and persons familiar with the route were entirely ignorant of the presence of mounds in the neighborhood of the water. As this agreed so well with our own experience of the neighboring portion of the coast investigated by us, we determined to abandon the remainder of the inland route, and to devote our attention to a more promising field.

Mounds Investigated.

Near Bluffton.	Little Island (2).
Callawassie Island.	Near Button Hill (4).
Hasell Point (2).	Indian Hill, St. Helena Island.
Guerard Point.	Polleewahnee Island.
Indian Hill.	

MOUND NEAR BLUFFTON, BEAUFORT COUNTY.

In a cultivated field belonging to the Cresson plantation, about 2.5 miles north of Bluffton, is a mound long under cultivation, having a height at the time of investigation of 3 feet 3 inches, a diameter of base of 58 feet. It was investigated by us by permission of Mrs. A. E. Coe, of Bluffton, under whose control it is. It had previously been dug into to a limited extent. The southern half was dug through by us and part of the central portion of the remainder. It was composed of dark yellow sand with no admixture of shell. No pits nor outlying graves were met with. A few chips of chert and scattered sherds, none with complicated decoration, were found. Almost at the center were fragments of a child's skull and two small deposits of calcined and unburnt bones together.

MOUND ON CALLAWASSIE ISLAND, BEAUFORT COUNTY.

This mound, in the pine woods near the northeastern end of Callawassie island, was investigated by us with the kind permission of Mr. William Pinckney, the lessee of the island. The mound, lying near a number of small deposits of oyster-shells, had a flattened appearance, presumably from previous cultivation; a part of the center had previously been dug out. The mound is 3 feet 4 inches in height and 48 feet across the base. The northern half was dug through by us, including considerable adjacent level territory, this last being done in a fruitless search for outlying pits or graves, which are so numerous near some mounds of the Georgia coast.

The mound consisted of dark sand containing a certain amount of clay. Scattered oyster-shells were present throughout. Along the base of the mound, at the level of the adjacent territory, was an irregular layer 8 to 12 inches thick, of crushed oyster-shells and fire-blackened sand. Beginning about 13 feet from the center, this layer increased somewhat in thickness, toward the center, and the oyster-shells lay loosely and unbroken. The superficial portion of the mound, to a depth of about 1 foot, was composed of oyster-shells, with a certain admixture of sand. Well in toward the center, sand alone lay above this layer, but whether or not the layer of sand was due to later cultivation of the mound, we could not determine.

Burials began almost at the margin, nine of human remains and two of dogs.

Burial No. 1, 20 feet N. E. by N. from the center, 2 feet 10 inches down, in a pit 3.5 feet deep, was the skeleton of a female, the trunk on the back, partly flexed, with knees to the left. The skull with all cervical vertebræ but one was missing. There had been no late disturbance. The head, if present, would have pointed E. S. E. There was a well-united fracture of the left radius.

Burial No. 2, 19 feet N. N. E., female, flexed on the right side, head E. S. E., in a grave-pit 3 feet deep, the body slanting upward, 2 feet 4 inches down.

Burial No. 3, a dog, in a small grave of its own, under unbroken layers. The skull and principal bones were sent to Professor Putnam, Peabody Museum, Cambridge, Mass.

Burial No. 4, a young dog. The cranium was sent to Professor Putnam. The remaining bones were badly decayed. In this mound we notice the custom which prevailed in certain mounds of the Georgia coast, namely: according the honor of sepulture to their canine friends by the aborigines.

Burial No. 5, 17 feet W. N. W., 3 feet down on the margin of a pit 3 feet 8 inches deep, was a skull with two cervical vertebræ. At the same level, but farther into the pit, were several scattered long bones. The skull, sex not determined, has an apical bone and double parietal foramina. It was sent to the Army Medical Museum, Washington, D. C.

Burial No. 6, 16 feet N. N. E., in a pit 4 feet 3 inches down, was the skeleton of a young male, flexed on the right, head E.

Burial No. 7, in the same pit about 1 foot farther out from the center of the mound, on a level just below Burial No. 6, was the skeleton of a child, flexed on the right side, heading E. N. E. The pit containing these two burials was 6 feet 5 inches in depth.

Burial No. 8, 15 feet W. N. W., just below the black base layer, 3 feet down, was the skeleton of an adult of uncertain sex, flexed on the left side, head N. E. by N.

Burial No. 9, 13 feet N. E. by E., on the base, 2 feet 4 inches down, was the skeleton of a male with trunk on back and knees flexed to the right, head S. S. E.

Burial No. 10, 12 feet N. N. E., on the bottom of a pit extending through the base layer, 3.5 feet down, were a tibia, a fibula and the foot bones with scattered bones of the other foot, all under an unbroken layer of oyster-shells.

Burial No. 11, 8 feet N. W. by W., 2 feet down, under a mass of small marine univalves (*Littorina irrorata*) was the skeleton of a female, partly flexed on the right side, head N. E. by E.

No artifacts lay with the burials. Near the surface, unassociated, was a disc of earthenware, evidently fashioned from a fragment of a broken earthenware vessel whose cord-marked decoration was apparent on the disc. These discs, if present at all in Florida, where the discoidal stone seems to be wanting, are extremely rare. They are numerous along the Georgia coast.[1] We found them in still greater numbers along the southernmost part of the coast of South Carolina. It is interesting to know that just such discs are found as far north as Canada, Mr. G. E. Laidlaw having met with great numbers in the ash-beds near Balsam lake, Ontario.[2] These discs were doubtless used in some sort of game. Mr. Laidlaw[3] thinks it probably resembled our "billy-button," which he has seen among the Crees and Salteaux of the Northwest British possessions. Mr. Stewart Culin[3] believes if they were used in a game it was one resembling our "checkers," and cites Mr. Cushing as to the existence of such a game among the Zuñis, and Mr. Fewkes as to a like game among the Mokis.

Sherds, which were fairly numerous, were undecorated or cord-marked, save one bearing a rude checked stamp.

In this mound was an unusual structural feature. The mound rested upon undisturbed grayish sand with a certain admixture of clay, and this stratum was above yellowish brown clay with a slight admixture of sand. At the center of the base of the mound a hole had been dug about 7 feet in diameter, extending down 5 feet 4 inches. In filling the pit, sand from the upper sand layer had been discarded, the material used being clay from the layer below, with a certain admixture of bits of charcoal and occasional oyster-shells. This mass of clay had somewhat the appearance of an altar, but careful. search showed neither bones, artifacts nor evidence of the use of fire.

Mounds near Hasell Point, Beaufort County (2).

A mound about three-quarters of a mile in a northwesterly direction from Hasell point, on the Colleton river, stood in woods on the edge of a cultivated field. Its shape was that of the usual truncated cone; its height, 4 feet 7 inches; its diameter of base, 34 feet. Shell deposits were nearby. A small trench had previously been dug. Considerably over one-half was dug away by us with the permission of Mrs. Sarah Hasell, of Hasell point.

The mound was made of yellow sand with irregular layers of oyster-shells. Nothing was found by us save a few sherds, undecorated or cord-marked. In the sand thrown out by the previous digger were a few fragments of calcined bones, probably belonging to a central deposit.

In the field by the woods in which was the mound just described and a comparatively short distance from it was what the plow had spared of a mound, also the property of Mrs. Hasell, 1 foot 4 inches in height and 32 feet across, at the time

---

[1] "Certain Aboriginal Mounds of the Georgia Coast," C. B. Moore, Jour. Acad. Nat. Sci., Vol. XI.

[2] "The Aboriginal Remains of Balsam lake, Ontario," "American Antiquarian," March, 1897, page 71.

[3] In private letters.

of our investigation. About one-half the mound and all the central part were dug through by us.

The mound was composed of dark brown sand with occasional pockets of oyster- and of mussel-shells. A central deposit of oyster-shells, with a diameter of about 15 feet, had a maximum thickness at the center of about 1 foot. Sherds were undecorated or cord-marked. Outlying burials were present as in some of the Georgia mounds.

Burial No. 1, 31 feet S. W. from the center of the mound, 15 inches down, were a pelvis and part of the thighs, apparently a late disturbance.

Burial No. 2, 29 feet W. S. W., a skeleton, full length on back, head N. N. W., 9 inches down, sex uncertain through decay.

Burial No. 3, 22 feet S. S. E., 10 inches down, a skeleton much decayed, flexed on the right side.

Burial No. 4, 16 feet E. S. E., on bottom of a pit, 3 feet down, was a skeleton of a male, partly flexed on the right side, head N. E.

Burial No. 5, 13 feet S. by W., 2 feet 5 inches down, in a pit with an undisturbed stratum of oyster-shells above, were leg and feet-bones in order, bones of the right arm also in order, sacrum, some vertebræ, the lower jaw and some ribs.

Burial No. 6, at the center, in a large pit, 3 feet 8 inches down, with charcoal and fragments of calcined human bones, were two femurs, two tibiæ and a fibula, not in order, all unburnt. Three feet away, at about the same level, were burnt fragments of bones, also ribs, part of a radius and a lower jaw, showing no trace of fire.

ABORIGINAL ENCLOSURE, GUERARD POINT, BEAUFORT COUNTY.

In sight of the water, on Guerard point, on the Oketeet river, is a roughly circular, aboriginal enclosure composed of marine shells, mainly those of the oyster. It has been greatly lowered by the plow and considerably spread out. The present maximum height of the walls is 28 inches, their average breadth about 33 feet. The inside diameter is 65 feet, approximately. No oyster-shells except those of the enclosure were discovered in the neighborhood. This enclosure (whose use we cannot determine) is of the same class as that on Bull island, S. C., and the great one on Sapelo island, Ga., figured and described by us in our previous Report.

We are indebted to Mrs. C. B. Guerard, of Bluffton, S. C., for permission to investigate on her property at Guerard point.

MOUND AT INDIAN HILL, BEAUFORT COUNTY.

In a cultivated field, on the property of Mrs. E. C. Paget, who kindly gave permission to investigate, was a mound greatly lowered and spread out by cultivation. Its height was 17 inches; its diameter, 47 feet. There had been some previous examination. The mound was carefully gone through by us without result, save the discovery of a central deposit of burnt and unburnt bones considerably disturbed and a few rough sherds, mostly cord-marked.

LARGER MOUND, LITTLE ISLAND, BEAUFORT COUNTY.

This mound, on the southeastern end of Little island, overlooking Whale branch, an arm of Broad river,[1] occupied the most prominent point of the eastern shore.   The mound was investigated by us with the kind permission of James M. Crofut, Esq., of Beaufort, S. C., under whose control the island now is.

The mound measured from the north, where the ground sloped upward, had a height of 11 feet; from the south its altitude was a trifle over 14 feet.   From the summit plateau to the base of the mound at the center was about 14 feet, showing there was no extension beneath the general level.

The base of the mound, elliptical in outline, had an east and west diameter of 100 feet, and a north and south diameter of 150 feet.   The summit plateau had diameters east and west and north and south of 38 feet and 61 feet, respectively. Its outline also was elliptical.   The plateau was markedly level, and the sides of the mound ascended at so steep an angle that evidently no cultivation had ever been attempted.   No previous investigation had been undertaken so far as known.

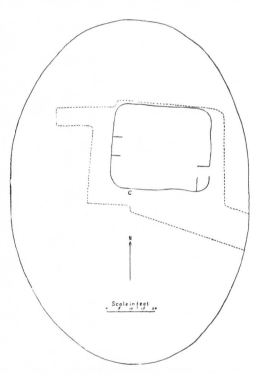

Fig. 1.—Ground plan of structure, excavation and mound. Little Island, S. C.

On the mound were a number of pines, some large, and live-oaks of moderate size.

To determine the nature of this mound a large trench was dug along the base toward the center resulting in the discovery of walls on the bottom of the mound, the investigation of which required extensive digging.

The material above was removed, the space enclosed by the walls completely excavated, parts of the exterior were laid bare and the walls carefully shored by the aid of planks. The work of excavation, irrespective of the survey, the artist's work and the filling, took twelve days of seven hours each, much of the material requiring quadruple handling.   During the work an increasing force of men was employed, the latter part requiring twenty-eight, exclusive of four engaged in superintendence.   The walls, the area excavated and the extent of the mound are shown on ground plan (Fig. 1), and the structure as it appeared looking down from the southeast corner of the excavation is shown in the frontispiece, which is drawn from a sketch made on the spot, from photographs and from sections of the wall which were brought home.

[1] Broad river, the Grande of the Huguenots, A. D., 1562.   For an interesting account of the aborigines of this vicinity see " History of Jean Ribault's First Voyage to Florida," by Réné Laudonnière.   Historical Collections of Louisiana and Florida, New York, 1869.

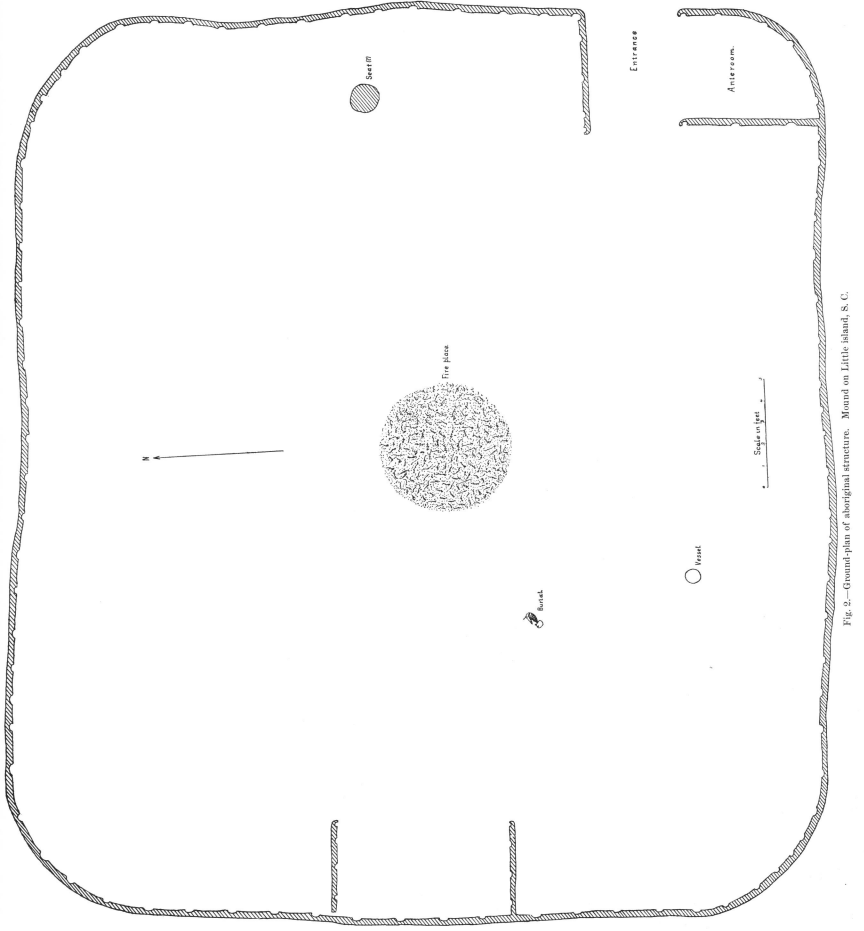

Fig. 2.—Ground-plan of aboriginal structure. Mound on Little island, S. C.

On the base of the mound and mainly to the north and east of the center (marked C on the ground plan) was a quadrilateral enclosure made by walls of clay, the northeast corner being 1 foot 7 inches, the northwest corner 7 feet 3 inches, the southeast corner 5 feet and the southwest corner 9 feet from the surface, respectively.

The enclosure was not exactly square, the sides varying slightly in length and the corners being rounded. Had it been quadrangular, the northern wall would have been 40 feet 2 inches in length; the southern, 41 feet 9 inches; the eastern wall, 35 feet 7 inches; the western wall, 36 feet 9 inches. The four walls in direction followed closely the cardinal points of the compass, the variation ranging between 2° and 4.5°. This orientation, however, was probably not intentional, as the eastern wall fronted, and was almost parallel to, the river, which at this point runs nearly north and south.

There were no windows. The entrance shown on the plan (Fig. 2) and marked **X** on the half-tone reproduction from a photograph (Fig. 3), was in the east wall near the southeastern corner. The width of the entrance was 4 feet 6 inches.

A partition of clay, the height of the wall and of similar structure, extended inward 5 feet 5 inches from the northern margin of the entrance. To the south of the entrance was a curious little three-sided compartment 5 feet wide at the entrance and 6 feet 3 inches in length, formed by the erection of a partition of clay and portions of the southern and eastern walls, including the southeastern corner. From the western wall were two parallel partitions of clay extending inward 4 feet 2 inches. These partitions practically enclosed the central 8 feet of the wall. Their use is problematic. They bore no marks of fire. During the excavation was found among the oyster-shells which covered the enclosure, a description of which will be given later, a cylindrical empty space, evidently the mold of a post, 8 inches in diameter and 6 feet in length, approximately. Starting from it on one side a layer of clay from 2 to 3 inches in thickness extended a number of feet. This layer contained, so far as we could determine, no holes showing former presence of supports, and it would hardly seem likely that such an area of clay could stand supported by a single post. For this reason and also from the fact that the clay did not lie upon the floor of the former structure but from 1 to 2 feet above in the shell, we cannot see how this layer could have been a partition, and are unable to suggest an explanation of its presence. Several other layers, unassociated with molds of posts, were met with in the shell within the enclosure.

The walls closely approximated 4 feet 3 inches in height. In thickness they varied from 2 to 3 inches, increasing to 4 or 5 inches at the top where a stringer had been enclosed. The wall had been supported by upright posts, which had been, in certain cases at least, covered with bark, as was plainly shown by the impression left in the clay. These uprights varied in diameter from 3.5 to 6 inches and projected 6 to 8 inches above the top of the wall. Some left molds in the clayey sand above the shell, indicating considerable enlargement around the top. We are unable to suggest a cause for this as no indication of anything extending from them was discovered. These uprights, which were from 14 to 19 inches apart, were held together by twelve parallel circular cross-pieces, probably vines, each about .3 of an inch in diameter, surmounted by a circular stringer about 1 inch in diameter, over

Fig. 3.—Entrance and compartment. Aboriginal structure. Mound on Little island, S. C.

which, as we have said, the clay had been turned and rounded. At places, marks in the clay plainly showed where the cross-pieces and the stringer had been attached to the uprights, probably by vines. The half-tone reproduction of a photograph of a portion of the wall (Fig. 4) shows the impression of the uprights and cross-pieces.

The molds in the sand above the wall are also plainly distinguishable The longitudinal lines are cracks which appeared in the clay on exposure to the sun, and have no connection with the process of manufacture of the wall.

Over this frame-work, with the exception of the inner portion of the uprights,

Fig. 4.—Portion of wall showing molds of uprights and cross-pieces. Aboriginal structure. Mound on Little island, S. C.

which were allowed to project from the wall, clay had been plastered, as shown in the cross-section of the upper part of the wall (Fig. 5); the space left by the stringer being marked A, those by the three upper cross-pieces B. The terminal posts of the partitions, however, had been enclosed in the clay. This clay, of a yellowish color but turning red on exposure, was moist and soft when uncovered but hardened to the consistency of a sun-dried brick upon contact with the air and sunlight. It was homogeneous, containing no admixture of sand, gravel, stones or vegetable fibre. In its moist condition, inside and out, it had received the impression of the oyster-shells over its entire surface, thus rendering impossible the determination as to any incised decoration or the like.

At irregular distances, usually but not always between consecutive uprights, on the top of the wall, were semi-circular depressions from 2 to 4 inches in diameter,

Fig. 5.—Cross-section of upper part of wall. (One quarter size.)

which had undoubtedly held ends of poles serving as rafters. A careful examination of the interior of some of these depressions indicated, by an increased height toward the inner surface of the wall, that the poles had slanted upward at a considerable angle. Other depressions were too much broken or indented by oyster-shells for any determination. It is probable that boughs rather than clay were used as a covering in the construction of the roof, as no fragments of clay lay upon the floor of the structure, and the sheets of clay in the shells, to which we have referred, were by no means sufficient in area to represent a roof.

There were present in the floor of the structure numerous circular holes representing ends of former supports, some of which probably upheld the roof.

Considerable excavations were made under the corners and doorway of the structure without result.

The entire floor of sand, darkened by admixture of charcoal, was dug through at a depth considerably below any marks of occupation, which extended from 3 to 5 inches in depth, except in the case of post-holes, to which reference has been made. Some of the holes, of considerable diameter, were filled with oyster-shells, and were probably open when the filling-in began, but the great majority, smaller as a rule, contained dark sand and midden refuse, bits of deer bone, charcoal, potsherds, etc. One of these sherds bore the familiar complicated stamp. Another was unusually good ware with dark and hard interior. In one post-hole were a number of carbonized fragments of very slender corn-cobs. These holes containing midden refuse, but no oyster-shell, we considered to belong to a period antedating the disuse of the structure and to have been filled before the bringing in of the oyster-shells.

Toward the center of the floor, as shown on the ground-plan, was a fire-place about 6 feet in diameter, showing considerable use, as the sand was hardened and reddened to a depth of about 5 inches. On the floor near the eastern wall was a projection or large knob of clay, like a seat, circular with rounded top, 9 inches in height and 1 foot 4 inches in diameter.

Fourteen inches from the surface, beneath where a fire had been, was the skeleton of a very young infant.

Just beneath the surface was a pot of about 8 inches diameter, the clay of which was so softened by moisture that it crumbled into pieces.

For some reason unknown to us it became the purpose of the aborigines to enclose their wall within a mound; and this they did apparently in the following manner: First they filled in the enclosure with a mass of shells (mainly of the oyster but containing those of the marine mussel, of the *Littorina irrorata* and doubtless of other shell fish), and midden debris (B) to about the height of the wall (A) allowing the deposit of shells (C) to continue a number of feet in a gradual slope beyond the wall, as may be seen by consulting the cross section (Fig. 6), taken about midway along the southern side of the enclosure. This shell deposit outside the

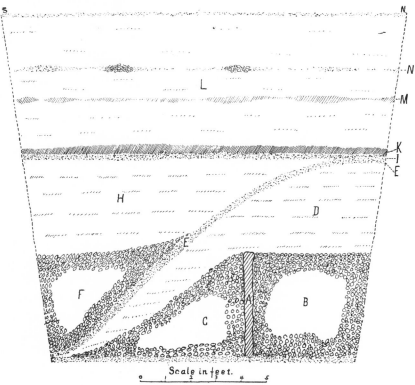

Fig 6.—Cross-section of part of mound. Little island, S. C.

wall extended a distances of about 8 feet, measured horizontally. The oyster-shells were not a deposit made by occupation, since they lay loosely together and were neither crushed nor tightly packed, and single calcined oyster-shells from fire-places in shell heaps at a distance were scattered among them. Throughout the entire deposit we noticed but one fire-place, a small one, and this was unquestionably made during the filling in of the shells. From these facts we know that the oyster-shells had been carried to the enclosure from some dwelling site [1] to form the initial stage in the construction of the mound.

[1] For data as to shell heaps in this country the reader is referred to Professor Jeffries Wyman's Memoir "Fresh Water Shell Mounds of the St. Johns river, Florida" and "Certain Shell Heaps of the St. Johns River, Florida, Hitherto Unexplored," Clarence B. Moore, "American Naturalist," Nov., 1892; Jan., 1893; Feb., 1893; July, 1893; Aug., 1893; Jan., 1894; July, 1894.

Next, over the mass of oyster-shells, was piled the clayey sand of the surrounding territory, mainly in thin horizontal layers of various shades of white, brown, yellow (D).   These layers were surmounted by what we took to be the layer of occupation (E) from 3 to 5 inches in thickness, consisting of clayey sand rendered black by action of fire and by admixture of charcoal.   The mound, now about 8 feet 3 inches in height, presumably having been occupied for a period, was enlarged by piling oyster-shells (F) around its margin for a considerable distance out, though not to the margin of the final mound.   Then the new mound was brought up to the level of the original one by the addition of layers of clayey sand (H).   This added portion, with the plateau of the first mound, had served as a place of abode, as a layer of occupation (I), merging with the similar layer (E) on the plateau of the original mound, was plainly discernible.   The plateau thus enlarged, so far as the investigation went, was covered with a layer of red clay devoid of sand (K) from 3 to 5 inches in thickness.   Above this stratum of clay came the remainder of the mound as found by us (L) consisting of less distinct strata of clayey sand, another band of red clay (M), not so clearly marked, of about the same thickness as the other, and about 2 feet above it, and about 1 foot higher, signs of occupation in places (N) consisting of the usual particles of charcoal and occasional small pockets of oyster-shells, with nearly 3 feet of less distinctly stratified clayey sand superimposed.

Immediately under the lower stratum of red clay were a number of circular spaces from 6 to 11 inches in diameter and about 3 feet in depth, distinctly cutting the layers through which they passed and filled with sand of a single shade. In some cases the layer of red clay above them was intact; in others fragments of the layer had fallen into, and lay on the top of, the sand filling the space.   It was, therefore, evident that the posts or stakes had disappeared, probably through decay before the imposition of the red clay layer.   These post-holes were present not alone on the mound originally piled over the wall, but were found in the added portion (H).

In spite of an earnest endeavor on our part to show all these post-holes on a ground-plan we were unable to do so; their exact recognition being extremely difficult.   That these posts had no connection with the clay wall beneath was distinctly shown by the fact that unbroken strata in every case lay between the bases of the holes and the level of the summit of the wall.

Beginning at the second layer of occupation, which, as we have stated, consisted of traces of fire and occasional small pockets of oyster-shells, a number of post-holes of somewhat greater diameter than those just described extended down about 3 feet terminating above, but never coming in contact with, the lower layer of red clay. They also were filled with sand, but were not nearly so numerous as the others and were not plotted by us.   They evidently had no connection with any of the spaces beneath, and doubtless at one time held supports during another period of occupation.

We have then various distinct periods of occupation as follows : that of the clay wall on the original surface ; that of the original mound ; that of the original mound with its enlargement on which was a perishable structure of some sort supported by wooden posts; a still later occupation during which wooden posts were again in use; and finally that of the surface of the mound as found by us.

At two or three feet from the surface of the mound began two extensive pockets of oyster-shells about 3 feet in depth. Nothing was discovered in association.

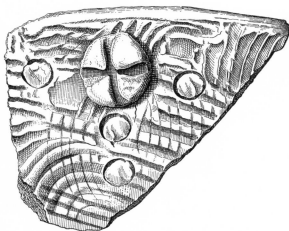

Fig. 7.—Sherd. Mound on Little island.   (Full size.)

With the oyster-shells within and surrounding the enclosure were numerous sherds, undecorated, also stamped in squares and with complicated stamp. One with complicated stamp and knob impressed with a cross is shown in Fig. 7.

In addition were: pebble hammers of quartz and quartz pebbles; smoothing stones; many fragments of chert; two arrowheads of chert; bone awls; and a considerable number of discs made from fragments of earthenware vessels. Loose in the sand were a graceful arrowhead of chert, and, near the surface, a polished chisel of volcanic rock, about 6 inches in length.

Just beneath the surface of the northern slope, in a small pit, was an intrusive burial, the remains of an adult male, heaped together, and in part calcined. With them were fragments of earthenware, a mass of sandy clay partly baked, and a quantity of carbonized maize.

Fortunately we know something of aboriginal structures which may throw some light upon this one. Gen. Gates P. Thruston, in his interesting "Antiquities of Tennessee" (Second edition, p. 68 *et al.*), has gathered much information on the subject. We quote at length:

"The ancient works of Tennessee were apparently of simple construction, but they indicate the existence of large family dwellings as a characteristic of aboriginal society. Early historical records are also in harmony with this view. From Garcilasso de la Vega we learn that some of the houses in the fortified native towns visited by De Soto were very large. He says, 'the whole number of houses' [in Mauvila, Alabama] 'did not exceed eighty, but they were of size capable of lodging from five to fifteen hundred persons each,' a statement probably extravagant, but generally sustained by the other chronicles.[1]

"Joutel, one of La Salle's companions in 1687, tells us that when they visited the village of the Cenis, west of the Mississippi, 'The Indian town, with its large thatched lodges, looked like a cluster of gigantic haycocks.' He declares that 'some of them were sixty feet in diameter.'[2] Joutel's description of one of these dwellings illustrates the house life of the southern Indians at that early period. 'These

---

[1] Garcilasso de la Vega, L. III, C. 20; Conquest of Florida (Irving), page 262.
[2] La Salle (Parkman), pages 415, 417.

lodges of the Cenis,' he says, 'often contained eight or ten families. They were made by firmly planting in a circle, tall, straight, young trees, such as grew in the swamps. The tops were then bent inward, and lashed together, and the frame thus constructed was thickly covered with thatch, a hole being left at the top for the escape of the smoke. The inmates were ranged around the circumference of the structure, each family in a kind of stall, open in front, but separated from those adjoining by partitions of mats. Here they placed their beds of cane, their painted robes of buffalo and deer skin, their cooking utensils of pottery, and other household goods, and here, too, the head of the family hung his bow, quiver, lance, and shield. There was nothing in common but the fire, which burned in the middle of the lodge, and was never suffered to go out.'[1]

"In Iberville's Journal, it is stated that the cabins of the Bayogoulas, a tribe of Louisiana, were circular in form, about thirty feet in diameter, and plastered with clay to the height of a man.[2] Adair says, the winter cabins, or hot houses of the Cherokees, and several other tribes, were circular, and covered six or seven inches thick with tough clay, mixed with grass. Father Gravier, speaking of the Tounicas of Arkansas, says, 'Their cabins were round and vaulted. They were lathed with cane, and plastered with mud from bottom to top, within and without, with a good covering of straw.'[3] Tonti, who accompanied La Salle, in 1682, describes his visit to the town of Taensas on the Lower Mississippi. He says the natives had 'large square dwellings, built of sun-baked mud, mixed with straw, arched over with a dome-shaped roof of canes and placed in regular order around an open area. Two of them were larger and better than the rest. One was the lodge of the chief, the other was the temple or house of the sun. The house of the chief was about forty feet square, with no opening but the door. The temple ' where they kept the bones of their departed chiefs,' in construction, was much like the chief's house ; a strong mud wall planted with stakes surrounded it. In the middle of the temple was a kind of an altar, before which a 'perpetual fire,' composed of large logs, was burning, and was watched by two old men devoted to their office.[4]

"Colonel Morris, an agent of the Bureau of Ethnology, some time since explored a group of earth-works in Butler county, Missouri, consisting of 'an inclosing wall and ditch, two large outer excavations, and four inside mounds.' The largest mound had an average diameter of about one hundred and thirty-five feet, and was twenty feet high. Deeply imbedded within the central portions of the mound were found two large upright charred posts, near the charred and decaying remains of horizontal or cross timbers, and in connection with burned clay, ashes, charcoal, and charred bones, indicating almost certainly the remains of a large house structure, built upon or in connection with this mound, or upon the smaller mound, upon which the main mound appears to have been subsequently erected. Within the different strata or layers of the mound were the remains of nine large fire-beds, indicating

[1] La Salle (Parkman), page 417.
[2] Professor Cyrus Thomas, Magazine of American History, February, 1884.
[3] Early French Voyages (Shea), page 135.
[4] La Salle (Parkman), page 281.

altars, sacrifices, burial ceremonies, or possibly, merely the fire-hearths used at different periods of occupation—Magazine of American History (Thomas), February, 1884. Gerard Fowke, an assistant of the Bureau of Ethnology, also reports that recently, in exploring a large mound on the Scioto river, in Ross county, Ohio, he discovered the remains of wooden ' posts set in pairs around the edge ; other posts at intervals within assisted [or may have assisted] in holding up the roof. The interior space was nearly forty feet across. A streak an inch thick of mingled ashes, charcoal, and black earth, spread over the floor, indicated the usual untidy appearance of the aboriginal housekeeping.' The skeleton remains of an elaborate burial were inclosed in the mound, and appearances indicated that the house had been torn away or burned, and the mound subsequently increased in size over the remains. —Gerard Fowke's Report in the Cincinnati Commercial Gazette, July 23, 1888.

" In 1876, Professor Carr, of the Peabody Museum, in exploring a large mound in Lee county, Virginia, discovered a series of decaying cedar posts, imbedded in a circle around the top of the mound, which the intelligent explorer regarded as the remains of a large house structure similar to the council-house Adair saw on a mound in the old Cherokee town of Cowe, Georgia, in 1773.—Tenth Annual Report Peabody Museum, page 75.

" Professor Putnam also found an upright cedar post still standing deeply planted in the large ancient mound of the Lebanon group, in Tennessee."

SMALLER MOUND, LITTLE ISLAND, BEAUFORT COUNTY.

This mound, about 35 yards south-southeast from the large domiciliary mound, had been about one-half washed away by the waters of Whale branch in times of storm. The mound, when whole, must have had a base diameter of about 50 feet. Its height, measured on the north, was 3 feet 7 inches; measured on the south, somewhat more, as the bank on which it was, had a downward slope. What remained of the mound was practically dug through by us with the exception of that part on the north on which a large tree was growing. We are indebted to Mr. Crofut for permission to investigate.

The mound had been composed, as nearly as we could judge, of a mass of oyster-shells 3 to 4 feet in thickness at the center and sloping to the margin. This mass of shell rested on a layer of disturbed clayey sand about 1 foot in thickness. This mass of oyster-shells was covered with a mixture of clay and sand, the sand predominating, containing oyster-shells in varying proportion. From the surface, at what seemed to be the center of the summit plateau, to undisturbed sand was a vertical distance of 8 feet 8 inches. Therefore, the base of the mound was about 5 feet under ground.

Occupying the central part of the mound, apparently dug into the oyster-shells to within 1 foot of the basal layer of disturbed sand, was a pit having a diameter of 24 feet where it entered the shell (see diagram Fig. 8.) This pit had been filled with material resembling that of the layer above the shell. With the exception of a shaft of a human tibia, found loose in the sand, the central part of the mound contained the only human remains met with by us. These consisted of four separate deposits of calcined fragments of human remains, each deposit representing the skeletons of several individuals. These deposits were closely associated; one lay at the center of the bottom of the pit, about 7 feet down; two, in the shell farther into the mound, 7.5 feet down; and one lay below these in the basal layer of sand, 8 feet 8 inches down. With one deposit were: shell beads, none over .5 of an inch in diameter; a perforated *Cardium ;* a number of small marine univalves (*Marginella*) ; one chert knife; one entire tooth of a fossil shark; two parts of fossil sharks' teeth, probably used for piercing purposes; a piercing implement of bone; a tooth of a large carnivore; a lot of small pebbles, probably from a rattle; twelve cockle-shells (*Arca incongrua*) perforated for suspension ; twelve marine shells (*Oliva literata*) pierced longitudinally for stringing; a pebble about one inch in diameter. With another deposit were small shell beads. Loose in the sand was a fossil shark's tooth and throughout the mound were earthenware discs of the type which we have already mentioned. Certain sherds present in the mound bore the complicated stamp.

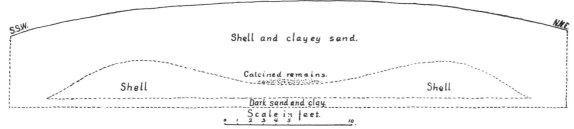

Fig. 8.—Cross-section through center of smaller mound. Little island, S. C.

MOUNDS NEAR BUTTON HILL, PORT ROYAL ISLAND, BEAUFORT COUNTY (4).

The settlement known as Button hill lies about three miles west of Beaufort. On the place of Mr. N. Christianson was a mound greatly lowered and spread out by cultivation. Its height was 1.5 feet; its diameter of base, 42 by 52 feet. Treasure seekers had dug considerably into marginal portions. The mound was trenched and the central part dug out by us without result.

A few yards distant was a somewhat smaller mound equally devoid of interest.

In a cultivated field about three-quarters of a mile south-by-west from the Christianson place, was a mound partly owned by Mr. Fred Carter and partly by Mr. James White, both colored. What the plough had spared of this mound was 2 feet 9 inches in height. The apparent diameter was 58 feet, but much material had been worked down from central portions. The southern half of the mound was worked through and the central portions were dug out. The mound was composed of yellow sand with the usual fire-places. A few loose sherds, plain and cord-marked, were met with. Four deposits of calcined and unburnt bones mixed, were found, the farthest from the center being at a distance of 13 feet. With one deposit was a small streak of hematite. Loose in the sand was a bird-arrow of chert.

About 300 yards southwest from the preceding mound, in a cultivated field, over which oyster-shells were scattered, was the remnant of a mound belonging in part to the estate of Mr. George Waterhouse and in part to Mr. Fred Carter, colored. Our thanks are tendered to Mr. William P. Waterhouse, of Beaufort, for permission to investigate. The mound was somewhat irregular in outline, its base having a diameter of 52 by 57 feet. Its height was 2 feet 10 inches. It was about three-fifths dug through. A few scattered bones lay near the center under hematite. Four deposits of calcined and unburnt bones mingled were met with toward the center. With one were quantities of hematite; with another, a little mica. One deposit lay at the bottom of a large central pit 6 feet 3 inches from the surface. On the surface, near the mound, was picked up an unusually gracefully shaped "celt" of polished volcanic rock, with beveled cutting edge, the opposite end tapering to a blunt point.

INDIAN HILL, ST. HELENA ISLAND, BEAUFORT COUNTY.

This mound, rising high above the flat surface of St. Helena island, is a land-mark known far and near as Indian hill. It stands in the midst of cultivated fields and is the property of a colored family named Chaplin.

The mound had seen but little previous investigation, practically none, if its size is taken into consideration, and the sides of the mound are too steep for cultivation. In shape the mound was the usual irregular truncated cone. The solid plateau was perfectly level. The height of the mound is 13 feet 2 inches; its diameter of base, east and west, 138 feet; north and south, 129 feet. The summit plateau, about circular, was 62 feet across.

From the northern side a trench 18 feet wide converging slightly toward the bottom and contracting somewhat, 15 feet farthest in, was run along the base to the center of the mound. The mound is composed, as far as our investigation enabled us to judge, of a tenacious mixture of sand and clay in small irregular streaks of different shades. Several small layers of clay were met with locally. No oyster-shells were found, though some were scattered around the surrounding fields.

A measurement from the center of the summit plateau, taken vertically to undisturbed soil, gave a depth of 15 feet or nearly 2 feet more than the height of the mound. As there were no signs of any basal pit to account for extra depth, it seems likely that the surrounding country, whose soil is a black loam filled with organic matter, was so long inhabited that a deposit two feet in thickness grew up around the mound.

Although no distinct evidence of long-continued periods of occupation was found in the mound, a number of post-holes from which the wood had rotted, still unfilled, were found at four distinct levels.

Sherds were infrequently found. Four pottery discs, one bearing a complicated stamp, came from midden-refuse, probably. On the base, doubtless left there by accident, was a handsomely wrought spearhead of chert, 5 inches in length.

No burials were met with and we must regard the mound at Indian hill as erected for domiciliary purposes.

Near the mound was a considerable rise in the ground having a height of about 2 feet. It was dug through to a certain extent and proved to be a dwelling site made up of rich clayey sand filled with organic matter and containing many bones of lower animals, also numerous sherds and a slight sprinkling of oyster-shells.

MOUND ON POLLEEWAHNEE ISLAND, BEAUFORT COUNTY.

Polleewahnee island, practically a part of St. Helena, is separated from that island by a small run. In a cultivated field containing shell deposits and having others in the vicinity, on the property of a colored family named Williams, about one mile north-northwest from Indian hill, is a mound 5 feet 10 inches in height, the sides of which, toward the base, have undergone extended cultivation. On the upper portion were good sized live-oaks and a palmetto. The mound was so spread out through continuous ploughing that it was impossible to determine its boundaries. A point judged to be the center of the summit was taken as the center of a circle having a diameter of 80 feet. The mound, thoroughly examined, proved to be without artifacts or burials.

A short distance away was a midden deposit similar to that near Indian hill.

The deposits of oyster-shells, evidence of dwelling sites throughout all the territory visited by us along the South Carolina coast were comparatively insignificant, being mainly confined to shells scattered over fields. It would seem then that the use of the oyster as an article of diet by the coast Indians decreased going northward, since the shell deposits of South Carolina are greatly exceeded by those of Georgia, which, in their turn, yield the palm to the mighty masses of shell along the Florida coast. Whether the restricted use of shell-fish for food on the South Carolina coast arose from a less bountiful supply of molluscs, a preference for other articles of diet on the part of the aborigines, or a sparse population, we are unable to decide.

A limited habitation would account for the scarcity of mounds domiciliary and sepulchral. The small number of mounds, however, could be explained under another hypothesis. The sea-islands of the Georgia coast in entirety or in large tracts are held by individual owners. Some islands are kept as game preserves and large parts of others lie fallow. Mounds on these islands have suffered less by cultivation than many on the sea-islands of South Carolina, where often the territory is divided into very small tracts, which are carefully and continuously tilled by their owners whose whole support they are. It is not unlikely, then, that what is left of some places of aboriginal sepulture along the South Carolina coast is no longer visible. Still, such mounds as have been investigated would doubtless be representative of those no longer evident.

These mounds, as may be seen from their description, may be divided into two classes: larger mounds used for domiciliary purposes and low mounds used for burial.

In the low burial mounds, as an almost invariable rule, burials were found well in toward the center, the only exceptions being a mound at Hasell point and the mound on Callawassie island and in these mounds alone were burials found in anatomical order, the chief method of disposing of the dead elsewhere being partial cremation ; that is, deposits where disconnected bones showing no mark of fire were mixed with charred and calcined fragments.   In the Little island burial mound calcined bones alone were met with.

Although in certain mounds fragments of pottery were found bearing a complicated stamp of the type of the Georgia coast, no evidence of urn burial was seen during our investigation.

The custom to inter artifacts with the dead, so universal among the aborigines, seems to have been little practised along the South Carolina coast, for only at Little island, as the reader may recall, did we find it in evidence, and then little beyond the customary beads was present.

On the whole, it would seem probable the South Carolina coast has little to offer from an archæological standpoint.

CERTAIN ABORIGINAL MOUNDS OF THE SAVANNAH RIVER.

By Clarence B. Moore.

The Savannah river, a narrow, muddy stream with rapid current, is navigable as far as Augusta, about 223 miles following the course of the stream, though the distance in a straight line is considerably less. Our investigation was limited to this portion of the river, which has South Carolina on the northern side and Georgia on the southern side.

The river runs between swamps extending a considerable distance back, the inhabitants, as a rule, living in the back country, though at places bluffs have a few inhabitants. All these high places were carefully examined by us during part of the winter of 1897–1898, in a rapid steamer of light draught, our work, moreover, being greatly facilitated through data acquired by George W. Rossignol, captain of our steamer, who has been employed in mound work for years, who during the previous summer went to Augusta and back to prepare the way for the winter's work.

It soon became apparent to us that the Savannah river, though no digging into the mounds had been attempted for scientific purposes, did not offer a promising field, for many rises in the ground known as mounds by the inhabitants proved to be roughly circular banks thrown up by the current, and this was notably so in the case of Little Patten and Big Patten, which are given as Indian mounds, even on the government chart. In addition, the few mounds found back from the river in cultivated fields were very small and had been rifled by seekers after treasure, and the swamp mounds seemed made for domiciliary purposes. Therefore, we did not pursue our usual custom, totally to demolish each mound discovered, as we had done, as a rule, in Florida and on the Georgia coast. No mounds of which we heard, however, except one on which stood a house, were left uninvestigated.

The mounds of the Savannah river, in the main, as we found them, were of two classes, namely : low burial mounds of sand, back on the high ground, and large mounds of clay in the swamp, having a great summit plateau as though made for habitation and refuge in periods of high water. In one case we found a burial in one of these swamp mounds, which, however, may have been incidental during its erection.

It is not likely that the swamps of the Savannah had a large population in prehistoric times, for the aborigines were good judges of dwelling sites. No shell heaps are visible along the banks of the river—at least, below Augusta. There were then probably comparatively few mounds in early times and of these, doubtless some of the smaller have been ploughed away. In addition, the river is ever encroaching on the Carolina shore. In 1776, William Bartram saw a number of mounds at Silver bluff,[1] about 27 miles by water below Augusta, of which no trace is now apparent. Colonel Jones[2] describes large mounds at Mason's plantation, below Augusta on the Carolina side, and examined a section of one which had been exposed by the river, finding no burials (page 155). He earnestly hopes that the mounds may be carefully watched during the process of destruction. All have totally disappeared. The archæological examination of the Savannah river has been too long deferred.

Mounds Investigated.

Near Pipemaker's creek, Chatham county, Georgia (2).
Near Hudson's ferry, Screven county, Georgia (2).
Near Mills' landing, Screven county, Georgia (2).
Near Brooks' landing, Barnwell county, South Carolina (2).
Near Demerie's ferry, Burke county, Georgia (2).
Near Shell bluff, Burke county, Georgia (3).

MOUNDS NEAR PIPEMAKER'S CREEK, CHATHAM COUNTY, GEORGIA (2).

At the union of Pipemaker's creek and the Savannah river, about four miles above Savannah, in view from the river, on property belonging to Henry Taylor, Esq., of Savannah, who kindly gave us permission to investigate, are two aboriginal mounds.

The larger, a truncated cone in shape, has a base irregularly circular in outline with a diameter of about 130 feet. The diameter of the summit plateau, which also is circular, is about 60 feet. The mound, which has a height of 19 feet, presents a picturesque appearance. The sides are steep and on them grow cedars and live-oaks, the oaks covered with trailing moss. A large excavation had been made previous to our visit, by treasure seekers, we were told. The exposed portions were carefully examined by us and a certain amount of digging done without showing traces of burials. The mound seemed to be composed of clayey sand with oyster-shells in places.

Contiguous to the southwest margin of the large mound was a rise in the ground, circular in a general way, with a diameter of about 60 feet and a height of 3 feet at the center. The mound, which was more than half dug through by us, seemed to have been a refuse heap formed by long-continued occupation. It had also been used as a place of burial. Human remains were met with at eighteen points—the usual flexed burials, the head as a rule, though not always, pointing to the east. With the burials were small shell beads on two occasions and with one was a pebble-hammer roughly pecked to leave a central encircling ridge. In the midden debris were: many pebbles, some broken; bits of chert; two earthenware discs; one-half of a discoidal stone; numerous sherds bearing the check, the diamond-shaped and the complicated, stamp.

[1] C. C. Jones, "Antiquities of the Southern Indians," page 150.
[2] *Ibid.* page 153, *et seq.*

MOUNDS NEAR HUDSON'S FERRY, SCREVEN COUNTY, GA. (2).

Hudson's ferry, about 68 miles by water above Savannah, is the steamboat landing for Enecks, a settlement and post-office about two miles inland. A man named Golden stated he had found two vessels of earthenware, one over the other, by the roadside at the landing, which contained cremated human bones. We visited Mr. T. J. Enecks, of Enecks, who showed us the vessels, which are of a type found on the Georgia coast.

In a field about 1 mile west of Hudson's ferry, on the property of Mr. William Prior, of Enecks, to whom we are indebted for permission to investigate, was a mound, much spread out by ploughing, in a cultivated field. Its diameter was 74 feet; its height, 2 feet 5 inches. The mound had been dug into previously to a certain extent. The holes remained unfilled. We were informed by the son of Mr. Prior that the digging was done by him and that he had found nothing except two skeletons. The mound was thoroughly investigated by us. It was of dark yellow sand without stratification or pits. A dark band ran through it at the level of the surrounding field.

Burial No. 1 was 4 feet S. E. by E. from the point taken by us as the center of the mound. The skeleton, of a male, heading S., was partly flexed, with trunk and face to the right. The legs were drawn up, the knees turned to the right, the upper arms lay along the body with the forearms bent across it. Near the skull was a chip of chert and a quantity of charcoal, though neither skull nor sand showed trace of fire. On either side of the right arm were two handsome discoidal stones each flat on one side and convex on the other, 2.3 inches and 2.7 inches in diameter, respectively. This skeleton had doubtless been buried, after exposure, with most of the parts held in place by the ligaments. The right foot, however, except the astragalus, was missing. The heel bone lay by the skull. The skeleton, which was 3 feet from the surface, had been let into the dark band at the base of the mound.

Burial No. 2 was 8 feet S. of the center and 2 feet 9 inches down, just through the black basal band. It was of a male, was flexed on the right and headed S. S. W. Back of the skull was a broken mussel shell and a tobacco pipe of earthenware covered as to the bowl with projecting knobs (Fig. 9).

Burial No. 3, 6 feet W. N. W., 2.5 feet down, head S., included the upper portion of a skeleton, the rest having been dug away during one of the excavations to which we have referred. In the sand, which had been thrown back and left, was an interesting tobacco pipe of light-colored clay consisting of an effigy of a bird, probably an owl. The wings, tail and "horns" are distinctly shown, as are the legs and eyes. Part of the bill is missing (Figs. 10, 11, 12). An interesting feature of this pipe is that the bird faces the smoker, the pipe evidently having been made more for the satisfaction of the owner than to attract the attention of others. We have before noticed this tendency in aboriginal pipes, notably in one found by us in the great Grant mound, Florida, where a small piece of copper had been fastened to the near side of the bowl.

Mr. J. D. McGuire, who has made an especial study of aboriginal tobacco pipes and whose memoir on the subject will shortly be brought out by the National Museum, says of this pipe that the specimen is the most interesting one of the pipes

Fig. 9.—Tobacco-pipe of earthenware. Mound near Hudson's ferry. (Full size.)

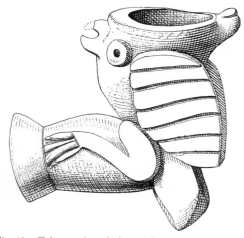

Fig. 10.—Tobacco-pipe of clay. Mound near Hudson's ferry. Side view. (Full size.)

of this type, which belongs to Georgia and South Carolina, that has come under his observation and by far the most elaborate one he knows of, though the pipe is related to other interesting pipes from the same locality and also from North Carolina and possibly from Tennessee.

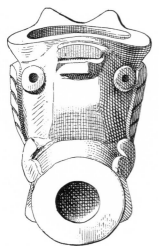

Fig. 11.—Tobacco-pipe of clay. Mound near Hudson's ferry. Showing front view. (Full size.)

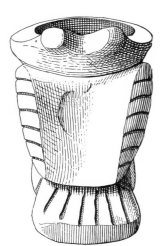

Fig. 12.—Tobacco-pipe of clay. Mound near Hudson's ferry. Showing rear view. (Full size.)

Mr. Andrew E. Douglass, whose superb collection of pipes may be seen at the Museum of Natural History, New York, writes of the bird-pipe as follows: "The pipe represented in the cuts is, so far as I know, entirely unique. It represents what I take to be a conventional owl, and, as you observe, the face is turned to the smoker, which would be considered a legitimate Indian conception. It is not likely to have any duplicate, as it is hand-work and the artist is not likely to have adhered to the same design in modelling another. I regard it a fine specimen of original Cherokee work."

Burial No. 4, 8 feet W. S. W., 10 inches from the surface had been disturbed in part by the second pit of the previous digging. Charcoal lay near the skull.

Together, and unassociated with human remains, were three fossil shark's teeth, each somewhat over one inch in length, with bases and points considerably worn, showing use in handles as pointed tools. With them was a mussel-shell containing two bones with cores of spurs, doubtless belonging to a wild turkey. A pitted smoothing stone lay loose in the sand, as did two arrow-points of chert.

In a field formerly under cultivation, about half a mile southeast from the mound just described, was a mound of sand 4 feet 5 inches high and 61 feet across the base. It had been somewhat spread out by cultivation. Previous to our visit a small hole had been dug into the top. A trench 30 feet wide was dug, in from the margin through the center. About the middle of the mound were calcined fragments of bones probably belonging to one individual. Similar fragments were seen in the sand thrown out by the former digger.

MOUNDS NEAR MILLS' LANDING, SCREVEN COUNTY, GA. (2).

In the thick cypress swamp bordering the river and accessible only at low stages of the river, is a mound with circular base and marked summit plateau, also circular. This mound, about one-quarter of a mile in a northwesterly direction from the landing, which is about 112 miles by the river from Savannah, is on the property of Dr. G. L. Mills of Hirschman, Ga., and serves as a refuge for live-stock in times of freshet. Its height is 11 feet. Across the base is a distance of 92 feet. Trenching showed it to be of clay, apparently without stratification. No burials were encountered.

About half a mile in a northwesterly direction from the other is a mound apparently of the same type, though somewhat smaller. A small amount of trenching showed it to be of clay, but yielded no other result.

MOUNDS NEAR BROOKS' LANDING, BARNWELL COUNTY, S. C. (2).

Brooks' Landing, not given on the government chart, is about 121 miles from Savannah by the river. About half a mile in an easterly direction from the landing, in the cypress swamp, are two mounds on the property of Mr. S. G. Lawton, of Allendale, S. C., who courteously placed them at our disposition. The mounds, about the same size and almost contiguous, stand close to the edge of the terrace, which borders the river in high water and is itself submerged in times of freshet. The northernmost mound was chosen for investigation. It was the usual shape, a greatly truncated cone with markedly level summit plateau. The diameter of base was 68 feet; of the summit plateau, 36 feet. Measured from the terrace on which it stands, its average height is 5 feet 4 inches, though, to an observer looking from the north and including the height of the terrace, its altitude would seem much greater. Trenches, aggregating 45 feet in length from 3 to 4 feet wide and from 5 to 6 feet deep, were dug into the summit plateau. About 5 feet down there seemed to be a black basal line indicating the original surface. The mound was of unstratified clay with occasional fire-places, perhaps in use during its construction. Three or four sherds were met with, and 5 feet from the surface was a deposit of small fragments of calcined bones, some of which were undoubtedly human. Probably this mound was domiciliary and the burial incidental.

STONY BLUFF, BURKE COUNTY, GA.

At Stony Bluff landing, about 131 miles by water above Savannah, the solid ground comes to the water's edge with masses of rock above the surface. This place has been the site of a great aboriginal workshop, the fields for acres around being covered with chips, spalls, cores, nodules and unfinished implements of chert. At places the deposit is such as to interfere with cultivation. The owner informed us that until recently, many interesting implements could be collected there and, as it was, we gathered a number of arrowheads and the like in the last stage of completion.

MOUNDS NEAR DEMERIE'S FERRY, BURKE COUNTY, GA. (2).

Demerie's ferry is about 161 miles by water, above Savannah. About three-quarters of a mile in a southerly direction from the ferry were two low mounds, kindly placed at our disposition by the owner, Mr. H. H. D'Antignac, of Augusta, Ga. These mounds had been dug into before. In the larger, human bones were at two points. Our investigation of the smaller was without result.

MOUNDS NEAR SHELL BLUFF, BURKE COUNTY, GA. (3).

Shell bluff, so called from a deposit of fossil oyster-shells, is 163 miles from Savannah, following the course of the river.

About half a mile in a west-southwesterly course from the river, in a cultivated field, were two low mounds greatly spread out by the plough and thoroughly dug through before our visit.

On the summit of a hill overlooking the field on one side and the river on the other, was a mound two feet in height and 52 feet across. The mound was made mainly of red clay which underlies the sand of the hill. We were not entirely satisfied as to the nature of the mound, which contained several modern burials with coffin-nails, etc. It may have been a domiciliary mound utilized in later times.

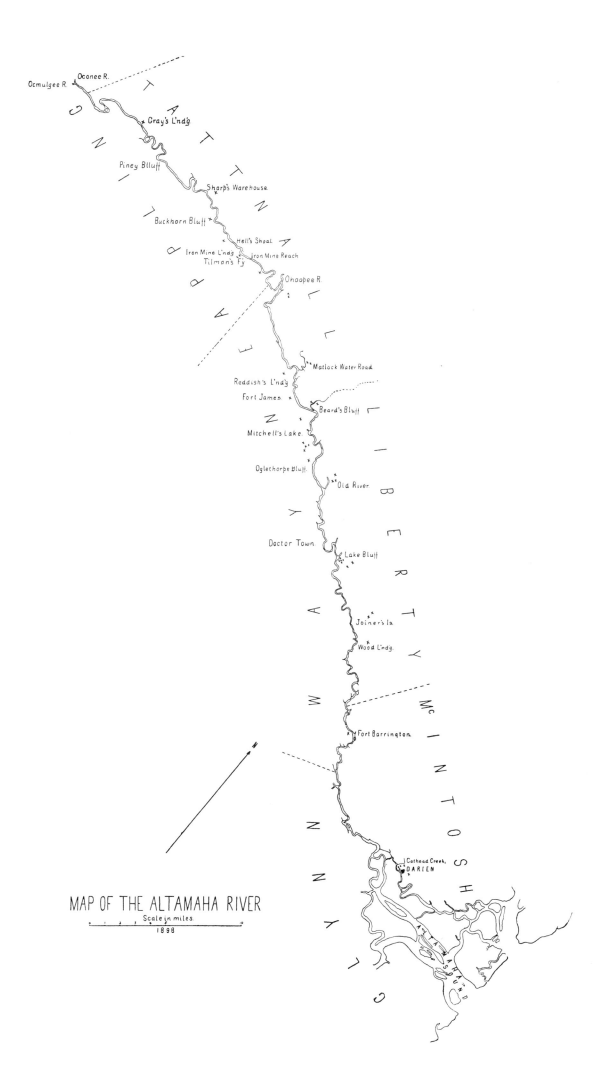

Ocmulgee R. Oconee R.

Cray's L'nd'g

Piney Bluff

Sharp's Warehouse

Buckhorn Bluff

Hell's Shoal

Iron Mine L'nd'g   Iron Mine Reach
Tilman's F'y

Ohoopee R.

Matlock Water Road

Reddish's L'nd'g
Fort James
Beard's Bluff

Mitchell's Lake.

Oglethorpe Bluff.
Old River.

Doctor Town.
Lake Bluff.

Joiner's Is.

Wood L'nd'g.

Fort Barrington.

Cathead Creek,
DARIEN

MAP OF THE ALTAMAHA RIVER
Scale in miles.
1898

CERTAIN ABORIGINAL MOUNDS OF THE ALTAMAHA RIVER.

By Clarence B. Moore.

The Altamaha river, formed by the union of the Oconee and Ocmulgee, takes a southeasterly course through part of the State of Georgia entering the ocean through Altamaha sound. From the Forks, as the confluence of the two rivers is called, to the town of Darien is 131 miles by water,[1] and from there to the sea is a farther distance of 16 miles.

The Altamaha river, like the Savannah, is narrow, crooked, shallow and muddy. It runs between cypress swamps with here and there a bit of high ground. No aboriginal shell-heaps are to be seen along the banks and no mussel-shells were scattered over such fields as were examined by us. Such territory as borders the river appears far from fruitful and it seems hardly likely that a considerable population inhabited the banks of the river in former times.

There has been no previous systematic exploration of the mounds of the Altamaha. Colonel C. C. Jones[2] refers to " the lonely mounds along the Altamaha," but makes no reference to exploration. Dr. J. F. Snyder describes an urn-burial[3] found at a point near the river. Beyond this we know of no investigation previous to our own.

In the spring of 1896 we went up the river as far as Lake Bluff, 50 miles by water above Darien, and in addition spent several weeks around Darien where five mounds were thoroughly examined. The result of our work at Darien has already appeared in our memoir of the Georgia coast. In the spring of 1898 we spent twenty-one days on the river carefully covering the territory as far as the Forks, including in our work only mounds within three miles of the river on either side. However, none of importance at even a greater distance was reported to us.

As the reader will see, the mounds of the Altamaha are mainly insignificant as to size and unimportant as to contents. Pits were rare and trans-marginal burials, so frequent on the Georgia coast, were wanting. Interments, as a rule, occupied a central position in the mounds which were unnecessarily great for their contents. Cremation obtained as did the bunched burial and the burial of skeletons in anatomical order, or but slightly disarranged. Urn-burials were found in but two localities.

Larger mounds of clay in the swamp, used as places of abode or of refuge, such as are found along the Savannah river, are wanting along the Altamaha.

[1] Chart of the Altamaha river. House of Representatives Ex. Doc. No. 283. We are indebted to Frederick R. Howard, Esq., U. S. Engineer's Office, Savannah, Ga., for charts which have greatly facilitated our investigations.

[2] *Op. Cit.* page 125.

[3] Smithsonian Report, 1890, page 609, *et seq.*

Mounds Investigated.

Near Darien (5).
Opposite Fort Barrington.
Near wood landing.
Joiner's Island (2).
Lake Bluff (7).
Old River (3).
Oglethorpe Bluff.
Near Mitchell's Lake (5).
Near Beard's Bluff (2).

Fort James.
Reddish's Landing.
Near Matlock Water Road (2).
Near Ohoopee River (2).
Below Tilman's Ferry.
Near Iron Mine Landing (2).
Hell's Shoal.
Buckhorn Bluff.
Gray's Landing.

MOUND OPPOSITE FORT BARRINGTON, WAYNE COUNTY.

Fort Barrington, in Liberty county, about 23 miles by water above Darien, has opposite to it a landing, about 300 yards in a westerly direction from which was a small mound greatly ploughed down. It was two-thirds dug through by us yielding nothing beyond a few decayed human bones here and there.

MOUNDS NEAR WOOD LANDING, LIBERTY COUNTY.

On the northern, or "White" side of the river, about 27 miles by water from Darien, is a nameless landing used by raftsmen. About 1 mile in a north-north-easterly direction from this landing, in thin woods, was a mound 2 feet 7 inches high and 40 feet across the base. The mound, which was of sand, like all those seen by us on the Altamaha, was trenched and dug centrally without result.

MOUNDS ON JOINER'S ISLAND, LIBERTY COUNTY (2).

Old landing, on Joiner's island, is about 40 miles by water from Darien. In the "scrub," about 1 mile in a northerly direction from the landing was a mound 3 feet in height and 38 feet across. It had been much dug into by treasure seekers. What was left contained one pocket of calcined human bones.

About 100 yards in a northerly direction from the other was a mound 68 feet across the base and 6 feet 8 inches in height. It was thoroughly trenched, the entire summit plateau was dug out and parts of the sides. It was composed of dry sand unstratified and, to our great disappointment, yielded but two or three sherds.

MOUNDS NEAR LAKE BLUFF, LIBERTY COUNTY (7).

In the "scrub," about three-quarters of a mile in a southwesterly direction from Lake Bluff, was a mound on the property of Messrs. J. R. McDuffie & Co., according to some, and of Messrs. Clarke Brothers, of Darien, according to others. Our thanks are tendered to both these firms, from whom we received a general permission to dig. The mound, which had been extensively dug into by others, had at the time of our visit a height of 5 feet 10 inches, a diameter of base of 52 feet.

All that remained of the mound was dug through by us. It was composed of yellow sand unstratified and had a distinct dark band 2 inches in thickness running along the base at the level of the surrounding territory. There were no pits.

Exclusive of scattered human remains in disturbed sand, seven interments were met with. Three of these were pockets of small fragments of calcined human bones,

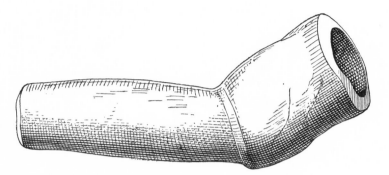

Fig. 13.—Tobacco-pipe of earthenware. Mound near Lake Bluff. (Full size.)

each presumably the remains of one skeleton. With two, no artifacts were present. With the third, lying immediately on top, was a hoe-shaped implement of calcareous rock, 8 inches in length. One side was much weathered. When new, this implement, polished and milk white, must have presented an attractive appearance. In all our mound work we have met with this type but once before, having found one

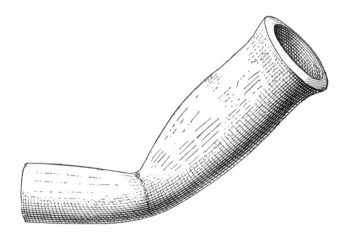

(Fig. 14.—Tobacco-pipe of earthenware. Mound near Lake Bluff. Full size.)

in the mound in the pine woods, back of Duval's landing, Blue creek, Lake county, Florida.[1]

The flexed skeleton of a child lay near the base. Close to the skull was a single vertebra of an adult. With the skeleton were a few shell beads.

[1] "Certain Sand Mounds of the St. Johns River, Florida," Part I, Journ. Acad. Nat. Sci., Vol. X.

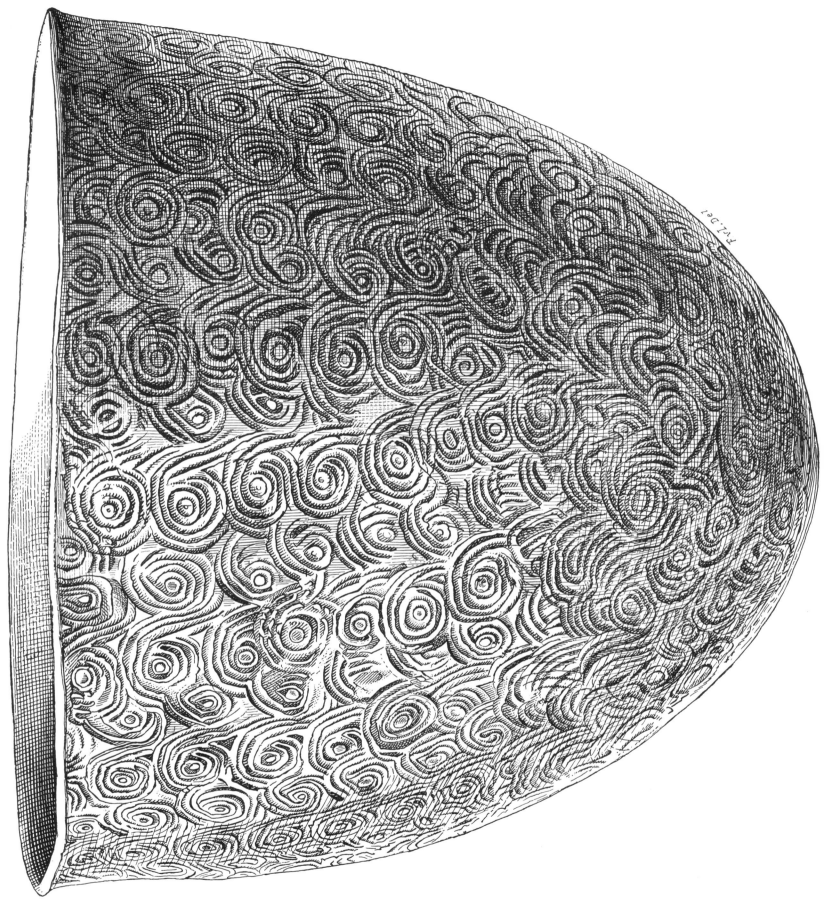

Fig. 15.—Vessel E. Mound near Lake Bluff. (One-half size.)

Thirty-eight inches from the surface was a pot (A) with rounded base and almost perpendicular sides faintly decorated with a complicated stamp. Its height is approximately 15 inches; its diameter, 13 inches. It was about two-thirds filled with good sized fragments of charred and calcined human bones, associated with small shell beads showing no mark of fire. This pot was capped and partly covered by an inverted undecorated pot (B), badly broken when discovered, but since suc-

Fig. 16.—Complicated stamped decoration on Vessel E. Mound near Lake Bluff. (Full size.)

cessfully put together. Its base was 19 inches from the surface. From a small flat base its sides extend out at a considerable angle. Its rim is almost horizontally inverted. Its maximum diameter is 17.25 inches; its diameter of aperture, 13.5 by 15.5 inches; its diameter of base, 3.5 inches; its height, 10.5 inches. Vessels A and B were presented to the Peabody Museum, Cambridge, Mass.

An undecorated bowl, somewhat resembling B in shape, was found upright with its base 40 inches from the surface. It contained cremated remains of probably one individual, associated with small shell beads. Approximate measurements: height, 6 inches; diameter of aperture, 12.5 inches; maximum diameter, 13.25 inches. This bowl was covered by a pot (D) of the same type as A as to shape, but with a check-stamped decoration. It was somewhat crushed. Vessels C and D also were sent to the Peabody Museum, where the broken parts have been carefully reunited.

Inverted, and covering a large deposit of calcined bits of human bone, among which lay a small polished chisel of volcanic rock, two tobacco pipes (Figs. 13, 14), and twenty-six perforated pearls, some of them large, was a great pot (E) (Fig. 15), having a diameter of mouth of 19 inches, a height of 17 inches. It was decorated with an interesting complicated stamp shown in Fig. 16.

The pipes found with the remains were undecorated. One had a peculiar metallic lustre, perhaps conferred by the use of plumbago. Unfortunately, there is not sufficient material for chemical determination. Both pipes had small mutilations. We have before called attention to the fact that tobacco pipes are practically never found entire in the mounds of the Georgia coast and probably the custom to mutilate pipes to a certain extent, previous to their interment, extended up the Altamaha. None of the vessels, however, had any perforation of base as is so often the case in Florida and sometimes along the Georgia coast, where the aborigines probably desired to "kill" the pot that its soul might accompany that of the departed. It is a curious and significant fact that this same custom prevailed in Yucatan where Mr. Thompson describes the basal perforation of mortuary pottery.[1] Vessel E and its contents may be seen, with the rest of the collection, at the Academy of Natural Sciences, of Philadelphia.

Six low mounds in the neighborhood of the preceding, some of which had been rifled, were dug through by us with little result. In one the unburnt bones of an infant lay under an inverted, undecorated bowl, in fragments, which was sent to the Peabody Museum. One mound, previously undisturbed, had a pit at the center at the bottom of which, 4 feet 9 inches from the surface, with hematite, was a mass of unburnt bones in no particular order, including parts of skulls of eight individuals.

MOUNDS NEAR OLD RIVER, LIBERTY COUNTY (3).

Old river, probably a former channel, joins the river proper about 60 miles above Darien. About one mile up Old river, on the east side, are the terminals of Hughes' lumber tramway and McDuffie's old tram. About 400 yards out from the lumber landing, a short distance to the left of McDuffie's tramway, going out, in the "scrub," were two mounds 15 feet apart. The mounds, the ordinary truncated cones, were unusually symmetrical. The smaller mound, 2.5 feet high, had a base diameter of 28 feet; the larger had a height of 3.5 feet, a base diameter of 32 feet. Both were thoroughly investigated, proving to be of sand. In the smaller mound

---

[1] "The Chultunes of Labna," Edward H. Thompson, page 11, Cambridge, 1897.

no bones were met with by us, though fragments were found in the sand thrown out from a small central hole previously made. The larger mound contained a central deposit, 3 feet 9 inches down, consisting of a few calcined fragments and bits of unburnt bones.

A low neighboring mound yielded nothing of importance.

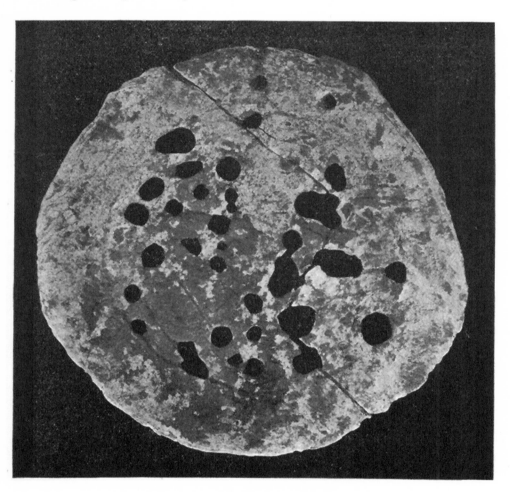

Fig. 17.—Shell gorget. Mound near Mitchell's lake. (Full size.)

MOUND NEAR OGLETHORPE BLUFF, WAYNE COUNTY.

A little mound thoroughly rifled was in the pine woods about 1 mile northwest of Oglethorpe bluff. Digging around the margin was without result.

MOUNDS NEAR MITCHELL'S LAKE, WAYNE COUNTY (5).

On the Altamaha, as on the Savannah, a dead river, which is an arm of the river coming to an abrupt ending, is called a lake. Mitchell's lake, about 69 miles from Darien, is such a one.

In a swamp-field, the property of Mr. R. J. Madry, of Pye, Georgia, to whom we are indebted for permission to dig, about 2 miles in a southerly direction from the swamp-landing, was a mound of sand. Its height was 2.5 feet; its diameter of base, 36 feet. About one-half was dug through and the central portion dug out. A circular implement of rough sandstone, pitted on either side, was loose in the sand; also a few sherds. Human remains, all near the center, were at three points as follows: an unburnt bunched burial; a deposit, 4 feet down, of calcined and unburnt bones, the unburnt and the calcined bones at first separate, then mingled; a pocket of calcined fragments with a streak of sand, colored with hematite at one side.

About 150 yards north-northwest from the preceding was a mound 2 feet 4 inches high with a basal diameter of 31 feet. It was practically dug through by us. Almost in the center, about 3 feet down, was a bunched burial.

Nearly contiguous was a mound 1 foot 8 inches high and 26 feet across. It was dug into without result. About one-half mile in a northwesterly direction from the last mound was a mound 14 inches high and 30 feet across the base. It was practically dug through, yielding one bunched burial almost in the center.

In an old field about 1.5 miles west by north from the swamp landing near Mitchell's lake was a mound 2 feet in height and 32 feet in diameter of base. The mound, which had been cultivated, was opened with the kind permission of Mr. M. A. Coleman, of Pye, Georgia. The mound which was of unstratified sand, like all the Altamaha mounds, was practically demolished by us. Human remains, all bunched burials, were encountered at six points, some out toward the margin. With an adult skull was a shell disc .8 of an inch in diameter, doubly perforated. With fragments of a child's skull were a shell pin 2.8 inches in length and shell gorget, roughly circular, 4.4 inches in diameter (Fig. 17). This gorget originally had on the concave side an engraved decoration now indistinguishable as to character through weathering and also—curiously enough—because numbers of irregularly shaped holes had been cut through the gorget.

MOUNDS NEAR BEARD'S BLUFF, LIBERTY COUNTY (2).

About one and one-half miles in a northwesterly direction from the landing, on the property of Mrs. Jack Jones, of Atlanta, Ga., who kindly permitted us to investigate, was a mound 3 feet high and 56 feet across the base. A considerable hole had been previously dug into the center. Our investigation showed the mound probably to be of a domiciliary character.

About one-half mile in a straight line from the preceding mound, in a northerly direction, across a small stream, the boundary of Tattnall county, in thick "scrub," also the property of Mrs. Jones, was a mound surrounded by hollows from which material for its construction had been taken. Its diameter of base was 36 feet. Its height, owing to neighboring depressions, was difficult to determine. Two and one-half feet would probably represent its average altitude. A small trench had been dug through the center previous to our visit. Considerably more than one-half the mound was dug away by us, resulting in the discovery of one small deposit of calcined human remains.

MOUND NEAR FORT JAMES, WAYNE COUNTY.

Near this place was a low mound whose investigation was without result.

MOUND NEAR REDDISH'S LANDING, WAYNE COUNTY.

Reddish's, a swamp-landing, under water when the river is high, is about 75 miles by water above Darien. About 2 miles in a northwesterly direction from the landing, in Spence's old field, formerly under cultivation, now the property of Mr. Hillhouse, was a mound, showing marks of cultivation. Its height was 4 feet and it is interesting to note, in connection with Altamaha mounds, that people living at considerable distances spoke of it as the largest mound that had come under their notice. Its original diameter of base was probably about 45 feet. A hole about 2 feet by 3.5 feet had been dug in the central portion almost to the base, and fragments of human remains lay in the marginal sand. About 5 feet from the center was a mass of unburnt bones, including parts of four skulls, also one calcined fragment of a skull. Charcoal was in association. One arrow-head was loose in the sand.

MOUNDS NEAR MATLOCK WATER ROAD, TATTNALL COUNTY (2).

Matlock water road is a sort of canal joining Bluff lake with the river, used for floating out lumber. The length of the "road" is about 1 mile and its confluence with the river is about 77 miles by water above Darien. At the end of the lake, not far from its union with the canal, is a lumber tramway. In sight of this tramway, near its terminus, were two mounds said to be on the property of Mr. James Durntz of Beard's creek. The larger mound, with the usual circular outline of base, had been much lowered by cultivation. Its height was 1 foot 8 inches; its basal diameter, 38 feet. The mound was practically dug through by us. Near the center was a considerable deposit, first of calcined bones, then of unburnt bones and finally a mixture of the two. Parts of seven skulls were recovered. A considerable number of shell beads were in association.

A short distance away was a mound almost levelled by cultivation. At the center were a few unburnt bones disturbed by cultivation.

MOUNDS NEAR THE OHOOPEE RIVER, TATTNALL COUNTY (2).

The Ohoopee river joins the Altamaha about 88 miles above Darien. In the "scrub," about one mile in, were two low mounds so dug into that no investigation was attempted by us.

MOUND BELOW TILMAN'S FERRY, APPLING COUNTY.

About 93 miles by water above Darien and a little over one mile below Tilman's ferry, in a cedar "hammock," about 50 yards in from the river, was a mound of sand 2 feet 4 inches in height and 28 feet through the base. A former visitor had left a hole 6 feet by 4 feet reaching almost to the base. In the sand thrown out were bits of calcined human remains. The remainder of the mound was demolished by us. A number of sherds, some having the complicated stamp, lay in the sand. About 8 feet from the center were a number of unburnt bones which apparently had been disturbed. Seven feet from the center were a skull and vertebræ with a number of shell beads, some two-thirds of an inch in diameter. Two feet down, about 7 feet from the center, was a skeleton of a female, flexed on the right side. Near the skull were a shell pin 3.25 inches in length, a part of another, and a considerable number of good-sized shell beads. Loose in the sand at various points, were two polished hatchets of volcanic rock and a small chisel.

Mounds near Iron Mine Landing, Appling County (2).

These mounds, about 15 yards apart, were one-quarter of a mile in a westerly direction from the landing. Apparently they had been under cultivation. They were on the property of Mr. John J. Robinson, residing not far from the landing, which is about 94 miles from Darien. Each had a diameter of base of 24 feet, a height of about 15 inches. About one-half of each and the central portions were dug through by us. A few feet from the center of one was a bunched burial containing parts of two individuals. In the other, near the center, was a bunched burial and a few bits of calcined bone. Shell beads were in association.

Mound near Hell's Shoal, Appling County.

Hell's shoal, a rocky and dangerous passage, is about 97 miles above Darien. Landing on the southern, or Indian side of the river, as it is still called, and going about one mile in a southwesterly direction, one comes to a mound on the border of a cultivated field. The mound also, in former times, had evidently been under cultivation. Its original diameter of base was probably about 35 feet; its height, at the time of our visit, a trifle over 2 feet. A hole 2 feet by 3 feet by 2 feet deep, with fragments of bone in the sand thrown out, had been made previous to our visit. A trench 21 feet by 26 feet was made from near the margin along the base through the center. The original central hole had cut through a skeleton. About 4 feet from the center, just below the surface, was an undecorated bowl of ordinary type with a diameter of 12 inches. Its original height had been about 8 inches. Part of the rim had been ploughed away. The vessel, to a depth of 3 inches was filled with small fragments of cremated bone. Beneath the bowl was charcoal and partly burnt wood, though the outside of the vessel showed no trace of fire.

Mound near Buckhorn Bluff, Appling County.

Buckhorn bluff is about 100 miles by water above Darien. The mound, in an old field now overgrown, was about 500 yards west of the landing. Its height was 3 feet 9 inches; its basal diameter, 38 feet. Two insignificant holes had been dug in it previous to our visit. Trees growing on the marginal parts encircled the mound. The clear portion, including all the center, was investigated by us with the kind permission of Mr. E. E. Mims, of Elliott, Ga. The mound, as usual, was of unstratified sand. A small pocket of calcined bones was about 6 feet from the center. Three feet and five feet from the center, respectively, were decaying fragments of a skull and of a skull and a humerus. Near one of these skulls was a handsome chisel of sedimentary rock about 7 inches long. Three feet from the center, on the base, was a flexed skeleton badly decayed. Near the cranium lay a well-made hatchet of polished rock about 8 inches long.

MOUND AT GRAY'S LANDING, TATTNALL COUNTY.

At Gray's landing, 120 miles by water from Darien, was a small mound 23 feet in diameter and 1 foot 4 inches in height. It was dug through by us with the permission of Mr. J. W. Matthews, the owner, resident nearby. It was composed of clayey sand. Sherds and fragments of chert were abundant, but no human bones were met with.

RECENT ACQUISITIONS.[1]

By Clarence B. Moore.

A Copper Gorget.

This gorget, shown in Fig. 18, is of hammered copper, undoubtedly native. It has a length of 8 inches, a maximum breadth of 3.1 inches. Its thickness, which is slightly irregular, has a maximum of .26 of an inch. Its weight is 17 ounces. It is covered with carbonate and has a perforation for suspension at one end. A small corner has been cut away since its discovery, doubtless to determine the nature of the metal.

This gorget has been examined by a number of experts in aboriginal copper, none of whom have seen a duplicate. It is certainly of extreme rarity.

Some time ago Professor J. W. Spencer, State Geologist of Georgia, heard of the discovery of the gorget and kindly put us in communication with the finder.

The gorget, we learned, was found with human remains and stone implements in an excavation made by the sons of Mr. James F. Dever, of Rockmart, Polk county, Ga., in a mound near that place. Polk county is on the Alabama line. The discovery of the gorget created considerable local excitement and at first an undue value was put upon it.

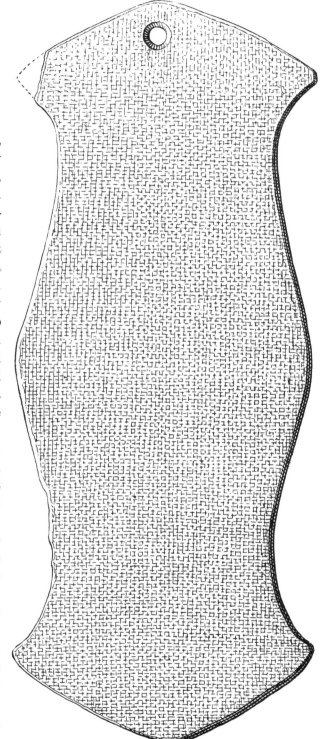

Fig. 18.—Copper gorget. Mound near Rockmart, Ga. (Full size.)

[1] Now on exhibition in the Moore Collection, Academy of Natural Sciences, Philadelphia.

Fig. 19.—Effigy water-bottle. Missouri. (Full size.)   Fig. 20.—Effigy water-bottle. Missouri. Side view. (Full size.)

A WATER BOTTLE FROM MISSOURI.

This vessel, well represented in Figs. 19, 20, has a height of 7 inches, a maximum diameter of 3.3 inches. It is made of clay of a light color and represents a figure with a peculiar style of head-dress. The ears are pierced, as is common in these effigy-bottles. The orifice is at the top. This vessel was obtained with a number of rare specimens from Mr. William J. Seever, of the Missouri Historical Society, who assures us that his collection was almost entirely obtained by himself during field-work. This particular vessel came from near the foot of a skeleton in a small mound which was the most easterly of a group known as the Richwood mounds, on the Whitehead farm, Stoddard county, Missouri.

The attention of the reader interested in prehistoric earthenware of Missouri is called to that excellent volume "Contributions to the Archæology of Missouri by the Archæological Section of the St. Louis Academy of Science, Part I, Pottery," Salem, Mass., 1880.

A "BANNER-STONE" OF SHELL.

In the swamp bordering the St. Johns river, near Volusia, Volusia county, Florida, is a huge aboriginal shell-heap known as Mt. Taylor.[1] Shell from Mt. Taylor is now being moved to Jacksonville for use on roads, by Mr. C. H. Curtis, of Bluffton, Florida, who has at times materially aided us during our archæological work on the river. Mr. Curtis has given strict instructions to those engaged in the demolition of Mt. Taylor carefully to save all objects found with the shells. We have been presented by Mr. Curtis with an interesting ornament, which, he informs us, was found by Albert Turner, a man in his employ, while clearing shell from roots of a tree. The specimen, therefore, occupied a position near the surface. The object, which is shown in Fig. 21, is a "banner-stone" of the bird-wing pattern,

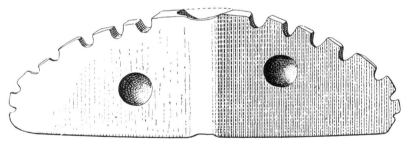

Fig. 21.—Shell "banner-stone," Florida. (Full size.)

carefully made. Its length is 4.1 inches; its height, 1.4 inches; its maximum thickness, .7 of an inch. The perforation, made by a circular drill, as is the case with "banner-stones," has a diameter of .6 by .7 of an inch at one aperture, where the drill has moved, and .6 of an inch at the other which is circular. One side of the ornament is practically flat over the perforation while the other presents two

[1] For details as to Mt. Taylor see our "Certain Shell-heaps of the St. Johns river, Florida, hitherto unexplored." American Naturalist, January, 1892, p. 12.

faces meeting in a transverse median ridge as shown in Fig. 22. This "banner-stone" has three peculiarities. Its upper margin is deeply notched; it has a semi-perforation, one lower than the other, on one side of either wing; and it is made of shell, probably the lip of the great marine univalve *Strombus gigas*.

In our mound work in Florida, Georgia and South Carolina we have seen nothing in shell resembling this ceremonial object.

Fig. 22.—"Banner-stone" of shell. Top view. (Full size.)

We have consulted a number of gentlemen as to this "banner-stone," including David Boyle, Esq., author of "Primitive Man in Ontario;" Andrew E. Douglass, Esq., whose great collection of prehistoric ornaments, pipes and the like may be seen at the Museum of Natural History, New York; Dr. Saville of the same institution; and Professor Putnam; all of whom agree that the type in shell is entirely new to them.

In "Art in Shell" nothing like this "banner-stone" is described or figured.

Index

Index

Certain Aboriginal Mounds of the Georgia Coast

(by Clarence B. Moore)

This section of the index is a facsimile of Moore's original. The page numbers are those at the tops of the pages.

Index

Certain Aboriginal Mounds of the Coast of South Carolina, the Savannah River, and the Altamaha River

(by Clarence B. Moore)

This section of the index is a facsimile of Moore's original. The page numbers are those at the tops of the pages.